Dictionary of
Music Education

Irma H. Collins

The Scarecrow Press, Inc.
Lanham • Toronto • Plymouth, UK
2013

Published by Scarecrow Press, Inc.
A wholly owned subsidiary of The Rowman & Littlefield Publishing Group, Inc.
4501 Forbes Boulevard, Suite 200, Lanham, Maryland 20706
www.rowman.com

10 Thornbury Road, Plymouth PL6 7PP, United Kingdom

British Library Cataloguing in Publication Information Available

Library of Congress Cataloging-in-Publication Data

Collins, Irma H.
  Dictionary of music education / Irma H. Collins.
      pages cm
  Includes bibliographical references.
  ISBN 978-0-8108-8651-3 (cloth : alk. paper) — ISBN 978-0-8108-8652-0 (ebook).
  1. Music—Instruction and study—Dictionaries. 2. Music—Instruction and study—Encyclopedias. 3. Music—Instruction and study—Bio-bibliography. I. Title.
  ML102.M76C65 2013
  780.71—dc23   2013012478

♾™ The paper used in this publication meets the minimum requirements of American National Standard for Information Sciences—Permanence of Paper for Printed Library Materials, ANSI/NISO Z39.48-1992.

Printed in the United States of America

To my mother, Irma Virginia Morgan Hopkins;
Thorndike's *Little Red Dictionary*, 1937;
and the teachers who inspired me.

Contents

Foreword   vii

Preface   ix

Acknowledgments   xi

Acronyms and Abbreviations   xiii

Organization Abbreviations   xv

Chronology   xxiii

Introduction   1

THE DICTIONARY   3

Appendix A: List of Organizations   291

Appendix B: List of Publications   309

Appendix C: Examining Institutions for Music   329

Bibliography   335

About the Author   339

Foreword

When a highly respected music educator with a passion for words envisions a professional resource to serve music teachers and learners worldwide, the result is a one-of-a-kind dictionary of music education. Irma Collins's *Dictionary of Music Education*, like any dictionary, is a reference book about words, presented in alphabetical order complete with definitions. However, this dictionary goes beyond just defining important words in music education. It focuses on *persons*, *terms*, *events*, and *organizations* that have affected and shaped the teaching and learning of music through the years. Furthermore, a chronology places these important persons, terms, events, and organizations in their historical contexts, while her extensive bibliography invites the reader to consult other sources for continued exploration. Remarkable throughout is the cross-referencing that connects the entries across the range of persons and terms, events, and organizations. This comprehensive compilation makes the *Dictionary of Music Education* a complete and practical resource for research and a landmark professional reference for exploring the evolution of music education through time.

A special feature is the inclusion of persons, terms, events, and organizations important to music education not only in the United States, but in Australia, Canada, and the United Kingdom as well. Collins identifies hundreds of *terms*—many familiar to music educators, some not so well known, and a number that cross geographic boundaries. The accomplishments of hundreds of outstanding music educators and musicians (*persons*) who have made or are still making significant contributions to music education are highlighted. Consider the enormous contribution of American Lowell Mason, who first introduced vocal music into the Boston schools in 1838, or Sir Frank Calloway (New Zealand/Australia), who was a founding member of the International Society for Music Education (ISME), then became its president, and finally its honorary president for life. *Organizations* such as ISME, the National Association for Music Education (NA*f*ME, United States, formerly MENC), the Canadian Music Educators' Association (CMEA), the Australian Society for Music Education (ASME), and the Music Education Council (MEC, United Kingdom) have all played major roles in advancing music education in their countries and throughout the world. Many of these organizations have sponsored significant *events* that have brought together music educators and decision makers to focus on critical topics in the profession and to consider visionary ways to ensure best practices in music teaching.

Bringing a dictionary of this magnitude from vision to reality required tremendous commitment, hours of painstaking research, and careful checking. All of us involved in the teaching and learning of music will reap the benefits of Irma Collins's in-depth work as we make the *Dictionary of Music Education* an important and practical resource in our professional lives.

Carolynn A. Lindeman
San Francisco State University and the
National Association for Music Education

Preface

One of the challenges of writing a *specific* field and *descriptive* dictionary is that the focus must consistently remain on topic. For a topic or subject such as music education, this can be a large part of the challenge. Music education represents two subject fields, and terms may vary in their definitions in moving between them. One must always be aware of the pervasive aspect of *music* when defining music education. (For example, without *music*, it would be *education*, and without *education*, it would just be *music*.) Coupled with this is the problem of changes over time in the terms and their meanings, tracking as they do changes in youth culture and technology. There is a danger also of listing too many, or not enough, people when trying to define the beginnings and the future of such an impressive subject as music education. These people have made, and are making, their indelible mark on the profession and were chosen for their specific contributions to the profession. From suggestions by experts—and from my own acquaintance with exceptional music educators—people were chosen because of their outstanding credentials. There are many other respected music educators, of course, but these I leave to a future biographical dictionary of music education.

Organizations change, and with them their acronyms; journals disappear almost as soon as they are recorded. Events come and go, but because of their import, music educators have recognized the more significant ones, such as the Tanglewood Symposium. The impact of national legislation on the discipline of education certainly affects music education, from budgets to charter schools, special education, and assessments of teachers and schools. And, once again, legislation often changes within ten to twenty years of enactment. This, too, adds to the problem of the inclusion of related terms in a dictionary.

A larger problem for this writer has been that of deciding what and how much to include from the discipline of music. There are many music dictionaries available, but they rarely, if at all, include music education entries. In this *Dictionary of Music Education*, you will find terms for music as well those interrelated from education. In the United Kingdom, for example, there are many educational reports that have affected music education. These are similar to those found in the United States. These reports were chosen because of their lasting impact on the teaching of music in overseas schools as well as ours. Fortunately, this has the benefit of enlarging our worldview of the ways in which music *and* education are disseminated by those who have devoted themselves to music education, from the earliest times to the present. In that regard, this dictionary provides a brief educational journey to many parts of the world through those music educators who chose to improve our understanding of music, regardless of culture and locale.

Basic technical information toward making the dictionary more readable includes the following:

- Words or acronyms/abbreviations in **boldface** within a definition direct the reader either to *entries* found elsewhere in the body of the dictionary or to *acronyms/abbreviations* listed in the beginning of the book.
- **Bib.:** at the end of a definition refers to sources to be found in the bibliography.
- **Lit.:** at the end of a definition refers to sources to be found beyond the dictionary.
- *See* at the end of a definition directs the reader to a term within the dictionary.
- *Entry* at the end of a definition directs the reader to a special entry by a contributor.
- *Italics* are used for book and journal titles, as well to emphasize certain words for better understanding.
- *Cross-referencing* is found in **boldface**, and is also indicated by the words *see* or *see also.*

Also included in this dictionary are abbreviations, acronyms, a chronology (i.e., time line), and bibliographic sources, both print and electronic. The appendix includes publications, and organizations from Australia, Canada, the United Kingdom, and the United States, as well as the international community. It also lists "examining boards" in Australia and the United Kingdom. All of these resources include as much contact information as could be found.

In writing a dictionary, one must rely on entries made by many scholars who have attempted to redefine older entries and to describe changing words and meanings over time with greater clarity. Their writing has impacted enormously this writer's own decisions for clear and descriptive definitions. Also, the use of Wikipedia, with its suggested bibliographical and reference sources, has been carefully noted to ensure basic accuracy in those entries.

The writing of this dictionary has been a solitary project, but the contributions from many specialists in the fields of music, music education, and education have been invaluable in my research and writing. The joy of writing this book has come from the wealth of knowledge I accrued from examining the spread of music *through* music education in the countries that are considered in this dictionary.

Acknowledgments

First and foremost, I wish to thank the many professionals who assisted me in collecting hard-to-find information for this dictionary. Their patience and perseverance were especially appreciated. I want to begin with the reference librarians at Shenandoah University: Rosemary Green, for the use of her personal book, the Australian *Macquarie Dictionary*; David McKinney, for his helpfulness with computer references; and Cindy Thomas, for her incredible overall support in locating important basic information, as well as the invaluable sources so needed in the international portion of the dictionary. Her technical support with new library equipment was greatly appreciated.

My deepest thanks go to Liz Maeshiro, who gave so much of her time to the typing of a large portion of the manuscript, and who returned each dictionary "letter" in record time; to Marsha Barley, a highly regarded general music teacher, who loaned me some of her classroom music books for "as long I needed them"; to Michael Rohrbacher, music therapist, for the use of his music therapy books; and to the Shenandoah University Learning Center, for securing Professor Mark Richardson's assistance with various citations.

It was one cold winter day, November 3, 2012, that Dr. Michael Jothen, an emeritus professor from Towson State University in Maryland, together with my former students, Dr. Kathleen Taylor, Eric Maeshiro, and Jane Daugherty—music teachers all—drove to Shenandoah University to participate in a day of sharing information about terms, persons, organizations, and events in music education from their teaching perspectives. I am grateful to them for their willingness to travel to Winchester for this meeting, which I, in fun, titled the "Untanglewood Conference."

I am indebted to Marlynn Likens at the NAfME headquarters, who graciously provided me with much-needed information. I am also most grateful to Vincent Navaro, curator of special collections in Performing Arts and Historical Center at the University of Maryland, for the many hours he spent searching for historical items. It is to my professional consultants, who respectfully consented to be my intellectual supporters in guiding me through the process of writing this dictionary, that I owe my deepest thanks. They are: Drs. Patricia Shehan Campbell, University of Washington; Jere Humphries,

Arizona State University; Carolynn Lindeman, San Francisco State University, retired, emerita; and Joanne Rutkowski, Pennsylvania State University. Their biographical information is found in the content of the dictionary.

To all my friends and family, especially Nadine, Diana, Kathleen, Wendy, Alison, Marilyn, and my sister-in-law Bobbie, I offer my sincere thanks for their personal support over the past two years. I am deeply grateful to my very capable friend and colleague Jo Pilette, who has spent an indefatigable amount of time at the computer carefully reading and editing each section of the manuscript. My appreciation for her assistance is immeasurable. And to my editor, Bennett Graff, who patiently answered my questions, and led me step by step along the way, I offer my sincerest thank-you.

Acronyms and Abbreviations

abbr.	abbreviation
AD	Anno Domini, current/calendar era
Aus.	Australia
Aust.	Austria
BA	Bachelor of Arts degree
BCE	Before the Common/Current/Christian Era
BM	Bachelor of Music degree
c.	century
ca.	circa, around
Can.	Canada
CO	Colorado
conf.	conference
DMA	Doctor of Musical Arts degree
e.g.	for example
Eng.	England
esp.	especially
est.	established
Eur.	Europe
exec.	Executive
FL	Florida
Fr.	France
GA	Georgia
gen.	general meaning for the definition
Ger.	Germany
gov.	government
Gr.	Greece
HI	Hawaii
hist.	history
i.e.	that is; in other words
int.	international
Ire.	Ireland
KY	Kentucky
Lit.:	further sources of literature beyond this dictionary

MA	Massachusetts
MD	Maryland
MM	Master of Music degree
MME	Master of Music Education degree
MI	Michigan
MN	Minnesota
NIre.	North Ireland
NSW	New South Wales, Australia
NT	Northern Territory, Australia
NY	New York
NZ	New Zealand
PA	Pennsylvania
RIre.	Republic of Ireland
SAus.	South Australia
Scot.	Scotland
Swz.	Switzerland
UK	United Kingdom (Great Britain and Northern Ireland)
Univ.	University
U.S.	United States of America
USO	United Service Organizations during World War II
WWI	World War 1
WWII	World War 2

Organization Abbreviations

AAB	Aboriginal Arts Board (Aus.)
AAC	Aboriginal Arts Committee (Aus.)
AAE	African American English
AAMT	American Association of Music Therapy (now AMTA)
AARME	Australian Association for Research in Music Education (See ANZARME)
AATEM	Association for the Advancement of Teacher Education in Music (UK)
ABA	American Band Masters Association
ABC	Australian Broadcasting Corporation
ABODA	Australian Band and Orchestra Directors Association
AC	Companion of the Order of Australia (an honor)
ACDA	American Choral Directors Association
ACE	Association for Cultural Equity (U.S.)
ACMT	Advanced Certified Music Therapist (Int.)
ACR	American Choral Review
ACT	*Action, Criticism, & Theory* (e-Journal for MayDay Group) (Int.)
ADA	Americans with Disabilities Act (U.S.: 1990)
ADCIS	Association for the Development of Computer-Based Instruction Systems (U.S.)
AEC	Aboriginal Education Council (Aus.) and Australian Education Council
AEP	Arts Education Partnership (U.S.)
AIATSIS	Australian Institute of Aboriginal and Torres Strait Islander Studies
AIDT	Aboriginal Islander Dance Theatre (Aus.)
AJME	*Australian Journal of Music Education*
AJMT	*Australian Journal of Music Therapy*
AM	Member of the Order of Australia
AMA	Australian Music Association
AMC	Australian Music Centre
AMEB	Australian Music Examinations Board

AMEL	Association of Music Education Lecturers (now ANZARME) (Aus.)
AMI	Association for Music and Imagery (U.S.)
AMTA	American Music Therapy Association
AMTA	Australian Music Therapy Association
ANATS	Australian National Association for Teachers of Singing
ANCOS	Australian National Council of Orff-Schulwerk
ANZARME	Australian and New Zealand Association for Research in Music Education
ANZATA	Australia and New Zealand National Art Therapy Association
AOSA	American Orff-Schulwerk Association
APMT	Association of Professional Music Therapists (now BAMT) (UK)
ARTATE	Australian Roundtable for Arts Training Excellence
ASA	Australian Strings Association
ASBDA	American School Band Directors Association
ASCAP	American Society of Composers, Authors and Publishers
ASCD	Association for Supervision and Curriculum Development (U.S.)
ASHE	Association for the Study of Higher Education
ASL	American Sign Language
ASME	Australian Society for Music Education
ASTA	American String Teachers Association (1948)
ATMI	Association for Technology in Music Instruction (U.S.)
AWSNA	Association of Waldorf Schools of North America
AYP	Adequate Yearly Progress (U.S.)
BAMT	British Association for Music Therapy
BCKSC	British Columbia Kodály Society of Canada
BCMEA	British Columbia Music Educators' Association
BFE	British Forum for Ethnomusicology
BJME	*British Journal of Music Education*
BKA	British Kodály Academy
BSI	British Suzuki Institute
BSMT	British Society for Music Therapy (now BAMT)
CA	Chorus America
CAAMA	Central Australian Aboriginal Media Association
CAI	Computer-Assisted Instruction
CAMT	Canadian Association of Music Therapy
CAUSM	Canadian Association of University Schools of Music (became the Canadian University Music Society, CUMS, in 1981)

CBA	Canadian Band Association
CBC	Canadian Broadcasting Corporation
CBDNA	College Band Directors National Association (U.S.)
CBE	Commander [of the Most Excellent Order of the] British Empire (an honor)
CBTE	Competency-Based Teacher Education (U.S.)
CCA	Canada Council for the Arts *and* Canadian Conference of the Arts
CCEA	Council for the Curriculum, Examinations and Assessment (UK)
CCMA	Canadian Country Music Association
CDIME	Cultural Diversity In Music Education
CEA	Canadian Education Association
CEMREL	Central Midwest Regional Educational Laboratory (U.S.)
CFMTA	Canadian Federation of Music Teachers' Associations
CfSA	Council for Subject Associations (UK)
CGM	Council for General Music (NA*f*ME—U.S.)
CHE	Australian Research Council's Centre of Excellence for the History of Emotions
CIDEM	Inter-American Music Council
CIRCME	Calloway International Resource Centre for Music Education (Aus.)
CJE	Council for Jazz Education, NA*f*ME (U.S.)
CJMT	*Canadian Journal of Music Therapy*
CMC	Canadian Music Council
CMEA	Canadian Music Educators Association
CMEJ	*Canadian Music Educator's Journal*
CMERC	Canadian Music Education Research Collaborative
CMP	Contemporary Music Project (U.S.)
CMRC	Canadian Music Research Centre *and* Canadian Music Research Council
CMS	College Music Society (U.S.)
CMT	Certified Music Therapist
CRME	Council for Research in Music Education (U.S.)
CSE	Certificate of Secondary Education (UK)
CSM	Canadian Society of Musicians
CSTM	Canadian Society for Traditional Music
CUMS	Canadian University Music Society (formerly Canadian Association of University Schools of Music, CAUSM)
DAW	Digital Audio Workstation
DBAE	Discipline-Based Art Education (U.S.)

DBE	Dame Commander of the Order of the British Empire (an honor)
DBME	Discipline-Based Music Education (U.S.)
DENI	Department for Education, Northern Ireland
DFE	Department for Education (UK)
DMUS	Doctor of Music (Aus.)
DSA	Dalcroze Society of America
ECMMA	Early Childhood Music and Movement Association (U.S.)
EFDSS	English Folk Dance and Song Society (UK)
EMA	Early Music America
ESCOM	European Society for the Cognitive Sciences of Music
ESEA	Elementary and Secondary Education Act of 1965 (U.S.)
ETM	Education Through Music (U.S.)
ETS	Educational Testing Service (U.S.)
FAPE	Free, Appropriate Public Education (ADA)
FCMF	Federation of Canadian Music Festivals
FLS	Folklore Society (UK)
GBE	Knight/Dame Grand Cross of the Order of the British Empire (an honor)
GCE	General Certificate of Education (UK)
GCEA	Getty Center for Education in the Arts
GCSE	General Certificate of Secondary Education (UK)
GIM	Guided Imagery and Music
GIML	Gordon Institute for Music Learning (U.S.)
GMT	General Music Today (NA*f*ME) (U.S.)
HMCP	Hawaii Music Curriculum Program
HRME	Historical Research in Music Education (U.S.)
IAJE	International Association of Jazz Education (no longer active)
ICTM	International Council on Traditional Music
IDEA	Individuals with Disabilities Education Act (U.S.)
IDES	Ireland Department of Education and Science (RIre.)
IEP	Individualized Education Program
IFCM	International Federation for Choral Music
IJME	*International Journal of Music Education*
IJRCS	*International Journal of Research in Choral Singing*
IKS	International Kodály Society
IMC	International Montessori Council *and* International Music Council
IMTA	Indiana Music Teachers Association (U.S.)
ISA	International Suzuki Association
ISM	Incorporated Society of Musicians (UK)

ISME	International Society of Music Education
ISPME	International Society for Philosophy of Music Education
JEN	Jazz Education Network
JHRME	*Journal of Historical Research in Music Education*
JIFSS	*Journal of the Irish Folk Song Society*
JMTE	*Journal for Music Teacher Education* (U.S.) and *Journal of Music, Technology & Education* (UK)
JMTP	*Journal of Music Theory Pedagogy*
JRIRE	*Journal of Research in International Music Education* (Int.)
JRME	*Journal of Research in Music Education* (U.S.)
JSMI	*Journal for the Society for Musicology in Ireland*
JWFSS	*Journal of the Welsh Folk-Song Society* (UK)
KCA	Kodály Center of America
KLA	Key Learning Area (Aus.-NSW Dept. of Ed.)
KMEIA	Kodály Music Education Institute of Australia
KMTI	Kodály Music Training Institute (U.S.)
KSC	Kodály Society of Canada
MANA	Music Advisers National Association (UK)
MAP	Musical Aptitude Profile
MBE	Member of the Order of the British Empire (an honor)
MCEECDYA	Ministerial Council for Education, Early Childhood Development and Youth Affairs (Aus.)
MCEETYA	Ministerial Council of Education, Employment, Training and Youth Affairs (Aus.)
MCVTE	Ministerial Council for Vocation and Technical Education (Aus.)
MEC	Music Education Council (UK)
MEJ	*Music Educators Journal* (U.S.)
MENC	Music Educators National Conference (now NA*f*ME) (U.S.)
MENZA	Music Education New Zealand Aotearoa
MERC	Music Education Research Council (U.S.)
MERI	Music Education Research International
MIOSM	Music In Our Schools Month (U.S.)
MIT	Massachusetts Institute of Technology
MMCP	Manhattanville Music Curriculum Project (U.S.)
MMEA	Manitoba Music Educators Association (Can.)
MSNC	Music Supervisors National Conference (later, MENC; now NA*f*ME) (U.S.)
MSOA	Maidstone School Orchestra Association (UK)

MTA   Music Teachers Association (UK-Aus.-NSW) *and* Musical
               Theater Academy (UK)
MTNA   Music Teachers National Association (U.S.)
MUSE   Musicians United for Superior Education (U.S.)
NAAE   National Advocates for Arts Education (Aus.) *and* National
               Affiliation of Arts Educators (Aus.)
NACWPI   National Association of College Wind and Percussion
               Instructors
NAEA   National Art Education Association (U.S.)
NAEP   National Assessment of Educational Progress (U.S.)
NAGB   National Assessment Governing Board (U.S.)
NA*f*ME   National Association for Music Education (formerly
               MENC) (U.S.)
NAISDA   National Aboriginal Islander Skills Development
               Association (Aus.)
NAJE   National Association of Jazz Educators (became IAJE)
NAME   National Association of Music Educators (UK)
NAMT   National Association of Music Therapy (now AMTA)
NASM   National Association of Schools of Music (U.S.)
NBA   National Band Association (U.S.)
NCATE   National Council for the Accreditation of Teacher
               Education (U.S.)
NCCAS   National Coalition for the Core Arts Standards (U.S.)
NCCATA   National Coalition of Creative Arts Therapies Associations
               (U.S.)
NCLB   No Child Left Behind (U.S.)
NEA   National Education Association (U.S.) *and* National
               Endowment for the Arts (U.S.)
NEH   National Endowment for the Humanities (U.S.)
NFAH   National Foundation of the Arts and Humanities (U.S.)
NHSO   National High School Orchestra and Band Camp (U.S.)
NMC   National Music Camp (Can.)
NNEB   National Nursery Examination Board (UK)
NSBOA   National School Band and Orchestra Association (U.S.)
NSMEA   Nova Scotia Music Educators' Association (Can.)
NSOA   National School Orchestra Association (joined with ASTA
               in 1990) (U.S.)
NSSE   National Society for the Study of Education
NTE   National Teacher Exam (U.S.)
NYB   National Youth Band of Canada
NYO   National Youth Orchestra (UK)
OAKE   Organization of American Kodály Educators (U.S.)

OBE	Outcomes-Based Education
OBE	Officer of the Order of the British Empire (an honor)
OFSTED	Office for Standards in Education, Children's Services and Skills (UK)
OFTA	Office for the Arts (Aus.)
OM	Order of Merit (an honor, UK)
OMEA	Ontario Music Educators' Association (Can.)
OSA	Orff-Schulwerk Association (after 1970 known as American Orff-Schulwerk Assoc.)
PCME	Parents Coalition for Music Education (U.S.)
PMMA	Primary Measures of Musical Audiation (U.S.)
POM	Psychology of Music (Aus.)
PPMTA	Post Primary Music Teachers Association (UK)
RAM	Royal Academy of Music (UK)
RCO	Register of Cultural Organizations (Aus.)
RMSM	Royal Military School of Music (UK)
RMT	Registered Music Therapist
RSME	Research Studies in Music Education
SAA	Suzuki Association of the Americas
SAI	Sigma Alpha Iota (Int.)
SAT	Scholastic Assessment Test (U.S.)
SCAA	School Curriculum and Assessment Authority (UK)
SCEA	Southeast Center for Education in the Arts (U.S.)
SCSEEC	Standing Council on School Education and Early Childhood (Aus.)
SEM	Society for Ethnomusicology (U.S.)
SEMPRE	Society for Education, Music and Psychology Research (Aus.)
SIEM	Southeast Institute for Education in Music (U.S.)
SIU	Southern Illinois University (U.S.)
SLSAP	Second Line Social Aid and Pleasure Society Brass Band (U.S.)
SMA	School of Music Association (UK)
SMEA	Saskatchewan Music Educators' Association (Can.)
SMEI	Society for Music Education in Ireland
SMENC	Student Music Education National Conference (U.S.)
SMI	Society for Musicology in Ireland
SMTE	Society for Music Teacher Education (U.S.)
SOSA	Scottish Orff Schulwerk Association
SPEBSQSA	Society for the Preservation and Encouragement of Barber Shop Quartet Singing in America
SRIG	Special Research Interest Groups (U.S.-NAƒME)

SRME	Society for Research in Music Education (U.S.)
TAFE	Technical and Further Education Colleges (Aus.)
TMSA	Traditional Music & Song Association of Scotland
T.MUS.A.	Teacher of Music Australia
UbD	Understanding by Design (U.S.)
UKCMET	United Kingdom Council for Music Education and Training
UNESCO	United Nations Educational, Scientific and Cultural Organization
USDE	United States Department of Education
UWA	University of Western Australia
WFMT	World Federation of Music Therapy (Int.)

Chronology
Precursors to the Discipline of Music Education

BCE

6th c. **(Gr.)** Music was taught as part of the core subjects (quadrivium)—at both a practical level (singing, dancing, instrumental music) and theoretical level. *See* GREEK EDUCATION.

6th c. **(Gr.)** Pythagoras, Ionian Greek philosopher and mathematician who experimented with musical overtones and ratios.

AD

Medieval/Middle Ages (5th–15th c.)

5th c. **(Eur.)** Musical notation, polyphony, plainchant, and organum (early form of counterpoint) began.

6th c. **(Italy)** Boethius. Wrote a treatise in five books, *De Institutione Musica* (Fundamentals of Music), the chief music sourcebook for monks.

11th c. **(Italy)** Method of teaching singing invented by Guido of Arezzo, a monk and choirmaster. Regarded as inventor of modern notation (staff notation).

1464 **(UK)** Cambridge University School of Music. Conferred the world's first music degrees.

1499 **(UK)** Madeline College at Oxford. Offered degrees in music.

1639 **(Can.)** Ecole des Ursulines and Ursuline Convent. First Canadian institutions to have music as part of the curriculum.

1640 **(U.S.)** *Bay Psalm Book*. Famous as the first real book to be published in the British colonies. A product of the Massachusetts Bay Colony.

1647 (Can.) First documented *choir* in Canada at Notre Dame de Quebec Cathedral, the primate church of Canada.

1678 (UK) The institution of the military band began in England.

1717 (U.S.) Beginning of singing schools. The first American school dedicated solely to singing was created at Brattle Street Church in Boston, Massachusetts.

1722 (Fr.) Jean Phillipe Rameau laid the foundation of the modern theory of harmony.

1732 (U.S.) Ephrata Cloister. A Protestant group in Pennsylvania, which, as a German-speaking communal society, believed strongly in music as an aid to worship.

1740s (UK) *Caledonia Pocket Companion*, the most important single source for old traditional Scottish music, compiled by James Oswald.

1741 (UK) Madrigal Society founded in London.

1775 (U.S.) United States Marine Band formed. Debuted in 1801 at reception for President John Adams.

1786 (U.S.) Stoughton Singing Society founded in Stoughton, Massachusetts (oldest singing society still in existence).

1782–1837 (UK) John Field (Dublin, Ireland). Pianist, composer, and teacher. Known for his contribution through concerts and teaching and to development of the Russian piano school.

Beginning of the Discipline of Music Education

1792–1872 (U.S.) Lowell Mason. Considered the "Father of Music Education" in the U.S.

1809 (Can.) New Union Singing Society founded, one of the earliest musical societies in Canada.

1815 (U.S.) Handel and Haydn Society organized in Boston. Its aims were the cultivating and improving of correct taste in the performance of sacred music.

1816–1880 (UK) John Curwen. Founder of the tonic sol-fa system of music education.

1820 (Can.) Quebec's Harmonic Society established. Among the earliest musical societies of Canada.

1822 **(UK)** Royal Academy of Music established.

1830 **(U.S.)** The Philadelphia Music Seminary established by Elan Ives Jr.

1831 **(UK)** Irish School System started by Lord Stanley.

1836 **(U.S.)** Dodsworth Band. Brass band popular prior to Civil War. One of the first of the professional bands that dominated the New York music scene from 1836 to 1891.

1838 **(U.S.)** The Magna Carta of Music Education passed by Boston School Board to contract with a vocal music teacher to teach in several public schools. Lowell Mason was hired to fill the position.

1846 **(UK)** The term *folklore* was introduced into scholarship by W. J. Thoms.

1853 **(UK)** Tonic Sol-Fa Association started by John Curwen.

1857 **(UK)** Royal Military School of Music (RMSM) formed at Kneller Hall for the purpose of training army bandsmen as bandmasters.

1857 **(U.S.)** National Teachers Association (NTA) founded.

1858 **(UK)** Music at Leeds. A music festival, mostly choral. Held triennially until 1970.

1858 **(UK)** Musical Society of London (1858–1867). Promoted social interaction among members and with musicians of other countries.

1859 **(U.S.)** April 9 was the date of the first performance of Gilmore's Band, founded in 1858 by Patrick Gilmore in Boston, Massachusetts.

1863 **(Aus.)** English-born James Churchill Fisher introduced the tonic sol-fa teaching method to Australian public schools. It was adopted as the official music teaching method in 1867.

1863 **(UK)** Tonic Sol-Fa College of Music opened.

1864 **(U.S.)** First basic music series, *The Song Garden* by Lowell Mason, to help elementary schoolchildren learn to read music.

1864 **(U.S.)** A Grand National Band of 500 army bandsmen and a chorus of 5,000 schoolchildren formed by Patrick Gilmore.

1865 **(U.S.)** After the Civil War, Benjamin Jepson persuaded the school to try the experiment of introducing music into the schools of New Haven, Connecticut.

1866 **(U.S.)** U.S. Department of Education created.

1867 **(Fr.)** World Band Contest in Paris. Greatest band contest of all time, following the rapid improvement of European bands at the beginning of the 19th century.

1869 **(U.S.)** National Peace Jubilee. A celebration in Boston to recognize the end of the Civil War. A 1,000-piece band, and a chorus of 10,000, created by Patrick Gilmore.

1870 **(UK)** Forster Act marked beginning of modern era of British education. The country was divided into school districts, and local school boards could levy taxes to support schools.

1872 **(U.S.)** World Peace Jubilee and International Band Festival organized by Patrick Gilmore to celebrate peace after the Franco-Prussian War.

1876 **(U.S.)** Music Teachers National Association (MTNA) founded. The oldest nonprofit music teachers' association in the U.S.

1877 **(U.S.)** Indiana Music Teachers Association (IMTA) formed. One of the first of the state MENC associations.

1879 **(UK)** Tonic Sol-Fa College opened by John Curwen.

1879 **(U.S.)** National Education Association (NEA) formed.

1880 **(U.S.)** John Philip Sousa appointed director of the Marine Band.

1882–1943 **(Can.)** Robert Nathaniel Dett, one of the first black Canadian composers during the early years of ASCAP.

1883 **(UK)** The Royal College of Music opened and was granted Royal Charter.

1883 **(U.S.)** *The Etude*. Publication developed for piano teachers and students. Provided articles and music for piano and instrumental students of all ages. Published from 1883 to 1957.

1884 **(Aus.)** Hugo Alpen. Transferred teaching of music from tonic sol-fa to movable doh, a method of his own devising.

1885 **(U.S.)** New England Public School Music Association was a movement to form independent bodies of school music teachers.

1886 **(U.S.)** Crane Normal Institute of Music (later Crane School of Music) founded by Julia E. Crane, referred to as a consummate music educator.

1890 **(NZ)** Elam School of Fine Arts. Founded by John Edward Elam. Students in Auckland studied for degrees in fine arts with an emphasis on a multidisciplinary approach.

1891 **(UK)** Elementary Education Act. Created free education for children.

1891 **(Aus.)** Thousand Voice Choir formed by Alexander Clark. Conducted for many years by music educator Francis Lymer Gratton.

1893 **(UK)** Royal Manchester College of Music founded in Manchester, England.

1897 **(UK)** Maidstone Movement began promoting instrumental class instruction (violin). Precursor of American public school instrumental classes.

1898 **(U.S.)** Phi Mu Alpha Sinfonia founded in Boston.

1898 **(UK)** Folk-Song Society founded.

1899 **(UK)** First volume of *The Journal of the Folk-Song Society* published.

Early 1900s **(U.S.)** Civic boys' bands begun by itinerant band directors who owned town bands, and who recruited and taught young boys who wanted to play band instruments.

1903 **(UK)** Royal Naval School of Music established to provide bands for the Royal Navy.

1904 **(U.S.)** Grade-school orchestras developed in California to provide good players for the high school organizations. Influenced by the Maidstone Movement in England.

1905 **(Can.)** Mary McCarthy introduced systematic instruction in music in the schools of Moncton, New Brunswick, Canada.

1906 **(UK)** Welsh Folk-Song Society founded. Its journal is *Canu Gwerin*.

1907 **(U.S.)** Music Supervisors National Conference (MSNC) was founded.

1908 **(UK)** Music Teachers Association (MTA) founded in London. Also in New South Wales, Australia.

1914 **(U.S.)** *Music Supervisors Journal* first published.

1918 **(UK)** Fisher Act was passed by Parliament, abolishing all fees and making an elementary education accessible to all children.

1918 **(U.S.)** MENC Education Council began.

1918– **(Aus.)** Doreen Bridges became the first person in Australia to receive a PhD in music education.

1921 **(Ire.)** Republic of Ireland established.

1921 **(U.S.)** Oberlin College Conservatory of Music established America's first four-year college degree program in music education.

1923 **(U.S.)** National Research Council (formerly MENC Education Council).

1923 **(U.S.)** National Band Contest. The first of these contests was held in Chicago.

1924 **(U.S.)** National Association of Schools of Music (NASM) formed.

1925 **(U.S.)** Westminster Choir College founded by John Finlay Williamson.

1928 **(U.S.)** National Music Camp founded at Interlochen, Michigan. A prestigious year-round arts academy that attracts students and faculty from many countries.

1929 **(UK)** Scottish Academy of Music established. "Royal" prefix added in 1944.

1932 **(U.S.)** Music Education Research Council (formerly National Research Council).

1932 **(UK)** English Folk Dance and Song Society (EFDSS) formed when two organizations merged—the Folk-Song Society and the English Folk Dance Society.

1934 **(U.S.)** Music Educators National Conference (MENC), formerly MSNC.

1934 **(U.S.)** John Dewey wrote *Art as Experience*, which later influenced music educators in the aesthetic education movement.

1940 **(U.S.)** College Band Directors National Association (CBDNA) organized through MENC.

1940s **(U.S.)** Music therapy moved forward as a profession with the help of Everett Thayer Gaston, "Father of Music Therapy."

1942 **(UK)** Music Advisors National Association (MANA), later National Association of Music Educators (NAME), founded in England.

1944 **(UK)** Butler Act marked the beginning of a national system of education.

1945 **(Aus.)** Musica Viva Australia founded, promoting chamber music.

1945 **(U.S.)** Sweet Adelines established.

1946 **(U.S.)** Midwest Band Clinic first held. In 1996, renamed *Mid-West Clinic*: *An International Band and Orchestra Conference.*

1946 **(U.S.)** *The Instrumentalist* magazine founded and published by Traugott Rohner.

1947 **(UK)** International Council on Traditional Music (ICTM) founded. Helped found the International Music Council.

1947 **(UK)** Music Advisers National Association formally established.

1947 **(U.S.)** Educational Testing Service (ETS) founded near Princeton, New Jersey.

1948 **(U.S.)** American String Teachers Association formed.

1949 **(Int.)** At UNESCO's request, the International Music Council (IMC) was formed.

1950 **(U.S.)** Child's Bill of Rights in Music. Adopted by MENC in the same year.

1950 **(U.S.)** The National Association of Music Therapy founded.

1953 **(U.S.)** Society for Ethnomusicology founded.

1953 **(Int.)** International Society for Music Education (ISME) founded in Brussels.

1956 **(U.S./Int.)** Inter-American Music Council (CIDEM) founded. Worked closely with the International Music Council of UNESCO.

1956 **(Can.)** Duncan McKenzie presented the alto-tenor plan for keeping adolescent boys singing in church and school choirs throughout the period when their voices are changing.

1958 **(U.S.)** College Music Society first met.

1958 **(UK)** British Society for Music Therapy founded by Juliette Alvin.

1959 **(Can.)** Founding of Canadian Music Educators Association (CMEA).

1959 **(U.S.)** Woods Hole Conference held in Massachusetts. Jerome Bruner, director.

1960s **(U.S.)** Aesthetic education introduced in the U.S.

1960 **(U.S.)** National Band Association (NBA) founded by Traugott Rohner to promote excellence in all aspects of wind bands.

1961 **(UK)** Welsh Harp Society formed to popularize the instrument in schools.

1963 **(U.S.)** Yale Seminar took place at Yale University, New Haven, Connecticut, to consider the problems facing music education and to propose possible solutions.

1965 **(U.S.)** Manhattanville Music Curriculum Project (MMCP) founded. Purpose was to develop a sequential music-learning program for public school students.

1965 **(U.S.)** Congress created the National Endowment for the Arts (NEA).

1965 **(U.S.)** Under President Lyndon Johnson's Great Society, Congress passed the Elementary and Secondary Education Act (ESEA), designed to improve the quality of educational opportunities for all children.

1965 **(UK)** Traditional Music and Song Associations of Scotland founded, which paved the way for folk festivals in Scotland.

1965 **(U.S.)** Musical aptitude profile (MAP) devised by Edwin E. Gordon.

1967 **(U.S.)** Tanglewood Symposium. Music educators and others met to examine music in American society.

1967 **(Aus.)** Australian Society for Music Education (ASME) initiated by Sir Frank Calloway.

1967 **(U.S.)** The Juilliard Repertory Project. Juilliard School received a grant to enrich the repertory available to music teachers in grades K–6.

1968 **(U.S.)** American Orff-Schulwerk Association founded in Indiana.

1968 **(U.S.)** Hawaii Music Curriculum Program was designed to implement comprehensive musicianship concepts and practices in the state's public school music program.

1968 **(UK)** Royal Scottish Academy of Music and Drama (formerly Royal Scottish Academy of Music).

1968 **(U.S.)** National Association of Jazz Educators (NAJE) formed. NAJE became IAJE in 1989 to reflect global outreach.

1969 **(U.S.)** Go Project centered around cultural diversity and ethnic and world music. In 1994 it played a role in MENC's development of National Standards for Music Education.

1971 **(UK)** Folk Music Society of Ireland founded.

1971 **(Aus.)** Kodály Pilot Project. As a result, Kodály teaching became well established in Australia as the Developmental Music Program.

1972 **(UK)** The Royal Northern College of Music established (formerly the Royal College of Music—1883).

1972 **(Aus.)** First Pacific Festival of the Arts.

1972 **(U.S.)** Title IX of the Education Amendment was implemented.

1973 **(Aus.)** Kodály Music Education Institute of Australia was established.

1975 **(U.S.)** Public Law 94-103, Education for All Handicapped Children Act. Music classes subject to this law. Went into effect in 1977.

1975 **(Aus.)** Australia Council was established (formerly Australian Council for the Arts, 1968).

1977 **(U.S.)** *Coming to Our Senses*, The Rockefeller Report. One of the recommendations was the employment of local artists and teachers in school systems.

1979–81 **(U.S.)** Ann Arbor Symposium. Sponsored by MENC with cosponsors the University of Michigan and the Theodor Presser Foundation.

1980 **(Can.)** "O Canada" adopted as national anthem of Canada.

1980 **(UK)** Education Act of 1980. Introduced several new concepts in public education policy.

1981 **(U.S.)** Society for General Music formed. (Currently Council for General Music.)

1984 **(U.S.)** Wesleyan Symposium held to examine the relationship between social anthropology and music education.

1986 **(U.S.)** Crane Symposium: Toward an Understanding of the Teaching and Learning of Music Performance held at Potsdam, New York.

1986–91 **(U.S.)** Arts Propel. A five-year collaborative effort involving Harvard, ETS, and the Pittsburgh (PA) Public Schools.

1987 **(U.S.)** *General Music Today* established as an official MENC publication for general music teachers.

1988 **(UK)** Education Reform Act of 1988. Brought a power shift from local education authorities to the national government.

1989 **(UK)** Education Reform Order of 1989. Curriculum was organized to facilitate a national system for assessing student programs.

1989 **(Int.)** International Association of Jazz Educators was founded (formerly NAJE).

1990 **(U.S.)** Adoption of Americans with Disabilities Act (expanded version of the Education for All Handicapped Children Act of 1975).

1990 **(U.S.)** MENC Symposium on Multicultural Approaches to Music Education.

1991 **(U.S.)** First issue of the *Journal of Music Teacher Education* (JMTE), founded by Irma H. Collins.

1991 **(U.S.)** Education through Music (ETM) founded by Edmund Schroeder and Eldon Mayer Jr. to promote integration of music into elementary and middle school curricula.

1993 **(UK)** Dearing Report. The official evaluation of the national curriculum by Sir Ron Dearing, streamlining the assessment system.

1993 **(U.S.)** First issue of *Teaching Music* (TM).

1994 **(Aus.)** National Curriculum for Australian Schools included music as one of the six subjects within the National Arts Curriculum.

1994 **(Can.)** National Youth Band of Canada, under the Canadian Band Association, offered musical opportunity for outstanding instrumentalists between the ages of 16 and 21.

1995 **(U.S.)** Establishment of the Arts Education Partnership (AEP).

1996 **(UK)** National Association of Music Educators (NAME) founded when the Association for the Advancement of Teacher Education in Music (AATEM) joined forces with the Music Advisers National Association (MANA).

1996 **(UK)** Society for the Traditional Instruments of Wales founded.

1998 **(U.S.)** MENC's national executive board adopted the name *MENC: National Association for Music Education.* (Later officially became *NAfME*.)

2000 **(U.S.)** Housewright Symposium: Vision 2020. First such symposium sponsored by MENC since the Tanglewood Symposium of 1967.

2001 **(U.S.)** No Child Left Behind Act (reauthorized the Elementary and Secondary Education Act of 1965 [ESEA]).

2005 **(U.S.)** National Anthem Project launched by MENC as a public awareness campaign "to restore America's voice through music education."

2005 **(Aus.)** National Review of School Music Education. As a result, the Guidelines for Effective Music Education were developed to provide tools for individual schools to improve the health of their own programs.

2007 **(U.S.)** Tanglewood Symposium II: Charting the Future. Music educators and scholars met to take up challenges for music in the new century.

2010 **(Ire.)** Founding of the Society for Music Education in Ireland (SMEI).

2011 **(U.S.)** National Coalition for Core Arts Standards formed.

2011 **(U.S.)** On September 1, National Association for Music Education officially changed its acronym from *MENC* to *NAfME*.

Introduction

From the Sumerians (ca. 2300 BCE) to the contemporary Western world (21st c. AD), people have wanted to know about words and their meanings. There are many works that are designed to introduce words and their meanings, from bilingual dictionaries to specific, descriptive works in specialized fields, in which lexical items are referred to as *terms* rather than as *words*. According to the now-ubiquitous Wikipedia, a dictionary—also called a *wordbook*, *lexicon*, or *vocabulary*—is a collection of words in one or more specific languages, often listed alphabetically, with usage information, definitions, etymologies, phonetics, pronunciations, and other information provided therein. This *Dictionary of Music Education* is descriptive and presents *terms*, *people*, *events*, and *organizations* in English, alphabetically, with etymologies, definitions, and occasionally historical information.

Music education has a long and diverse history, dating from the history of humanity itself, that shows *music making* as a basic and universal instinct. While performing and listening to music are major parts of this history, it is the passionate and indomitable spirit of music education that has cultivated and spread the beauty and importance of music in our lives. The history of music is, in many ways, the history of music education. When a musician speaks to another person about music (whether or not the other person is a musician) and begins to explain the process of *music making*, in a sense, that musician has become a music teacher.

This dictionary includes many *people* who have devoted their lives to the promotion of music *as educators*. These individuals, over at least 1,000 years, have had as a guiding philosophy the importance of teaching and learning music and an intense belief in the sharing of their musical gifts with children and adults. They have used their own personal resources to create events for like-minded individuals that, in their coming together, have resulted in long-standing music *organizations*, such as MENC, founded in 1907 (now NA*f*ME), and its concomitant associations. From Julia Crane and the Potsdam Musical Institute (also known as the Crane Normal Institute, 1884), to Philip C. Haydn and his advertisement of the supervisors meeting in Keokuk, Iowa (1907), to Charles Leonhard and Robert W. House's *Foundations and Principles of Music Education* (1949) and Bennett Reimer's own challenging

A Philosophy of Music Education (1970), all have demonstrated their importance to the history of American music education. These events and books, along with Richard Colwell's impressive *Handbook of Research on Music Teaching and Learning*, published in 1992, highlight only a few of those educators (*people*) who chose to spend their lives in the creation of *events*, *organizations*, and *publications* in the name of music education.

Events such as the Go Project, the Tanglewood Symposium, the Ann Arbor Symposium, and the Task Force on Music Teaching Education for the Nineties (and its publication in 1987 of *Music Teacher Education: Partnership and Process*) were catalysts for the formation of many programs created by music educators in the development and spread of the best in music education.

Many reports from government agencies in the United States, as well as in Australia, Canada, the United Kingdom, and Northern Ireland, have had a lasting impact on music education. In the U.S. there is the Elementary and Secondary Education Act of 1965, which continues to influence the work of music educators. The Lynn and Dearing Reports on curriculum and assessment in the UK (1993), the Massey Report in Canada (1949), and the National Review of School Music Education in Australia (2004) have brought about changes in the music curriculum and the organization of schools. All have had far-reaching consequences for the teaching of music in schools.

You will find music terms from all parts of the UK that have found their way into the teaching and learning vocabulary of music educators globally. There are terms from Scotland and Wales that are indigenous to those countries because of their specific cultures. And there is, of course, a mixture of terms found in folk music that have spread throughout the world and are readily grasped by all. While there is continuing debate over the claim that music is a *universal language*, certainly musicians and music educators do practice a universal music language of their own.

As first noted, music is a basic and universal instinct. In this dictionary of music education, you will find terms invented and developed by people who committed themselves to the discipline of music. These people came together to create events that have been important to the spread of music through special organizations focused on the best that can be found in music education practices.

While we now have an immense system of events and organizations throughout the world, it is still people—music educators—who continue to devote their time and energy to the ongoing success of music programs everywhere. The history of many of these people, along with terms, events, and organizations, is found in this *Dictionary of Music Education*.

A

ABBOT, ERIC OSCAR (1929–1988). (Can.) Bandmaster, cornetist, pianist, organist, composer, arranger. *See also* CANADIAN MUSIC FESTIVAL MOVEMENT.

ABORIGINAL ARTS BOARD (AAB). (Aus.) Est. 1973. In 1975 it was made one of the seven boards of the Australia Council. In 1989 it was replaced by the **Aboriginal Arts Committee** (AAC).

ABORIGINAL ARTS COMMITTEE (AAC). (Aus.) One of two major committees of the **Australia Council** that was formed by the minister for the arts, tourism, and territories in 1989 to replace the **Aboriginal Arts Board**. AAC has its own three specialized art-form committees—Performing Arts, Literature, and Visual Arts/Craft—each comprising practitioners from these fields. *See also* ARTS COUNCIL OF AUSTRALIA.

ABORIGINAL ENGLISH. (Aus.) One of a number of variants converging on Australian English. It is especially characterized by the pronunciation, lexis, and idiom that are typical of many Aboriginal people. It includes distinctive elements of vocabulary and grammar that are taken from Aboriginal languages and alternative, or obsolete, uses of Australian English.

ABORIGINAL ISLANDER DANCE THEATRE (AIDT). (Aus.) An Australian dance company formed in 1976 that constitutes the performing wing of the **National Aboriginal Islander Skills Development Association**; presents a fusion of Western classical and contemporary dance and traditional dance.

ABSOLUTE PITCH. (Perfect pitch.) The ability of persons who know the musical alphabet to name any note struck or plucked on a musical instrument without any prompt.

ACADEMY SCHOOLS. (UK.) *Originally*, a school of philosophy founded by Plato. *Currently*, a school above the elementary level; a private high school that includes music and the arts.

A CAPPELLA TRADITION. In church style, choral singing without accompaniment. Generally, any unaccompanied vocal performance. This early choral form reappeared in the early 20th century when **Peter C. Lutkin** used this title with the first university choir, the A Cappella Choir of Northwestern University. In 1928 this nationally prominent choir sang for the convention of the **Music Supervisors National Conference**. Three other prominent choirs emerged immediately: the **St. Olaf Lutheran Choir** (1912), **F. Melius Christiansen**, conductor; the **Westminster Choir** (1925), John Finley Williamson, conductor; and the Paulist Choristers, Father William J. Finn, conductor. The St. Olaf Choir set standards that became the performance practices of the "a cappella tradition" in high schools and colleges. Soon, strong state organizations promoted excellence in choral singing by sponsoring contests, festivals, and honor choruses at regional and state levels.

ACCORDION. A portable wind instrument with a small keyboard and free metal reeds that sound when air is forced past them through pleated bellows operated by the player.

ACCULTURATION. Cultural modification of an individual or group by borrowing and adapting traits from another culture.

ACOUSTIC INSTRUMENTS. The production of sound on a musical instrument without the aid of electronic means. Classical or Spanish guitar is generally understood to be an acoustic instrument. Stringed instruments, violin, viola, cello (short for violoncello), and bass are also found in this category.

ACTION RESEARCH. Trying out ideas in practice as a means of improvement and as a means of increasing knowledge about a given topic. It is a four-step process: 1) plan, 2) action, 3) observation, and 4) reflection. A research spiral is when the cycle of these four steps has been completed and the process repeated in revised form until the objectives of study are met. Kurt Lewin is often cited as the "father" of action research.
  Lit.: Regelski, Thomas A. *Teaching General Music: Action Learning for Middle and Secondary Schools*, 1981.

ACTION SONG. Children's songs in which bodily movements depict the action of the words.

ADASKIN, MURRAY (1906–2002). (Can.) Toronto-born, Adaskin was a violinist, composer, conductor, and teacher at the University of Saskatchewan. From 1923 to 1936 he was an orchestral and chamber musician with the Toronto Symphony Orchestra. Later named head of music at the University of Saskatchewan. He was a composer-in-residence at this university, the *first* appointment of this type in Canada.

ADEQUATE YEARLY PROGRESS (AYP). The measure by which schools, districts, and states are held accountable for student performance under Title I of the **No Child Left Behind Act of 2001** (NCLB), the current version of the **Elementary and Secondary Education Act**.

AYP is used to determine if schools are successfully educating their students. The law requires states to use a single accountability system for public schools to determine whether all students, as well as individual subgroups of students, are making progress toward meeting state academic content standards. The goal is to have all students reaching proficient levels in reading and math by 2014 as measured by performance on state tests. Progress on those standards must be tested yearly in grades three through eight, and in one grade in high school. The results are then compared to prior years, and, based on state-determined AYP standards, used to determine if the school has made adequate progress toward the proficiency goal (Department of Education, 2001).

ADJUDICATION. The act of adjudicating; the making of musical judgments about solo or ensemble performances in contests or festivals.

ADOLESCENT BASS THEORY. *See* SWANSON, FREDERICK.

ADVANCED PLACEMENT. A course, or courses, offered in many high schools with the course content similar to that found in many freshman-level university courses.

AEROPHONE. An ancient to modern classification of music instruments that produce their sounds by the vibration of air, including the accordion, pipe and reed organ families, flute, and mouth-blown reed instruments.

AESTHETIC EDUCATION. A teaching approach that focuses on the deeper artistic qualities of music and the other arts by showing students where and how to find these deeper qualities through interactive and feelingful experiences. Aesthetic education involves two disciplines: *aesthetics*, known in earlier times as "a study of the beautiful"; and *education*, which addresses methods of teaching and learning for all instructional levels.

In the fourth century BCE, music education was actually quite well developed through the writings of Aristotle and Plato, but eventually lost its way and focus. Through the years scholars have changed their position regarding aesthetics, from a study solely of the beautiful to that of the relationship of music to human senses and the intellect.

While arguments continued about the philosophical basis for the teaching of music, scholars such as **Alexander Baumgarten** and Friedrich Schiller in the 1700s explored the concept of aesthetic education more deeply. (They were the first to use the term "aesthetic education.") Much later, through the works of Victor Zuckerkandl, Leonard Meyer, and **Susanne Langer**, scholars in music education began to examine a different approach to the philosophical foundation of music education. From the 1950s through the 1970s, scholars such as **Abraham Schwadron**, **Charles Leonhard**, **Bennett Reimer**, and **Harry Broudy** explored the idea of teaching music experientially and involving students in "making music" rather than through the older approach of lectures and readings about music. They began to seriously challenge the idea of music being taught for reasons other than the nature of music itself. Music was being taught for utilitarian reasons: for health, citizenship, and entertainment. As a result of these scholars, the music-education profession began to move toward teaching music for aesthetics, or musical aesthetics. These artistic qualities are found in the very foundation of the structure of music and promote a more feelingful approach to its understanding and enjoyment. Today, a curriculum in *aesthetic education* provides students with reasons why the teaching and learning of music are important to their personal and professional lives through an exploration of their beliefs about music and music education.

For a greater understanding of the historical development of the *aesthetic education movement*, see the books listed below.

Bib.: Abeles, H., C. H. Hoffer, and R. Klotman, *Foundations of Music Education*, 1984; Broudy, Harry, *Enlightened Cherishing: An Essay on Aesthetic Education*, 1974; Henry, Nelson, ed., *Basic Concepts in Music Education*, 1957; Mark, Michael, and C. Gary, *A History of American Music Education*, 3rd ed., 2007; Reimer, Bennett, *A Philosophy of Music Education*, 2nd ed., 1989.

Lit.: Alperson, Philip, ed., *What Is Music?: An Introduction to the Philosophy of Music*, 1987 and 1994; Leonhard, C., and R. W. House, *Foundations and Principles of Music Education*, 2nd ed., 1972; Schiller, Friedrich, *Letters upon the Aesthetic Education of Man*, trans. Reginald Snell, 1909–14; Schwadron, Abraham, *Aesthetics: Dimensions for Music Education*, 1967; Reimer, Bennett, *A Philosophy of Music Education: Advancing the Vision*, 3rd ed., 2003; Reimer, Bennett, ed., *Toward an Aesthetic Education*, 1971; Runes, Dagobert, ed., *A Dictionary of Philosophy*, 1962.

AFRICAN DRUMMING ENSEMBLES. Instrumental ensembles that consist of several drums, a bell, and a rattle. Each ensemble usually has a master drum, a bell-like instrument called a **gankogui,** and a group of secondary drummers. Since the early 1980s, these ensembles have been strongly integrated into music classes for children as well as middle and high schools.

AGROTOU. Improvised music in music therapy. Music created by the patient, therapist, or both; reflects the state of the patient-therapist relationship at any given moment.

AIKEN, CHARLES (1818–1892). (Cincinnati, OH.) Music educator. Taught in primary grades in the early part of 1855 but had begun teaching in high schools when the Hughes and Woodward high schools opened in 1852, thus providing the city with music instruction for all public school students. **Edward Birge** called Aiken "the most striking figure with the exception of **Lowell Mason**." Upon Aiken's retirement he was credited with laying "the foundation of a high musical culture, not only with the pupils but also with the public at large." His marble bust stands in Cincinnati's Music Hall, a memorial contributed by his former pupils in love and in recognition of the contribution he made for the establishment of the city's musical reputation; a music educator with the highest of ideals, both musical and personal; lived a life worthy of reexamination by his followers in the profession.

AINSWORTH PSALTER. A collection of psalms that Rev. Henry Ainsworth collected, translated, and published in 1612 for his congregation of English Separatists in Amsterdam, Holland. Referred to as the *Ainsworth Psalter*, it included both prose and poetic translations, extensively annotated, of the entire Book of Psalms; it also included 29 melodies borrowed by Ainsworth from "our former English Psalms [and from] the French and Dutch Psalms." In variety of length, meter, and rhythm, Ainsworth's choices were remarkable. The psalter was used by the Pilgrims of the Plymouth Colony, and also by settlers at Ipswich and Salem. Another psalter, the ***Bay Psalm Book***, published by the Massachusetts Bay Colony, finally replaced the *Ainsworth Psalter* in 1692.

ALEATORY MUSIC. (From Latin *alea*, a dice game.) Random notes, chance music, either in compositional process or in the performer's realization. Random composition generated by the throw of dice or another way of producing members by chance. Used as early as 18th century by Mozart. A more serious approach in modern times was cultivated by **John Cage** (1912–1992), who often used the Chinese *I Ching*, from which he derived numbers. Related subjects are probability, information theory, experimental music, computer music, and indeterminacy.

ALEXANDER TECHNIQUE. A relaxation technique developed by F. Matthias Alexander (1869–1953). This involves identifying and correcting posture positions and body movements that cause tension and inhibit flexibility of movement. Most often used in the teaching of singing but may be, and is, used by other music teachers. *See also* CONABLE, BARBARA.

ALICE SPRINGS. (Aus.) Desert town situated in the geographic center of Australia. The Arrernt Aboriginal people have lived in and around this area for thousands of years. The Aboriginal name for Alice Springs is *Mparntwe*. Situated on the Todd River, surveyed in 1888, and officially called Stuart until 1933, then renamed after *Alice* Todd, wife of Sir Charles Todd. Founded as a telegraph post in 1871 and known primarily for its annual Country Music Festival for Aborigines throughout the region. Also there is the Central Australian Aboriginal Media Association (CAAMA), founded in 1980, which through its radio and television stations broadcasts an array of Aboriginal bands and choirs. For a town this size (approximately 21,000), local music activity is strong: a town band, Desert Harmony Chorus, Junior Singers, Country Music Association, and Central Australian Folk Society. The Alice Springs Music Teachers' Association presents regular recitals, and the Centralian **Eisteddfod** is held there each May.

ALLEN, GEORGE LEAVIS (1827–1897). (Aus.) An itinerant music teacher in the colonial/early federation period in Victoria. He used the **fixed doh** method of **John Hullah**.

ALLENTOWN CIVIC BAND (1828). An early American **wind band** from Pennsylvania that still performs today; usual size of early bands was between eight and 15 players: two oboes, two clarinets, two horns, a bassoon, and a drum.

ALOUETTE. Popular French Canadian children's song about plucking feathers from a lark; originated in France. First published in 1879 in a *Pocket Song Book* for the use of students and graduates of McGill College (Montreal). Folklorist Marius Barbeau (1883–1969) claimed the song's ultimate origin was France. Today, the song is used to teach French to English-speaking children in Canada and other English-speaking countries, by singing names of body parts (e.g., *je te plumerai la tete* ["I shall pluck your head"]).

ALPEN, HUGO (1842–1917). (Aus.) Born in Germany, immigrated to Australia in 1858 as choral conductor, pianist, and public school singing master in rural NSW. Appointed superintendent of music in Australia in 1884. Gradually transferred teaching of music from **tonic sol-fa** to a **movable-doh** staff notation method of his own devising, which preempted similar developments in English music education by almost a decade.

ALTDORF. (Swz.) A town in central Switzerland; the legendary home of William Tell, a Swiss patriot said to have been forced by the Austrian governor to use a bow and arrow to shoot an apple off the head of Tell's son, Walter (ca. 1307). The subject of the *William Tell Overture* by G. Rossini.

ALTO-TENOR PLAN. The term *alto-tenor* was first used by **Ralph Baldwin** (1899) to refer to his decision to place boys' changing voices on the third, or tenor part, of the vocal score. By placing them on the "tenor" part, Baldwin referred to them as *alto-tenor*, so that it would not be confused with the mature tenor voice. The earliest published music in which *alto-tenor* appears seems to be the *Beacon Song Collection*, edited by Herbert Griggs, **Silver Burdett**, 1895. The alto-tenor plan was first conceived by **Duncan McKenzie** in his book *Training the Boy's Changing Voice* (1956), which promoted the idea of adolescent boys continuing to sing in church and school choirs throughout the period of their voice change. McKenzie writes that the term *alto-tenor* is used to describe and classify the boy's voice after it has lowered to the stage when the changed voice begins to develop. The voice is still *alto* in quality and range, but it has not yet become masculine in terms of *tenor* or *bass*. It is a gradual process, and in moving through the mutational process, he will gradually lose the upper notes and add lower notes until the voice settles.

ALYAWARRA. (Aus.) An Aboriginal language from the Sandover River area in Central Australia.

AMBIENT SOUNDS. Existing on all sides; surrounding of sound as in an echo. Quality of room construction determines quality of musical sounds, as described in the subject *acoustics*.

AMBROSE, ROBERT S. (1824–1908). (UK.) Born in Chelmsford, England, he received early music training from his father, an organist at Chelmsford Cathedral. Family immigrated to Hamilton, Ontario, Canada, in 1845. Ambrose left Canada in 1857 only to return in 1863 to become musical director of what is now Hamilton Ladies College until 1889. In 1891 Ambrose served as president of the Canadian Society of Musicians. The formation of several conservatories in the 1870s led to the opportunity for all class levels of society to learn music; Ambrose's song, *One Sweetly Solemn Thought*, became one of the most popular songs ever to be published in the 19th century.

AMERICAN BANDMASTERS ASSOCIATION (ABA). Founded in 1929 by **Edwin Franko Goldman**, with **John Philip Sousa** as honorary life president. It recognizes outstanding achievement on the part of concert band conductors and composers. The current membership (invitational) comprises approximately 300 band conductors and composers in the U.S. and Canada. It includes 70 associate members from music businesses and corporations that provide significant services to bands and through the publication of band music.

AMERICAN CHORAL DIRECTORS ASSOCIATION (ACDA). The strongest supporter of choral music in America. Founded in 1959, it holds biennial meetings and publishes *The Choral Journal* each month (excluding summer months). Membership now exceeds 18,000. ACDA is a strong supporter of choral music education in the public schools.

***AMERICAN HIGH SCHOOL TODAY* (1959).** A book written by **James Conant**, influential education critic from Harvard University, that stressed the need for stronger academic preparation. While he promoted the need for strong math and science programs, he urged the inclusion of art and music in high school elective programs.

AMERICAN MUSIC THERAPY ASSOCIATION (AMTA). As of January 1, 1998, the **NAMT** (1950–1997) and AAMT (1971–1997) unified to become the AMTA. There are a variety of definitions for the term *music therapy*. As **Kenneth Bruscia** asserts, "music therapy is a systematic process of intervention wherein the therapist helps the client to achieve health, using musical experiences and the relationships that develop through them as dynamic forces of change." Leslie Bunt concludes: "Music therapy is the use of organized sounds and music within an evolving relationship between client and therapist to support and encourage physical, mental, social and emotional well-being."

A music therapist may also hold the designations CMT, ACMT, or RMT—designations that were previously conferred by the now-defunct AAMT and NAMT, and that will remain legitimate until 2020.

Bib.: Bruscia, Kenneth E., *Defining Music Therapy*, 2nd ed., 1998, p. 54; Ockelford, Adam, *Music for Children and Young People with Complex Needs*, 2008, p. 38.

AMERICAN ORFF-SCHULWERK ASSOCIATION (AOSA). Founded in Muncie, Indiana, on May 11, 1968. Its formation was the result of 10 passionate and dedicated music educators who recognized the value and potential of the Orff-Schulwerk music and movement pedagogy developed by **Carl Orff** (1895–1982) and Gunild Keetman (1904–1990). The AOSA founders acted in hopes of organizing the excitement that was building for this approach, which was spreading across the country, and to promote its implementation in American music education. Known as the Orff-Schulwerk Association (OSA) until 1970, AOSA grew from 10 founding members to an enrollment of 332 in its first year. Seven chartered local chapters expanded through the years to more than 90 today, with current membership at approximately 4,500.

AMERICAN SIGN LANGUAGE (ASL). Once called *Amesian*, it is the dominant sign language of deaf (hearing impaired, hearing loss) Americans, including deaf communities in the U.S., in the English-speaking parts of Canada, and in some regions of Mexico. British Sign Language (BSL) is unlike ASL, and the two are not mutually intelligible. ASL is related to French Sign Language. The story of deaf education in America had its beginnings in Martha's Vineyard with a minister, Thomas Hopkins Gallaudet, who was enlisted by a father to educate his deaf daughter, Alice Cogswell. Little is known of sign language in the U.S. before 1817. In Canada there are five broad regions of ASL: the Pacific, Prairie, Ontario, Quebec, and Atlantic regions. Black ASL is influenced by African-American English (AAE). This influence is evident in the younger black deaf community, with the use of signs for AAE words such as *my bad* and *whassup*. Black ASL evolved out of racial segregation in the U.S., especially in the South. At that time only black teachers were permitted to instruct black deaf children. (Currently, according to ASL, the deaf community prefers the terminology, "Americans who have a hearing loss," or "a child who has a hearing loss.")

AMERICAN STRING TEACHERS ASSOCIATION (ASTA). Formed in 1948 in Cleveland, Ohio, by a concerned group of string educators as a professional organization of string teachers, orchestra directors, and professional players that promotes excellence in string music. The **National School Orchestra Association** (NSOA) merged with ASTA in the 1990s.

AMERICANS WITH DISABILITIES ACT (ADA). Public Law 101-336. Legislation enacted in 1990 to establish a comprehensive prohibition of discrimination based on disability. Public schools are subject to the ADA, and the statute mandates that school districts provide a "free and appropriate public education" to disabled students who fall under its protection.

ANCIENT AND MODERN SCOTTISH SONGS **(1769, 1776).** Scholarly work by David Herd (1732–1810) and George Paton (1721–1807). Scotland has one of the longest European traditions of studying its native music. Song scholarship under the direction of David Herd is considered trustworthy.

ANCIENT BRITISH MUSIC (1742). The 1700s saw the earliest appearance in print of Welsh music for the harp. The first important publication for the harp was the 1742 collection of 24 untitled tunes, *Antient [sic] British Music*, compiled in London by the blind John Parry (master of the triple harp) and Evan Williams.

ANCIENT CONSORT (1776). (UK.) A company of musicians who regularly performed together; an early form of *concert*.

ANCIENT NATIONAL AIRS OF GWENT AND MORGANWQ. Welsh folk song. Generally, Welsh folk songs have no ornamentation (passing tones, slurs, long melismas); however, older ballads and carols are highly ornamented, especially in South Wales. The level of ornamentation in the "Ancient National Airs" is high (Huws, 1988). This probably owes more to the art music of the period than to the folk tradition.

ANDERSON, WILLIAM M. (1948–). (U.S.) Music educator and professor emeritus at Kent State University; was founding director of the Kent Center for the Study of **World Musics** there, where he established a distinctive PhD program that combines music education and world musics. He is author, compiler, and editor of books, accompanying recordings, and articles, many relating to the intersection of music education and world musics. At the 1990 MENC conference, he led a national symposium on multicultural approaches to music education. Anderson has been president of the 6,000-member Ohio Music Education Association and board president of the Ohio Foundation for Music Education. He received the Ohio Music Education Association Distinguished Service Award. The book *Integrating Music into the Elementary Classroom* by Anderson and Joy E. Lawrence is one of the more popular college texts that includes curriculum guides on world music.

ANDOVER EDUCATORS. Founded by **Barbara Conable**; a network of music-education teachers dedicated to placing music education on a sound somatic (physical or anatomical) foundation for all time. Each is trained to present the six-hour course *What Every Musician Needs to Know about the Body*, which uses an innovative and specific technique called **body mapping** to enhance musicians' abilities and to help those in pain or discomfort. *See also* ALEXANDER TECHNIQUE.

ANDRESS, BARBARA (1929–). Internationally known music educator, author, clinician, and organizational leader who devoted much of her career to early-childhood education. She has been an elementary music teacher, instrumental music teacher, district supervisor, and college professor. After a highly successful career as district supervisor in the public schools of Arizona, she was recruited for an associate professorship in music education at Arizona State University in 1972. She retired in 1990, which completed her 36-year career in **music education**. In 2002 she was inducted into the **Music Educators Hall of Fame**. She is the author of a very popular book for early childhood, *Music Experiences in Early Childhood*, published by Holt, Rinehart and Winston.

ANGKLUNG. (Aus.) A generic term for sets of tuned, shaken bamboo rattles attached to a bamboo frame. Tubes are carved to have a resonant pitch when struck, and are tuned in octaves. The base of the frame is held in one hand, while the other hand shakes the instrument rapidly. Popular throughout Southeast Asia, it originated in today's Indonesia and has been played by the Sudanese for many centuries. At least one Sudanese *angklung buncis* ensemble exists in the U.S.: "Angklung Buncis Sukahejo" is an ensemble at Evergreen State College (WA). Videos are available on YouTube. On July 9, 2011, there were 5,182 people from many nations that played the *angklung* together in Washington, DC. They were listed in the *Guinness Book of Records* as the largest *angklung* ensemble in the world.

ANN ARBOR SYMPOSIUM. Meetings sponsored by **MENC**, cosponsored by the University of Michigan and the Theodore Presser Foundation between 1979 and 1981. Meetings were held at the University of Michigan. History: There were three sessions:

1. (1978) Papers presented by music educators to acquaint psychologists with music-education practices. A response was made by a *psychologist*.
2. (1979) Presentation of papers by psychologists on topics discussed by music educators in the previous year. A response was made by a *music educator*.
3. (1981) Music educators and psychologists summarized current knowledge and theory in motivation and creativity, and they applied this to the teaching and learning of music at all levels. Responses were made by *music educator panelists*.

Lit.: Music Educators National Conference, *Documentary Report of the Ann Arbor Symposium*, 1981; Music Educators National Conference, *Ann*

Arbor Symposium on the Applications of Psychology to the Teaching and Learning of Music, 1983.

ANTHEM. English-speaking Protestant churches' equivalent of the Latin motet. An Anglican creation with a place in the Church of England liturgy. Usually, but not necessarily, accompanied by organ; frequently includes passages for solo voice. The term is also less strictly used, as in the phrase "national anthem," to denote a solemn, hymnlike song.

ANTILL, JOHN HENRY (1904–1986). Australian musician and prolific composer; best known for the ballet suite *Corroboree* (1944). At age 16, he designed a multitoned steam whistle for the C-36 class locomotive for the New South Wales Government. A singer, conductor, and composer of several operas, he became the Australian Broadcasting Corporation's music supervisor for NSW. He encouraged Australian composers and promoted their work. A bronze bust of Antill by Dawn Swayne is held at the Sydney Conservatorium of Music.

APOLLO. The great Olympian god of prophecy and oracles, healing, plague and disease, **music**, song and poetry, archery, and the protection of the young.

APPLE ON A STICK. (U.S. and Can.) Long-standing interactive chant in which children stand in pairs or occasionally in a circle or lines, clapping, patting, stomping, snapping fingers, and moving their bodies in complex patterns that complement the chant or song.

ARIRANG. (Korea.) A favorite Korean folk song, a song of love and longing. The title is the name of a mountain in Korea. The *Kayakum*, a harp-like instrument, is widely used. This song appears in several basic school music series both in the English and the Korean languages. A greater melodic embellishment occurs in the Korean version. Dr. Kan-sook Lee, a Korean music educator, writes that "Korean modes are not based on equally tempered scales . . . the pentatonic scale as found on the piano is fundamentally different from that of the Korean mode."

  Lit.: Swanson, Bessie, *Music in the Education of Children*, 4th ed., 1969, pp. 265–67; Wolfe, Irving, Beatrice Krone, and Margaret Fullerton, *Voices of the World*, 1960.

ARTISTS-IN-SCHOOLS PROGRAM. (U.S.). A program funded by the National Endowment for the Arts that involved bringing artists into classrooms to share their talents and abilities with students. Funding began in 1970 after the success of the visual artist-in-residence program in 1969. Because the program is federally funded, some limiting policies have been imposed on schools and artists.

ART MUSIC. (Aus.) Music that has a theoretical foundation and consequently some form of notation, as distinct from folk music. In Australia, most composers from ca. 1850 to 1890 worked within European models, and many undertook compositional training in Europe or the United Kingdom. Percy Grainger's "English Country Gardens" (1908) is a good example of the influence of folk music written in the English tradition. From the 1960s, strong influences emerged from Aboriginal and Southeast Asian music and instruments, American jazz and blues, to the belated discovery of European atonality and the avant-garde. State-based symphony orchestras, originally managed by the Australian Broadcasting Corporation (ABC), but now operating independently, have played a major role in performing mainstream orchestral repertoire, as well as commissioning new works from Australian composers. **Musica Viva Australia** is the largest entrepreneur of chamber music in the world.

ARTS COUNCIL OF AUSTRALIA. A nongovernmental organization, founded in Sydney in 1946, which aimed to promote public appreciation of the arts.

ARTS EDUCATION. (Can.) From a report (*Learning to Live; Living to Learn: Perspectives on Arts Education in Canada*) of the Canadian Conference for the Arts (2005), a project of **Canada Council** and **UNESCO** that outlines 50 values that the arts bring to Canadian society. Arts education allows one to learn in, about, and through the arts in formal and informal ways, in schools and communities.

ARTS EDUCATION PARTNERSHIP (AEP). (U.S.) Est. 1995 through an agreement between the **NEA** (National Endowment for the Arts) and the U.S. Department of Education based on research that shows that the arts (music, dance, theater, and visual arts) help students to develop in areas such as creativity, critical thinking, communication, and academic achievement. AEP is a national coalition of more than 100 education, arts, business, cultural, government, and philanthropic organizations committed to making high-quality arts education accessible to all U.S. students.

ARTS INTEGRATION. 1. A term used generally to describe arts courses, typically including music, visual art, drama, and dance, that are included in the school curricula. In 1980, the **Discipline-Based Art Education** (DBAE) program attempted to establish the arts as a more meaningful part of school curricula. (*See also* DISCIPLINE-BASED MUSIC EDUCATION.) **2.** Instruction combining two or more content areas, wherein the arts constitute one or more of the integrated areas. The integration is based on shared or related concepts, and instruction in each content area has depth and integrity reflected by embedded assessments, standards, and objectives; it uses the fine and performing arts as primary pathways to learning. An integrated curriculum with the arts involves:

- organizing instruction to allow students to question and engage in real-life issues;
- combining subject areas, not separating them;
- developing skills and applying knowledge in more than one area of study—education through the arts allows students to learn how to analyze, evaluate, and draw reasoned conclusions from what they see and hear.

ARTS PROPEL. A five-year collaborative effort involving Harvard's **Project Zero**, the **Educational Testing Service** (ETS), and teachers and administrators of the Pittsburgh (PA) public schools (1986–1991). Model programs combining instruction and assessment developed for middle and high school students in three art forms: music, visual arts, and imaginative writing. In the classroom, students approached the art form along three crisscrossing pathways that gave Arts Propel its name: 1) *production*—students were inspired to learn the basic skills and principles of the art form by putting their ideas into music, words, or visual form; 2) *perception*—students studied works of art to understand the kinds of choices artists make and to see connections between their own and others' work; 3) *reflection*—students assessed their work according to personal goals and standards of excellence in the field.

ARTS TRAINING AUSTRALIA. An elite national arts training institute that produces a new wave of artists and teachers, as found at Southern Cross University at Lismore, New South Wales. The Office for the Arts (OFTA) develops and administers programs and policies for this and other arts organizations. Arts Training Australia is a member of the Australian Roundtable for Arts Training Excellence, founded in 2003. Arts Training's primary purpose is to promote and enhance the quality and effectiveness of vocational training and education by providing a forum through which industry can express its vocational education and training needs. Currently, as a $15 billion a year industry, the arts are a powerful 21st-century megatrend.

ASH GROVE. (UK.) A traditional Welsh folk song that has provided the melody for numerous sets of lyrics. The most well-known version was written in English by John Oxenford in the 19th century. The first published tune was in 1802 in *The Bardic Museum.* The tune might be much older, as a similar tune appears in *The Beggar's Opera* by John Gay (1728), in the song *Cease Your Funning.* In 1922, however, **Frank Kidson** claimed that John Gay's tune derives from the Morris dance tune, *Constant Billing*, which is first known in John Playford's *Dancing is Master.*

ASME TRUST FUND. (Aus.) (Est. 1993.) Registered as a tax-deductible fund on the **Register of Cultural Organizations** (est. 1991). The fund is used to:

- encourage young Australians in performance and composition;
- sponsor the development of young music educators;
- house resource material; and
- provide professional development activities for music educators.

See also AUSTRALIAN SOCIETY FOR MUSIC EDUCATION.

ASSESSMENT. A term used to describe an evaluative process for determining what has been learned and levels of competency; encompasses a variety of techniques and methods and is often used interchangeably with the terms *evaluation*, *testing*, or *measurement.*

ASSIMILATION. Process by which an individual or group is able to adapt and become part of a new culture. In **Jean Piaget**'s *Theory of Cognitive Development*, *assimilation* refers to the individual's ability to internalize and conceptualize environmental experiences. Piaget used *assimilation* in conjunction with *accommodation*, which refers to the adjustment an individual makes to environmental *stimuli. See also* ZIMMERMAN, MARILYN PFLEDERER.

ASSOCIATION FOR CULTURAL EQUITY (ACE). (U.S.) Founded by **Alan Lomax** to explore and preserve the world's expressive traditions with humanistic commitment and scientific engagement. Housed at the Fine Arts campus of Hunter College, NY, it was chartered as a charitable organization in the state of New York in 1983.

ASSOCIATION FOR TECHNOLOGY IN MUSIC INSTRUCTION (ATMI). (U.S.) Formed in 1975 as a special interest group of the Association for the Development of Computer-Based Instruction Systems (ADCIS).

Since 1992, ATMI has been an independent professional organization. Its mission is to improve music teaching and learning through introducing technologies into the music-learning environment. It does this by providing a forum for the scholarly presentation of pedagogical and technical information for music teachers in higher education.

AUDIATION. A term devised by **Edwin E. Gordon** for the process of hearing and comprehending music internally when no physical sound is present. According to Gordon, audiation is fundamental to music aptitude and music achievement, and it is the basis of his music learning theory. Though not accepted by Gordon, **inner hearing** is a similar process that is used by proponents of **Zoltan Kodály**.

AUDITION. A performance test given to an aspiring singer, instrumentalist, or symphony conductor, preliminary to the offer of a place in a conservatory (school) or a performance contract.

AURAL TRANSMISSIONS. This refers to the means by which musical compositions, performing practices, and knowledge are passed from musician to musician. *Oral transmission* implies transmission by mouth in the medium of words. *Aural transmission* refers to learning music by ear from sound itself, without the aid of words. *See also* GORDON, EDWIN ELIAS; SYSTEMATIC AURAL TRANSMISSION.

AUSDANCE. Australia's professional dance advocacy; part of a network of Ausdance organizations delivering integrated programs across the country, anticipating industry issues, and providing innovative and inclusive responses. Its mission is to educate, inspire, and support the dance community to reach its potential as a dynamic force within local, national, and international communities.

AUSMUSIC. (Aus.) A training and promotion organization encouraging popular musical training in secondary schools and technical colleges.

AUSTRALIA COUNCIL. Est. 1975 (formerly the Australian Council for the Arts, an advisory body formed in 1968); an organization through the federal government made up of several boards representing different arts (including the performing arts board) and differently constituted boards; awards grants to individuals and organizations and creative-arts fellowships to selected artists. It is paralleled by smaller programs at the state level. (Informally known as *Australia Council for the Arts*.)

AUSTRALIAN AND NEW ZEALAND ASSOCIATION FOR RESEARCH IN MUSIC EDUCATION (ANZARME). Established at the organization's first annual general meeting in 2007. Formerly the Australian Association for Research in Music Education (est. 1995), and before that the Association of Music Education Lecturers (est. 1977). Primary objective is to promote communication between music-education researchers and music educators.

AUSTRALIAN COUNTRY MUSIC. Part of the music of Australia. There is a broad range of styles, from bluegrass, to yodeling, to folk, to the more popular. The genre has been influenced by Celtic and English folk music, by the traditions of Australian bush balladeers, as well as by popular American country music. Themes include outback life; the lives of stockmen, truckers, and outlaws; songs of romance and political protest; and songs about the "beauty and the terror" of the Australian bush. *See also* COUNTRY MUSIC.

AUSTRALIAN EDUCATION COUNCIL (AEC). (Aus.) A former body comprising the ministers of education in each state and territory and in the commonwealth. In 1989 a decision was made for a national curriculum to be published in 1994 that included music as one of the six subject strands within the national arts curriculum. This reaffirmed the place of music as an integral element in the general education of young people in Australia.

AUSTRALIAN INSTITUTE OF ABORIGINAL AND TORRES STRAIT ISLANDER STUDIES (AIATSIS). An organization that sponsors research and collects documentation on all aspects of indigenous culture and history; programs include publishing a semiannual journal, and commercial recordings of indigenous music; houses large collections of unpublished manuscripts, published material, tapes, film, and photos with major musicological research potential.

***AUSTRALIAN JOURNAL OF MUSIC EDUCATION* (AJME).** (1967–1982.) A biannual journal of the **Australian Society for Music Education** (ASME); a fully refereed journal that aimed to provide clear, stimulating, and readable accounts of current issues in music education. In particular, it strove to strengthen professional development and improve practice within the field of music education. Its last issue was published in 1982. A new series of the journal, in association with the **International Society for Music Education** (ISME), appeared in 1984, published by ASME.

***AUSTRALIAN JOURNAL OF MUSIC THERAPY* (AJMT).** An annual refereed journal reflecting research and debate in the profession. Indexed in the *Australian Medical Index*, *Cumulative Index to Nursing*, and *Allied Health Literature*; *Music Therapy World Journal Index*; and *Psyc INFO*. Published by the **Australian Music Therapy Association**.

AUSTRALIAN MUSIC THERAPY ASSOCIATION (AMTA). Music therapy is an allied health profession practiced throughout Australia and in more than 40 countries around the world; it is the planned and creative use of music to attain and maintain health and well-being. People of any age or ability may benefit from a music therapy program, regardless of musical skill or background. Focuses on meeting therapeutic aims, which distinguishes it from musical entertainment or music education; allows an individual's abilities to be strengthened and new skills to be transferred to other areas of a person's life. The purpose of AMTA is the progressive development of the therapeutic use of music in rehabilitation, special education, and community settings.

AUSTRALIAN ROUNDTABLE FOR ARTS TRAINING EXCEL- LENCE (ARTATE). An initiative between the national performing arts training organizations and the Australian government; committed to providing unique and high-level training for emerging artists.

AUSTRALIAN SOCIETY FOR MUSIC EDUCATION (ASME). Est. 1967 following discussions between nationwide representatives after the successful **UNESCO** Conference on Music Education held in Sydney in July 1965. ASME has a national council and chapters in Australian states. The society is the representative in Australia of the **International Society for Music Education** (ISME) and publisher of the *Australian Journal of Music Education* (AJME). The purpose of ASME is to encourage and advance music education at all levels as an integral part of general education and community life, and as a profession within the broad field of music. It is Australia's only affiliate organization of the ISME, which exists under the auspices of UNESCO's **International Music Council** (IMC). ASME also represents music education on the National Advocates for Arts Education (NAAE).

AUSTRALIAN SOCIETY FOR MUSIC EDUCATION TRUST FUND. *See* ASME TRUST FUND.

AUTOHARP. (Chorded zither.) A 19th-century zither. Buttons attached to bars (or bars only) that, when pressed, dampen strings that are not needed for a desired chord. Player strums soft or plastic plectrum with thumb. Also used in the United States to accompany simple songs or Appalachian traditional music. Extensive research indicates that Karl August Gutter (1823–1900) was the real inventor of the autoharp, while Charles Zimmerman popularized it in the United States.

Lit. Stiles, Ivan, *Autoharp Quarterly* 3, no. 3.

AXATSE. (Africa.) A bead-covered gourd used in African percussion ensembles; often used in elementary and middle school general music and chorus classes. Used in American ensembles from elementary to professional musician ensembles. *See also* INTEGRATION OF MUSIC.

B

BACON, DENISE. Music educator. A 1952 graduate of the New England Conservatory with a BM in piano performance, and in 1954 an MM in chamber music. In 1957 she founded the Dana School of Music in Wellesley, Massachusetts, at the request of local parents needing musical instruction for children and adults. She became interested in the new Kodály and Orff methods in the 1960s, and as a result was awarded a Braitmayer Fellowship to study at the Lizst Academy in Budapest and the Orff Institution in Salzburg. In 1969, through a Ford Foundation Grant, she established the Kodály Music Training Institute (KMTI) in Wellesley. In 1977 she founded the **Kodály Center of America** (KCA). The KMTI is now the Kodály Institute at Capital University in Columbus, Ohio. KCA continues independently as a resource center offering only short early childhood and advanced refresher courses. Ms. Bacon continues her work on the KCA archives for the material to be housed at the International Kodály Institute in Hungary. A more complete U.S. collection will go to the University of Maryland libraries.

BALALAIKA. A popular Russian instrument of the guitar type, with a triangular body, long neck, and three strings. It became popular in the 18th century.

BALDWIN, LILLIAN (1888–1960). (U.S.) A music educator who served the Cleveland public schools for 25 years as supervisor of music appreciation. Her principal duty with the Cleveland school system was to supervise the annual series of children's concerts on assignment with the Cleveland Orchestra. She wrote study booklets for the 50,000 or more students who attended the concerts. Some of her study materials were published by the Kulas Foundation as *A Listener's Anthology of Music* in two volumes (1946). **Silver Burdett** published *Music to Remember: A Book for Listeners* (1951). Baldwin took several pieces of classical music and explained the musical principles at work in each one. These books were used in many music-education classes in colleges and universities until the late 1950s and early 1960s.

BALDWIN, RALPH (1872–1943). (U.S.) A music educator who in 1899 was the first to use the term *alto-tenor*. He placed boys' changing voices on the third, or tenor part, of the vocal score. While they were placed on the tenor part, Baldwin referred to them as *alto-tenor*, so that it would not be confused with the mature tenor voice. The earliest published music in which *alto-tenor* appears seems to be the *Beacon Song Collection*, edited by Herbert Griggs (**Silver Burdett**, 1895). *See also* ALTO-TENOR PLAN.

BALLET. A theatrical performance by a dancing group, usually with costumes and scenery, accompanied by music but generally without singing or spoken words; a dance introduced in an opera or other stage work from the 15th century.

BAMBOO BAND. (Aus.) A band of guitars and tuned lengths of bamboo, the open ends of which players strike with a rubber thong or thongs in patterns evoking a "boogie-woogie" bass.

BAND. Instrumental ensemble consisting of brass, woodwind, and percussion instruments, excluding string instruments; applied to military bands, jazz bands, dance bands, and brass bands.
   Lit.: Keene, James A., *A History of Music Education in the United States*, 1982.

BAND CONTEST IN PARIS (1867). (Fr.) The greatest band contest of all time was that held in Paris, France, in 1867, with nine nations competing. The rapid improvement of European bands in the first half of the 19th century reached its peak with the international contests of the 1860s and 1870s.

BAND OF THE WELSH GUARDS. (UK.) The youngest of the five bands in the Foot Guards Regiments in the Household Division that primarily guard the British monarch. The band is based at Wellington Barracks in St. James London; formed in 1915, it plays regularly for occasions and events and was honored with playing at the investiture of Prince Charles as Prince of Wales. Highly regarded British band that has played extensively in Canada to large numbers of people. In 1965 they visited Milan to play at British Week, and were also accompanied by the Pipes, Drums and Dancers of the Scots Guard for a long tour of America two years later. The band has toured Seattle, WA, Australia, Japan, and Paris among other cities and countries.

BARBEAU, MARIUS (1883–1969). (Can.) Canadian sociologist/ethnomusicologist. He carried out extensive fieldwork recording songs of warriors, medicine men, and coastal and mountain Indians, including the Huron and Iroquois tribes. In 1925, with Edward Sapir, he wrote *Folksongs of French Canada* (New Haven: Yale University Press).

BARBERSHOP HARMONY ASSOCIATION. (Formerly SPEBSQUSA, **Society for the Preservation and Encouragement of Barbershop Quartet Singing in America**.) First of several organizations to promote and preserve barbershop music as an art form. Founded by Owen C. Cash in 1938 in Tulsa, Oklahoma. As of 2007, just under 30,000 men of all ages in the U.S. and Canada are members; the organization's focus is on **a cappella** music. National headquarters was in Kenosha, WI, for 50 years until moving to Nashville, Tennessee, in 2007. For purposes of administration (particularly of local schools and contests), the society is organized into geographical districts.

BARD. (UK.) Pre-Christian and medieval poet-musician(s) of the Celts, esp. the Irish and Welsh. In the early Middle Ages, bards exercised great political power, serving as historians, heralds, ambassadors, officers of the king's household, and in brief, constituting the highest intellectual class. Their activities are documented as early as the pre-Christian era by Greek writers. Annual congregations of the Welsh bards, called *eisteddfod*, were revived as a regular practice in the early 19th century after an interruption of about 150 years. The music of the Welsh bards has been the subject of much discussion and controversy.

BARRESI, ANTHONY. (U.S.) Professor emeritus of choral music education at the University of Wisconsin–Madison. A proponent of contemporary information about the adolescent changing voice; has written numerous articles and produced a videotape titled *Barresi on Adolescent Voice*. It includes demonstrations by adolescent singers (both male and female) in various stages of vocal mutation.

BARRETT, MARGARET. (Aus.) Music educator; head of the University of Queensland School of Music, Dr. Barrett is a recognized scholar and teacher with a number of awards for her several abilities; editor of *Research Studies in Music Education*, associate editor of *Psychology of Music*, and a member of the editorial boards of key journals in music and arts education. She is a former national president of the **Australian Society for Music Education** (1999–2001), and chair of the Asia-Pacific Symposium for Music Education Research (2009–2011).

Barrett is professor of music education at the University of Tasmania. She holds a PhD (Monash University, 1996), MEd (UTAS, 1990), and BA Mus.

Ed. (1981). An ISME member since 1988, Barrett is a commissioner for the Research Commission. Barrett has an extensive record of service to the music-education community.

BARTON, WILLIAM (1981–). Australian Aboriginal **didgeridoo** player. Learned to play from his uncle, an elder of the Wannyi, Lardil, and Kaikadunga tribes of Queensland; a leading didgeridoo player in the classical world; Australia's first didgeridoo artist in residence with a symphony orchestra—the Queensland Symphony. He has collaborated with orchestras, choral directors, and composers in Australia, America, and Europe; was featured on the ABC (Australian) television program *Australian Story*, in an episode titled "William the Conqueror."

***BASIC CONCEPTS IN MUSIC EDUCATION* (1958).** A yearbook published by the National Society for the Study of Education designed to emphasize the trend toward more effective orientation of instructional programs to accepted goals of formal education. Organized in two parts, this book presents a series of chapters written by outstanding **MENC** members that gathered together the essential knowledge and motivation for successful performance by students in training for careers in the field of music as well as for music teachers now in service. Based on the work of the MENC Commission on Basic Concepts, it included a variety of articles related to music education.

    Bib.: Henry, Nelson B., *Basic Concepts in Music Education*, The Fifty-Seventh Yearbook of the National Society for the Study of Education, 1958.

BASIC MUSIC SERIES. (Basal and graded music series.) A music series for public school elementary grades was introduced shortly after the Civil War in order to satisfy the need for materials to help children learn to read music. **Lowell Mason** wrote what many regard as the first American "graded music series," *The Song Garden*, a three-volume set that began in 1864. **George Loomis** produced *First Steps in Music* in 1866, a three-book series introducing music reading by placing notes above or around a single line. Just prior to the 20th-century series, **Clarence C. Birchard**'s *Laurel Series* (1900) provided folk and composed song literature of high quality.

    It was 1923 before *Songs of Childhood*, the first book of Ginn and Company's Music Education Series, appeared. In the 1920s Ginn published *The World of Music*, with **Mabelle Glenn** as editor. In 1927 **Silver Burdett** published the *Music Hour Series*. From these early books to the present, book publishers such as the American Book Company, Ginn, Silver Burdett, Holt (later Holt Rinehart; and now Holt, Rinehart and Winston), Follett, Allyn Bacon, and others have created many books to meet the demand for the changing music scene in public school music.

BAUMGARTEN, ALEXANDER GOTTLIEB (1714–1762). Early music educator who in 1750 first used the term *aesthetics* to denote the science of sensuous knowledge, as contrasted with *logic*, the aim of which is truth. *See also* AESTHETIC EDUCATION.

***BAY PSALM BOOK* (1640).** Revision of the *Ainsworth Psalter*, and famous as the first real book to be published in the British colonies. A product of the Massachusetts Bay Colony, from which a committee of 30 compiled it and sought not only to make "a plain and familiar translation" of the **psalter** more accurate than the Sternhold-Hopkins version they had brought with them from England, but also to differentiate their Puritan, Bay Colony psalter from that of the Pilgrims at Plymouth (*Ainsworth Psalter*). First printed in 1640, the *Bay Psalm Book* (or "New England version") originally included no music, but directed that most of its verses could be sung either to Ravenscroft's tunes or those of "our English psalm books" (i.e., Sternhold-Hopkins). The *Bay Psalm Book* relied on the *lining out* method (call and response) used in colonial times.

BEATTIE, JOHN W. (1885–1962). (U.S.) Dean, School of Music, Northwestern University. One of the founders of **MENC**, when the name changed from **MSNC** (1934), and also the fourteenth president; a member of the National Council of Music Education and Research Council, as well as a member of the *Music Supervisors Journal* editorial board. When MSNC became MENC, the *Music Supervisors Journal* became the *Music Educators Journal*. Beattie believed that music does more to strengthen democratic procedures and uplift the soul than any other subject taught in school. He also believed that only well-trained, properly qualified music educators should be in "school teaching." Beattie wrote more than 400 songs for children, either words or music; however, few of these bear his name.

BEISSEL, CONRAD (1691–1768). *See* EPHRATA CLOISTER.

BENTLEY, ARNOLD (1913–2001). (UK.) A pioneer of research in music education. At the University of Reading for most of his working life, he developed Britain's first postgraduate course for secondary school music teachers. His book *Musical Ability in Children and Its Measurement* (1966) became a widely cited and translated text, establishing his international influence in the field. He established the research commission of the **International Society for Music Education**. In 1966 he wrote *Aural Foundations of Music Reading*, which advocated the adoption of **John Curwen**'s **sol-fa method** as a means of teaching sight singing in schools. He lectured in several European countries, the U.S., Australia, and New Zealand. After some

50 years of teaching in music education, Reading University awarded him an honorary doctorate of letters.

BETHLEHEM BACH CHOIR (1898). (U.S.) Oldest and continuing Bach choir of Moravian tradition. Organized to study Bach's *Mass in B Minor*. The choir performed the American premiere of the complete mass on March 27, 1900, in Bethlehem, Pennsylvania; toured internationally in London, Leipzig, and Munich. In the U.S. they have performed at Carnegie Hall and the Kennedy Center.

BILINGUAL EDUCATION ACT (1965). Also known as Title VII of the **Elementary and Secondary Education Act** (ESEA). Intended to address the needs of American children whose native language is not English. The act provides federal assistance to schools for children learning English.

BI-MUSICALITY. An ethnomusicological term that has come to mean fluency in two or more musics. The inspiration for the term *bi-musical* was *bilingual*. Mantle Hood (1918–2005) applied the term to music the same way a linguist would when describing someone who spoke two languages. While Hood was not the first ethnomusicologist to attempt to learn to perform the music being studied, he gave the approach a name in his 1960 article on bi-musicality. It has been an important ethnomusicological research tool ever since. Hood required that his students learn to play the music they were studying. The approach enabled them to, in some manner, learn about music "from the inside," and thereby experience its technical, conceptual, and aesthetic challenges. The student is also able to better connect socially with the community being studied and have better access to the community's rituals and performances. Hood considered bi-musicality to be a means of acquiring musicianship in the performance of "cultivated," non-Western music.

    Lit.: Hood, Mantle, "The Challenge of *Bi-Musicality*," *Ethnomusicology* 4, no. 2 (May 1960): 55–59.

BIRCHARD, CLARENCE C. (1866–1946). A music educator and publisher; founder and president of the Boston music and textbook publishing company that bears his name. Among the composers whose works he published were Bloch, Cadman, Copland, and Hanson. He was closely associated with school music since the early days of summer schools sponsored by book companies; advocated an independent professional organization such as the **Music Supervisors National Conference** (MSNC) for some time; and was an ardent supporter of this new organization for almost 40 years. The early *Music Supervisors Bulletin* was financially supported by publishers such as the Birchard Company and its successor, Summy-Birchard, for 52 years:

from vol. 1, no. 1, to vol. 52, no. 9, in 1966. His philosophy: "We are teaching music not to make musicians, but to make Americans."

BIRGE, EDWARD BAILEY (1868–1952). An early music educator recognized for his exceptional contributions to the field of music education; a founding member of the **Music Supervisors National Conference** (MSNC), which later became the **Music Educators National Conference** (MENC). Birge served as president of the organization from 1910 to 1911, and also as chairman of the editorial board for the *Music Educators Journal* (MEJ) for many years. He originated the "MEJ Clubs" on college campuses that made possible student memberships. Through the clubs, the journal was used in classes for prospective teachers. This greatly increased the circulation of the magazine. In recognition of his long service to the journal and to the conference, the MENC board of directors named him chairman emeritus. Birge is also remembered for writing the first history of American music education. He was a member of **Phi Mu Alpha Sinfonia** fraternity for men in music, initiated with Paul J. Weaver and **Clarence C. Birchard** in April 1924 at the national convention of MENC. Birge was a music supervisor in Indianapolis and was one of the first teachers of music appreciation in the early 20th century.

Bib.: Birge, Edward Bailey, *History of Public School Music in the United States*, 1928; 1937.

BLOCK SCHEDULING. A method of scheduling the six-hour school day into "blocks" of class time. Sometimes referred to as extended-period schedules, block scheduling is supported by advocates because it keeps students in class for longer periods of time, reduces the amount of time students spend transitioning between classes, and gives students and teachers more opportunities to get to know each other.

Of school schedules with fewer but longer daily class periods, there are three types:

- 4/4 accelerated block—Each day has four 90-minute class periods. Courses change each semester; therefore, students can take eight courses a year.
- A/B, eight-block (expanded)—Two four-period blocks rotate every other day for a year.
- Modified block—Block scheduling and traditional scheduling are mixed.

BLOOM, BENJAMIN SAMUEL (1913–1999). An American educational psychologist who made contributions to the classification of educational objectives and to the theory of mastery-learning. He taught at the University of

Chicago for 30 years and wrote a book titled *Stability and Change in Human Characteristics*. In his work he tried to resolve the nature/nurture controversy, studied the process of gifted and talented performance, and supported the critical importance of early learning and experience in intellectual growth and development. He also directed a research team that conducted a major investigation into the development of exceptional talent; the results of this study are relevant to the questions of eminence, exceptional achievement, and greatness. *See also* BLOOM'S TAXONOMY.

BLOOM'S TAXONOMY. A classification of learning objectives within education proposed in 1956 by a committee of educators chaired by **Benjamin Bloom**, who also edited the first volume of the standard text *Taxonomy of Educational Objectives: The Classification of Educational Goals*. Although named for Bloom, the publication followed a series of conferences from 1949 to 1953 that were designed to improve communication between educators on the design of curricula and examinations.

Bloom's *Taxonomy of Educational Objectives in the Cognitive Domain* is a taxonomy (classification) of educational objectives that emphasizes the development of cognitive skills. A committee of colleagues led by Benjamin Bloom (1956) identified three domains (categories) of educational activities:

- Cognitive: mental skills (*Knowledge*—sometimes described as *knowing/ head*)
- Affective: growth in feelings or emotional areas (*Attitude*—described as *feeling/heart*)
- Psychomotor: manual or physical skills (*Skills*—described as *doing/ hands*)

Within the domains, learning at the higher levels is dependent on having attained prerequisite knowledge and skills at lower levels. A goal of Bloom's taxonomy is to motivate educators to focus on all three domains, creating a more holistic form of education.

This taxonomy was revised in 2001 and is titled *A Taxonomy for Learning, Teaching and Assessing: A Revision of Bloom's Taxonomy of Educational Objectives*, edited by Lorin W. Anderson and David Krathwahl.

BLUES. (12-bar blues, blue note, rhythm & blues.) (U.S.) A traditional African-American ballad-style or slow jazz song of lamentation, usually for an unhappy love affair. It is in 4/4 time and is based on major tonality. Made up of groups of 12 bars, instead of the traditional 8 or 16 bars, each stanza being 3 lines covering 4 bars of music, mostly in major but with the flattened 3rd and 7th of the key (the "blue notes"). Harmony tends toward plagal or subdominant cadence. Can be traced by oral tradition as far back as the 1860s. The African-American composer and trumpet player W. C. Handy claimed to have "discovered" the blues; he published *Memphis Blues* (1911) and *St. Louis Blues* (1914).

BLÜME, FRIEDRICH (1893–1975). German musicologist; his invention of the valve for brass instruments was of major significance to the band movement. From 1943 he directed the preparation of the encyclopedia *Die Musik in Geschichte und Gegenwart*, 14 volumes of which appeared between 1949 and 1968, containing 9,414 articles for which he was personally responsible. An authority on Bach and Mozart.

BLUME, HELMUT (1914–1998). A naturalized Canadian (1945) pianist, broadcaster, administrator, and educator. He gave radio and public recitals. In 1958 the CBC (Canadian Broadcasting Co.) won an Ohio State Award for his eight-lecture TV series, "Music to See." Also associated with Edith Fowke and Alan Mills in the preparation of "Canada's Story in Song." He became dean of McGill University in 1964, which, under his leadership, became one of the leading music schools in the country. He undertook a study of music training in Canada for the Canada Council, published in 1978 as *A National Music School for Canada*.

BOARDMAN, EUNICE (1926–2009). A music educator and author specializing in elementary music education. Served as chair of the Department of Music at the University of Wisconsin in Madison (1980). In 1988 she became chair of the Graduate Committee for Music Education at the University of Illinois. Retired in 1998.

Prolific author of textbooks, including *Exploring Music* (1966), *The Music Book* (1980), and *Holt Music* (1987). *Musical Growth in the Elementary School* (1963) was a popular elementary text coauthored with Bjornar Bergethon. Active member of several music organizations, she was the first national chair of the Society for Music Teacher Education, founded by **Charles Leonhard** (1982). Inducted into **Music Educators Hall of Fame** in 2004.

BODHRÁN. (UK.) An Irish frame drum. A goatskin head is tacked to one side (synthetic heads or other animal skins are sometimes used). The other side is open ended, for one hand to be placed against the inside of the drumhead to control the pitch and timbre. It is similar to the tambourine. There are some who believe the *bodhrán* to be the native drum of the Celts, with a musical history predating Christianity.

BODY MAPPING. A concept developed by **William Conable**. He began developing the concept of body mapping in the mid-1970s. The method is widely recognized as a major contribution to the theory and pedagogy of the **Alexander Technique**; it is a somatic (mind-body) discipline based on the scientific fact that the brain contains neural maps of bodily functions and structures that govern body usage. Body mapping has been described in detail by **Barbara Conable** in her books *How to Learn the Alexander Technique* and *What Every Musician Needs to Know about the Body*, and has formed the basis for courses that are taught around the world.

Body mapping, as used in **conducting**, is more than the basics of learning the appropriate gestures for "beating time." Although traditional conducting courses involve manual and bodily motions and facial expressions, the concept of body mapping involves a greater understanding of the mind and body. It is the conscious correction of one's body map to produce efficient, graceful, and coordinated movement. Body mapping, according to teachers, over time with application allows any musician to play like a natural. It also assists conductors toward greater communication with ensemble members. *See also* BUCHANAN, HEATHER.

BOETHIUS, ANICIUS MANLIUS SEVERINUS (480–524). A philosopher who wrote a treatise in five books, *De Institutione Musica* (Fundamentals of Music), the chief sourcebook for the theorizing monks of the Middle Ages.

BONNY, HELEN LINQUIST (1921–2010). A music educator who studied with **Everett Thayer Gaston** at the University of Kansas in the early 1960s, where she received her bachelor's degree in music education, with a major in music therapy. She received a master's degree in music education, with an emphasis in research. After completing her PhD in the late 1960s, and after an unexpected encounter with music, Bonny was inspired to explore the transformative power of music. She began researching the effects of music on imagination, and in 1973 authored a book, cowritten with Louis Savary, titled *Music and Your Mind: Listening with a New Consciousness*. Although drawn from various schools of psychology, Bonny cited as its main influences the humanistic and the transpersonal psychology of Carl Rogers and Abraham Maslow; she was also profoundly influenced by the work of Carl Jung. Founder of the **Bonny method of guided imagery and music** (GIM), she is now recognized internationally as a major model of **music therapy**.

> Music, as a structured envelope of sound, is probably the most effective and safe opener to the doors of the psyche. It reaches beyond personal defenses to the realities and beauties of the person. Music gives access to

the discovery of inner strength, uncovers the potential for creativity, and manifests ways in which life can be lived from a center of inner security.

—Helen Bonny, World Congress of Music Therapy

BONNY INSTITUTE. Helen Bonny first created the Bonny Foundation in 1988 for the purpose of promoting the legacy of her work. Initially it provided training in the **Bonny method of guided imagery and music**. In 2004 it shifted its focus to other educational projects and changed its name to the Bonny Institute.

BONNY METHOD OF GUIDED IMAGERY AND MUSIC. (Founded by **Helen Bonny**.) Music therapist **Kenneth Bruscia** uses the following definition to describe guided imagery and music: "(GIM) refers to all forms of music-imaging in an expanded state of consciousness, including not only the specific individual and group forms that Bonny developed, but also all variations and modifications in those forms created by her followers."

BONYNGE, RICHARD ALAN (1930–). (Aus.) A conductor and researcher into *bel canto* operatic repertoire. In 1964 made his debut with the San Francisco Opera, Covent Garden, and the Met in New York with *Lucia di Lammermoor* in 1966. Returned to Australia as artistic director and chief conductor of the Sutherland-Williamson International Grand Opera Co., and in 1975 became musical director of the Australian Opera. He frequently accompanied his wife, Dame Joan Sutherland, in recital, and recorded numerous recitals. The Australian Opera's young artists development program was established during his time as musical director, and he has remained involved in the training of young singers' *repetiteurs* (coaches of singers) and conductors.

BOOMERANG CLAPSTICKS. (Aus.) Two boomerangs held in the middle and clapped together at the tips as an accompaniment to Aboriginal singing. The beat pattern may consist of even strokes throughout the song or two adjacent strokes followed by a rest in triple meter. End of song may be marked by rapidly rattling the tips of the boomerang together.

BOOSE JOURNAL-CHAPPEL ARMY JOURNAL. (UK.) A journal that contains published band arrangements. British firms were able to publish band arrangements of generally high quality that stimulated and influenced the course of band music in both Great Britain and the United States. The size and scope of the band movement would not have been possible without the British band libraries.

BORN TO GROOVE (2011). A movement spearheaded by Charles Keil, anthropologist-ethnomusicologist, dedicated to nurturing and enhancing the musical capacities of children, especially young children, with attention to highlighting their rhythmic sensibilities through drumming, dancing, poetry, and the like. *Born to Grove* is played out through projects funded by the Jubilation Foundation, which supports community music projects for children that center on *rhythmicking*. This work is jointly written with Dr. **Patricia Campbell** and was first published on the Web. It is an application of Keil's findings over many years in ethnomusicology.

BOSTON BRIGADE BAND. Evolved from the Massachusetts Band (1783) and the **Green Dragon Band**. In 1859 this band acquired the director **Patrick Gilmore**, who again changed the name to **Gilmore's Band**, took it to war, and made it famous.

BOSTON SCHOOL COMMITTEE. A committee of the Boston Board of Education that approved the inclusion of music in the public school curriculum as a regular subject in 1838. The committee, influenced by **Lowell Mason**, stated that music classes would benefit children intellectually, morally, and physically, and would also improve recreation, worship, and discipline.

BOULANGER, NADIA (1887–1979). A French composer, conductor, and teacher who taught many of the leading composers and musicians of the 20th century, such as Aaron Copland, Roy Harris, Virgil Thomson, Elliott Carter, and Walter Piston. She herself won first prizes in harmony, counterpoint, fugue, and orchestration at the Paris Conservatory. She was principally known as an outstanding, influential teacher of composition. She taught at the Paris Conservatory, in the U.S. at Juilliard, and at the American Conservatory at Fontainebleau. She was the first woman to conduct many London and European orchestras.

BOWEN, ROBIN HUW (1957–). (UK.) A musician who is a foremost professional now specializing solely on playing the triple harp. Recognized internationally as the leading exponent of the Welsh national instrument and ranks among the most important figures that Welsh traditional music has produced. His repertoire closely reflects that of the Welsh harp in its heyday (mid-17th to the end of the 19th centuries).

BOWMAN, WAYNE. Canadian music educator; primary research interests involve philosophy of music and the philosophical exploration of issues in music education. His work is extensively influenced by pragmatism, critical theory, and conceptions of music and music education as social practices. He is particularly concerned with music's sociopolitical power, music and social justice, and ethically informed understandings of musical practice. Dr. Bowman's publications include *Philosophical Perspectives on Music* (Oxford, 1998), the *Oxford Handbook of Philosophy in Music Education* (2012), numerous book chapters, and articles in prominent scholarly journals. Former editor of the journal *Action, Criticism, and Theory for Music Education*. His university teaching experience includes positions at Brandon University (Manitoba, Canada), Mars Hill College (NC), and the University of Toronto. An accomplished trombonist and jazz educator, Dr. Bowman earned his graduate degrees at the University of Illinois at Urbana.

BRAILLE MUSIC. Developed by Louis Braille (1809–1952) in France. Braille cells (raised dots) allow music to be read by visually impaired musicians. Braille music uses the same six-position Braille cells as literary Braille and has its own syntax and abbreviations. Largest collection of Braille music is found in the National Library for the Blind in Stockport, UK.

BRANDON, J. RAYMOND (1907–2005). An exemplary band director and music educator in the state of Arkansas, whose work as a band director culminated in North Little Rock from 1949 to 1974. While there, he helped design the new fine arts building (1954), which became a model for other band programs. A unique feature of the building included walls that could be removed for a combined band and choir rehearsal. It also had practice rooms and a lecture room.

In 1973 Brandon wrote a curriculum guide for the American School Band Directors Association (ASBDA) that became an important addition to the personal libraries of many band directors. He was selected as one of the Top Ten Outstanding Band Directors in the Nation by the magazine *The School Musician*. In 1976 he received the MAC Award from *First Chair of America*. He was awarded the Goldman Award from the American School Band Directors Association, and is ASBDA president and executive secretary emeritus. In 1992 he was inducted into the Outstanding Bandmasters Hall of Fame by Phi Beta Mu International Bandmasters Fraternity.

Bib.: Meredith, Samuel Maurice, Jr. "An Historical Study of J. Raymond Brandon and His Contribution to the History and Development of Arkansas School Band Programs."

BRASS BAND. Wind band consisting entirely of brass instruments and percussion; originated in the 1820s. They constituted mounted bands for many cavalry regiments and became the most popular type of band for amateur music making, particularly in Great Britain and the U.S. In Great Britain the brass band tradition has continued alongside the mixed-wind band; in the U.S. the brass and **woodwind** instrumentation was used almost exclusively by the late 1800s.

BRASS INSTRUMENTS. Section of the **orchestra** consisting of the instruments made of brass or other metal, such as trumpets, horns, and trombones, as distinguished from those made of wood. *See also* WIND INSTRUMENTS; WOODWINDS.

BRASS METHODS FOR PUBLIC SCHOOLS. (U.S.) Specific references to the teaching of brass in the public schools may be found in a number of instrumental methods books. A suggested text is *The Teaching of Instrumental Music* by **Richard Colwell** and Thomas Goolsby. Their opening description of brass instruments is as follows: "All brass instruments produce a sound from a vibrating column of air set in motion by the lips. All brass instruments play pitches based on the overtone series and are fitted with mechanical means to play a complete chromatic scale. With the exception of fiberglass used for some sousaphones and the plastic trumpets that were a short-lived fad in the early 1970s, all brass instruments are constructed of a brass alloy."

BRASSWIND. Term used to denote European brass instruments, including those made in the European tradition on other continents, but excluding instruments used purely for signaling and those of folk traditions that have not been integrated into the mainstream of "art" music. The term *brasswind* is used in much the same way as *woodwind*.

BREATHNACH, BREANDÁN (1912–1986). (Or Brendan Walsh, as many people knew him.) (UK.) An Irish music collector and uilleann piper; worked as a civil servant with the Department of Education and was responsible for collecting music from around Ireland. His efforts were responsible for saving numerous tunes, and he is generally recognized as a major figure in the preservation and continuation of Irish music. Best known for his three-volume series, *Ceol Rince na hÉireann*, a collection of Irish traditional dance music. Founder of the journal *CEOL* and closely involved with uilleann pipers, and in 1968 was the prime mover of the piper's society, Na Piobairi Uilleann. In 1971, he and others founded the Folk Music Society of Ireland. The society publishes an occasional journal, *Irish Folk Music Studies*. Unfortunately, Irish traditional music is not well covered in higher institutions in Ireland.

BRESLER, LIORA (1915–2005). Professor at the College of Education at the University of Illinois at Urbana-Champaign, and affiliate professor in the School of Music. Her research includes art and aesthetic education, international issues, and qualitative research methodology. Bresler was involved in a number of national research projects and served as an editor for the book series *Landscapes: Aesthetics, Arts and Education* (Springer). She was also the cofounder and coeditor of the electronic *International Journal for Arts and Education* with Tom Barone (1999). She won many prestigious awards from the University of Illinois and was invited internationally to give talks, seminars, and short courses in 30 universities.

BRIDGE. (Strings.) A thin, upright piece of wood in some stringed instruments that supports the strings above the soundboard. Material varies from hardwood (violins) to bone, ivory, metal, plastic, vegetable pith, or even hair (as is the case with some African fiddles). It serves the purpose of raising strings to the required distance above the soundtable or fingerboard and transmits vibrations to the body of the instrument.

BRIDGES, DOREEN (1918–). Australian music educator and researcher. Her PhD was the first in music education in Australia. With the Australian Council for Educational Research, she developed a test of acquired perceptual-cognitive abilities of potential tertiary music students—the Australian Test for Advanced Music Studies. She collaborated with Deanna Hoemann in rewriting the Developmental Music Program, and compiled *Catch a Song*, a popular children's song collection. She held office in ASME and was made fellow of the Australian College of Education for services to music education (1982). Recognized both in Australia and internationally for her work as a distinguished music educator.

BRITISH ASSOCIATION FOR MUSIC THERAPY (BAMT). Replaced the Association of Professional Music Therapists (APMT) and the British Society for Music Therapy (BSMT) in 2011; acts as a central point for information about music therapy—health benefits experienced by people, young and old, who receive music therapy; latest research information; books, videos, and events related to music therapy. Associate membership available for students interested in a career in music therapy.

BRITISH BAND LIBRARIES. The size and scope of the band movement would not have been possible without the British band libraries. Published arrangements included in the libraries had become possible due to the standardized instrumentation encouraged by Kneller Hall, the **Royal Military School of Music**.

BRITISH BRASS BAND. This combination of instruments is found all over Europe and in countries settled by Europeans. Highest standard is possibly reached in the north of England, Lancashire, and Yorkshire. Usual instrumentation: cornets, flugelhorn, saxhorns, euphoniums, trombones, and basses (formerly *bombardons*), with percussion. Currently, saxes (not strictly a brass instrument) are not included. The brass band movement in Britain has a history (almost a folklore) stretching back to the start of the 19th century.

***BRITISH JOURNAL OF MUSIC EDUCATION* (BJME).** A fully refereed international journal that aims to provide clear, stimulating, and readable accounts of contemporary research in music education worldwide, together with a section containing extended book reviews that further current debates. In particular, the journal strives to strengthen connections between research and practice, enhancing professional development and improving practice within the field of music education. The range of subjects covers music teaching and learning in formal and informal contexts including classroom, individual, group, and whole-class instrumental and vocal teaching, music in higher education, international comparative music education, music in community settings, and teacher education. Contributors include researchers and practitioners from schools, colleges, and universities. Where appropriate, authors are encouraged to include supplementary sound files and other multimedia material. These accompany articles in electronic format in *Cambridge Journals Online*.

BRITTON, ALLEN PERDUE (1914–2003). American music educator. Through his many passions in life, he contributed to elevating the field of music education to the same stature as the field of musicology. He developed the doctoral program in music education at the University of Michigan, where he directed 51 dissertations. He contributed heavily to the history of music pedagogy in early America, especially singing schools. To combine his two interests of music education and history, he joined with Marguerite V. Hood, Warren S. Freeman, and Theodore F. Normann to create the ***Journal of Research in Music Education*** (JRME). Less than a decade after developing the journal for **Music Educators National Conference** (MENC), he became its president from 1960 to 1962. It was during this time that Russia had launched Sputnik, and the United States tried to counteract that advancement by going "back to the basics." This meant that there was little monetary support for music. As the president of the Music Educators National Conference, he took it upon himself to harness the full potential of this organization's political power. MENC, now the **National Association for Music Education** (NA/ME), has since exercised its influence over numerous political and social actions.

BROADWOOD, JOHN (1732–1812). (UK.) A pianoforte maker in London. The firm was originally founded in 1728 by Burkat Shudi, whose daughter married John Broadwood, a joiner and cabinetmaker in the firm. Broadwood became Shudi's partner in 1700. The firm was renamed John Broadwood and Son in 1795, and *Sons* in 1807. Earliest Broadwood grand was built in 1781 and reached production of 2,500 instruments a year in the 1850s but declined after 1890. These were a form of square pianos, but improvements over **Johannes Zumpe** pianos.

BROLGA. (Aus.) An Australian bird, a crane, that performs elaborate movements, possibly as part of a courtship display; often the subject of singing and dancing by Aboriginal Australians.

BRONSON, BERTRAND (1902–1986). *See* ENGLISH AND SCOTTISH POPULAR BALLADS.

BROUDY, HARRY S. (1905–1998). Educator. Professor emeritus of philosophy of education at the University of Illinois–Urbana-Champaign. Born in Poland, he came to the U.S. at age seven. Educated at MIT and at Boston and Harvard Universities. Retired in 1974 as professor emeritus. A well-known speaker and writer on the subject of the arts and **aesthetic education**, he was a longtime leader in promoting the cause of the arts in public education. Among his many publications, a most exceptional contribution is *Enlightened Cherishing: An Essay on Aesthetic Education.*
   Bib.: Broudy, Harry, *Enlightened Cherishing: An Essay on Aesthetic Education*, 1974.

BROWNLEE, JOHN (1901–1969). (Aus.) A baritone who was recognized by **Dame Nellie Melba**, who advised him to study in Europe. He established himself on the international opera scene in Paris and with the Metropolitan Opera company. While in New York, he taught at the Manhattan School of Music, and in 1956 was appointed director. He established a highly regarded opera workshop and directed many productions. He returned to Australia with the Melba Grand Opera. A John Brownlee Vocal Scholarship in Melbourne commemorates his distinguished career as a singer and teacher.

BROWN V. BOARD OF EDUCATION. Supreme Court decision (1954) that desegregated American public schools. Music teachers began to include ethnic music and jazz in their classes, even though there was not total integration in the schools.

BRUNER, JEROME (1915–). One of the best-known and most influential psychologists of the 20th century; a key figure in the so-called cognitive revolution. He was the director of the 1959 **Woods Hole Conference**, and his book *The Process of Education* is his account of what took place during the conference. This and his following book, *Toward a Theory of Instruction*, have become classics. In his *Process of Education*, two major ideas influenced the direction of music education: 1) any subject can be taught effectively in some intellectually honest form to any child at any stage of development; 2) the spiral curriculum, a curriculum as it develops, should revisit these basic ideas repeatedly, building upon them until the student has grasped the full formal apparatus that goes with them. In other words, each subject or skill area is revisited at intervals, at a more sophisticated and advanced level each time. The idea of the spiral curriculum greatly affected music educators in their teaching and publications. *See also* MANHATTANVILLE MUSIC CURRICULUM PROJECT.

BRUSCIA, KENNETH (1944–). Professor of music therapy, retired, Temple University (PA); board-certified in music therapy; fellow of Association for Music and Imagery (AMI); past president of AAMT and NCATA; author of several books and articles regarding music therapy; specialist in music psychotherapy using improvisation and imagery. *See also* BONNY METHOD.

BUCHANAN, HEATHER. (Aus./U.S.) Australian-born conductor with degrees from Queensland Conservatorium (Aus.), Westminster Choir College (U.S.), and the University of New England (New South Wales, Aus.); director of choral activities at Montclair State University, NJ. A vibrant choral musician and pedagogue, her choirs have consistently received glowing reviews for their performances. A certified **Andover Educator** who specializes in the teaching of **body mapping** and somatic pedagogy for choral musicians with the University of New England and researches the impact of body mapping on student musicians. Her PhD dissertation, *The Impact of Body Mapping: How Student Musicians' Perception of Their Performance and Development Are Influenced by Somatic Pedagogy*, is the first qualitative research study in the field of body mapping.

BULLETIN OF THE COUNCIL FOR RESEARCH IN MUSIC EDUCATION (CRME). (U.S.) A periodical founded in 1963 through the University of Illinois and the Illinois Office of the Superintendent of Public Instruction to provide a source of information about research being conducted in music education. The *CRME Bulletin* is published quarterly and contains critiques of doctoral dissertations, as well as book reviews and original articles.

BULLROARER OR THUNDERSTICK. (Aus.) A small piece of carved or notched wood tied to a string, swung in circles, creating a sound of considerable eeriness. In Australia it is sometimes sold as a children's toy, but it is chiefly found in certain Aboriginal rituals, where its use and significance are secret.

BURNS, ROBERT (1759–1796). (UK.) Scotland's favorite son, and in Scotland simply referred to as *The Bard*, a poet and lyricist. Widely regarded as the national poet of Scotland and celebrated throughout the world. A pioneer of the Romantic movement who became a great source of inspiration to the founders of both liberalism and socialism. As well as making original compositions, Burns also collected folk songs from across Scotland, often revising or adapting them. His poem and song "Auld Lang Syne" is often sung at Hogmanny (the last day of the year). "A Red, Red Rose" is one of his well-known poems across the world.

BUTLER ACT (1944). (UK.) Marked the beginning of a truly national system of education. In addition to mandating free compulsory education through age 15, it restructured the national administration of schools. The old Board of Education was renamed the Ministry of Education. The act included preschool and community-based education and recreation. Thus, nutrition and health care became part of the mission of state-supported education.

BUTTLEMAN, CLIFFORD (1930–1955). (U.S.) First executive secretary and business manager of **MENC**. He was dedicated to bringing quality professional literature to American music educators. Director of publications from 1930 to 1960 and editor of the *Music Educators Journal*. As a member of the National Interscholastic Music Activities Committee Executive Council, Buttleman was influential in distributing literature and materials to band, orchestra, and choral directors throughout the nation. He was a famous writer, teacher, graphic artist, and publisher, and a significant influence for good for MENC and music educators of the United States.

BUTTON ACCORDION. A type of accordion on which the melody-side keyboard consists of a series of buttons rather than piano-style keys. There exists a wide variation in keyboard systems, tuning, action, and construction of these instruments. *See also* ACCORDION.

BYATT, JOHN (1862–1930). (UK and Aus.) Educator. Born in London; a graduate, licentiate, and examiner of the **Tonic Sol-fa College of Music**, organizing and conducting at many musical festivals. Moved to Australia. Lectured and taught woodworking in Victoria, New South Wales, and Tasmania. Asked in 1915 to reorganize their school music. Byatt revitalized the teaching of singing and promoted the **tonic sol-fa** system; not until 1925 was he officially appointed as an inspector of the teaching of singing.

C

CAGE, JOHN (1912–1992). American composer, music theorist, writer, philosopher, and artist. A pioneer of indeterminacy in music, electro-acoustic music, and nonstandard use of musical instruments, Cage was one of the leading figures of the postwar avant-garde. Critics have lauded him as one of the most influential American composers of the 20th century. He was also instrumental in the development of modern dance, mostly through his association with choreographer Merce Cunningham, who was also Cage's romantic partner for most of their lives.

Cage is perhaps best known for his 1952 composition *4'33"* (four minutes and 33 seconds), the three movements of which are performed without a single note being played. The content of the composition is meant to be perceived as the sounds of the environment that the listeners hear while it is performed, rather than merely as four minutes and 33 seconds of silence, and the piece became one of the most controversial compositions of the 20th century. Another famous creation of Cage's is the *prepared piano* (a piano with its sound altered by placing various objects in the strings), for which he wrote numerous dance-related works and a few concert pieces, the best known of which is *Sonatas and Interludes* (1946–1948).

His teachers included Henry Cowell (1933) and Arnold Schoenberg (1933–1935), both known for their radical innovations in music, but Cage's major influences lay in various Eastern cultures. Through his studies of Indian philosophy and Zen Buddhism in the late 1940s, Cage came to the idea of chance-controlled or **aleatory music**, which he started composing in 1951. The *I Ching*, an ancient Chinese classic text on changing events, became Cage's standard composition tool for the rest of his life. In a 1957 lecture, *Experimental Music*, he described music as "a purposeless play" that is "an affirmation of life—not an attempt to bring order out of chaos nor to suggest improvements in creation, but simply a way of waking up to the very life we're living."

Bib.: Slonimsky, Nicolas, and Richard Kassel, *Webster's New World Dictionary of Music*, 1998.

CAKEWALK. African-American dance in quick 2/4 time, popular with blackface minstrels in the latter 19th century. Its vogue soon spread all over the world. Used in the walk-around finale of the minstrel show; syncopated rhythm is that of ragtime. Debussy included a cakewalk in his piano suite, *Golliwog's Cakewalk.*

THE CALEDONIA POCKET COMPANION. (UK.) The most important single source for old traditional Scottish music. Scotland has one of the longest European traditions of studying its native music. Published in the 1740s, the 15 volumes by James Oswald constituted a landmark publication embodying the rediscovery and performance of traditional tunes. It contains a large number of tunes as melody line only, including many Gaelic harp tunes.

CALENNIG. (UK-Wales.) Word meaning "New Year celebration/gift," though literally translates to "the first day of the month," deriving from the Latin *kalends.* The English word *calendar* also has its root in this word. Until the early decades of the 20th century, New Year's in Wales was considered more important than Christmas. It was an occasion for luck visiting, which included songs asking for calennig money, food, wassail, and wishing luck to family in return.

CALL-AND-RESPONSE. A leader-and-chorus approach to singing, as originated in the African-American community. Often referred to as antiphonal or responsorial singing. "Kye, Kye, Kule" is an African children's song sung in this fashion.

CALLOWAY, SIR FRANK (1919–2003). (Aus.-NZ.) Music educator and conductor. Born in New Zealand. In 1939 entered the Dunedin Teachers' Training College. At the outbreak of World War II a few months later, he volunteered for overseas service, was rejected due to poor eyesight, but was invited to join the full-time military band as a bassoonist. In 1942 he was appointed as head of music at King Edward Technical College in Dunedin, where he also enrolled as a bachelor of music student. For eight years he was a part-time member of the orchestras for the New Zealand Broadcasting Service. In 1947 a postgraduate traveling scholarship took him to study at the **Royal Academy of Music** in London, where he studied conducting, composition, and general musicianship; and met **Percy Grainger**, who was prominent as a choral and orchestral conductor, particularly as a guest conductor of the ABC orchestra. Calloway was also awarded a Carnegie Travel Grant to observe music education in the United States. He returned to King Edward Technical College as musical director in 1949.

Callaway was a founding member of the **International Society for Music Education** (ISME) shortly after World War II. He became its president in 1988 and was later an honorary president. He was president of UNESCO's **International Music Council**; created the **Australian Society for Music Education** (ASME) in 1967; helped create the Indian Ocean Arts Festival, held in Perth in 1979 and 1984. He was on the founding committee of the Commonwealth Assistance to Australian Composers scheme before its activities were absorbed into the **Australia Council**. He founded the *Australian Journal of Music Education* (AJME) and cofounded the musicological journal *Studies in Music*. In 1984 the University of Western Australia (UWA) established the Frank Calloway Foundation for Music, which supports the Calloway International Resource Centre for Music Education (CIRCME).

CALLWOOD, JUNE (1924–2007). (Can.) Journalist, author, and activist known as Canada's *conscience*; national icon. One of the most exceptional and respected voices in Canada, she was a proud career journalist and writer, and a founding member of the Writers' Union of Canada. She lectured at numerous Canadian universities and received 17 honorary degrees. She was a passionate supporter of a variety of children's causes.

CAMBIATA. A term borrowed from the theory term *changing note* by **Irvin Cooper** (ca. 1900–1971), a Canadian music educator, when describing his concept of the changing voice. Carl Fischer published his many works for the **cambiata** voice. Cooper was a professor at Florida State University for many years.

CAMBIATA CONCEPT. An approach to the changing voice researched, devised, and promoted by **Irvin Cooper**, professor of music education at Florida State University (1950–1970). Cooper supported his ideas with choral literature of octavos and booklets that were used by thousands of adolescent singers in middle and high schools throughout the country during the 1950s and 1960s. Since that time a specialty publishing company, *Cambiata Press*, has received wide acceptance nationally by producing music based on the tenets of the cambiata concept.

Cooper trained several disciples who have been prominent in providing workshops nationally since his death in 1971. They have kept his concept alive by promoting its use in secondary schools and churches as well as by seeing it used by various universities throughout the nation. This concept has been a part of the music education and church music scenes for 50 years or more.

CAMBIATA VOCAL MUSIC INSTITUTE OF AMERICA. A nonprofit, state-chartered educational institution founded in the spring of 1979 by **Don L. Collins**. In 2009 it became the Cambiata Vocal Institute of America for Early Vocal Music Education, under the auspices of the College of Music at the University of Texas in Denton. Dr. Alan McClung is the executive director. The primary purpose of the institute is to train music educators in the comprehensive philosophy and methodology of the **cambiata concept** by providing a sound basis for teaching vocal music to adolescents.

CAMBRIDGE UNIVERSITY SCHOOL OF MUSIC (13th c.). (UK.) Earliest collegiate foundation was Kings College, which was provided with "a choir of 24 singing men and boys." The world's first music degrees were conferred at Cambridge in 1463–1464. Practical music making occurred with the Peterhouse Music Society (founded 1843), which then became Cambridge University Musical Society in 1844 (for amateurs and professional performers). It then added the Cambridge Musical Club Society in 1899 for small-scale activities. There are 24 undergraduate colleges with chapels, organ scholarships, and maintained chapel choirs.

CAMPBELL, PATRICIA SHEHAN. (U.S.) A prolific researcher-writer and teacher of undergraduate and graduate courses in music education at the University of Washington, including music for children, world music pedagogy, sociology of music, and research methods. Appointed chair of the **ethnomusicology** program (2010), with a dual appointment in **music education**. Was named the Donald E. Petersen Professor of Music, an honor that is offered to accomplished faculty at the University of Washington. She has delivered lectures and conducted clinics across the U.S., Europe, Asia, Latin America, Australia, New Zealand, and South Africa. Campbell is widely published on issues of cross-cultural music learning, children's musical development, music methods for children, and the study of world music in K–12 schools and university courses. The term *world music pedagogy* was coined by Campbell to describe world music content and practice in elementary and secondary school programs.

CANADA COUNCIL. *See* CANADIAN COUNCIL FOR THE ARTS.

CANADA'S FIRST NATIONS. Collectively, this refers to various Aboriginal peoples in Canada who are neither Inuit nor Métis. There are currently over 630 recognized First Nations governments or bands spread across Canada, roughly half of which are in the provinces of Ontario and British Columbia.

In order to have greater knowledge of the indigenous peoples of Canada (except the Arctic-situated Inuit and Métis), an important group, the Canadian Music Education Research Collaborative, is supporting the further development of arts education through the linking of musicians, practitioners, and researchers. Edited, peer-reviewed books—the first of their kind ever in Canadian music education—are being disseminated to policy developers in government, funding agencies, and the public. Canadians are seen as leaders in this important international process of collaboration. *See also* CANADIAN MUSIC RESEARCH COUNCIL.

CANADIAN ASSOCIATION OF MUSIC THERAPY (CAMT). A federally incorporated, self-regulated, nonprofit professional association dedicated to fostering the practice of music therapy in clinical, educational, and community settings throughout Canada; serves as a forum for its members providing advice, guidance, information, and exchanges of professional experience concerning music therapy; represents the interests of music therapists in matters related to standards of professional practice, salary scales, and government legislation.

CANADIAN ASSOCIATION OF UNIVERSITY SCHOOLS OF MUSIC (CAUSM). *See* CANADIAN UNIVERSITY MUSIC SOCIETY.

CANADIAN BAND ASSOCIATION (CBA). (1934.) A national organization representing and supporting school, university, military, and community bands; band directors; students, parents, and administrators; the music industry; and composers, arrangers, and all those interested in bands and band music across Canada. An incorporated nonprofit organization that hosts several workshops and concert venues each year.

CANADIAN BOAT SONG. A folk melody based on a poem composed by the Irish poet **Thomas Moore** during his visit to Canada in 1804. The "Canadian Boat Song" was so popular that it was published several times over the next 40 years in Boston, New York, and Philadelphia.

CANADIAN COMMISSION FOR UNESCO. Operates under the **Canada Council**, a Crown corporation established in 1957 to act as an arts council of the Canadian government. The commission's title includes the Public Lending Right Commission and operates the Musical Instrument Bank. This bank has acquired many valuable stringed instruments that are mostly loaned to Canadian musicians, often as a result of juried competitions. In 2005, the commission sponsored a report of the **Canadian Conference for the Arts**

(a project of Canada Council and **UNESCO**), *Learning to Live; Living to Learn: Perspectives on Arts Education in Canada* that outlines 50 values that the arts bring to Canadian society.

CANADIAN CONFERENCE FOR THE ARTS (CCA). A dynamic group of artists came together in the early 1940s with a common vision for the sustained growth of the arts and artistic expression in Canada. In 1945, this vision fostered the establishment of a national arts advocacy body, the Canada Arts Council, which later evolved to become the Canadian Conference for the Arts (CCA). Its first major national conference, which called for increased funding and support for the arts, was organized in 1961. Thereafter, national conferences were held every few years, becoming biennial events in the 1980s and early 1990s. Issues tackled include taxation, status of the artist, new technologies, cultural funding, and arts and education.

CANADIAN COUNCIL FOR THE ARTS (CCA). An organization in support of the arts and arts education that deals specifically with evaluation and assessment in arts education; commonly called the *Canada Council*; established in 1957 to act as an arts council of the government of Canada, created to foster and promote the study and enjoyment of, and the production of works in, the arts. It funds Canadian artists and encourages the production of art in Canada.

CANADIAN COUNTRY MUSIC. *See* COUNTRY MUSIC.

CANADIAN FEDERATION OF MUSIC TEACHERS' ASSOCIATIONS (CFMTA). An organization whose purpose is to strengthen the work of provincial registered music teacher associations through collaboration. They promote and support high standards of education among their provincial and territorial members.

CANADIAN MUSIC COUNCIL (CMC). (1947–1990.) An umbrella organization founded in 1944, the council adopted its permanent name in 1945 and received a federal charter in 1949. It acquired a permanent secretariat in Ottawa in 1976. Its objectives were as follows:

- to provide information on music in Canada;
- to provoke discussion on musical subjects of general interest;
- to represent the musical community to governments and international agencies;
- to contribute to the development of music in Canada; and
- to be concerned with the status of music in Canada.

The establishment of the **Canadian Council for the Arts** in 1957 did not change the status of the CMC as an "unofficial" voice of Canadian musicians, but at least it enabled the organization to reimburse its members' travel expenses and to ask for funds for some major projects. The largest and most far-reaching project was the Canadian Music Centre (1959) for the promotion of Canadian compositions. Until 1965 the center remained under the direct control of the council, which received and passed on the Canada Council's annual grants.

The CMC became the Canadian committee of the **International Music Council** in 1952, and of the **Inter-American Music Council** (CIDEM) in 1959. In the next few years it welcomed several new organizations to its own ranks. The council ceased its activities in 1990 but still retains its charter.

CANADIAN MUSIC EDUCATION RESEARCH COLLABORATIVE. An organization that seeks to examine and promote music and arts education in Canada by first examining the current state of music education in Canada. Some 40 of Canada's leading scholars in music-education research have been involved in this process in order to make the report accessible to all, from teachers, to musicians, to policy makers.

CANADIAN MUSIC EDUCATORS ASSOCIATION (CMEA). (1959.) An organization founded to support the interests of public school music teachers; represents the music educators' associations of the provinces: Alberta, British Columbia, Manitoba, New Brunswick, Newfoundland, Nova Scotia, Ontario, Prince Edward Island, Quebec, and Saskatchewan. The CMEA and its members, which represent school music educators and teachers, should not be confused with the **CFMTA** and its provincial associations, which represent private music teachers.

The CMEA's chief aim—unifying and informing Canada's musicians and music educators—has been carried out mainly through publications and conventions. The CMEA is a member organization of the **Canadian Conference for the Arts** (CCA), and in 1989 became the official Canadian representative to the **International Society of Music Education** (ISME).

CANADIAN MUSIC FESTIVAL MOVEMENT (1969). A doctoral dissertation by **Eric Oscar Abbot** titled *The Evolution of the Canadian Music Festival Movement as an Instrument of Musical Education*; traced the growth and development of the Canadian music festival movement. It was suggested that the British Federation of Musical Competition Festivals and the **Eisteddfodau** of Wales be studied in order to ascertain their value as instruments of musical education.

CANADIAN MUSIC FESTIVALS, FEDERATON OF (FCMF). *See* FEDERATION OF CANADIAN MUSIC FESTIVALS (FCMF).

CANADIAN MUSIC RESEARCH CENTRE (CMRC). A synergistic and collaborative group of researchers who explore connections of sound to human experience. The most evident form of sound is music, but the interests of this center extend to the scientific study of sound connections in the broad areas of neurology, physiology, medicine, education, and performance; and narrow applications like semiotics, acoustics, digital representation, biophysical pulsation, and neurological response. Research in CMRC is organized into five spheres: 1) sound; 2) health, therapy, and medicine; 3) body, brain, and mind; 4) culture and society; and 5) teaching, learning, and performing.

CANADIAN MUSIC RESEARCH COUNCIL (CMRC). Adjunct of the **CMEA**, organized by Frank Churchley (University of Victoria) and G. Campbell Trowsdale (University of British Columbia) and founded at the 1973 CMEA convention in Ottawa. Initially the council merely convened for research sessions every two years at CMEA conferences, but it then began to function on a more regular basis and cover an expanding range of activities. Its primary goal has been the collection and dissemination of information concerning music research activity in Canada in the fields of education, musicology, ethnomusicology, and bibliography.

CANADIAN POPULAR MUSIC. The American and British counterculture explosion and "hippie movement" diverted music to that which was dominated by socially and American politically incisive lyrics by the late 1960s. The music was an attempt to reflect upon the events of the time. Things changed course in the 1980s and 1990s. An explosion in youth culture accompanied the fast-paced changes in the broader culture. Canadian publications began to devote attention to all types of music, with more content devoted to young readers. The influence and innovations of Canadian hip-hop came to the foreground in Canada when music videos became an important marketing tool for Canadian musicians—*Much Music* debuted in 1984, and *Musique-Plus* in 1986. Now both English and French Canadian musicians have outlets to promote all forms of music through video in Canada.

CANADIAN UNIVERSITY MUSIC SOCIETY (CUMS). (Formerly the **Canadian Association of University Schools of Music**, CAUSM.) A national organization of university schools, faculties, and departments of music and of music professors and others in the profession of music. Proposed in 1964 at a meeting of Toronto, Montreal, and McGill Universities, CAUSM was established in 1965. Facilitated the exchange of views regarding minimum standards for music degree programs, and encouragement and assistance of the professional development of both institutional and individual members of the society. The name was changed in 1981 to Canadian University Music Society (CUMS). It publishes the *Canadian University Music Review*.

CANDELMAS. (UK-Wales.) A festival, *Gwyi Fairy Canhwyllan*, to celebrate the change from winter to spring beginning on February 2. This festival was a musical contest between outdoor wassailers and indoor responders in the form of musical tests of memory or ability to sing long sections on a single breath. Though the festival has not survived, many of its songs give glimpses of their role of accompanying a dressing in animal costumes and masks.

CANTATA. ("Work to be sung.") Originally, a solo vocal work with basso continuo; gradually enlarged to include solo voices, chorus, and instruments.

CANV'R PWNC. (UK-Wales.) Declamation in the Welsh folk tradition, "singing the text." It is connected with reciting biblical scriptures at catechetical festivals as early as 1800. A presenter sounds the note, one group enters on that note, a second part comes in at a fifth above, and the two parts chant together.

CAPER. (Dance.) To leap or skip about in a spritely manner; a playful leap or skip.

CAPER SECTIONS. Parts of some English dances that require the instrumentalist to play at a slower tempo, or at half the speed while the dancers perform high leaps.

CAPO. Wood, ivory, or metal bar placed on the fingerboard of guitars or lutes to shorten the length of all strings and thus raise their pitch, enabling transition to other keys without changing fingerings.

CARABO-CONE METHOD. (U.S.) An early-childhood approach to learning music, sometimes referred to as the sensory-motor approach to music, was developed by the violinist Madeleine Carabo-Cone (1915–1988). This approach involves using props, costumes, and toys for children to learn basic musical concepts of staff, note duration, and the piano keyboard. Her sensory-motor approach to music learning includes audio, visual, and tactile learning tools. Her approach is basically for preschool children to assist them in learning the fundamentals of music. The planned classroom allows the child to learn the fundamentals of music by exploring through touch. Structured subject matter can be assimilated if translated into a concrete explorable environment. Comparison is made with other methods (**Montessori**, **Dalcroze**, **Orff**, **Suzuki**, and **Kodály**). The arrangement of the room is important as a learning environment. The musical staff as a mental gymnasium is considered. Attention is given to the child's own body as a learning aid, his motivation, the mental and visual focus of attention.

CARLSEN, JAMES C. A professor of music at the University of Washington, Seattle, where he organizes and directs the graduate program in systematic musicology and serves as coordinator of music education. Carlsen holds a BA from Whitworth College, an MA from the University of Washington, and a PhD from Northwestern University. He is the author of *Melodic Perception*, a programmed text in ear training; is a member of the Music Educators National Research Council; is an editorial associate for the *Journal of Research in Music Education*; and has recently been appointed to the Research Commission for the **International Society for Music Education**. His current research is a study of the relationship of *expectancy* to *perceptual error* in melodic music.

CARVER, HAZEL O. (1918–2009). Music educator. Carver has been called a "living legend in music education." A graduate of Western Kentucky University (WKU) at Bowling Green with a BA and an MME. Her work as a music teacher, both vocal and instrumental, touched thousands of lives during her 35 years at Russellville High School, Kentucky. Her students were judged and assessed at Kentucky Music Educators Association (KMEA) Festivals, where they consistently received certificates for top performance grades. She also taught piano privately and was inducted into the National Piano Guild Hall of Fame. Her lifetime achievement in the arts and education and KMEA (a federated unit of **NA∫ME**) brought her many honors and accolades. As a music teacher she received the Governor's Award in Arts Education, KMEA's Prism of Excellence Award, WKU Department of Music Wall of Fame, and was honored as Teacher of the Year by KMEA. She was recognized twice as a Kentucky Colonel (a state award from the governor) and received citations of recognition from both the Kentucky House of Representatives and Senate.

After Carver's retirement from teaching, she became editor of the *Bluegrass Music News*, the official journal of KMEA. Her tireless work in this capacity transformed this original newsletter into an award-winning journal. After winning first place among the conference's state publications, she was elected chair of **MENC** (now NA∫ME) National Editor's Association.

Hazel Oates Carver was considered by many to be one of the most talented musicians ever to come out of Kentucky.

CASTRATO. (Italy.) A young male whose voice was preserved by castration before puberty. In great demand in Italian opera in the 17th and 18th centuries, this voice was brilliant, flexible, and often sensuous. Castrati survived in the Vatican Chapel and Roman churches until the 20th century.

CBC NATIONAL COMPETITION FOR YOUNG PERFORMERS. (Can.) Every other year the Canadian Broadcasting Corporation (CBC) offers cash prizes and public exposure to classical musicians in their twenties and thirties from across the country; categories change from event to event.

CELT. (UK.) A member of any of a group of peoples (as the Scots, Irish, or Welsh) of western Europe. (The term also refers to Bronze Age civilizations that expanded their territorial hold throughout Europe until the early years of Christianity.)

CELTIC MUSIC. (UK.) A term applied to music unique to, or typical of, each of the countries called *Celtic* because the Celtic languages remain part of the cultural heritage transmitted from ancient times. No scholar has established a set of sonic traits that can qualify or disqualify music as Celtic.

CELTIC MUSIC IN CANADA. Celtic musical styles and techniques are known throughout Canada, including the folk music of Newfoundland and Canada's Maritimes, especially on Cape Breton Island. Instrumentation in Newfoundland includes button accordion, guitar, violin, tin whistle, and more recently the **bodhrán**. Some, with an Irish leaning, use the mandolin and *bouzouki*. Cape Breton is internationally known for unusual styles of fiddling, which are derived from Scottish techniques. There are strong ties between traditional Québécois music and the music of Brittany, Ireland, Scotland, and the Maritimes. Songs are drawn from the French tradition, and dance tunes are more closely related to Celtic traditions. Fiddle and accordion are the most common lead instruments.

CENTRAL MIDWEST REGIONAL EDUCATION LABORATORY (CEMREL). These research laboratories were created through the use of **ESEA** Title IV research funding to develop and implement research data on **aesthetic education** (1966).

CEOL: A JOURNAL OF IRISH MUSIC. Edited, published, and written by **Breandán Breathnach**. (Ceol: *music, song*.)

CERTIFICATION AND LICENSING. (U.S.) A process that qualifies individuals to become music teachers in public schools. This process is generally controlled by state departments of education. Programs and requirements vary from state to state and are evaluated and changed periodically. A praxis test is one of a series of American teacher-certification exams written and administered by the **Educational Testing Service** (ETS). Various praxis tests are usually required before, during, and after teacher training courses in the U.S. The **Praxis Series** replaced the **National Teacher Examination** (NTE). The **Praxis II** exam relates specifically to music teaching. *See also* NATIONAL ASSOCIATION OF SCHOOLS OF MUSIC.

CHAMBER CHOIR. Label describing an accompanied or unaccompanied vocal ensemble consisting of a limited number of auditioned members; generally refers to having more members than those in a quartet, quintet, or octet, but fewer than in a larger ensemble, such as a **chorale**; may be all female, all male, or mixed voices; repertoire emphasizes works most appropriate to smaller venues and includes existing, newer, and/or experimental selections from various cultural settings; contrasts with **glee club** and **symphonic choir**.
(Entry by **Michael Jothen**, Nov. 2012.)

CHAMBER ENSEMBLES. Groups performing vocal or instrumental music suitable for performance in a room or small hall. These ensembles use limited numbers of performers.

CHAMPLAIN, SAMUEL DE (1574–1635). (Can.) A French explorer who arrived in 1605 and established the first permanent Canadian settlements at Port Royal and Quebec City in 1608.
Quebec was a French colony that, while slow to develop, was to become the French capital in North America.

CHANGING VOICE. Changes in the vocal mechanism of both boys and girls that occur during puberty as they mature physically. This concept was originated by music teacher **Irvin Cooper**. *See also* CAMBIATA CONCEPT.

CHAPBOOKS. (UK.) **1.** A small book or pamphlet containing poems, ballads, stories, or religious tracts. The term is still used today to refer to short, inexpensive booklets. **2.** An influential popular journal in the mid-1960s that grew out of the *Aberdeen Folk Club Newsletter*. Folk clubs such as this were involved with antigovernment and antinuclear songs due to the neglect of Scottish affairs.

CHARTER SCHOOLS. (U.S.) Schools operated by independent private organizations and typically supported by state funds, exempt from many district and state regulations governing traditional public schools. They are based on a contract or charter between school organizers (parents, teachers, or other concerned citizens) and a sponsor (a local or state board of education). Responsible for their own curriculum, staffing, instructional goals, and objectives. Organizers have almost total autonomy in running the school as they see fit in terms of curriculum, hiring and firing, and budget money. Critics argue that charter schools take money away from regular public schools. They do not have to follow state regulations and have not been shown to be more effective than regular schools.

CHEST REGISTER. Lower register of the male or female voice, the tones of which produce sympathetic vibrations in the chest.

CHEST VOICE. (Chest tone.) **1.** Vocal quality of the **chest register**. **2.** Manner of voice production recommended by Italian teachers for tenors and basses, subjectively felt as though traveling into the chest from the larynx; it is said that the corresponding expansion of the lungs produces a richer tone.

CHEVÉ, EMILE-JOSEPH-MAURICE (1804–1864). A French music teacher and theorist who helped develop a **sight-singing** system based on **movable-doh** lines and with a practical device for acquiring time-values of notes. *See also* GALIN-PARIS-CHEVÉ METHOD.

CHILD-CARE CENTER. A place where children, especially young children, may be watched while their parents work or are otherwise occupied.

CHILD-CENTERED CURRICULUM. An instructional approach that focuses on the child's active participation in the learning process. The **Montessori** method and **Carabo-Cone method** are child-centered approaches.

CHILD ENDOWMENT. (Aus.) A family allowance for children (term considered obsolete).

CHILDERS, HUGH CULLING EARLELLEY (1827–1896). (Aus.) Politician born in England; founder of Melbourne University in 1853. Taken together, the university and the City of Melbourne have continued to be considered the Arts Capital of Australia. Founded in 1895, the University of Melbourne Music Faculty is the oldest music school in Australia.

CHILD GUIDANCE. (Aus.) The readjustment, with psychiatric help, of difficult "mental retardation" in children.

CHILD-MINDER. (Aus.) One who looks after children, usually without having formal training.

CHILDREN OF PEACE (1820). (Can.) One of the first registered all-civilian musical ensembles of a religious sect organized from Upper Canada.

CHILDREN'S CHOIRS. (U.S.-Can.) Select children's choirs have flourished in the U.S. and Canada over the past several decades. Tuition-based, they usually include several levels of groups of children who must qualify in auditions. Children's choirs from Toronto to San Francisco have gained public attention through concerts and professionally produced CDs. Choral series from music publishers such as Boosey-Hawkes and Oxford are found under the names of distinguished children's choral directors. *See also* GOETZE, MARY.

CHILDREN'S MUSICAL DEVELOPMENT. (Aus.) Children mimic adults. They borrow musical material and texts from adults, manipulating them, parodying them, and ultimately claiming ownership. They may borrow whole texts or melodies, or may combine fragments to produce new creations; use playground songs and rhymes to learn basic elements of verbal, aural, and kinesthetic arts that reflect the culture from which they spring. Australian society of the late 1990s provides a rich and diverse source of cross-cultural material.

CHILD'S BILL OF RIGHTS IN MUSIC. (U.S.) (1950; revised 1991.) Based on Articles XXVI and XXVII of the Bill of Rights adopted by the General Assembly of the United Nations, it is contained in a resolution adopted by the **Music Educators National Conference** (now NA*f*ME) in 1950.

CHIME, CHIMING, CHIMER. 1. A set of vertical metal tubes struck with a hammer, as used in the modern band or orchestra. **2.** To sound harmoniously or in chimes, as a set of bells. **3.** One who chimes.

CHINESE WOOD BLOCK. (Clog box, tap box.) A percussion instrument consisting of a resonant hollow block of wood that is struck with a drumstick, giving a hard, hollow tone.

CHIN REST. A device attached to a viola or violin for controlling its position under the chin. Also an oval plate of ebony attached to the edge of the violin or viola, to the left of the tailpiece.

CHOATE, ROBERT ALONZO (1910–1975). (U.S.) Dean, Fine and Applied Arts, Boston University, 1954–1960. Consultant to the **Manhattanville Music Curriculum Project** (1964) and one of the directors of the **Tanglewood Symposium** (1967). He made a major contribution to the music-education curriculum in the public schools and higher education. MENC president 1954–1956, and director of International Relationship Board 1946–1950. Important publications include:

> *Music of Our Time*, an anthology of 20th-century composers.
> *Music in American Society: Documentary Report of the Tanglewood Symposium*, 1967.
> *New Dimensions in Music*, 1970, music texts. Senior author.

CHOIR. A generic label most frequently attached to a vocal ensemble in a church but also a group of like instruments (e.g., brass choir, woodwind choir, etc.). Vocal ensembles vary in size, voices (i.e., unchanged, changing, changed, female, male, mixed, etc.), requirements for membership, and repertoire performed; examples include **chamber choir**, **concert choir**, and **symphonic choir**, as well as numerous ensembles including community choir, church choir, festival choir, etc. A blurring of definitions between the labels *choir* and *chorus* has resulted in the gradual use of either term to label a vocal ensemble.
(Entry by **Michael Jothen**, Nov. 2012.)

CHOOKIE. (Aus.) (Chook: *colloquial*, a domesticated chicken.) Regarding children: a *chook* is an endearment or affectionate name, and is used as a term in children's songs. Also, *chooky*.

CHOPS. 1. *Colloquial*: The jaw. **2.** *Jazz*: a. **embouchure**, b. musical ability, and c. technical prowess. **3.** "In the chops"—in the mouth; instrumentalists use this term when referring to their lips when they have become tired in performance.

CHORALE. Label describing an accompanied or unaccompanied vocal ensemble of mixed voices consisting of auditioned members; generally refers to having more members than found in a **chamber choir** and fewer than found in a **concert choir**; repertoire exhibits a wide diversity ranging from that for smaller venues and smaller ensembles, to that performed by larger ensembles in larger venues.

(Entry by **Michael Jothen**, Nov. 2012.)

CHORALOGRAPHY. (U.S.) A blend of *choral* and *choreography*; addition of a visual aspect to traditional choral ensembles. A term coined by Frank Pooler of California State University–Long Beach: ways of adding simple body movements such as leaning, turning, bending, bowing, and using the hands, arms, and head to add a visual dimension of expression to the text and music of traditional choral music. Singers usually stand in one place on or off risers.

Lit.: Albrecht, Sally, *Choral Music in Motion*, 1989.

CHORDOPHONE. A musical instrument with stretched strings that are either plucked, bowed, or struck; includes zithers, lyres, and harps.

CHORUS. A generic label most frequently attached to a vocal ensemble in a nonchurch setting. Vocal ensembles vary in size, voices (i.e., unchanged, changing, changed, female, male, mixed, etc.), requirements for membership, and repertoire performed. Examples include elementary school chorus, festival chorus, community chorus, **symphonic choir**, etc.; a blurring of definitions between the labels *chorus* and *choir* has resulted in the gradual use of either term to label a vocal ensemble.

(Entry by **Michael Jothen**, Nov. 2012.)

CHRISTIANSEN, F. MELIUS (1871–1955). A Norwegian-born violinist and choral conductor in the Lutheran choral tradition. For 30 years he led the **St. Olaf Lutheran Choir**, striving for perfect intonation, blend, diction, and phrasing. A pioneer in the art of **a cappella** choral music. He composed and arranged over 250 musical selections, and his choral techniques, especially his trademark "straightness of tone achieved throughout the vocal range," were spread throughout the U.S. by St. Olaf graduates.

CHRISTMAS BOX. (UK.) A wooden or clay container where people place gifts; a gift of money, traditionally given at Christmas to people who provide services, such as milk delivery, garbage collection, etc.; a Christmas present.

CHRISTMAS ISLAND. An island in the Line Islands in the central Pacific; the largest atoll in the world.

CHROMATIC. A progression by semitones, especially to a tone having the same letter name, as in C to C sharp; involving a modification of the normal scale by the use of accidentals.

CHROMATICISM. The extending of the diatonic style of composition to include all the semitones of the scale.

CHROMATIC NOTES. Music notes outside the normal diatonic scale in which the piece or passage is written.

CHROMATIC SCALE. A scale progressing entirely by semitones or half-steps, as in white to black keys, black to white keys, or white to white without a black key in between on the piano.

THE CHURCH. Australian pop group, formed in 1980.

CHURCH AND SCHOOL CORPORATION. A body established by the Church of England in Australia in 1826 to maintain religion and education.

CHUTTIE. (Aus.) *Colloquial*, chewing gum. Also, chutty.

CIVIC BOYS BAND. (U.S.) Bands made up of boys in the community that served as feeder programs for the town bands. At the turn of the century (1900s), band directors were owners of town bands in various communities, and young boys who wanted to play band instruments were recruited and taught by these itinerant band directors. These civic bands played for town functions such as parades and athletic events.

CLANSONGS. ("Manikay.") (Aus.). Aboriginal music from *Arnhem Land* song series. Associated with public ceremonial performance at funerals, memorial ceremonies, male circumcision, and cleansing or purification rites in northeastern and north-central Arnhem Land. Sung by one or more men playing pairs of wood **clapstick**s with a single male accompanying on **didgeridoo**; they may be sung both with and without corresponding women's and men's mimetic dances.
    Bib.: Bebbington, Warren, ed., *The Oxford Companion to Australian Music*, 1997.

CLAPPING CHANTS. A children's rhythm game. American and Canadian children by school age enter into the realm of singing games, clapping chants, and regular and purposeful rhythms. "**Apple on a Stick**" is an example of a long-standing interactive clapping chant.

CLAPSTICK. (Aus.) *See* BOOMERANG CLAPSTICKS.

CLARK, ALEXANDER (1843–1913). (Aus.) Music educator. Although born in Scotland, he migrated to Sydney in 1867. From 1884 to 1902 he championed the cause of music in state schools. Introduced the **tonic sol-fa** school syllables and encouraged the training of teachers. In 1890 he cofounded the Public School Decoration Society's concert (Adelaide 1927–1937) and inaugurated the annual Thousand Voices Choir concerts, which he conducted until his demise. He was an inspirational music educator who formed the Australian state music curriculum.

CLARK, FRANCES ELLIOTT (1860–1958). (U.S.) An early music-appreciation advocate. As a teacher in 19th-century Ottumwa, Iowa, Clark spent 10 minutes in each of her chorus rehearsals telling students about composers or helping them recognize the stylistic features of the work that made it possible to place it in its correct historical context. Shortly thereafter, the phonograph added new opportunities for students to listen to music. Clark, who by 1903 had moved to Milwaukee, told of her introduction to the potential of Edison's invention. She realized the difference it could make to her students if they could hear professional recordings. Her principal agreed and approved the purchase of a machine for the schools.

Clark made herself an authority on the use of the phonograph (**Victrola**) to teach music to children and in 1910 spoke to the Wisconsin Teachers Association on "Victrolas in the Schools." **Edward Bailey Birge**, president of the **Music Supervisors National Conference** (MSNC), invited her to present this subject at his MSNC program in Detroit. Within a year she had moved to Camden, New Jersey, where she established an educational department for the Victor Talking Machine Company. She supervised the preparation of recordings designed for use in the classroom. Recordings were also developed to correlate music with English and American literature. Among other responsibilities, Clark assisted record and Victrola dealers in setting up educational displays to help music educators learn the benefits of the phonograph. Victor issued a number of instructional booklets prepared by Clark and assistants. Clark remained with Victor for the rest of her professional career but kept up with the times in the 1920s, when she promoted the radio as an avenue to music appreciation.

CLÀRSACH. Gaelic for *Irish harp*.

CLASS INSTRUMENTAL MUSIC INSTRUCTION. (U.S.) The early 20th century brought about the idea of class instruction. **Charles H. Farnsworth** (1859–1947) visited the schools in England in 1908 and made this report: "The idea of teaching violin classes strikes one as impossible, but here it is being done." In 1910 **Albert G. Mitchell** studied instruction in England for one year. The result was the creation of the Mitchell class method. The emphasis was on the ensemble idea—drilling the class as an orchestral section, strings, woodwind, or brass—then combining to form an orchestra or band. *See also* MAIDSTONE MOVEMENT.

CLASSICAL. (*music*) Deemed to be serious or of intrinsic worth, often taking one of several traditional forms, such as a sonata, symphony, etc., and distinguished from simpler and more widely popular music, such as pop, folk, rock, etc., thought to be inferior, ephemeral, and frivolous.

CLASS METHOD FOR VIOLIN. A classroom method pioneered by the **Maidstone movement**, England, in 1911. **Albert G. Mitchell** studied this violin class method at Maidstone. When he returned to the U.S., he organized five classes of violin students with 16 to 20 students in each class. These were free lessons. After using books from England for several years, he became dissatisfied with their content. He then wrote the *Violin Class Method*, 1924.

CLOGGING. A type of folk dance with roots in traditional European dancing, early African-American dance, and traditional Cherokee dance, in which the dancer's footwear is used musically by striking the heel, the toe, or both in unison against a floor or each other to create audible percussive rhythms. The dance has fused with similar dances such as the Peruvian dance "zapateo" (which may in itself be a derivative of very early European clog dances); this resulted in the birth of newer street dances, such as tap, locking, jump, hakken, stomping, and the Nordic track dance. The use of clogs is more rare in modern dances, since clog shoes seem no longer to be a fashion in urban society (in which most dances are now evolving). Clogging in its main form is often considered the first dance to be classed as a street dance, since it evolved in urban environments during the Industrial Revolution due to urbanization. Clogging was a social dance in the Appalachian Mountains as early as the 18th century.

As the clogging style has migrated over the years, many localities have made contributions by adding local steps and rhythms to the style. Welsh seamen appear to have adopted the dance very early on and may have been those who introduced it to the British Isles. As the dance migrated to England in the 15th century, the all-wooden clog was replaced by a leather-topped shoe with a one-piece wooden bottom. By the 16th century, a more conventional leather shoe with separate wooden pieces on the heel and toe called *flats* became popular, from which the terms *heel and toe* and *flat footing* derive.

In later periods it was not always called *clogging*, being known variously as *flat-footing*, *foot-stomping*, *buck dancing*, *clog dancing*, *jigging*, or other local terms. What all these had in common was emphasizing the downbeat of the music by enthusiastic footwork. As for the shoes, many old clogging shoes had no taps, and some were made of leather and velvet, while the soles of the shoes were either wooden or hard leather.

COCKLES AND MUSSELS. An expressive Irish folk song based on an old street cry. The words are about a young girl in Dublin, Molly Malone, who was a fishmonger. She died of a "faver" (fever), and her ghost continued wheeling her barrow, crying, "cockles and mussels alive!"

COLDSTREAM GUARDS BAND. One of the oldest and best-known bands in the British Army, having been officially formed on May 16, 1785, under the command of Major C. F. Eley, reflecting the fact that the Coldstream Guards regiment is the oldest of the guards regiments. Although the band is not technically the oldest in the army, it has the longest-standing tradition of music, as from its earliest days the officers of the Coldstream Guards hired eight musicians to provide music for the regiment during the changing of the guard. This is an event that still occurs today, every day at eleven thirty in the summer outside Buckingham Palace.

COLI [cOli, Australian spelling]. (Aus.) An evening gathering usually held monthly by people of Irish ancestry, and often involving social dances (including the waltz), solo or group displays, and vocal solos.

COLLEGE BAND DIRECTORS NATIONAL ASSOCIATION (CBDNA). A group organized in 1940 through **MENC** as the College Band Directors National Conference. Nine years later (1949), a constitution was written with a name change from *Conference* to *Association*. This group of band directors is one of several specialist groups within MENC that was formed to satisfy their particular needs. CBDNA and other groups are considered associated organizations of MENC.

COLLEGE MUSIC SOCIETY (CMS). A consortium of college, conservatory, university, and independent musicians and scholars whose mission is to promote music teaching and learning, musical creativity and expression, research and dialogue, and diversity and interdisciplinary interaction. First meeting took place in 1958.

COLLINS, DON L. (U.S.) Music educator, conductor, author, clinician, arranger, church musician, and publisher. Studied with **Irvin Cooper**, founder of the **cambiata** approach to teaching adolescent boys' voices. On the faculty of Central Arkansas University, where he founded the Cambiata Institute of America for Early Adolescent Vocal Music (1979), a nonprofit organization. Two major contributions to choral music education by Don Collins are the *Changing Voice Library*, five volumes of literature for adolescent singers, and the textbook *Teaching Choral Music* (Prentice-Hall, 1999).

COLORED MUSIC NOTATION. A technique used to facilitate enhanced learning in young music students by adding visual color to written musical notation. It is based on the concept that color can affect the observer in various ways, and combines this with standard learning of basic notation.

COLWELL, RICHARD. Professor emeritus of the University of Illinois and the New England Conservatory of Music; has long been involved with assessment and evaluation in music education. In 1970 he published *An Evaluation of Music Teaching and Learning*. Beginning in the late 1960s and continuing into the 1980s, he published 22 music-achievement tests. He served as a consultant to the states of New York, Illinois, Indiana, and Minnesota in the development of the state music tests, as well as consulting with the Boston Public Schools. He was the editor of the first *Handbook of Music Teaching and Learning*, and coeditor of the *New Handbook*. His *Teaching Instrumental Music* is in its third edition. He also published, with Lizabeth Wing, *An Orientation to Music Education: Structural Knowledge for Teaching Music*.

COMING TO OUR SENSES: **THE ROCKEFELLER REPORT.** (U.S.) A report in 1977 by the Arts, Education, and Americans Panel, chaired by David Rockefeller Jr., titled *Coming to Our Senses: The Significance of the Arts for American Education*. It summarized the panel's position regarding the importance of art in education and the schools. One of the basic recommendations was the employment of local artists and teachers to offset budget cuts and job losses. The report reflected America's cultural values and attitudes at that time.

COMMISSION ON TEACHER EDUCATION, MENC. A commission appointed by **Wiley Housewright** in 1972, then president of the **Music Educators National Conference**, to make recommendations for improving music education. They suggested that teacher certification should be based on demonstration of competencies rather than satisfactory completion of a course or set of courses. Competences recommended were: 1) personal qualities, 2) musical competencies, and 3) professional qualities.

COMMUNITY SCHOOLS. Locally supported schools in which the educational program is an outgrowth of the life of a particular community. All segments of the community are involved in determining *curricular* content.

COMPARATIVE EDUCATION IN SCOTLAND AND THE UNITED STATES. Education in Scotland has many similarities to education in the U.S. Scotland has more in common with the U.S. than with England and Wales. Some of these similarities are:

1. They have local control as a result of the Act of Union in 1707.
2. They have local education committees that operate similarly to local boards of education in the U.S.
3. The national curriculum, technically, is advisory.
4. The use of a national assessment system is optional.
5. Professional preparation of teachers resembles the design of teacher education in the U.S. The teaching profession has a strong voice in all matters affecting the quality of teaching in Scottish schools.

COMPENSATORY EDUCATION. Educational programs that offer supplementary instruction to at-risk students and/or students performing significantly below expected achievement levels, particularly in language, mathematics, and/or reading (e.g., Title I, Upward Bound, and Success for All). *See also* ELEMENTARY AND SECONDARY EDUCATION ACT (ESEA) (1965).

COMPETENCY-BASED TEACHER EDUCATION (CBTE). The idea that prospective teachers must meet predetermined competencies, and the process of learning and developing those abilities. Most prospective teachers are required to demonstrate predetermined competencies as part of teacher-training programs. This approach began in the 1970s and continues today.

COMPETITIONS. (*music*) In music education, formal competition is common, especially as it relates to performance-based classes and activities. Full ensembles, small ensembles, and soloists compete at a variety of festivals, contests, and competitions.

COMPREHENSIVE HIGH SCHOOLS. (U.S.) The most common form of public high schools in the United States, meant to serve the needs of all students. Some high schools specialize in academic preparation for university, some in remedial instruction, and some in vocational instruction. A typical comprehensive high school offers more than one course of specialization in its program. Comprehensive high schools usually have a college preparatory course and one or more scientific or vocational courses. *See also* COMPREHENSIVE SCHOOLS (UK).

COMPREHENSIVE MUSICIANSHIP. An interdisciplinary approach to studying music, in which students learn and understand the relationship among a variety of music courses rather than treating each course separately. The original intent was to develop students' abilities to analyze, organize, and perform music. The emphasis shifted to improving teacher-education programs, and in 1965 the Contemporary Music Project (CMP) sponsored a four-day Seminar on Comprehensive Musicianship: The Foundation for College Education in Music. After many years of use, the term has become debatable among music educators, in that most music courses are still structured independently in the curriculum. There are faculty members who subscribe to teaching comprehensively within their own courses, which underscores the idea that comprehensive musicianship is almost synonymous with the teaching of music from the holistic, comprehensive perspective.

COMPREHENSIVE SCHOOLS. (UK.) The system for secondary education in the UK has consisted of two tracks: *grammar schools* for students seeking admission to a university, and *secondary modern schools* for students who are not preparing for a university admission. In the past two decades, these two tracks have combined into the *comprehensive school*, which students of all abilities may attend. *See also* COMPREHENSIVE HIGH SCHOOLS (U.S.).

COMPUTER-ASSISTED INSTRUCTION (CAI). A type of instruction in which students interact with computers to learn materials. CAI is a form of individualized instruction in that it allows each student to progress at his or her own rate. Sometimes referred to as "programmed instruction." One of the most influential projects in computer-based instruction has been the PLATO system developed at the University of Illinois in the early 1960s. The PLATO Music Project, with its specialized peripherals, has provided leadership in the development of computer-based instruction.

COMPUTER MUSIC. Music generated by computer, whether directly, through interaction with live instruments, or as the product of pre-compositional data.

CONABLE, BARBARA. Founded the **Andover Educators**. During her 30-plus years as an **Alexander Technique** teacher, Barbara Conable helped to save hundreds of musical careers and to enhance hundreds more. She experienced frustration, however, because she knew that thousands more musicians were losing careers and capacity. To enhance her effectiveness, she wrote the book *What Every Musician Needs to Know about the Body* and developed a **body-mapping** course by the same name that is now taught by Andover educators around the world. Conable is also the author of *How to Learn the Alexander Technique: A Manual for Students*, and *The Structures and Movement of Breathing*. Now retired from teaching, she continues to develop the theory and practice of body mapping.

CONABLE, WILLIAM. Alexander Technique teacher; developed the concept of **body mapping** in the 1970s.

CONANT, JAMES (1893–1978). (U.S.) An influential education critic and former president of Harvard University who stressed the need for stronger academic preparation in high schools. Conant focused on the need for stronger math and science programs, but he recommended that students be urged to include art and music in their high school elective programs. Unfortunately, little emphasis was placed on this recommendation, which was one of many that he made for improving American high schools. As the president of Harvard University, he reformed the university as a research institution. Many American colleges followed Conant's lead. Conant became an advocate for educational reform in society generally, and this campaign led eventually to the adoption of the Scholastic Assessment Test (SAT). He was active throughout his career on issues of education and scientific policy on both the secondary and collegiate level, being a strong advocate for the establishment of community colleges. In 1959 he authored the book *The American High School Today*.

CONCERT "A." The note to which concert performers tune their instruments.

CONCERT BAND. A wind band consisting of woodwind, brass, and percussion instruments for the performance of concert pieces.

CONCERT CHOIR. Label describing an accompanied or unaccompanied vocal ensemble of auditioned or unauditioned mixed voices; generally refers to having more members than a **chorale** and fewer than a **symphonic choir**; repertoire includes works of varying lengths from varied historical and cultural settings.
(Entry by **Michael Jothen**, Nov. 2012.)

CONCERTINA. A small accordion, usually hexagonal in cross-section.

CONCERT PITCH. The standard pitch to which instruments are tuned, where the frequency of A above middle C is 440 hertz, at 18˚c.

CONCH TRUMPET. (Aus.) A *conch*, or *conque*, is a musical wind instrument that is made from a seashell—the shells of several different kinds of very large sea snails are used. These instruments are sometimes referred to as *shell trumpets*. The shells of large marine gastropods are prepared by cutting a hole in the spire of the shell near the apex, then blowing into the shell as if it were a trumpet, as in blowing a horn. Sometimes a mouthpiece is used, but some shell trumpets are blown without one.

CONDUCTING. Leadership directed toward helping others achieve a depth of musical experiences beyond the obvious; involves using nonverbal physical movements, gestures, and expressions for the purpose of guiding performing musicians to heightened experiencing of the expressive content in musical works; can also assist in guiding and helping focus the responses, involvement, and engagement of audience members.
   (Entry by **Michael Jothen**, Nov. 2012.)

CONDUCTOR [DIRECTOR]. One who practices the art of rehearsing and directing a performing group of musicians. Through knowledge and experience of history and literature, and a solid theoretical foundation of musicianship, the conductor will usually possess a mental image of what he or she wants from the group. A conductor will also have an understanding of the developmental aspects of student/adult music learners.

CONDUCTOR'S COPY. A substitution for a full score in which the parts are condensed into two staves, and the names of the various instruments are inscribed as they enter, or a leading part such as the first violin, on a single stave, fully cued for the other instruments.

CONJUNTO. Group music; the enculturation of children into the music of their varied communities—enclaves of ethnicities, races, classes, and social groups. Communities embrace their music, giving much effort to the creation, maintenance, and transfer of individual and group identity through the music they make. Some of these are: **mariachi** (California, Southwest); conjunto (Texas); polka bands (Midwest); group step-dance lessons (Irish-American/ Celtic roots); and African-American gospel choirs.

CONNECTIONISM (1918). Also known as *associationism*; was one of the early influential schools of thought about learning. Connectionism represents psychology's first comprehensive theory of learning. It was introduced by Herbert Spencer, with William James and his student **E. L. Thorndike** in the very beginning of the 20th century, although its roots are older. Thorndike held that learning occurs by establishing bonds between specific stimuli and responses. His law of learning included the idea that learning bonds would be stronger if the effect of the response were pleasant rather than disappointing. This principle worked well and became the basis for S. L. Pressey's "teaching machines" and later of computer-assisted instruction. John B. Watson of Johns Hopkins and **B. F. Skinner** of Harvard were leaders in what eventually became known as the "behaviorist" school. This had great appeal for music educators.

CONSTRUCTIVISM. A theory of knowledge (epistemology) that argues that humans generate knowledge and meaning from an interaction between their experiences and their ideas. In education, this term is sometimes used to describe a movement to modify the curriculum and instruction to reflect a cognitive or student-centered point of view. Constructivists favor *student-centered instruction* over *teacher-centered instruction*. They promote teaching students to think for themselves and to develop effective study skills and problem-solving strategies. In **music education** constructivism works well in areas such as listening, performing, composing, and improvising.

CONTEMPORARY ECLECTIC THEORY. [Eclectic: choosing from among different sources.] A theory developed and promoted by John Cooksey, who researched the boy's changing voice while teaching at California State University–Fullerton. While some of his research corresponds to other researchers in this field—McKenzie, Cooper, Swanson, and Barresi—there is enough variation to cause other researchers to question his findings. One difference occurs in his ideas of range and vocabulary. While **Irvin Cooper** speaks of *cambiata* and *baritone*, Cooksey uses the following terminology: *boy soprano*, *midvoice I*, *midvoice II*, *midvoice IIA*, *new baritone*, and *settled baritone.* Barresi's classifications are similar in name only.

CONTEST. A musical competition involving two or more individuals or ensembles with the goal of identifying and ranking participants from strongest to weakest; a musical event organized to identify the best, having one winner; common in the United States during the time period from before WWI to after WWII; contributed to the development and refinement of instrumental instrumentation and repertoire.

(Entry by **Michael Jothen**, Nov. 2012.)

CONTROLLED SCHOOLS. (NIre.) One of five categories of school organization in Northern Ireland. These schools are fully funded by the state and under the control of education and library boards. As a result of the history of controlled schools, with few exceptions, students and faculty are Protestant. Controlled schools include primary, secondary, or grammar schools. They do not charge tuition or fees.

COOPERATIVE LEARNING IN MUSIC. Learning that occurs in groups in which students are encouraged to work together toward achieving common goals. It can be adapted to almost any group setting, such as band, orchestra, or choir. Nearly all performance-based classes involve cooperative learning. Also, cooperative learning is more conducive to lower-level, fact-based activities. It has been used for many years in elementary classrooms.

COOPER, IRVIN (ca. 1900–1971). Music educator born in England who went to Canada after college to teach public school music. He received his undergraduate degree from the University of Manchester, and worked for 15 years in Montreal as a high school choral and instrumental director. In his 40s he became supervisor of music for the entire Montreal system and finished his doctorate at McGill University, where he later became director of the McGill University Orchestra and the University Choral and Operatic Society.

During his years as supervisor of music, he became involved with early-adolescent singers and changing-voice problems. While supervising middle-level classrooms, he became aware that most of the boys were not singing, but instead were having a study period during music class. This lack of involvement in music by the young singers led him to investigate ways in which their participation could be improved. Ultimately he engaged in an in-depth study of early-adolescent voices. He soon determined that the young men could sing completely throughout vocal mutation as long as they sang music written in accordance with their unique range and tessitura limitations. He felt that no attempt should be made to make the voice fit already existing music, but that the music should be made to fit the voice.

The approach to the changing voice that has received the greatest exposure, acceptance, and application worldwide is the **cambiata concept**, which Cooper researched, devised, and promoted while professor of music education at Florida State University (1950–1970).

Cooper devoted the last 30 years of his life to working with the early-adolescent voice. Eventually, he was to see his ideas used in 30 states in the U.S., as well as in Canada, England, France, Russia, Brazil, Japan, and Hungary during his lifetime. His publications include 22 books of song collections arranged for changing voices; *Letters to Pat* [his nephew], a professional book for middle-level school music teachers; *Teaching Junior High School*

Music, a college textbook; *The Reading Singer*, a sight-reading method for adolescents; and a sound-color movie, *The Changing Voice*, which was a blue-ribbon winner at the American Film Festival. At the time of his death in 1971, he was chairman of the International Research Committee for the Study of Changing Voice Phenomena with the **International Society of Music Education.**

COPPER FAMILY OF ROTTINGDEAN. (UK.) A family of singers of traditional, unaccompanied English folk song. They were originally from Rottingdean, England; the nucleus of the family now lives in the neighboring village of Peacehaven. English traditional (folk) song has been thought to be pure melody; however, some of the folk singing has included harmony, as found in the example of the Copper family, whose style has been explained as being derived from 18th-century **glee singing**, a form of amateur music making in three or more unaccompanied parts. The Copper family has been recorded extensively. They have a tradition of the unaccompanied singing of traditional local songs that has been passed down through several generations. In 1898, they came to the attention of Kate Lee (d. 1904), one of the founders of the Folk Song Society (later the **English Folk Dance and Song Society**), who knew she had found something special when she encountered the Coppers. Vic Gammon, who wrote notes to accompany the Copper family's recent archive CD *Come Write Me Down*, notes that both the collecting of songs and their unaccompanied singing were less common than is often imagined.

CORE CURRICULUM. This curriculum is commonly used in the context of public school education and refers to academic courses that all students must complete prior to graduation. Individual states determine which courses are in the core curriculum. These decisions are often based on budgetary and political factors that, unfortunately, eliminate music and arts courses from the core curriculum.

CORK GREASE. A lubricant used on the corks of woodwind and reed instruments in order for the mouthpiece to fit together tightly with the neck-piece.

CORNET. A wind instrument of the trumpet class, with valves and pistons. It has a smaller conical tube and larger cupped mouthpiece than the trumpet, resulting in a more mellow timbre and greater technical facilities; evolved from the old post horn by the addition of three valves; range covers two octaves plus three more tones.

CORPS-STYLE MARCHING. A marching style of bands that began to appear in the early 1970s. They adopted changes to the activity that paralleled developments with modern drum and bugle corps. Some of these changes are:

- Instead of marching with a traditional high step, they tend to march with a fluid glide step and keep torsos completely still.
- The use of flag, rifle, and saber units that provide visual flair by spinning and tossing flags or mock weapons.
- Moving marching timpani and keyboard percussion into a stationary sideline percussion section.

CORROBOREE. (Aus.) **1.** An Australian Aboriginal dance with music, generally one that is performed publicly. Intended for all members of the community, held after sunset, when large fires are lit for illumination. Word coined by European settlers of Australia in imitation of an east-coast local Aboriginal Australian word, "caribberie," which is a nocturnal festivity with songs and symbolic dances by which the Australian aborigines celebrate important events. **2.** A ballet by John Antil. Its first performance in 1946 was a concert piece. Rex Reid was the first chorographer, but Beth Dean revamped it in 1954 and included an array of Aboriginal dance movements. For a time, Antil became the musical voice of Australia.

COTSWOLD'S MORRIS DANCING. (UK.) An exception to English traditional dance music, which is typically more regular in shape than tunes not meant for dancing. The music follows this dance closely. The pattern of sections can be complex, and many dances contain **caper sections** that require the instrumentalist to play at a slower tempo, or at half-speed (with note values doubled), while the dancers perform high leaps.

COUNCIL FOR GENERAL MUSIC (CGM). (Formerly **Society for General Music**.) A council devoted to promoting general music education. The official publication is *General Music Today* (GMT). The CGM is under the auspices of **NAfME**, formerly **MENC**.

COUNCIL FOR JAZZ EDUCATION (CJE). Founded by Willy L. Hill in 2009 to supplant the **International Association of Jazz Educators** organization (IAJE), which ceased operation in 2009. Hill is the chairperson of this organization and will serve from 2012 to 2014. The council's mission statement is: "To support the members of the **National Association for Music Education** (NAfME), and the jazz community by serving as a resource to improve the quality of teaching and research in jazz education at all levels."

There are representatives from each of the six divisions of NA∫ME, and three at-large representatives. The council is a member of the NA∫ME association of organizations.

COUNCIL FOR RESEARCH IN MUSIC EDUCATION (CRME). *See* BULLETIN OF THE COUNCIL FOR RESEARCH IN MUSIC EDUCATION.

COUNCIL FOR THE CURRICULUM, EXAMINATIONS AND ASSESSMENT (CCEA). (UK.) The council responsible for curriculum and assessment in Northern Ireland, which is under the **Department for Education in Northern Ireland** (DENI). CCEA's chief purpose is to advise schools on the content of the curriculum; also administers the national assessment system to monitor pupil progress through the primary years and administers examinations to students at various levels on completion of secondary school or grammar school.

COUNTRY MUSIC. (Aus./Can./UK/U.S.) Music beginning in rural areas. In all countries involved in country music, the genre's beginnings are similar:

In Australia, *country music* means rurally based music. From the 19th century, when settlers first left Sydney Cone or Hobart Town for the bush, rural ballads appeared, usually based on the folk tunes of the British Isles, but adapted to reflect the struggles, aspirations, discoveries, and unique emerging lifestyle of the bush.

After the U.S., Canada has the largest base of country music fans and artists. Mainstream country music is culturally ingrained in the **Maritimes** and the **Prairie Provinces**, areas with large numbers of rural residents. Canadian country music originated in Atlantic Canada in the form of British and Irish folk music popular among Irish and Scottish immigrants to Canada's Maritime Provinces (Nova Scotia, New Brunswick, and Prince Edward Island). Like the southern United States and Appalachia, all three regions are rural and heavily populated by people of British Isles stock; as such, the development of country music in the Maritimes mirrored the development of country music in the U.S. South and Appalachia.

The United Kingdom, immersed in its own folk tradition, was slow to recognize the idea of country music as found in the American musical culture. It was the electronic medium, radio and recordings, along with country-western groups and soloists from the U.S., that gradually began to influence the popular wave of music in the UK.

Once again, popular country music began in the rural areas of the South and West of the United States. It was negatively referred to as "hillbilly" music by the urban areas that rejected it. Country music, a mixture of narrative ballads; lively instrumental dance music played on the fiddle, guitar, and banjo; and religious music in the form of hymns and gospel tunes, is highly emotional and personal. Much of this music reflected the Scottish traditions that immigrants had brought to the U.S. The music was homespun and largely amateur. Country-western music has since splintered into several styles, including *outlaw country*, *countrypolitan*, *folk revival*, *country-rock*, and *new country*.

Music education has been affected by this genre in that it is often included in middle school and high school curricula, both in subject matter and in choral music.

COX, GORDON (1923–1999). (UK.) Music educator who was formerly senior lecturer in **music education** at the University of Reading, UK. He served on the History Standing Committee of the **International Society of Music Education** (ISME), and he taught for some years in England and Canada. His main research interest was in the history of music education, and his books included *A History of Music Education in England*, 1872–1928 (1993) and *Living Music in Schools*, 1923–1999 (2002). His last publication was *The Origins and Foundations of Music Education* (2010), coedited with Robin Stevens. He presented papers and organized symposia at the ISME World Conferences in the UK, South Africa, Norway, Spain, Malaysia, Italy, and China. He is a former coeditor of the ***British Journal of Music Education*** and a member of a number of editorial boards. Cox studied the remarkable expansion of school music that took place in England in the late 19th and early 20th centuries.

CRANE, JULIA ETTA (1855–1923). A consummate music educator, singer, conductor, and businesswoman in a time when leadership among women was unlikely. From early childhood she loved music, learned to play the piano, and was also fascinated by bands, concerts, opera, and singing groups.

Crane graduated in 1874 from the State Normal and Training School in Potsdam, New York. Each summer she traveled to Boston to take courses in music education. In 1877, Julia moved to Shippensburg, Pennsylvania, where she taught music, but returned to Potsdam in 1880 and opened a vocal school on Elm Street. It was during this time that she went to England to study under the talented and well-known singer Manuel Garcia, who also taught the famous Jenny Lind, "the Swedish Nightingale." She was constantly trying to discover ways by which students could get the best music education possible.

She was invited in 1884 to join the faculty of the Potsdam Normal School, and was delighted at the opportunity to try her own ideas and theories of teaching music. Two years later (1886) she founded the now-famous **Crane School of Music**, then called the **Crane Normal Institute of Music**, which was located in her studio on Elm Street. She was the first person to set up a school specifically for the training of public school music teachers.

She wrote instructional books for teaching primary grades through college. Her life's philosophy remained unchanged: She believed in the total impact of music on the development of every individual. Ultimately, this led her to establish a program of training for public school music teachers.

Julia Crane's philosophy is addressed in an article by William D. Claudson, "The Philosophy of Julia E. Crane and the Origin of Music Teacher Training," in the *Journal of Research in Music Education*. Briefly, her guiding tenets were based on Aristotle's conclusion regarding happiness. She believed that the highest form of joy resulted from successful achievement by the student. The greatest good to be realized in any teaching situation was to lead the child in such a way as to help him find the fullest measure of himself. Self-realization, she believed, was just as possible in music as in any other school subject. Crane also believed that music could be taught in the classroom using established principles of methodology similar to those in other subject areas.

In the *Music Teachers' Manual*, which she wrote in 1887, the basic elements were found in the activity of the child, training the ear and then the eye. Physical motion, singing, and notation in combination were needed for success; but the progress made by the child depended on his individual effort and positive motivation.

She believed that music is both an art and a science and must be taught as such.

The welfare of the child was the foundation of Crane's philosophy, and that placed heavy responsibility on the teacher to provide the proper setting for self-realization. Crane had two basic axioms in the development of her philosophy:

1. The democratic concept of the individual.
2. Public schools should make music a possession of the masses.

Hers was not a radically new philosophy, but it found expression in the training of America's first music supervisors and laid the foundations for a sound philosophy based on the democratic educational ideal of the freedom and equality of man. Her philosophy echoed universal truths. Even today her philosophy sounds remarkably similar to those who subscribe to the concept of aesthetic education in the teaching and learning of music.

Bib.: Bailey, Edward Birge, *History of Public School Music in the United States*, 1966; Claudson, William D., "The Philosophy of Julia E. Crane and the Origin of Music Teacher Training," 1969; Mark, Michael L., and Charles L. Gary, *A History of American Music Education*, 3rd ed., 2007.

Lit.: Howe, Sondra Wieland, "A Historical View of Women in Music Education Careers," *Philosophy of Music Education Review*, 2009.

CRANE NORMAL INSTITUTE OF MUSIC. Became the **Crane School of Music** of Potsdam College in 1886, under the leadership of Julia Etta Crane. The institute's mission was to provide the specialized training needed by those who aimed to teach music in the public school. Potsdam College is a part of the New York State University system. *See also* NORMAL INSTITUTES.

Bib.: Fowler, Charles, ed., *The Crane Symposium: Toward an Understanding of the Teaching and Learning of Music Performance*, 1988.

CRANE SCHOOL OF MUSIC. Founded in 1886 by Julia Etta Crane (1855–1923) as the **Crane Normal Institute of Music**, it was one of the first institutions in the country to have programs dedicated to training public school music teachers. It continues today as a leader in the field of music education.

CRANE SYMPOSIUM: TOWARD AN UNDERSTANDING OF THE TEACHING AND LEARNING OF MUSIC PERFORMANCE (1986). A symposium in honor of Julia Etta Crane, who built her institute of music in a remote village in New York's north country a century earlier. Her precepts were that:

- Everyone was entitled to a musical education.
- Music should be taught by specially trained teachers.
- Those teachers must be competent, practicing musicians, whose education included a broad base of studies in the liberal and fine arts.

This special symposium sought to synthesize what was known about the teaching and learning of music, and to chart the next 100 years of leadership in music education. Scholars such as **Harry Broudy** and **Richard Colwell** presented papers regarding teaching and learning in answer to a selection of prepared questions. Symposium sessions included presentations by study writers, panel responses to the papers and presentations, small-group discussions, and full-group discussions. **Charles Fowler** acted as editor for the preparation of the Crane Symposium documents, published by Potsdam College of the State University of New York.

CREATIVE NATION. (Aus.) A policy implemented in 1994 by the Australian government that made a commitment to promoting and supporting "cultural industry," tourism, and new technology in the arts, and to assisting emerging artists. This continued an era in Australian cultural development that began emerging in the 1980s.

CREATIVE THINKING IN MUSIC. A type of thinking usually associated with being innovative or productive. Creative thinkers are usually good at problem solving in unusual ways. Creative thinking involves a combination of cognitive and affective processes. This process works in music as in *composing* and *improvisation* at any level, and in all areas of teaching from elementary through higher education.

CREMIN, LAWRENCE A. (1925–1990). (U.S.) Educator; holds enormous stature in 20th-century American education. His parents founded the New York Schools of Music and hoped that Lawrence might become a concert pianist (this, of course, was not in his future). After earning his masters and doctoral degrees from Teachers College, Columbia University, he joined their faculty and subsequently spent his entire professional career there. He founded the History of Education Society and the National Academy of Education. He also served as president of Teachers College from 1974 to 1984. Through his work as a writer and editor, Cremin sought to improve scholarship and teaching, with specific emphasis on the field of educational history.

While a prolific author of 16 books and countless articles, there are two works that stand out as groundbreaking:

- *The Transformation of the School: Progressivism in American Education, 1876–1957.*
- His three-volume history of American education: *American Education: The Colonial Experience, 1607–1783*; *American Education: The National Experience, 1783–1876* (won 1981 Pulitzer Prize in History); and *American Education: The Metropolitan, 1876–1980.*

Cremin broadly defined education as "the deliberate, systematic, and sustained effort to transmit, evoke, or acquire knowledge, values, attitudes, skills, or sensibilities, as well as any learning that results from the effort, direct or indirect, intended or unintended." By using this all-embracing understanding of education, Cremin was able to detail a wide range of American cultural and intellectual history.

For music educators as graduate students, *The Genius of American Education*, delivered as an essay at the University of Pittsburgh in 1965, is a comprehensive overview of Cremin's belief: "With all its limitations, man's rationality remains his best instrument for comprehending and dealing with his experience . . . men will learn to face their problems more intelligently in the future than they have in the past."

CRISIS IN THE CLASSROOM: THE REMAKING OF AMERICAN EDUCATION (1970). An important book by Charles E. Silberman regarding an examination and criticism of traditional education. This book includes an excellent section on "open education," and also a section on teacher education as an aspect of the education crises at that time.

CRITICAL THINKING IN MUSIC. A general term for a conceptual mode of thinking that can involve a variety of processes, including reflection, logic, analysis, synthesis, problem solving, directed thought, forms, evaluation, investigation, and thoughtful consideration. In music, studies involving critical thinking tend to focus on problem-solving skills and identifying relationships between musical and nonmusical variables on measures of critical thinking tasks.

CRME BULLETIN. *See* BULLETIN OF THE COUNCIL FOR RESEARCH IN MUSIC EDUCATION.

CRUIT. (UK-Scotland.) A small, triangular handheld harp or lyre that accompanied missionaries from Ireland. Early history shows Scotland to have a shared musical culture with Ireland.

CRWTH. (Pronounced "crowd.") (UK-Wales.) An instrument developed from the Celtic lyre, which accompanied bardic declamation as early as the first century BCE. Rectangular in shape. It had from three to six strings, probably of horsehair, stopped by fingers of the left hand. The bridge was flat, which enabled the performer to produce chords; it had one leg lengthened to go through a sound hole and act as a sound post. It was used to accompany the voice in declamation of poetry, to play melodies, to accompany dancing, or as a solo instrument. By the 1700s it had been replaced by the **fiddle**.

CULTURAL DIVERSITY IN MUSIC EDUCATION (CDIME). An international network for researchers, teachers, and learners in the field of cultural diversity in music education; an informal network for institutions and individuals working in this field. It is a platform for exchange of ideas, experience, and practice in an area that is still gaining ground in music education.

CULTURE BEARER. A person who carries knowledge and understanding of a culture. Culture bearers keep the culture alive by helping new members of the group to learn its skills, language, and values (e.g., in **music education** this could be **general music** teachers [K–12]; and band, choral and orchestra directors).

CURRICULAR ALIGNMENT. A coherent and consistent progression of content, instruction, and assessment within a course of study. Instructional materials will be designed to meet cultural relevance and accessibility standards, and will incorporate methods for teaching all students, including those receiving special education, bilingual education, or advanced learning services.

CURWEN, JOHN (1816–1880). (UK.) An English Congregationalist minister and the founder of the **tonic sol-fa** system of music education. He was educated at Wymondley College (subsequently Coward College) and University College London. Curwen gave up full-time ministry in order to devote himself to his new method of musical nomenclature. Curwen's system was designed to aid in sight-reading of the stave with its lines and spaces. Curwen felt the need for a simple way of teaching how to sing by note through his experiences among Sunday school teachers. Stemming from his religious and social beliefs, Curwen thought that music should be easily accessible to all classes and ages of people.

Curwen made use of **Sarah Glover**'s sol-fa "ladder," which he adopted into the tonic sol-fa modulator. He incorporated French solfege time names into his method, as in *ta* for quarter notes and *ti* for eighth notes. **Mary Helen Richards** also used this approach. Similar ideas had been elaborated in France by **Pierre Galin** (1786–1821), Aimé Paris (1798–1866), and **Emile Chevé** (1804–1864), whose methods of teaching how to read on sight also depended on the principle of tonic relationship being taught by the reference of every sound to its tonic, and by the use of a numeric notation.

Curwen brought out his *Grammar of Vocal Music* in 1843, and in 1853 started the **Tonic Sol-Fa Association**. The *Standard Course of Lessons on the Tonic Sol-fa Method of Teaching to Sing* was published in 1858. In 1879 the **Tonic Sol-Fa College** was opened. Curwen also began publishing, and brought out a periodical called the *Tonic Sol-fa Reporter and Magazine of Vocal Music for the People*, and in his later life was occupied in directing the spreading organization of his system. *See also* HAND SIGNS.

CYMRU. (UK-Wales.) The name for Wales in the Welsh language. Wales occupies a mountainous peninsula along the central west coast of Great Britain. Musically, Wales is most famous for its traditional harp playing and choral singing, and for its annual competitive music festivals, The Royal National **Eisteddfod** (festival) and the International Music Eisteddfod.

D

DALCROZE, EMILE. *See* JAQUES-DALCROZE, EMILE.

DALCROZE METHOD. (Dalcroze eurhythmics.) (Swz.) The method incorporates the basic elements of music—rhythm, melody, harmony—with body movement, to provide a multidimensional approach to music learning. Unlike most traditional methods, improvisation is a major component of the Dalcroze approach and one of its three aspects:

- **Eurhythmics** trains the body in rhythm and dynamics.
- **Solfège** (sight singing) trains the ear, eye, and voice in pitch, melody, and harmony.
- **Improvisation** brings all elements together according to the student's own invention, in movement, with voice, at an instrument (**Dalcroze Society of America**).

Beyond musical intelligence, the Dalcroze approach engages and exercises several other aspects of intelligence. Musical games and experiments engage logical thinking. Eurhythmics appeals to kinesthetic and spatial types of learners. The social quality of music making develops communication, feeling, and empathy. It has the physicality of sports and the aesthetic appeal of the arts, and is mentally challenging for all ages. Unfortunately, programs are not widespread, and where they exist, they are frequently for children only.

The Dalcroze concept of improvisation is close to the nature of childhood play. According to Dictionary.com, *improvisation* means to compose and perform or deliver without previous preparation; to compose, play, recite, or sing (verse, music, etc.) on the spur of the moment. Improvisation frees a child to relate directly and spontaneously to music within a range of musical knowledge. Improvising with full-body movement, singing, or playing an instrument helps the child internalize complex elements of rhythm, pitch, tone, and dynamics without having to read a musical score. Through improvisation, composing becomes a personal and immediate creative act. A child enhances his creative spirit through improvisation and carries that spirit into his daily life.

Emile Jaques-Dalcroze was a visionary 19th-century pedagogue. He did not like his approach to be labeled as a method. In fact, there is really no set curriculum. Teachers are trained in techniques and principles, which they adapt to the characteristics, needs, and abilities of their students. Dalcroze certificates and licenses are conferred by master Dalcroze teachers who hold the diploma from the Dalcroze Institute in Geneva, Switzerland (http://www.dalcrozeusa.org/). In California, two established musical institutions that teach the Dalcroze method are:

- The San Francisco Conservatory of Music.
- The School of Performing Arts Division of the Colburn School.

DALCROZE SOCIETY OF AMERICA (DSA). An organization founded on **Emile Jaques-Dalcroze**'s approach to teaching music education.

DANN, HOLLIS ELLSWORTH (1861–1939). Teacher, author, editor, choral conductor, and leader of public school music in the United States. The thirteenth president of **MENC** (1919–1920), with official responsibilities from 1910 to 1939. He believed that music teachers must be sound musicians, with excellent performance as their goal and standard. He helped standardize the teaching of music as chairman of the New York State Music Examination Committee and was a member of the New York State Music Syllabus Committee, and chairman of the New York State Music Council (1910–1921).

Professional career included: principal and supervisor of music, Ithaca Public Schools (1887–1905); director of Cornell University **Glee Club** for 32 years; head of Cornell Music Department; and state director of music, Pennsylvania (1921–1925).

Publications include: *Hollis Dann Music Course*, 1912; *New Manual for Teachers*, 1929; *Hollis Dann Song Series*, 1935–1936; *School Hymnal*, 1910 (New York: American Book Company); and *Spirituals* (1924–1934) (New York: H. W. Gray Co.).

DAVIDSON, JANE W. (Aus.) Chair of Music Department at the University of Western Australia, and deputy director of the Australian Research Council's Centre of Excellence for the History of Emotions (CHE). She has written in excess of 100 international scholarly publications and secured $24.5 million in external funding. Her pioneering work on expressive body movement in the early 1990s set a research agenda many have pursued and developed. Her latest book is *Music and the Mind*.

DAVISON, ARCHIBALD T. (1888–1961). American music educator and choral director, organist, and choirmaster at Harvard University. Taught at Harvard University from 1909 to 1955. Known for many choral arrangements and for his book *The Technique of Choral Composition* (1966). He was also the editor of the two-volume *Historical Anthology of Music*.

DAWNSIO HA'. (UK-Wales.) May dancing. This is a boisterous element in May celebrations that included *Cadi*, a man dressed in women's clothes and wielding a broom, accompanied by dancers with blackened faces.

DEAD STRING. (False string.) A string on a violin, viola, cello, or bass that does not sound right; it does not produce the correct pitch, or does not produce a natural resonance commonly heard when bowed.

DEARING REPORT. (UK.) This 1993 report was the official evaluation of the national curriculum by Sir Ron Dearing, chairman of the School Curriculum and Assessment Authority. Dearing made a firm case for streamlining the assessment system. He reported that the national curriculum relied too heavily on standardized tests, tended to "fragment teaching and learning," and trivialized the process of education assessment to a "meaningless ticking of myriad boxes." Dearing's report resulted in the simplifying of the mechanism for assessment, while helping to keep the broad goals of standardization and accountability intact.

DEPARTMENT FOR EDUCATION (DFE). (UK.) The central agency for education in England and Wales (Wales has its own central agency, the Welsh Office Education Department) that is responsible for all state-maintained schools and certain aspects of independent schools. DFE is responsible for educational standards achieved, the efficiency of financial management, and the "spiritual, moral, social and cultural development" of pupils.

DEPARTMENT FOR EDUCATION NORTHERN IRELAND (DENI). (UK-NIre.) The central government agency responsible for education in Northern Ireland. The minister of education, a member of the Northern Ireland Parliament, is the chief spokesperson for education policy.

DETT, ROBERT NATHANIEL (1882–1943). (Can.) One of the first black Canadian composers during the early years of the American Society of Composers, Authors and Publishers (ASCAP). His works often appeared among the programs of William Marion Cook's New York Syncopated Orchestra. Dett performed at Carnegie Hall and with the Boston Symphony as a pianist and choir director. He studied at Eastman and in Paris with **Nadia Bou-langer**; taught at Hampton Institute, Virginia (1913–1932), and was active in the study of Negro music and in promoting the interests of Negro musicians. He compiled the Dett Collection of Negro Spirituals (four vols. 1936).

Bib.: Slonimsky, Nicolas, and Richard Kassel, *Webster's New World Dictionary of Music*, 1998.

DEWEY, JOHN (1859–1952). Leading American philosopher. The spirit of democracy and an abiding faith in the efficacy of human intelligence run through his diverse works in the fields of metaphysics, aesthetics, religion, ethics, politics, and education. Progressive education owes its impetus to his guidance and its tenets largely to his formulations.

Dewey received his undergraduate degree from the University of Vermont in 1979 and his PhD from Johns Hopkins in 1884. He taught at the University of Michigan, the University of Chicago, and Columbia University. Among his many important works is *Art as Experience* (1934), which influenced the thinking of many philosophical writers. *See* BROUDY, HARRY; REIMER, BENNETT.

DIATONIC HARMONICA. (Can.) A melodic instrument of the folk music tradition that appeared in the late 18th century; limited to pitches belonging to a single scale, whose generating **fundamental** is the tonic of the scale. Other names are *French harp* and *mouth organ*.

A small, flat metal box with openings on one of its long sides. The player places the instrument against his lips and moves it back and forth according to the desired notes by blowing or inhaling against the openings of the instrument.

DICKEY, FRANCES M. A president of the Northwest Music Supervisors Conference (1931) who wrote a valuable paper on "The Early History of Public School Music in the United States." This paper contained the dates that marked the introduction of music into the public schools in the cities that followed the example of Boston.

Bib.: Birge, Edward Bailey, *History of Public School Music in the United States*, 1966, p. 65.

DIDGERIDOO OR DIDJERIDU. (Aus.) Australian Aboriginal wind instrument. End-blown, trumpet-like **aerophone**, without the mouthpiece. It is played using a circular breathing technique, while buzzing the lips. Although basically mono-tonal, it is also capable of producing overtones, and when combined with vocalizations, tonguing, and guttural shrieks, complex sounds and rhythms can be created. It can be seen in rock paintings at least 1,500 years old. Originally made out of bored-out bamboo or termite-hollowed wood.

In education, it is used by musicians, storytellers, and dancers who present Aboriginal culture to students at the primary, secondary, and tertiary levels.

Bib.: Kennedy, Michael, *Oxford Concise Dictionary of Music*, 2004, p. 199.

DIFFERENTIATED INSTRUCTION OR EDUCATION. Implementation of instruction and learning activities designed specifically for gifted or advanced students, as in **Gifted and Talented** programs.

DIRECTOR. *See* CONDUCTOR.

DIRECT TEACHING. (UK.) Also known as *direct instruction* or the *didactic method*. Direct teaching involves the whole class or small groups within the whole class as the teacher sets the pace of a lesson. The pace is modified when students fail to grasp key points. There is regular interaction with students and perceptive questioning by the teachers. Activities include class discussions, debate, singing, drama, parachute games, circle time, and many more. It may also involve the teachers using concrete objects to aid in learning and encouraging students to learn from handling objects and materials.

DISCIPLINE-BASED ART EDUCATION. A program intended to establish the arts as a more meaningful part of school curricula by broadening content, emphasizing the relationship between and among the arts, helping students understand the place of arts in the history of civilization, and making course requirements more rigorous. Founded in 1980 by the Getty Center for Education in the Arts (GCEA), an entity of the J. Paul Getty Trust.

DISCIPLINE-BASED MUSIC EDUCATION (DBME). An approach that places music as a core subject in the general education of all students using Western and non-Western music of various cultures. This includes four areas of discipline: aesthetics, criticism, history, and production.

In October 1992, the Southeast Institute for Education in Music (SIEM) hosted the nation's first invitational conference on DBME, sponsored by a major grant from the Getty Center for Education in the Arts and the Southeast Center for Education in the Arts. New funding from Chattanooga's Benwood Foundation, the University of Chattanooga Foundation, and the **National Endowment for the Arts** allowed SIEM to continue its groundbreaking research and implementation efforts with teachers, schools, and students throughout the Southeast. *See also* DISCIPLINE-BASED ART EDUCATION.

DISCOVERY LEARNING. A teaching technique in which teachers question students about a topic. Students are led to discover (learn) things for themselves through the thinking process.

DISTANCE LEARNING. An approach or method of teaching in which teachers interact with students over a long distance. This includes any and all aspects of Internet activity. Best used in nonperformance music courses such as music theory, music history, and music appreciation.

DJAMBIDJ. (Aus.) Aboriginal clan song series in north-central Arnhem Land. It consists of 21 song subjects, the most important being "Hollow Log" and "Wild Honeybees." The bees make their nests in hollow logs, which are also used to contain the bones of deceased humans—symbolizes both life and death. Performed by at least one singer accompanying himself with a clapstick and a didjeridoo.

DJEMBE. (Aus.) Rope-tuned, skin-covered, goblet-shaped drum played with bare hands.

DOANE UKULELE SYSTEM (1971). (Can.) **1.** *Ukulele Method for Classroom Teaching*, published in 1971 and revised in 1980 by J. Chalmers Doane, director of music education, Halifax School Board. **2.** Comprehensive approaches to the teaching and learning of the **ukulele** individually and in classes. **3.** Areas such as *picking*, rhythmic strumming, sight-reading, and changing chords by ear are emphasized.

DODSWORTH BAND. A brass band popular prior to the Civil War that dominated the New York music scene from 1836 to 1891. One of the first professional bands, and perhaps the best band in New York prior to the advent of **Patrick Gilmore**'s inventive genius in 1869.

DOLMETSCH, ARNOLD (1858–1940). Swiss musician and maker of old instruments. Restored old instruments, and made his first flute in 1893, clavichord in 1894, and harpsichord in 1896. Worked at Chickerings' piano factory in Boston (1902–1909). Following his introduction of recorder playing to English schools, recorder groups were established in Australian schools from 1940.

DOLMETSCH, CARL (1911–1997). English recorder player, son of **Arnold Dolmetsch**. Was a virtuoso performer touring the world; also a maker of recorders and player of violin and lute. In 1940, after his father's death, he became director of the Haslemere Festival.

DONKEY RIDING. (Can.) A Canadian dock-loaders' song. The engines for loading are called donkey engines, because they have less horsepower. A "donkey" is a small steam engine used in loading lumber onto a ship.

DRAGOON GUARDS. (UK.) A member of a military unit formerly composed of such cavalrymen as in the British Army. One who carries the regimental color of the Dragoon Guards is a "guide." The purpose of the Prince of Wales Dragoon Guards was to march into battle or perform for those who were marching. *See also* GUIDON.

DRUM AND FIFE. *See* FIFE AND DRUM (Int.).

DRUM AND FIFE BANDS. (Aus.)

Drum: A *side drum*, also called a *snare*, is a small cylindrical drum with two heads stretching over a shell of metal. The upper head struck with two drumsticks in the *batter head*; the lower, across which are stretched the taut snares, is called the *snare head*. In Australia, instrumental music in schools during the colonial period (early 1840s) was limited to drum and fife bands that were viewed as an extensive military drill that was taught in many schools.

Fife: A small flute, usually wood, still used as in centuries past, is found in the drum and fife band. It is built a tone lower than the orchestral piccolo, and with six to eight finger holes and no key. Used chiefly in military bands.

DUKE, JOHN WOODS (1899–1984). American composer and pianist best known for his art songs. After WWII he became a concert pianist with the New York Philharmonic. In 1923 he joined the faculty at Smith College (MA), where he remained until his retirement in 1967. Pursuing compositional studies with **Nadia Boulanger** (Paris) and Artur Schnabel (Berlin), he returned to the U.S., where he continued to lecture and to write some 260 art songs that became very popular. His lectures took him to college campuses, where students worked with him and performed his songs in recital. He covered a wide range of styles but was influenced by 19th-century German lieder. Although a pianist, he mostly wrote art songs because he "believed that vocal utterance is the basis of music's mystery." Duke's "Loveliest of Trees" (based on a poem by A. E. Housman) is considered to be a classic, and is essential to young singers' art-song education. He received the Peabody Alumni Association Award for Distinguished Service in the field of music upon his retirement in 1967.

DUKE, ROBERT A. Distinguished fellow in teacher education and director of the Center for Music Learning, he is also an adviser to the Psychology of Learning Program at Colburn Conservatory in Los Angeles. A recipient of the **MENC** Senior Researcher Award, he has directed national research efforts sponsored by the National Piano Foundation and the International Suzuki Institute. His research has focused on human learning and behavior that spans multiple disciplines, including motor skill learning, cognitive psychology, and neuroscience. Recently, he has explored procedural memory consolidation and the cognitive processes engaged during musical improvisation. A former studio musician and public school music teacher, he has worked closely with children at risk, both in the public schools and through the juvenile justice system. He is the author of *Scribe 4* behavior-analysis software; and his most recent books are *Intelligent Music Teaching: Essays On the Core Principles of Effective Instruction* and *The Habits of Musicianship*, which he coauthored with Jim Byo of Louisiana State University.

DWIGHT'S JOURNAL OF MUSIC. A periodical with some 1,051 issues in nearly 30 years of publication. It was the most substantial and long-lived music periodical in America, but not necessarily the first. *See also* SULLIVAN, JOHN DWIGHT.

DYKEMA, PETER WILLIAM (1873–1951). (U.S.) Dykema's prolific writing, teaching, conducting, and leadership were major forces in public school music. He was extremely popular as a lecturer, conductor, and teacher. He worked with **Jacob Kwalwasser** of Syracuse University in music psychology and, as a result, produced a series of music tests corresponding to intelligence tests in general education. He served as editor of the first official **MENC** publication, *The Bulletin* (1914), later named the *Music Supervisors Journal*. He remained as editor for many years. Among his list of influential publications are *Music for School Administrators*, *School Music Handbook*, *Kwalwasser-Dykema Music Tests* (1930, 1954), and *Twice 55 Community Song Books*.

Dykema's philosophy was built on the premise that everyone should learn to love and enjoy good music. "*Music for every child, and every child for Music*" (a **NAfME** slogan) does not mean the same music for every child; rather, what is best suited for the student's own development. He believed that music education had been too long a process of *training* and not one of *education*. The more important aspect of teaching is to have the student express something within himself that has been stimulated by outward influences. Dykema was chairman of the Music Education Department at the University of Wisconsin (1913–1924), and head of the Music Education Department at Teachers College, Columbia University (1924–1939).

E

EARHART, WILL (1871–1960). (U.S.) An influential member of **MENC** for 50 years, and a highly respected conductor, violinist, pianist, music educator, and author. Promoted instrumental music in the public schools and was the first to teach instrumental methods by any school in the summer of 1911. Among his great contributions to music education were his prolific philosophical writings based on sound reasoning. He believed that music, more than any other academic subject, is able to develop in people the finer inner life and provide aesthetic experiences. In the 1958 *Music Educator's Journal*, he wrote, "The role of music education should be the cultivation of fine taste and appreciation of the beautiful; a concept of beauty of tone, understanding of form, content and expressiveness."

Most of Earhart's professional career was spent in Pittsburgh, Pennsylvania, as a music supervisor, professor of music at the University of Pittsburgh, and professor of music at Carnegie Mellon University (previously named Carnegie Institute of Technology). His important publications include:

- *Music in the Public Schools* (1914)
- *Music in the Secondary Schools* (1917)
- *The School Credit Piano Course* (1918)
- *The Meaning and Teaching of Music* (1935)
- *Choral Techniques* (1937, 1938)

EARLY CHILDHOOD MUSIC AND MOVEMENT ASSOCIATION (ECMMA). (U.S.) An organization that seeks to promote developmentally appropriate practices for all early-childhood music and movement specialists for the good of children (birth through age seven).

EARLY MARK. (Aus.) A permission for pupils, usually in infants' or primary schools, to leave class a little early as a reward for good behavior or work.

EAR-TRAINING. A generic description of music educational methods used to improve the ability of students to learn and remember intervals and rhythms.

EASTMAN WIND ENSEMBLE. A group organized in 1952 by Frederick Fennell at the Eastman School of Music as an adjunct to the Eastman Symphonic Band. This **wind ensemble** began with the premise that they could make music with the minimum (one on a part) rather than the maximum number of players. This ensemble confined their rehearsals and performances to the study of original music written for the larger band. They embarked upon an active program to stimulate the composition of music for wind ensembles by contemporary composers everywhere. Ensembles playing this original music written for winds sprang up at the University of Illinois and Northwestern University, and were quickly emulated by other colleges and the larger public schools.

EASY INSTRUCTOR. (U.S.) Publication by William Little and William Smith in 1801. *See also* SHAPE-NOTE.

EBBINGHOUSE, HERMAN (1850–1909). German psychologist. An early pioneer in the study of memory. He devised a set of items to be committed to memory that would have no previous associations, so-called "nonsense syllables." Using himself as a subject, he explored the memory process for several years. He has been referred to as the "father of the experimental study of learning" and is best known for developing a curve of forgetting:

- Individuals remember best immediately after learning new information.
- After a brief period of time, there is a relatively rapid decrease in memory abilities.
- After the rapid decrease, an individual's ability to remember information declines steadily with the passage of time.

This information is extremely helpful for music teachers when assisting students in memorizing for performances.

E-BOOK. *See* E-READER.

ECOLE DES URSULINES AND URSULINE CONVENT. (Can.) One of North America's oldest schools and the first institution of learning for women in North America. Both were founded in 1639 by French nun, **Marie de l'Incarnation** (1599–1672), alongside laywoman Marie-Madeline de

Chauvigny de la Peltrie (1603–1671). They were the first Canadian institutions to have music as part of the curriculum.

EDITH COWAN UNIVERSITY. (Aus.) A university with campuses in Perth and Bunbury; formed in 1991 from Western Australian College of Advanced Education, est. 1982.

EDUCATION ACT OF 1980. (UK.) This act introduced several new concepts in public education policy:

- Declared that parents had the right to choose which school their children would attend.
- Recognized the unique cultural character of Wales.
- The Wales chief education officer was authorized to fund bilingual education—English and Welsh—for elementary and secondary education.

EDUCATIONAL PSYCHOLOGY. The study of educational growth and behavior in all its aspects: intellectual, emotional, social, and physical. *See also* THORNDIKE, E. L.

EDUCATIONAL TESTING SERVICE (ETS). Founded in 1947 near Princeton, New Jersey. The world's largest private nonprofit educational testing and assessment organization. *See also* PRAXIS SERIES.

EDUCATION FOR ALL HANDICAPPED CHILDREN ACT OF 1975. *See* MAINSTREAMING.

EDUCATION REFORM ACT OF 1988. (UK.) This act brought a power shift from local education authorities to the national government. Important provisions were:

- A national curriculum was instituted when Parliament created the National Curriculum Council for England and the Curriculum for Wales. Parliament prescribed in specific terms the kind of education desired.
- The act set up a system of "grant-maintained schools" to complement the existing system of "maintained schools."
- Tenure was abolished for faculty in universities.

EDUCATION REFORM ORDER OF 1989. (UK.) This order follows the 1988 Reform Act. The curriculum is organized to facilitate a national system for assessing student progress. Assessment has been the main part of the platform for education reform. It prescribes assessment points and methods, with the stakes growing higher as students progress through the key stages. The content of the curriculum includes art and design, music, and physical education.

EDUCATION THROUGH MUSIC (ETM). (U.S.) A nonprofit corporation that promotes the integration of music into elementary and middle school curricula to enhance student development and academic performance. Founded in 1991 by Edmund R. Schroeder and Eldon C. Mayer. Music instruction consists of a sequential skills-based curriculum that includes learning frameworks, sample lesson plans, integration strategies, and assessment tools. Several elementary and middle schools in the New York area, Connecticut, and Pennsylvania are a part of this program. The program was developed by **Mary Helen Richards** through the Richards Institute of Music Education and Research, to use the language and songs native to the people living in the United States. Advised by **Kodály**, Richards personally used American folk songs and games to reflect the rhythm, accents, and inflections of English as spoken in the United States.

EDUCATION WEEK. (Aus.) A week set aside each year during which special school displays, functions, etc., are held in order to foster community involvement and interest in schools.

EDUCOLOGY. (Aus.) A study of methods of teaching based on observation of teaching practices and the application of that theory in order to enhance teaching skills.

EISNER, ELLIOT W. (1933–). (U.S.) Professor of art and education at Stanford University. Works in three fields: arts education, curriculum studies, and qualitative research methods. He has advanced the role of the arts in American education and by using the arts as models for improving educational practice in other fields. His background in teaching extends from the University of Chicago, to Ohio State, and ultimately to Stanford University, where he has spent most of his educational career. As a prolific writer and lecturer, he has made the case for developing attention to the cognitive in art rather than art education being only driven by emotional and "creative" forces. Eisner's influence has stemmed not only from his writings and lectures, but also from his involvement in key projects and initiatives. One of the most important has been the Getty Center for Education in the Arts, where he has served on the advisory board from 1982 to the present. As a result of his work with the Getty Center, his contribution to **aesthetic education** has been an important part of music education and has influenced thinkers and practitioners in this sister field of the arts. Eisner is a fellow of the Royal Society of Art in the United Kingdom, the Royal Norwegian Society of Arts and Science, and the National Academy of Education in the United States.

EISTEDDFOD. (UK-Wales.) (Plural *eisteddfodau*.) A Welsh festival of music, literature, and performance. The tradition of such a meeting of Welsh artists dates back to at least the 12th century, when a festival of poetry and music was held by Rhysap Gruffydd of Deheubarth at his court in Cardigan in 1176, but, with the decline of the bardic tradition, the festival tradition also fell into decline. The present-day format owes much to an 18th-century revival arising out of a number of informal *eisteddfodau*. The closest English equivalent to *eisteddfod* is "session"; the word is formed from two Welsh morphemes: *eistedd*, meaning "sit," and *bod*, meaning "be."

In its modern form, the eisteddfod is a competition festival, not always confined to music. The **Royal National Eisteddfod**, the most important, is a revival dating from the early 19th century. It takes place annually in August, alternately in northern and southern towns in Wales. An International Eisteddfod, at which choirs and dancers from all over the world compete, has been held annually in Llangollen since 1947.

ELAM, JOHN EDWARD (1823–1888). *See* ELAM SCHOOL OF FINE ARTS.

ELAM SCHOOL OF FINE ARTS. This Auckland school was founded in 1890 by John Edward Elam as a result of money that was bequeathed by an English philanthropist in New Zealand. Students study for degrees in fine art, with an emphasis on a multidisciplinary approach.

ELASTICS. (Aus.) A game in which children jump in sets of patterns over stretched pieces of elastic.

ELECTOPHONE. A term for music instruments that produce sound by electronic means, either by oscillation or by electronic/electromagnetic/electrostatic methods.

ELECTRONIC MUSIC. Music produced by electronic means, which may include organized nonmusical sounds. Electronic music has served a variety of functions in music education. Attempts to produce electronic sounds began in the U.S. and Canada in the 1890s, and the field has proceeded step-by-step with the invention of a variety of types of electronic equipment. Electronic music was revolutionized in the 1960s by the invention of voltage-controlled sound **synthesizers**, especially the model developed in 1964–65 by the American Robert A. Moog. A smaller synthesizer, the Putney synthesizer (ca. 1970), was developed in Britain and was used in college music-education classes.

(Aus.) The first electronic music made by an Australian occurred in the University of Southern Australia with the "**free music**" experiments of Percy Grainger and Burnett Cross from 1945. The free music machines that they built produced a small amount of music recorded on acetate discs. These examples, made exclusively with sine waves, were the world's first pieces made with these materials. The earliest electronic music studios in Australia were at the University of Adelaide, set up in 1969 by Peter Tahourdin, and the Melbourne University studio, founded in 1972 by Keith Humble. The earliest commercial studio, and perhaps the first electronic music studio in Australia, was Bruce Clarke's Recording Workshop, est. in 1962.

ELECTRONIC POP. A style of pop music originating in Britain and Europe in which musicians are reduced to a minimum in favor of computer-driven, synthesized-backing track.

ELECTRONIC TUNER. A device used by band directors to have students match pitch with their specific instrument, when needed. The Kong electronic tuner is preferred by many band directors.

ELEMENTARY AND SECONDARY EDUCATION ACT (ESEA) (1965). (U.S.) Public Law 89-10, Titles I, II, III, IV, V. (1965–1970). Federal legislation designed to improve the quality of education and to equalize educational opportunities for all children.

Titles II and III were important for the arts and music-education programs. For example, Pittsburgh (PA) Board of Education administrators developed a Center for the Creatively Talented through Title III, in which students from city high schools were able to participate in special after-school instrumental and vocal programs.

ELEMENTARY EDUCATION ACT (1891). (UK.) An important act that created free education for children, even though parents were responsible for the payment of incidental fees.

ELGAR, SIR EDWARD (1857–1934). (UK.) English composer and conductor. For a number of years, he earned his living as a violin teacher. His first large-scale London success came in 1899, when Hans Richter conducted the *Variations on an Original Theme (Enigma)*, one of Elgar's greatest and best-known works. After the second performance of his choral work *The Dream of Gerontius*, Richard Strauss hailed Elgar as the foremost English composer of the day.

From 1901 until 1914 were the years of Elgar's greatest acclaim. His *1st Symphony* had an astonishing success after having been performed more than 100 times in a variety of European cities; however, the work, which to this day makes him a well-known musical name, was the first of a set of *Pomp and Circumstances Marches* written in 1901. The tune of the trio section was acknowledged by King Edward VII, who suggested that it should be set to words. In 1902 it emerged in the *Coronation Ode* as *Land of Hope and Glory*, and it soon became clear that Elgar had composed an alternative national anthem. Elgar was knighted in 1904 at the age of 47, and in 1911 he became a member of the Order of Merit. He wrote successful compositions for theater, orchestra, voices and orchestra, part songs and church music, chamber music, short pieces for small orchestra, solo songs, piano, organ, and transcriptions for orchestra.

Elgar's greatness as a composer lies in his ability to combine nobility and spirituality of utterance with a popular style. He was one of the first great composers to realize the possibilities of the *gramophone*, and from 1914 to 1933 made many recordings of his own music, which are important historical documents. The most celebrated recording was that of the violin concerto made in 1932 with the 16-year-old Yehudi Menuhin, American-born violinist.

ELKINS, MARGRETA ANN ENID (1930–). Mezzo-soprano who, at 17, won a Queensland Government scholarship to study dramatic art and musical theory. A highly successful opera artist who became principal artist with the Australia Opera in 1975 and performed in Australia and throughout Europe, the U.S., and Canada. Since 1988 she has lectured in vocal studies at the University of Queensland Conservatorium, and in 1991–1994 she was head of vocal studies at the Hong Kong Academy of Performing Arts. She was awarded an honorary DMus by the University of Queensland.

ELLIOTT, DAVID. (Can.) Philosopher. Born in Toronto and educated in their schools, including the University of Toronto. He taught in Toronto secondary schools as well as the University of Toronto. After 28 years, he joined the faculty at New York University in 2002. He has given more than 200 lectures at university music schools around the world. He has presented numerous research papers at international, national, and local conferences. Several of his compositions and arrangements are published by Boosey and

Hawkes (New York). Two of his best-known works among music educators in particular are *A New Philosophy of Music Education: Music Matters* and *Praxial Music Education: Reflections and Dialogues.* Elliott emphasized participation in music over listening, as defined by **Bennett Reimer**. This was a criticism of Reimer's definition of aesthetic education as a foundation of a philosophy of music education. Elliott's new view of music-education philosophy gained widespread acceptance as more music educators became interested in philosophy.

ELLIS, CATHERINE (1936–1996). (Aus.) Music educator who specialized in Aboriginal music. She studied pitch in Central Australian vocal music. In the 1990s, she and Udo Will devised methods for measuring and analyzing pitch. Studying unfiltered, complex waves, they analyzed song lines from Central Australia and songs from Northern Australia. She found that small intervals (multiples of three to five herz) consistently occurred in Central Australian singing. She interpreted these intervals as building blocks for arithmetic (equidistant) scales. A more complete discussion of these findings can be found in *The Garland Encyclopedia of World Music*, vol. 9, *Australia and the Pacific Islands*, pp. 292–93.

ELMS, LAURIS MARGARET (1931–). (Aus.) A contralto and a violinist. Sang folk songs and ballads with an ABC radio station and the National Theatre Movement Opera Co. She has performed in Paris, in a Covent Garden (UK) regional tour, in Israel, and with the Australian Opera Company. An intelligent and musical performer, her roles have included works from Mozart, Bartok, and Honegger. She was honored with the OBE in 1974 and the AM in 1982.

ELOUERAN. (Aus.) A cultural period of Aboriginal development recognized in eastern Australia, which follows the Bondaian period and extends to the present.

ELYOT, SIR THOMAS (1490–1546). English scholar and diplomat remembered for his treatise on education, *The Boke Named the Governour* (1531).

EMBOUCHURE. (*music*) **1.** Mouthpiece of a wind instrument. **2.** The adjustment of a player's mouth to such a mouthpiece.

EMERGENCY TEACHER. (Aus.) Sometimes called a *relief teacher*; a school teacher who temporarily replaces regular teachers who are absent.

ENCULTURATION. (*Also* **acculturation**, socialization.) The by-product of the normal, daily functioning of any given society; the process through which individuals learn and internalize a society's rules and norms.

ENGLISH. The people of England collectively, especially as distinguished from the Scots, Welsh, and Irish. Sometimes referred to as "The Queen's [or] King's English," educated or correct English speech or usage.

ENGLISH AND SCOTTISH POPULAR BALLADS (1882–1898). (U.S.) The American ballad scholar and anthologist Francis J. Child published and annotated texts, mostly older narrative pieces with the characteristic features of oral transmission. Though Child included a few tunes, the American scholar Bertrand Bronson (1902–1986) compiled the tunes extant for many of these ballads in *The Traditional Tunes of the Child Ballads* (1959–1972), printing additional texts. Most ballads are narrative, and many deal with fabulous, miraculous, or gruesome deeds. Ballad singers made a living by singing their newest production in the streets and at country fairs, and by selling the printed sheets, which usually gave a direction: "to be sung to the tune of . . ." (e.g., "Greensleeves"). Mostly written in common meter as in 8.6.8.6.

ENGLISH COUNTRY MUSIC. A term that gained acceptance in the 1960s and early 1970s to specifically describe a genre of instrumental music then receiving attention from the folk revival.

This was a deliberate attempt to avoid both the term *folk*, at the time being used widely to include much acoustically performed music with or without genuine folk origins, and the term *traditional*, which would strictly preclude the more recent material country musicians performed. *See also* COUNTRY MUSIC.

ENGLISH FOLK DANCE AND SONG SOCIETY (EFDSS). Formed in 1932 when two organizations merged—the **Folk-Song Society** (1898) and the English Folk Dance Society (1911). One of the greatest contributions that the EFDSS made to the folk movement, both dance and song, was the folk festival, starting with the Stratford-upon-Avon Festival in the 1940s and later festivals in Whitby, Sidmouth, Holmfirth, Chippenham, and elsewhere. In 1998, with the folk movement strongly supported by a number of other organizations and the seeds planted by EFDSS thriving, the EFDSS altered its strategy to focus on education and archiving, with its primary goal the development of the Vaughan Williams Memorial Library as the country's national archive and resource center for folk music, dance, and song.

***ENGLISH FOLK-SONG: SOME CONCLUSIONS* (1907).** An influential book by Cecil J. Sharp, who characterized English tunes as being cast in the dorian, phrygian, mixolydian, aeolian, and ionian (major) modes, and occasionally in the minor. He accepted a modal theory of English folk song that he used to classify melodies.

ENGLISHNESS. The quality of being English; a romantic nationalism that values the spirit of the nation and seeks out those things that expressed it. During the late Romantic period, ca. 1900, musical nationalism was prominent. English composers saw the need to incorporate the English traditional music into their compositions. Their goal was twofold: to lay the basis for a national school of composition and to give the folk song back to the people as a cultural and social renaissance. As a result, Ralph Vaughn Williams's and Percy Grainger's music became examples of Englishness in music.

ENTERTAINMENT. (Can.) In Canada, particularly in urban areas, the responsibility for teaching music may rest in the hands of classroom teachers, who increasingly use music as *entertainment*, as a pervading atmosphere for other classroom activities, or as a means of setting the scene for a particular season or special event.

EPHRATA CLOISTER. (U.S.) A musical group of German-speaking Protestants in Pennsylvania who lived as a communal society. German-born **Conrad Beissel** founded the Ephrata Cloister in 1732, and by the late 1750s the community had grown to over 300 members. They were Seventh-Day Baptists who believed strongly in music as an aid to worship. They used their own homespun music based on principles set forth by Beissel in his *Dissertation on Harmony*. He established choirs and singing schools, and even prescribed special diets for each of the SATB choral sections. The choral music of these Seventh-Day Baptists was usually in four parts, and some of their hymnbooks were published by Benjamin Franklin in the 1730s. Beissel's work is generally considered an example of "primitive" art in musical Americana. One can still visit this small community in Ephrata, Pennsylvania, thanks to the research work of Dr. Russell Getz, former **MENC** president and supervisor of music for the state of Pennsylvania.

E-READER. An electronic device that allows individuals to download and read digital books (e-books), newspapers, magazines, and other electronic publications and programs. It is approximately the size of a small paperback book, lightweight, and easily carried from place to place. There are several brands on the market, including the **Kindle** (Amazon Books) and the **Nook** (Barnes & Noble Booksellers).

ERNST, KARL D. (1910–2000). An outstanding music educator who spent his teaching career at the University of Washington and the University of Oregon from 1932 to 1974. He held positions as president of **MENC** from 1958 to 1960 and the **International Society for Music Education** (ISME) from 1964 to 1968. He served on several music-education committees, including the **Tanglewood Symposium** in 1967. He was an outstanding performing musician as a trumpet soloist and as guest conductor of the Portland Symphony Orchestra.

Ernst believed that the public schools should provide opportunities in music for all students, including the talented, the special aptitude, and the general student body. He was also a proponent for designing general music classes for all students. Ernst, with Charles Gary, published *Music in General Education* in 1965.

ERNST, ROY (1938–). Professor emeritus, taught at Eastman School of Music for 25 years and chaired the Music Education Department for 12 years. In 1991, Dr. Ernst started the first New Horizons Band at Eastman for the purpose of creating a model program to teach music making for older adults. The New Horizons Band was a model that assisted in starting more than 60 similar programs in the United States and Canada. Dr. Ernst has been recognized as a Grand Master of Music Education by **MENC**, and he has published books and articles on conducting, flute performance, and music education. He is the founding director of the Aesthetic Education Institute in Rochester, New York.

ETHNOMUSICOLOGY. A relatively new term to describe rigorous study of traditional music of all peoples. The primary area of research has been non-European music that once would have been labeled "exotic" in times past, such as music of Asia, Africa, and South America. The invention of videotape allowed dance, ceremony, and other visually oriented elements to be recorded for study. This term was coined by J. Kunst to replace *comparative musicology*, on the grounds that the comparative method is employed in every scientific discipline.

THE ETUDE. A popular publication (1883–1957) developed for piano teachers and students to provide practical articles and music for piano and instrumental students of all ages.

EURHYTHMICS. A system of musical training introduced by **Emile Jaques-Dalcroze** (in 1910) in which pupils were taught to represent and experience complex rhythmic movement with their entire bodies, to the accompaniment of specially composed or improvised music. *See also* DALCROZE METHOD.

EXTENSION MUSIC. (UK.) The Cliff Richard Law, a directive that would extend music copyright from 50 to 70 years.

EYE MUSIC. Certain 15th- and 16th-century compositions in which the affective meaning of the music is made visible to the eye by the use of special notational methods, such as blackened notes to express grief, lament, night, dark, or shade. An early example is found in Ockeghem's *Missa Mi-Mi*, where black notation is used at the end of the Credo for the word "mortuorum." Eye music is also applied to examples of word painting, as in ascending or descending notes for words meaning "heaven" or "dying."

FADO. A popular Portuguese song and dance genre.

FALSE STRING. *See* DEAD STRING.

FALSETTO. 1. "False" voice; an artificially produced high voice, free of overtones. **2.** (Aus.) A vocal timbre from many areas of **Oceania**. Its use enables singers to reach pitches above their full-voice range. Falsetto singing by males occurs throughout Oceania in solo and ensemble singing to **chordophone** accompaniment. It may be unusually loud, but it more typically occurs at subdued levels. In some societies, men and women sing in falsetto; in others, falsetto is typical of one sex, usually males. It may be a singer's improvisational choice.

FARM AND TRADE SCHOOL BAND OF BOSTON HARBOR (1858). An early group in Boston that met after school and received no academic recognition or credit.

FARNSWORTH, CHARLES HUBERT (1859–1947). A pioneer in music teacher education and later a professor at Teachers College, Columbia University, the leading pedagogical institution in the nation in the early years of the 20th century. He wrote one of the earliest scholarly papers on the value of music in American secondary schools. In "Music in the Secondary School," he outlined the major problems and aims of American music education at the secondary school level and suggested music's place in the secondary curriculum. This essay marked the beginning of a century of growth in American music education, and was a benchmark paper on the aims of music in secondary education.

FARNUM MUSIC TEST. Developed in 1969 by Stephen E. Farnum. The purpose of this test is to select beginners for all musical instruments; it is considered by Farnum to be a predictive measure. From a pilot study of 170 high school students, four important factors were identified: 1) eye and hand coordination, 2) recognition of music notation, 3) tests of musical memory (tonal patterns), and 4) tonal movement (cadence).

FA SO LA (OR FASOLA). A method of teaching singing popular in England and colonial America using only three syllables of the **Guidonian hand**—*fa*, *sol*, and *la*. These were used to form a major **hexachord** (*fa*, *sol*, *la*, *fa*, *sol*, *la*), and by adding the syllable *mi* for the seventh degree, a major scale was obtained (*fa*, *sol*, *la*, *fa*, *sol*, *la*, *mi*). *See also* SHAPE-NOTE.

"FATHER OF MUSIC EDUCATION." *See* MASON, LOWELL.

FEDERATION OF CANADIAN MUSIC FESTIVALS (FCMF). An organization designed to develop the amateur competitive festival movement in Canada. First convened in 1926 when representatives from four western provinces met in Calgary. Occasionally joined by Quebec and northwestern Ontario until 1945. In 1946 eastern Canadian festivals were invited to join. Their main objective is the development and encouragement of Canadian talent in the performance and knowledge of classical music.

FEDERATION OF FESTIVALS. (UK/Int.) The British and International Federation of Festivals for Music, Dance and Speech offers a platform for performance and the opportunity to hear the work of others and the chance to receive feedback from professional adjudicators. It is the member body for amateur competitive festivals of performing arts and provides information, support, advice, and services to members.

FEIERABEND, JOHN. One of the leading authorities on music and movement development in early childhood. He is committed to collecting, preserving, and teaching diverse folk music of the U.S. and using that folk music as a bridge to help children understand and enjoy classical music. Dr. Feierabend makes frequent presentations both in the U.S. and abroad and is the author or creator of over 60 books, articles, CDs, DVDs, and videotapes. He is professor of music and the director of the Music Education Division of the Hartt School of the University of Hartford (CT) and is past president of the **Organization of American Kodály Educators**.

FENNELL, FREDERICK (1914–2004). *See* EASTMAN WIND ENSEMBLE.

FIDDLE. 1. Often, an affectionate name for a violin. **2.** Any European bowed string instrument from the Middle Ages onward. Applied to instruments that do not conform to standardized patterns; colloquial name for violin, particularly one of rustic origin; found in many European and American folk musics. **3.** (UK-Ire.) Violin, always called *fiddle* by traditional musicians, was always found at the Sunday dancing. It is not played in the classical manner. It is held lower and at a different angle, and the upper end of the bow is used most of the time for playing. "**Country music**" fiddlers tend to hold their instruments in a similar manner. **4.** (Can.) In the late 18th century, the *fiddle* was the instrument of the lower class. Fiddles were a fixture in most public drinking establishments; they were held and played much like in the Irish tradition.

FIELD, JOHN (1782–1837). (Ire.) An Irish pianist, composer, and teacher who studied with Muzio Clementi. An extended visit to St. Petersburg, the Russian capital, impressed him so much that he stayed very active there from about 1804. Field was highly regarded by his contemporaries, and his playing and compositions influenced many major composers, including Chopin, Brahms, Schumann, and Liszt. He is best known for originating the piano *nocturne*, a form later made famous by Chopin, as well as for his substantial contribution, through concerts and teaching, to the development of the Russian piano school. Although born in Dublin, because of his love of the Russian artistic life and his rescue by his Russian patrons, Field remained there until his death. He died and was buried in 1837 in Moscow.

FIFE AND DRUM. (Int.) The fife and the drum are prehistoric musical instruments. Simple in design, they were and are used in various forms and combination in nearly every culture and period of history.

The first time they were used together in a form that we would recognize today as *fife and drum* was in Switzerland in the 15th century. The needs of extended marches and camp life encouraged the development of fife and drum music in the 1400s. The rest of Europe took notice of this military music at the climatic Battle of Marignano (near Milan, Italy) in 1515.

The Germanic principalities adopted this military music in the 1500s and 1600s. The French employed Swiss mercenaries in the 1600s and 1700s, who brought their fife and drum music with them and influenced the rest of the French army. During the reign of Queen Anne of Great Britain, the English army had become very disorganized and undisciplined. The Hanoverians, who succeeded Queen Anne beginning with George I in 1714, reorganized the English army, requiring troops to march in step to proper military music, which took the form of fife and drum (excepting Scottish Highland regiments, which used bagpipe and drum). This was the model that the English colonists in North America followed when they formed their local military organizations.

Both the British Army and the English colonists used fife and drum in the Revolutionary War. This music is strongly associated with the birth of America. It was still used by the American military into the Civil War, but by then the increased range, accuracy, and rapidity of firearms; the extension and rapid movement of battle lines; and the replacement of long marches by transport on railway and steamship made fife and drum obsolete. After the Civil War, the bugle was preferred, though fife and drum was used by shipboard Marine detachments until 1921.

Fife and drum, however, blossomed as a folk tradition around the year 1876, the centennial of American independence. Nostalgic, patriotic Americans of this era re-created this music. Many local militia companies had become fire brigades and supported fife and drum corps as a town **band**. They are now primarily located on the East Coast between Virginia and Massachusetts, most heavily in Connecticut. Groups are scattered elsewhere in the U.S., and a few are in Switzerland, where they play in the American "ancient" style, thus returning this musical form to its original homeland.

FIFE AND DRUM BANDS. (Aus.) *See* DRUM AND FIFE BANDS.

FILM MUSIC. (U.S.) There are approximately three periods of development in film music, beginning with what is called the era of "silent films."

1. At the beginning of the 20th century and motion-picture production, theater owners would hire pianists or organists to provide appropriate music for images on screen, from romantic scenes to mournful minor keys for scenes. Most played music from the classical repertoire. Some improvised their own or other composer's works.

2. With the advent of sound in motion pictures, music was provided with the dialogue on the sound track. Sometimes producers would hire "ghost" composers. Eventually, legitimate composers were hired, such as Max Steiner and Alfred Newman. Sometimes composers would incorporate music quotations from Wagner, Tchaikovsky, and Rachmaninoff. Eventually, as movie making with sound became more sophisticated, electronic music or avant-garde composers supplied the aural background, such as Ligeti and Ussachevsky. Then John T. Williams became highly successful with his *Star Wars* trilogy and *Close Encounters of the Third Kind*. (The use of Kodály's *solfege* in this movie excited many schoolchildren and music teachers.)

3. The third period of composing for films requires precise synchronization with the changing images and actions on screen. As a result, digital technology has refined this process further.

FIPPLE FLUTES. (UK.) These are various kinds of six-holed pipes. Early examples are made of wood, but in the 19th century, instruments such as the tin whistle or penny whistle were widely produced commercially.

FISHER ACT (1918). (UK.) An act passed by Parliament in which all fees were abolished, and an elementary education became truly accessible to all children. (Secondary education at this time was available only to those who could afford to pay for it.)

FISHER, JAMES CHURCHILL (1826–1891). Music educator. Born in England and died in Australia, he introduced the **tonic sol-fa** teaching method to NSW (Aus.) through adult singing classes. After various positions as a schoolmaster, he was appointed as singing master to Sydney (Aus.) schools and teacher-training colleges. Initiated tonic sol-fa in public schools in 1863; this was adopted as the official music teaching method in 1867. He composed school songs and cantatas and published several tonic sol-fa songbooks and textbooks.

FISK JUBILEE SINGERS. In 1870 a choir was formed at Fisk University under the direction of a northern-born faculty member, George L. White. The original Fisk Jubilee Singers were former slaves or children of former slaves and were the first group to publicly perform the songs of slaves and share them with the world. In order to raise money for the newly created Fisk University in Nashville, Tennessee (1865), White chose singers from a select group of Fisk University Singers. On their first tour they emphasized Negro spirituals and were very well received. The Jubilee Singers were a sensation in New York and New England. Eventually, their journeys included the British Isles and the European continent. Their performances during those years raised a total of $150,000 for the university. The Jubilee Singers continue performing today.

FIVE-LINE STAFF (OR STAVES). A set of five horizontal lines and four spaces in which each line and space represents a different musical pitch; or, in the case of a percussion staff, different percussion instruments. In Western music this shows time as running from left to right.

FIXED DOH. A system of solmization in which tone C, and all of its chromatic derivatives, are called *doh*; D and the following tones are called *re*, *mi*, *fa*, *so*, *la*, *ti*, *doh*, no matter what key or harmony in which they appear. It is the opposite of **movable doh**, in which the tonic note moves within the scale and regardless of the line or space on the staff. It is also called *do[h]*, whatever the key. Most *music-education professionals* use the movable-doh system. *Performance professionals* tend to use fixed doh.

FLAGG, JOSIAH (1737–1794). The publisher of important tune books such as *Collection of the Best Psalm Tunes* (1764) and *Sixteen Anthems* (1766).

FLAMENCO. (Spain.) Popular Andalusian art of singing and dancing, accompanied mainly by guitar and castanets. It gradually developed into an important folk art form. The singing is usually introduced by exclamations ("ay! ay!") and accompanied by vigorous heel stomping and passionate gesticulation; the resulting dance is called *zapateado* (shoe dance).

FLEMING REPORT (1944). (UK.) This report (England and Wales) represented a concentrated effort to integrate the "public" schools into the state-supported education system. It proposed a system of government grants to students who attended these private, independent schools. While this recommendation was well received, it was never implemented because of the unwillingness of either the national government or the local education authorities to fund grants. The report, however, indicated a desire by education policy makers to break down the social-class divisions so apparent in English society.

FOLK DANCE. A dance that originated among, and has been transmitted through, the common people.

FOLKLORE. (UK.) When the term *folklore* was introduced in 1846 by the English scholar William J. Thoms, scholars of that time felt satisfied that it gave a proper name to their investigations of vernacular tales, customs, and beliefs that were in danger of vanishing.

FOLKLORE INSTITUTE OF SCOTLAND (1947). An important organization in the collection and dissemination of Gaelic songs. John Lorne Campbell and Margaret Fay Shaw gathered traditions in South Uist and Barra, and Alan Lomax recorded material later published on the Columbia World Library label. The Folklore Institute began to record Gaelic songs in 1947.

FOLKLORE SOCIETY (FLS). A learned society founded in London in 1878 and devoted to the study of all aspects of folklore and tradition, including ballads, folktales, fairy tales, myths, legends, traditional song and dance, folk plays, games, seasonal events, calendar customs, child lore and children's folklore, folk arts and crafts, popular belief, folk religion, material culture, vernacular language, sayings, proverbs and nursery rhymes, folk medicine, plant lore and weather lore.

FOLK MUSIC, FOLK SONG. 1. The musical repertory and tradition of communities (particularly rural) as opposed to art music, which is the work of musically trained composers. It generally develops anonymously, usually among less-educated classes, and it was originally (and may still be) transmitted aurally, thereby becoming subject to modification. **2.** The music of usually simple character, originating and being handed down among the common people using songs, dances, and instruments such as fiddle and dulcimer. **3.** Music originating in the urban American beat generation of the 1940s and 1950s, which concentrated on lyrics of social comment.

    Bib.: Apel, Willi, *Harvard Dictionary of Music*, 2nd ed., 1973.

FOLK MUSIC JOURNAL. Scholarly journal of the **English Folk Dance and Song Society** (EFDSS).

FOLK MUSIC SOCIETY OF IRELAND (FMSI). (NIre.) **Breandán Breathnach** and others founded the Folk Music Society of Ireland (1971) and the Pipers Society (1968), *Na Píobairí Uilleann* (The Uilleann Pipers). The Folk Music Society publishes an occasional journal, *Irish Folk Music Studies*, and both societies have produced books, pamphlets, and tapes.

***FOLK SONGS IN ENGLAND* (1967).** A publication by A. L. Lloyd. It is considered a heroic attempt to understand English folk song musically, socially, and historically. The book drew on three intellectual traditions: Sharpian folk song scholarship, international folklore scholarship (especially from eastern Europe, on the work of Bartok and Brailoui), and radical Marxist historical writings. Lloyd tried to comprehend folk song as a historical process, one that was not divorced from the experiential world, not relegated to some mythical past, nor the product of mythical folk, but as the product of men and women engaged in real social relations, experiencing a range of human emotions. Lloyd's book is considered by many to have an elegant command of English folk song material.

FOLK-SONG SOCIETY (1898). (UK.) The term *folklore*, derived from the German *Vokskurde*, was introduced into scholarship by the antiquarian W. J. Thoms in 1846. Cognate terms *folk song* and ***folk music*** followed, and growing interest in musical idioms led to the founding of the Folk-Song Society in 1898. The first volume of the *Journal of the Folk-Song Society* was published in 1899.

FOLK-SONG SOCIETY (1906). (UK-Wales.) *See* WELSH FOLK-SONG SOCIETY.

FOLK SONGS OF THE UPPER THAMES. (UK-Eng.) A publication in 1923 edited by Alfred Williams, who wanted "to describe how the people spent their days and nights, in what employments, recreations and amusements." He argued that a representative collection of folk songs would be the best and only way to obtain this information. He was the first collector from a working-class background. Williams wanted to gain an understanding of the social context in which the songs were performed. This desire led more recent researchers toward the study of English social history.

FOLLETT SERIES. In 1950, the Follett Publishing Co. of Chicago brought out the first book with the title *Together We Sing*. The authors were **Irving Wolfe** and Margaret Fullerton, daughter of **Charles A. Fullerton**, who was the original coauthor of this series. This series contained a teacher's guide and a series of educational records designed and produced by Dr. Wolfe. A Carnegie grant paid for the translation of songs he had collected. As Wolfe explained in an interview, "We were using recordings as a means of bringing music, the sound of music, into the experience of the classroom." Prior to this, Fullerton and Wolfe had been working on a revision of Fullerton's book, *A One Book Course in Elementary Music*, but Fullerton died before the publication.

The Follett Series continued to expand, and new titles appeared: *Music Round the Clock*, *Music Across Our Country*, *Voices of the World*, *Music Round the Town*, *Voices of America*, *Music Sounds Afar*, and *Proudly We Sing*. In 1964 the editors published a book especially for kindergarten called *Music Round About Us*.

The Follett Series is important to music education because it represents the first use of educational recordings and an invaluable source of folk songs from around the world.

Bib.: Goss, Donald R., "Irving W. Wolfe, His Life and Contributions to Music Education," 1972, 1980.

FORRAI, KATALIN (1926–2004). One of the most well-known Hungarian music pedagogues, she was internationally connected to early childhood music education. She devoted her life to the **Kodály** concept of music education, working with children at the kindergarten level with attention to the artistic values of children's songs. She selected and edited Hungarian children's songs and other nations' materials, advancing Kodály's ideas by giving lectures and in-service courses for teachers worldwide. Her best-known work is her book *Music in Preschool*, as well as a set of videotapes. As a board member of the **International Society of Music Education**, she was the promoter and leader of the Early Childhood Commission. Katalin Forrai's devoted activity was recognized with many awards in Hungary and abroad, including the award from the Kodály Institute in 1994.

FORSTER ACT OF 1870. (UK.) This act marked the beginning of the modern era of British education. The Forster Act divided the country into school districts and made provisions for local school boards to levy taxes to support schools for areas in which none existed. Unfortunately, even with these sweeping changes of the "board schools," there were neither general curriculum guidelines nor requirements for teachers. Schools could still assess fees, which meant that many children did not attend because their parents could not afford to send them.

FOUNDATION SUBJECTS. (UK.) National curriculum subjects that are compulsory and form the core of the curriculum. In all key stages these include English, mathematics, and science. In Wales, Welsh is an additional foundation subject in all maintained schools.

The administration of the national curriculum rests with two national agencies created by the **Education Reform Act of 1988**.

FOWLER, CHARLES B. (1931–1995). Musician, arts educator, and writer, he voiced the challenge of change and reform. He urged teachers to experience their work with students as creative encounters that were alive, inventive, and filled with mutual discovery. Fowler, in donating his papers to the University of Maryland–College Park, stated: "I was not satisfied as a teacher with merely passing on the culture. I wanted a role in creating it. The classroom is not just a place for learning about yesterday, but a laboratory for inventing tomorrow." As a writer, one of his most important books was *Can We Rescue the Arts for America's Children?*

Fowler received the MM degree from Northwestern University and a DMA from Boston University. For 15 years he served as education editor of *Musical America* magazine, and was also editor of **Music Educators Journal**. He also published *Sing!*, a textbook for secondary school choral classes, and *Music! Its Role and Importance in Our Lives*. He was director of National Cultural Resources in Washington, DC.

FREE MUSIC. Percy Grainger introduced the idea of *free music* to critic Olin Downes in 1942. He wrote:

In this music, a melody is as free to roam thru space as a painter is free to draw and paint free lines, free curves, create free shapes. . . . In FREE MUSIC the various tone-strands (melodic lines) may each have their own rhythmic pulse (or not), if they like; but one tone strand is not enslaved to the other (as in current music) by rhythmic same-beatedness. In FREE MUSIC there are no scales—the melodic lines may glide from & to any depths & heights of (practical) tonal space, just as they may hover about any "note" without ever alighting upon it. . . . In FREE MUSIC harmony will consist of free combinations (when desired) of all free intervals—not merely concordant or discordant combinations of set intervals (as in current music), but free combinations of all the intervals (but in a gliding state, not needfully in an anchored state between present intervals).

THE FREE SCHOOL. (UK.) A school in England funded by the taxpayer, nonselective and free to attend, but not controlled by a local authority. The concept is based on similar schools found in Sweden and the U.S., where they are known as **charter schools**. The Academies Act of 2010 authorized the creation of free schools and allows all existing state schools to become **academy schools**. The first 24 of these schools opened in autumn 2011. They are subject to Office for Standards in Education, Children's Services and Skills (OFSTED), inspections and are expected to comply with standard performance measures.

FREIRE, PAULO (1921–1997). A Brazilian educator and influential theorist of critical pedagogy. He became familiar with poverty and hunger during the Great Depression of the 1930s. In school, he ended up four grades behind, and his social life revolved around playing pickup football with other poor children. These experiences shaped his concerns for the poor and would help to construct his educational viewpoint. He dedicated his life to improving the lives of the poor. After his family's financial prospects improved, he enrolled at the University of Recife, Brazil, where he studied law, philosophy (phenomenology), and the psychology of language. His most important book, *Pedagogy of the Oppressed*, was first published in Portuguese in 1968. His work was always about education reform, especially among the illiterate poor in Brazil, Chile, the U.S., Switzerland, and Africa. He held important posts, including a visiting professorship at Harvard in 1969, and finally as secretary of education for São Paulo. He stated that "there is no such thing as a neutral education process." Education is used to facilitate the integrations of a system that brings about conformity to it, or it becomes the "practice of freedom," the means by which persons deal critically with reality and discover how to participate in the transformation of their world.

FRENCH HARP. Colloquialism for **diatonic harmonica**.

FRÈRE JACQUES. A famous French nursery melody that is traditionally sung as a round. An approach by Janet Wills suggests starting on C and singing simultaneously with "Three Blind Mice," much like the concept of **partner songs**, which can be sung together.

FRÖBEL, FRIEDRICH W. (1782–1852). A German pedagogue and a student of Pestalozzi who laid the foundation for modern education based on the notion that children have unique needs and capabilities. As an educator in 1805 he learned about Pestalozzi's ideas and later worked with him in Switzerland. Throughout his career he dedicated himself exclusively to preschool child education. Some of his important contributions to childhood education include the following:

1. Created play materials for small children called Fröbel Gifts: geometric building blocks and pattern activity blocks.
2. Developed the concept of the **kindergarten** and coined the word *kindergarten*, which is now used in German and English, for the Play and Activity Institute, founded in 1837.
3. Introduced the concept of "free work" into pedagogy with activities that included singing, dancing, gardening, and self-directed play with Fröbel Gifts.
4. Published a songbook, *Mutter- und Kose-Lieder*, to introduce children to the adult world.
5. The first to train women as kindergarten teachers, called *Kindergärtnerinnen*.

As a result of his work, Fröbel's student Margaretha Schurz founded the first **kindergarten** in the U.S. at Watertown, Wisconsin, in 1856, and she inspired Elizabeth Peabody to found the first English-speaking kindergarten in Boston in the 1860s. (The first American kindergarten in a public school system was established in St. Louis in 1873.) Music played an important role in the growth of the kindergarten movement. The kindergarten songbook was one of the principal vehicles for the spread of the kindergarten idea.

THE FROG AND THE MOUSE. (UK.) A folk song; part of the actual repertory of English songs that was current in the Tudor period (1485–1603) and survives into the present.

FULLERTON, CHARLES A. (1861–1945). A lifelong participant in the **Music Supervisors National Conference** and president in 1912. Associated with the Iowa State Teachers College for 48 years. He gained international recognition for his work with music in rural schools. He developed the Fullerton Choir Plan, which included selected phonograph records used to teach rural school students; they learned by imitating great artists. He was author of a number of textbooks that have been widely used in public schools. One in particular was the *Together We Sing* series published by Follett Publishing Co. of Chicago. There were several books in this series, which was the first to use recordings of children singing the selected songs. He teamed with **Irving Wolfe**, Beatrice Krone, and his daughter, Ruth, in writing some of the **Follett Series**. Fullerton's *One Book Course* (1925) with accompanying records filled a particular need for rural schools, bringing music to those schools earlier than might have been possible otherwise.

FUNDAMENTAL. Root of chord; a tone generating harmonic series. A *fundamental position* is any arrangement of chordal tones in which root remains lowest in pitch; root position.

G

GACKLE, LYNNE. (U.S.) Has contributed significantly to current knowledge about the adolescent female voice change. Background information comes from **Irvin Cooper** and other pioneers of adolescent voice theory, but her research has secured and alerted music educators to this strategic area of the female voice. She indicates that girls pass through four specific stages of change in their development. She provides vocal descriptions for each stage, including approximate age and ranges. Active in **ACDA** and **MENC** as an officer, writer, and editorial consultant for women's choral series, such as the *Lynn Gackle Choral Series* for Colla Voce Music. She has conducted both national and international women's choral groups.

    Bib.: Collins, Don, *Teaching Choral Music*, 2nd ed., 1999.

GAELIC. (UK-Scot.) Scotland maintains two languages, Gaelic and Scots. Gaelic has receded since the 1700s, but it is still spoken in the Hebridean Islands and pockets of the western mainland. Both languages have given rise to musical genres that interact and overlap in melody and theme. The presence of history in songs of clan warfare and overtones of natural magic in Gaelic songs have kept them alive, despite the predicted demise of the language. Gaelic speakers perpetuate musical genres attached to the life cycle and the pastoral, clan-based society before 1700. Lullabies and laments can be related to two of three ancient divisions of **Celtic music**: those for sorrow (lament) and sleep (lullaby); that for laughter (dance music) was the third. In many Gaelic songs, the refrain precedes the verses.

GAELIC LULLABY. (UK-Scot.) Old Gaelic folk song. The melody of this song is modal in that there is no F, nor B. It is also similar to the normal, or folk, minor, in that C natural is used rather than C sharp, as found in the harmonic form. This song is found in *Voices of the Worlds* by Follett Publishing Co., 1960.

GAGNÉ, ROBERT (1916–2002). An American experimental psychologist who was a pioneer in instructional design. His work significantly impacted contemporary educational technology. Gagné developed tests and instructional design models for the military during WWII, as well as in the early 1950s and 1960s. His most important book for education, including music education, was his *Conditions of Learning*, which was published four times between 1965 and 1985. He describes a taxonomy of learning objectives and eight conditions of learning that include nine instructional events and provide specific strategies based on a hierarchy of intellectual skills.

GALIN, PIERRE (1786–1822). A French music educator. He used the principles of **movable-doh solfège**. He also taught the study of pitch and rhythm and devised a numbered music-notation system, but recommended that students learn staff notation as well. He never published an explanation of his teaching system, although *Explanation of a New Way of Teaching Music* (1818), addressed to the teacher, sets out many of his ideas. *See also* GALIN-PARIS-CHEVÉ METHOD.

GALIN-PARIS-CHEVÉ METHOD. A music-notation system that was developed by **Pierre Galin**. After Galin's death, his work was propagated by his assistant, Aimé Paris, and further developed by **Emile Chevé**, a French music teacher and theorist. The system was brought to English-speaking countries by **John Curwen**, and carried to America by **Lowell Mason**. The Hungarian music educator **Zoltan Kodály** adapted the system in his **Kodály method**.

GALLAUDET, THOMAS HOPKINS (1787–1851). An American pioneer in the education of the deaf. *See also* AMERICAN SIGN LANGUAGE.

GAMELAN. Generic Indonesian orchestra, composed of tuned gongs, chimes, drums, flute, chordophones, xylophones, and small cymbals. It is heard on its own or accompanies dance and theater performances, some lasting all night. The survival of gamelan music is due to the work of ethnomusicologists.

GANKOGUI. A bell or gong instrument played with a wooden stick. It is made out of forged iron and consists of a low-pitched bell (often referred as the parent bell) and a high-pitched bell (or the child bell, which is said to rest on the bosom of the protective parent), which are permanently bound together. The gankogui is the foundation of all traditional Ewe music in West Africa.

GARAGE BAND. A software application for Mac OS X and iOS that allows users to create music or podcasts. It was developed by Apple, Inc. It is a streamlined digital audio workstation (DAW) and music sequencer that can record and play back multiple tracks of audio.

GARAMUT. (Aus.) Any hollowed log **idiophone** of Papua, New Guinea.

GARDEN, MARY (1874–1967). (UK.) American soprano of Scottish birth. Created role of *Mélisande* in Debussy's opera at the composer's request (1902). Massenet wrote *Chérubin* (1905) for her. Joined Manhattan opera, New York, 1907–1910, with debut of American premier of *Thaïs*. Chicago opera from 1910, becoming director 1921–1922, and remained until 1931. Taught at Chicago Musical College, 1935, and was an adviser on opera scenes in Hollywood films. Returned to Scotland in 1939. She wrote *Mary Garden's Story* (NY, 1951).

GARDNER, HOWARD (1943–). An American developmental psychologist and professor of cognition and education at Harvard Graduate School of Education, senior director of **Project Zero**, and author of over 20 books, which have been translated into 30 languages. He is best known for his theory of multiple intelligences (*Frames of Mind*), for which he received the Prince of Asturias Award (Spain) in 2011 for the development of his theory. This theory states that human beings have several different ways of learning and processing information, all independent of each other. Since 1999, Gardner has identified eight intelligences: linguistic, logic-mathematical, musical, spatial, bodily/kinesthetic, interpersonal, intrapersonal, and naturalistic. Although there have been scholarly criticisms of his work, music educators have embraced his research as an important support for their profession. His background in developmental psychology bodes well for K–12 music teachers. In his chapter on musical intelligence in *Frames of Mind*, he wrote: "of all the gifts with which individuals may be endowed, none emerges earlier than musical talent." In terms of his basic premise, "a study of musical intelligence may help us understand the special flavor of music and at the same time illuminate its relation to other forms of intellect."

GASTON, EVERETT THAYER (1901–1970). A psychologist active in the 1940s–1960s who helped develop **music therapy** in the U.S., he worked at the University of Kansas as professor of music education and director of music therapy. Gaston was one of the founding fathers of music therapy, describing the value of music in therapy and the qualities of music expression that could be therapeutic. His theories and ideas were grounded in the works of Plato, Aristotle, Skinner, Pavlov, and Jung. Gaston realized that great works could be accomplished by incorporating music and psychological therapy.

His educational background included music, pre-medicine, and eventually a doctorate in educational psychology. His seminal work, *Music Therapy*, has influenced the entire field of music therapy in the U.S. Gaston was named to the **Music Educators Hall of Fame** in 1986.

G-BEQUEST (1926). (Aus.) The *Gilliés Bequest* provided funds for the purchase of instruments for use in schools, and was an important factor in promoting instrumental teaching and ensemble performances in Victorian state schools.

GEERDES, HAROLD P. (1916–2002). Author of an important book on the design and equipping of rehearsal and practice rooms, *Music Facilities: Building, Equipping, and Renovating*, published by **MENC** in 1987.

GEHRKENS, KARL WILSON (1882–1975). One of the founders of the **Music Educators National Conference**, Gehrkens believed all children should be taught to love good music and to have an intelligent approach to listening, and should have the opportunity to express themselves in music. He was a pioneer in the teaching of music through music itself, rather than by means of abstraction of symbols and intervals.

Gehrkens made outstanding contributions to music education as an author and editor. Some of his important publications include: *Music in the Grade Schools*, 1934; *Music in the Junior High School*, 1936; and *Teaching and Administration of High School Music*, 1941.

GEILWAD. ("Plowboy.") (UK.) The oldest known category of Welsh work songs is the oxen songs, mentioned in the 1100s and still used in plowing until about 1900. The singer was the plowboy (g*eilwad*), whose job was to walk backward facing the oxen and sing to keep the oxen calm. Some 21 of these songs survive.

GELL, HEATHER (1896–1988). (Aus.) Music educator and kindergarten teacher, she became an expert **Dalcroze eurhythmics** teacher, completing a teacher's certificate at the London School of Dalcroze Eurhythmics in 1923. In 1940 she began broadcasting the ABC national educational program **Music and Movement**. Gell was the first Australian to gain a diploma at the Institut **Jaques-Dalcroze** Geneve (1970), and was honored with the MBE (1977) for services to music and education.

GENERAL CERTIFICATE OF EDUCATION (GCE). (UK.) A national exit examination, which was instituted in 1951 and later modified in 1965.

Includes three levels of qualifications: 1) certificate of secondary education (CSE), designed so that top 60 percent would pass; 2) general certificate of education (GCE) "O-levels", designed so that the top 30 percent would pass; and 3) general certificate of education "A-level" exam system. In 1988 the CSE and GCE were replaced by the GCSE, giving England, Wales, and Northern Ireland a single examination system at the end of compulsory schooling.

GENERAL MUSIC. (U.S., Can.) Often referred to as vocal/general, these classes are most common in junior high or middle school and grade nine and ten of secondary schools. Certification usually includes elementary K–5. A wide variety of curricula offerings occur among schools at the discretion of the teacher, including choral singing, history, listening, and some type of performance.

GENERAL MUSIC TEACHER. A certified music teacher for public school, grades K–8. Requirements for this degree typically involve study of an applied instrument (vocal or instrumental), theoretical/musicianship studies, music literature, music history, arranging and composing, and participation in a choral organization. Methods courses are also required for Pre-K through secondary classes. A separate class in the teacher-education curriculum is a required class in special education, to fulfill the **Individuals with Disabilities Education Act** of 1990 (IDEA), and the **Education for All Handicapped Children Act** of 1975/Public Law 94-142. They are also required to fulfill at least one semester of student or practice teaching.

While general music teachers need not be outstanding performers, they should be able to demonstrate musically on an instrument or voice within at least a sophomore or junior level of ability. Basic accompanying skills on a keyboard instrument are highly recommended. General music teachers are of exceptional value to the disciplines of music and music education, for it is through them that children and young people are introduced to the value of music and the arts for the rest of their lives.

GENERAL MUSIC TODAY (1987). An official **MENC** publication for general music teachers of the **Society for General Music**, now referred to as the *Council for General Music*. It is a refereed journal of articles pertaining to any and all aspects of teaching general music.

GESTALT PSYCHOLOGY. A school of psychology founded in Germany in the 1910s. The primary focus is on unified wholes. A well-known aphorism used among educators is: "the whole is different from, or greater than, the sum of its parts." Music educators embraced some parts of this theory in a variety of ways, especially in the teaching of theory and performance. Koffka, Wertheimer, and Köhler developed Gestalt psychology based on the tendency of the mind for wholes rather than fragments. This theory emphasized insight and problem solving. **James Mursell** brought the Gestalt message to music education.

GIDDINGS, THADDEUS PHILANDER (1869–1954). One of the founders of **MENC**, National Education Association, and along with **Joseph Maddy**, a cofounder of the **National Music Camp** at Interlochen, Michigan (1928). Giddings was an advocate of a systematic approach to the teaching of music. He believed that vocal music is the foundation of music and at the heart of the school curriculum. Giddings believed that the **sol-fa method** was one of the best ways to teach the reading of music, and that this system should precede the beginning of instrumental instruction. Giddings believed that *all* teachers should know the discipline of music. During his career, he was a strong advocate for the teacher and supervisor to be a musician and teacher, and above all to be a musician.

GIFTED AND TALENTED PROGRAMS. These are designed to provide advanced educational opportunities for students with extraordinary abilities in one or more areas. There are generally two categories: 1) enrichment programs beyond regular instruction; and 2) acceleration programs, which allow students to progress more quickly through traditional curricula. Advanced placement (AP) courses are often available to gifted students.

GILLESPIE, ROBERT. Professor of music at Ohio State who is responsible for string teacher education; Ohio State has one of the largest and most extensive string pedagogy degree programs in the U.S. Dr. Gillespie obtained his doctorate from the University of Michigan, and is past national president of the **American String Teachers Association**. He is a frequent guest conductor of all-state, regional, and festival orchestras throughout the country, Canada, and Europe. His string education articles appear in all major music journals, and his major publications include: *Essential Elements for Strings*; *Strategies for Teaching Strings: Building a Successful School Orchestra Program*; *String Clinics to Go DVD Series*; and *Teaching Music through Performance*. Dr. Gillespie received the Distinguished Scholar award in the School of Music at OSU in 2002–2003, and is an editorial committee member of the MENC *Journal of Research in Music Education*.

GILMORE, PATRICK S. (1829–1892). (UK-Ire.) "Father of American Bands." A gifted cornetist, bandleader, composer, and impresario who devoted his life to the audacious dream that music had the power to change the world, that it could be used as an instrument of peace. Born in Ireland, he became a member of a local **band** in Athlone. He learned music from military bands stationed in Athlone and was taught classical music and trumpet by the great bandleader Patrick Keating (1795–1875). He immigrated to Boston in 1849 and was a successful bandleader through the 1850s, forming his own *Patrick Gilmore's Band* in 1858. In 1861, at the outset of the Civil War, Gilmore enlisted in the Union army with the 24th Massachusetts Volunteers, where he learned firsthand the transformative power of music, playing for the troops on both sides of the conflict (after the Battle of Gettysburg, Gilmore wrote the well-known song "When Johnny Comes Marching Home"). Following the war and the temporary discharge of bands from the field, the governor of Massachusetts entrusted Gilmore with the task of reorganizing military music making, and he was made bandmaster general. In 1863 Gilmore was put in charge of training bands in Massachusetts. Gilmore took over the 22nd Regimental Band in 1873 and directed it until his death in 1892.

Following the Civil War, Gilmore organized several large concerts/festivals, most of them for the purpose of celebrating peace:

- **1864** Gilmore formed a **Grand National Band** of 500 army bandsmen and a chorus of 5,000 schoolchildren.
- **1865** Gilmore was asked to organize and perform a celebration of peace in New Orleans.
- **1869** Gilmore organized Boston's **National Peace Jubilee**.
- **1872** After the Franco-Prussian War, Gilmore visited with European bandleaders and went to Europe's capital cities and royal courts, imploring presidents and kings to send their finest musicians to Boston to celebrate world peace. With their cooperation, he organized Boston's **World Peace Jubilee and International Music Festival**, with an audience of 50,000, containing 20,000 choristers and almost 2,000 instrumentalists.

GILMORE'S BAND. In 1858 **Patrick Gilmore** founded *Patrick Gilmore's Band*, which featured two woodwinds to each brass instrument (a model that would become the modern concert band). April 9, 1859, was the date of the first performance of Gilmore's Band.

GLANVILLE-HICKS, PEGGY (1912–1990). (Aus.) Critic, composer, studied composition from age 15 with such notables as Fritz Hart, Vaughn Williams, Egon Wellesz, and **Nadia Boulanger**. She and her husband eventually settled in New York in 1941. In 1948 Virgil Thomson, chief critic of the *New York Herald Tribune*, employed her as a stringer (freelance journalist).

Thomson was to remain her greatest friend and benefactor. In 1953 she was offered a commission for an opera by the Louisville Philharmonic Society, the first such offer made to a woman. In 1954 she was invited to contribute 98 articles to the fifth edition of *Grove's Dictionary of Music and Musicians*. She moved to Athens, Greece, in 1959, where she was involved in preparations for her opera *Nausicaa*. This opera received international attention. She returned to New York in 1967, where she had major surgery on a brain tumor. This illness destroyed her ability to compose. She lived in Greece until the early 1970s, when she returned to Sydney, Australia. Although familiar with the avant-garde, her music always retained a romantic and impressionist quality, while being inspired by the sounds of Asian music.

GLASGOW SCHOOL TEACHERS. Morris Blythman (Allan Glen's School) and Norman Buchan (Rutherglen Academy) started folk song clubs at the classroom level. In 1965, the founding of the **Traditional Music and Song Association of Scotland** paved the way for folk festivals that still flourish.

GLASS ARMONICA. *See* GLASS HARMONICA.

GLASS HARMONICA. (Glass armonica, or musical glasses.) Now obsolete. Consisting of drinking glasses filled with water to different heights in order to leave a larger or smaller area of glass free to vibrate. Sound is produced by rubbing the rims of glasses with a wet finger. Several composers used these for special effects.

GLEE CLUB. (UK.) In England this was a club formed in 1783 to encourage the production of new music. Choral societies in America in the 19th century were styled after the English glee clubs. These were originally all male, but some grew into large choruses that included women and featured mostly art music.

GLEE SINGING. (UK.) A form of amateur music making in three or more unaccompanied parts, derived from the 18th-century English traditional songs.

GLENN, MABELLE (1881–1969). MENC president, 1929–1930, president of the National School Vocal Association in 1936, and acting president of the Anglo-American conference in Lausanne, Switzerland, 1929. During her MENC presidency, she established a national executive secretary position and a constitution revision that allowed any music teacher to become a member of the organization. Her greatest successes came when she served as director of music for the Kansas City Public Schools. Her music programs were models for the country. She believed that only the best of material and literature has a place in the classroom. Her most significant contribution in music curriculum was in the field of appreciation.

Her publications include the *Psychology of School Music Teaching* (with James L. Mursell), 1931; *Music Appreciation for Every Child*, 1935; and the *Our Singing World* series (with Lilla Belle Pitts and Lorrain Watters), 1950.

GLOTTIS. Anatomically, the opening between the vocal folds in vocal production.

Bib.: Collins, Don, *Teaching Choral Music*, 2nd ed., 1999.

GLOVER, SARAH ANNE (1785–1867). Invented the **Norwich Sol-fa** singing system of music teaching in the 1830s in Norwich, England, using traditional **solfège** syllables based on movable doh and using a "tone ladder" to teach tonal relationships, followed by the introduction of syllable notation. No staff was used. She developed her learning system in the English primary schools to aid teachers with **a cappella** singing. Her instructional book *Scheme for Rendering Psalmody Congregational* met with great success. Her system was later refined and developed by John Curwen and others over the years.

GOETZE, MARY. (U.S.) Professor emerita of Indiana University and the Jacob School of Music, Mary has been one of the driving forces of the children's choir movement in the U.S. for decades. Her composition and arrangements have reached multitudes of children's choirs primarily through the *Mary Goetze Choral Series*, Boosey & Hawkes. Her research and presentations on children's voices have influenced music teachers throughout the world. She served as coordinating author for two series of books published by Macmillan/McGraw-Hill: *Spotlight on Music* (2005) and *Share the Music* (1995). In 1995, she founded the International Vocal Ensemble, an ensemble that re-creates vocal music from around the globe.

During her tenure at Indiana University, Mary was instrumental in founding the Music in General Music Studies program. She also founded two choral programs, the International Vocal Ensemble and the Indiana University Children's Choir.

Throughout her long and distinguished career, she has been the recipient of numerous awards. Some of these are: Distinguished Alumna, Oberlin Conservatory and University of Colorado; Distinguished Teaching Award from

Indiana University; and Outstanding Educator of the Year by the **Organization of American Kodály Educators**.

GOLDMAN, EDWIN FRANKO (1878–1956). One of America's prominent band composers of the early 20th century, he composed over 150 works, mostly marches. Goldman was born in Louisville, Kentucky, but the family eventually moved to New York City, where he attended the National Conservatory of Music. He became a professional trumpet player, performing with the Metropolitan Opera House orchestra. In 1911 Goldman founded the New York Military Band, later known as the *Goldman Band* (1918), and in 1929 he founded the American Bandmasters Association. Because of his contribution to the radio industry, he was awarded a star on the Hollywood Walk of Fame. The Goldman Band shell in Allentown, Pennsylvania, is named in his honor, and he was guest conductor there in 1927.

GOLDMAN, RICHARD (1910–1980). Son of **Edwin Franko Goldman**, he was a conductor, educator, author, music critic, and composer. He was a graduate of Columbia University (NY) and studied composition in Paris with **Nadia Boulanger**. He was associate conductor, 1937–1956, and then succeeded his father as conductor of the Goldman Band of New York City. Among his achievements, he taught at the Juilliard School, 1947–1960; was visiting professor at Princeton, 1952–1956; was director of the Peabody Conservatory of Music in Baltimore, 1968–1977; and served as president of the Peabody Institute, 1969–1977. His contributions to the *Musical Quarterly* as New York critic ensured early acquaintance with Wallingford Riegger (with whom he studied), Henry Cowell, and Elliott Carter. Among his compositions are the *Sonata for Violin and Piano* (1964), and a *Duo for Tubas or Bassoons* (1950).

GOODLAD, JOHN I. (1920–). (Can.) Educational researcher who has published influential models for renewing schools and teacher education. He has designed and promoted several educational reform programs, and has conducted major studies of educational change. His best-known book, *A Place Called School* (1984), had a profound effect on all educational thought. Music educators were influenced by his thinking on curriculum. Goodlad wrote: "Children should be introduced to the structure of music through a carefully planned sequential curriculum as rigorous and well-organized as the best math curriculum." His book *School, Curriculum, and the Individual* also provided approaches to organizing general music curriculum around structural and expressive concepts. Goodlad and **Bennett Reimer** have expressed similar philosophies regarding the importance of a qualified music teacher for music classes. Reimer writes: "The subject matter chosen for study must be fundamental to the discipline *as the discipline is conceived by the expert in the discipline.*" And John Goodlad stated: "The content used in the organizing center must be authentic and important to the field, as *determined by leading scholars in it.*"

Goodlad, with Robert Anderson, was responsible for introducing the concept of the nongraded school in the book *The Non-Graded Elementary School* in 1963. A variety of concepts and approaches have been developed from Goodlad's writing on the nongraded school (see, e.g., Mursell's *cyclical* approach and Bruner's *spiral* approach and *structural curriculum*); yet, it has not continued to gain acceptance according to its original intent.

Goodlad is currently professor emeritus of education and codirector of the Center for Educational Renewal at the University of Washington.

GO PROJECT. A **MENC G**oals and **O**bjectives Project was implemented in 1969 in response to recommendations made at the **Tanglewood Symposium**. The GO Project centered around cultural diversity, ethnic and world music, changing demographics in American society, and music education in urban settings. MENC adopted the goals and objectives of the GO Project in 1970. The project had great influence on music education and played a role in the development of the **National Standards for Music Education** adopted by MENC in 1994.

GORDON, EDWIN ELIAS (1927–). A well-known researcher in the field of music education, Gordon has made significant contributions to the study of music aptitudes, audition, music learning theory, and musical development in infants and very young children. He has authored six musical aptitude tests and several publications, including *Learning Sequences in Music: Skills and Contents Patterns* (1989), *A Music Learning Theory for Newborn and Young Children* (1990), and *Guiding Your Child's Musical Development* (1991). The complete collection of Gordon's professional materials is housed at the University of South Carolina Music Library in the Edwin E. Gordon Archive. *See also* SKILL LEARNING SEQUENCE.

GOSPEL MUSIC. While *gospel music* can be an extremely broad term, most ethnomusicologists pursue the roots to Europe and Africa from church music to rural folk music traditions. Gospel music of the African American experience can be traced to the early 17th century. Its oral tradition uses a great deal of repetition, which promoted group participation. Hymns and sacred songs were *lined* and repeated in a **call-and-response** fashion, and the Negro spiritual and work songs emerged. When slaves attended their masters' worship services, they were influenced by traditional hymns, and reading from the apostle Paul's writings about being good servants and loving, obeying, and trusting one's master.

Gospel music generally is characterized by dominant vocals (often with strong use of harmony) and reference to religious lyrics, particularly Christian. Several groups use choirs, piano or Hammond organ, drums, bass guitar, and increasingly, electric guitar. The music is tuneful and easy to grasp, has rudimentary harmonies, uses the chorus, and often has motor rhythms.

The southern gospel music that is called *quartet music*, due to the original all-male, tenor-lead-baritone-bass quartet makeup, is probably the most popular style of gospel music, due to the proliferation of TV musical programs. The music has strong harmonies, often with extremely wide ranges (extremely low bass and falsetto tenor); examples include the Statesman Quartet (ca. 1940–1950) to the Cathedrals and the current signature Sound Quartet.

Thomas Andrew Dorsey (1889–1993) was known as "the father of black gospel music," which was a formulation of Christian praise with the rhythm of jazz and the blues. Dorsey began recording gospel music alongside blues in the mid-1920s. Dorsey's works have proliferated beyond performance into the hymnals of virtually all American churches and of English-speaking churches worldwide. Two of Dorsey's best-known compositions are *Take My Hand, Precious Lord* and *Peace in the Valley*.

Dorsey's papers are preserved at Fisk University in Nashville, Tennessee, along with those of W. C. Handy, George Gershwin, and the **Fisk Jubilee Singers**.

GRADE SCHOOL ORCHESTRAS. In Los Angeles, California (1904), grade school orchestras were formed to provide good players for the high school organizations. Some influence on the grade school orchestra movement has been attributed to the **Maidstone movement** in England around 1908, which presented instrumental instruction to children.

GRAINGER, PERCY (GEORGE PERCY ALDRIDGE) (1882–1961). (Aus./U.S.) Pianist, composer, and ethnologist who was born in Melbourne and died in New York. Grainger's education began in a homeschool setting with his mother from 1882 to 1895. He appeared in Melbourne as a concert pianist, and with benefit support, studied in Germany from 1859 to 1901 at the Hoch Conservatory in Frankfurt. There he became a member of the Frankfurt Group, consisting of Cyril Scott, Balfour Gardiner, and Roger Quilter, all English students. He also came in contact with Rudyard Kipling and Walt Whitman, who inspired many of his settings of their works.

In 1901 Grainger moved to London, where he became a concert pianist (1901–1914) and sometime accompanist for vocal recitalists. He also took lengthy tours of Australia (1903–1904 and 1908–1909). His composing was not launched until his reputation as a pianist was secure; Stanford, Grieg, Delius, and critic R. Legge promoted his work.

Grainger left for the U.S. at the outbreak of WWI in 1914; he settled in New York and his reputation there as pianist and composer surpassed his London status. He signed lucrative contracts for piano rolls and gramophone recordings, and settled on G. Shirmer as publisher of his works. Later, he enlisted in the U.S. Army (1917), where he played oboe and soprano sax in an army band and was later appointed a band instructor. In 1918 he became an American citizen, and in that same year completed his most popular composition, *Country Gardens*, a setting for piano of a Morris dance tune collected by Cecil J. Sharp.

During the 1920s he developed the principles of "elastic scoring," whereby music was written for "tone strands" rather than for inflexible combinations of instruments. It was the conductor's role to assign available instruments so as to ensure an appropriate overall balance of sound.

In the 1930s Grainger's educational and promotional work overshadowed his performing and compositions. He promoted the work of **Arnold Dolmetsch** and later became head of the Music Department at New York University, where his lecture course on "The Manifold Nature of Music" became the basis of the twelve radio lectures on "Music: A Commonsense View of all Types," which was presented over the ABC in 1934–1935 while he was on tour in Australia. Grainger's *Lincolnshire Posy* (1937) is a setting of six English folk songs and remains today a cornerstone of American band repertoire. He also taught each summer at the **National Music Camp**, Interlochen until 1944. He also worked with physicist Burnett Cross during 1945–1960 on various **free music** machines, designed to introduce Hogarth's curve of beauty into music with their gliding intervals and freedoms of rhythm and harmony.

Grainger was never technically an Australian. During his childhood he was a citizen of the self-governing British colony of Victoria, and he remained British until he took American citizenship in 1918. His influence upon Australian music and culture has been more conceptual than stylistic. He influenced the next generation of British composers, especially Benjamin Britten. Grainger's innovations in scoring and balancing of instrumental timbres have a vibrant legacy in the music of subsequent generations of American composers of band music.

Lit.: Gilles, M., and D. Pear, eds., *The All-Round Man*: *Selected Letters of Percy Grainger*, 1994; Josephson, D., "Grainger, (George) Percy (Aldridge)" in the *New Grove Dictionary of American Music*, ed. H. Wiley Hitchcock and Stanley Sadie, 1986; Mellers, W., *Percy Grainger*, 1992.

GRAMMAR SCHOOLS. (UK.) A secondary school corresponding to a U.S. high school, and one of two tracks leading to a university. Generally considered high-level academic preparation.

GRAND NATIONAL BAND (1864). Designed to celebrate a gubernatorial inauguration, **Patrick Gilmore** formed a "grand national band" of 500 army bandsmen and a chorus of 5,000 schoolchildren. This encouraged him to continue organizing massed festival performances, as in the **National Peace Jubilee**.

GRATTON, FRANCIS "FRANK" LYMER (1871–1946). (Aus.) Music educator, musician, conductor. Born in Halifax, England, and died in Seacliff, South Australia (SA). He was a product of the SA state school system in which he trained and taught, apart from his six-year sojourn as first assistant at the Charles Street State School in Launceston, Tasmania. He demonstrated musical aptitude in the prevailing **tonic sol-fa** pedagogy, eventually becoming an associate of The Tonic Sol-fa College, London (1906). In 1914 he was appointed inspector of music at the Adelaide Training College and was supervisor of music in the SA Education Department, 1920–1936. He was also the acclaimed conductor of the massed children's **Thousand Voice Choir** for concerts 1920–1937.

GREAT MIGRATION OF CANADA (1815–1850). This was largely due to the arrival of the Irish, British, and Scottish immigrants that considerably broadened the Canadian musical culture through the opening of music stores, selling pianos, and publishing engraved sheet music.

THE GREAT SOCIETY (1965). Under the influence of President Lyndon Johnson's *Great Society* program, Congress passed the **Elementary and Secondary Education Act** (ESEA), which provided renewed support for the arts through cultural enrichment programs. Other events strengthening the music-education process were the Contemporary Music Project, the **Yale Seminar**, **MMCP**, and the **Tanglewood Symposium** (1967).

GREEK EDUCATION, MUSIC IN (6th century BCE). In early Greek culture, music played a major role in education and was taught as part of the core subjects—**quadrivium**. It was as essential as reading, writing, and arithmetic, and Greek boys began learning music as early as six years old. The Greek musical modes were taught in Greek music theory, and eventually, the Greek musical modes were the foundation for classical music as well as Western religious music. Students used singing to assist in memorizing odes such as the *Iliad* and the *Odyssey*. Intrigued with the harmony of music, one exceptional student, **Pythagoras**, designed a mathematical theory behind musical tones in the 6th century BCE that is still used in modern times. Some of our fundamental musical terms—*tone*, *rhythm*, *lyrics*, *harmony*, *orchestra*—are of Greek origin. The word *music* has its origin in Greek religion, and music is the only art form named after a Greek god, **Apollo**.

It is highly probable that the Greek initiates gained their knowledge of the philosophic and therapeutic aspects of music from the Egyptians, who, in turn, considered Hermes the founder of the art. According to one legend, this god constructed the first lyre by stretching strings across the concavity of a turtle shell. Both Isis and Osiris were patrons of **music** and poetry. Plato, in describing the antiquity of these arts among the Egyptians, declared that songs and poetry had existed in Egypt for at least 10,000 years, and that these were of such an exalted and inspiring nature that only gods or godlike men could have composed them.

Lessons in Greek music theory concentrated solely on numbers and ratios and the role music played in the big cosmic picture. The ancient Greeks laid the foundation of scholarship in music, its terminology and notation, its theory and philosophy. Broad currents of tradition flowed from their music and music theory into Rome, Byzantium, and the Arabian Empire, and farther to the Far East.

GREEN DRAGON BAND. This originally named Massachusetts Band was formed in 1783; it was known as the Green Dragon Band beginning in about 1812, changing its name around 1820 to the **Boston Brigade Band**. The name apparently came from the Green Dragon Tavern. In 1859 it became **Gilmore's Band**, the first great American band and considered one of the finest that has ever played.

GREEN, ELIZABETH A. H. (1906–1995). She is recognized as one of the most important and highly esteemed teachers of stringed instruments and conducting in America. Her books are used in classrooms of major universities, and her associations with some of the greatest violinists and conductors in the world put her in high demand as a lecturer. She studied violin from the age of five, and later the viola. Her education included Wheaton, Northwestern University, and Eastern Michigan University. Two of her greatest challenges were the Waterloo, Iowa, public schools and the Ann Arbor public schools. In Waterloo, she organized the Waterloo Symphony, and in Ann Arbor, she transformed the Ann Arbor High School Orchestra into a 60-piece symphony.

Two of her most important books are *The Teaching of Stringed Instruments in Classes* and *The Modern Conductor* (7th ed.).

GRENADIER GUARDS. (UK.) A modern, forward-thinking infantry regiment, despite being one of the oldest regiments in the British Army and the most senior of the five Regiments of Foot Guards. Originally known as the First Regiment of Foot Guards for the exiled King Charles II at Bruges in 1656. The first formed band of the regiment became the *Grenadier Guards* after the Battle of Waterloo in 1815. After the death of King Charles, the musicians wore a dark blue cloth halfway around a sleeve of their scarlet tunic as a sign of mourning. The band never uses bugles on parade, nor do the drummers flourish their sticks.

***THE GRIEG-DUNCAN FOLK SONG COLLECTION* (1981–2003).** (UK/Scot.) The most extensive collection of Anglophone (native speaker of English) songs, with the entire collection currently appearing in eight volumes.

***GROWING UP COMPLETE: THE IMPERATIVE FOR MUSIC EDUCATION* (1991).** A published report from the **MENC** National Commission on Music Education that was a key element in the effort to have the arts included in the GOALS 2000 legislation. This report was distributed to Congress, the White House, parent groups, arts and education organizations, major corporations, advocacy groups, and individuals concerned about the status of the arts in education. The national standards were a product of the Congressional act GOALS 2000.

GUIDELINES FOR EFFECTIVE MUSIC EDUCATION. (Aus.) A major focus of the National Review of School Music Education by the Australian government in 2005. The guidelines are based on two broad assumptions:

1. Every Australian child is capable of learning music.
2. Every Australian school is capable of supporting effective learning in music.

The guidelines were developed through a review of international and national research and current effective practice. They were validated through consultation with **ASME** and individual music teachers. It has been found that most parents believe that music should be taught as a separate subject rather than integrated with other subjects.

GUIDO OF AREZZO (ca. 990–1050). A music theorist, regarded as the inventor of modern notation (staff notation) that replaced neumatic notation. His early career was spent in a Benedictine monastery. He saw that some of the singers had difficulty remembering the Gregorian chants and came up with a method of helping them to learn the chants more easily. He left the monastery in 1025 and was invited by Bishop Tedald of Arezzo to train and conduct a group of cathedral singers. While at Arezzo, he developed new techniques for teaching, such as staff notation and the use of the "ut-re-mi-fa-so-la" (do-re-mi-fa-so-la) mnemonic solmization. He is credited with the invention of the **Guidonian hand**, and his text *Micrologus* was the second most widely distributed treatise on music in the Middle Ages, after the writings of **Boethius**.

GUIDON. A small flag or streamer carried for marking or signaling. *See also* DRAGOON GUARDS.

GUIDONIAN HAND. Named after **Guido of Arezzo** (ca. 900–1050), inventor of syllabic solmization. Didactic method of teaching by relating hexachordal degrees to places on the palm of the left hand. The names of the major hexachord were ut, re, mi, fa, sol, la, from syllables in the opening lines of the "Hymn of St. Johns" ("Jesus Shall Reign").

In the Middle Ages, the choir director indicated the points on the different joints of each finger to dictate the required notes to the singers.

GUILDHALL. (UK-London.) The hall built or used by guilds or corporations for their assemblies; town hall.

GUILDHALL SCHOOL OF MUSIC. A music academy established in 1880 by the Corporation of the City of London in a warehouse at Aldermanbury. Moved in 1887 to Blackfriar when student population grew from 62 to 2,700. Moved to present center in Barbican Arts Center and changed name to include *Drama* in 1935.

GUITARS IN THE CLASSROOM. In general music classes, the guitar is an excellent instrument to learn experientially about notation, basic keys, and enough playing technique (usually strumming to accompany singing) to continue independent instruction. It is not necessary for each student to have a guitar; they can work in terms of two to an instrument. Basic guitars are inexpensive and can be managed within the classroom budget. There are a number of guitar method books that are easy to use and accessible to students outside the classroom. Generally, guitar instruction can begin as early as fifth grade general music class.

GYPSY FIDDLERS. (UK-Wales.) The *fiddle* in Wales never attained the status of the harp, but these two instruments were most often heard together. Throughout the 1800s fiddlers were indispensable at fairs, weddings, wakes, feasts, and dances. During the 1800s and early 1900s, the Welsh fiddling tradition became increasingly confined to Gypsy players who played on street corners.

H

HABITANTS AND METIS. (Can.) *Habitant* is a Canadian of French speech and culture, especially one residing in Quebec, and *Metis* in Canada is the offspring of an American Indian and a white person, especially one of French ancestry. In the 18th century this group transmitted traditional songs and dances orally from generation to generation and from village to village, and they felt no need to transcribe or publish them.

HAIKU. A major form of Japanese verse written in 17 syllables divided into three lines of five, seven, and five syllables, employing the subject of nature or one of the seasons. Often used in music-education classes with Orff instruments for creative activities.

HALL OF FAME. *See* MUSIC EDUCATORS HALL OF FAME.

HANDBELL CHOIRS. (Also handbell ensemble or team.) A group that rings recognizable music with melodies and harmony, as opposed to the mathematical permutation used in *change* ringing. The bells used generally include all notes of the chromatic scale within the range of the bell set. Bells are typically arranged chromatically on foam-covered tables; these tables protect the bronze surface of the bell. Each musician is responsible for particular notes, sounding his or her assigned bells whenever that note appears in score. Handbells and chimes are currently popular in churches and schools.

HANDBELLS. Designed to be rung by hand; a ringer grasps the bell by its slightly flexible handle—traditionally made of leather—and moves the wrist to make the hinged clapper inside the bell strike. Handbells are generally heard in tuned sets. They were first brought to the U.S. from England by Margaret Shurcliff in 1902. Bells used in America are almost always English handbells, a reference to a specific type. American handbells are either made by Malmark Bellcraftsman or by Schulmerich Carillons, both based in Pennsylvania. Handbells (and handchimes) are deliberately transposed and sound one octave higher than their displayed **pitch**. Piano middle C4 is the same as handbell C5.

HANDBOOK OF RESEARCH ON MUSIC TEACHING AND LEARN-ING **(1992).** Edited by **Richard Colwell**. This handbook contains some 55 chapters written by more than 70 scholars and researchers. *The New Handbook on Music Teaching and Learning* (2002), edited by Richard Colwell and Carol Richardson, contains 61 chapters written by 101 scholars and researchers. These two books "provide information on topics ranging from policy to partnerships by scholars in many fields who are in a position to influence and enrich music pedagogy, its research and its place in the larger cultural/educational scene."

HANDEL AND HAYDN SOCIETY. Organized in 1815 by Gottlieb Graupner (1767–1836), who had settled in Boston in 1797 to become an entrepreneur of concerts and musical organizations. Its aims were to cultivate and improve a correct taste in the performance of sacred music, and also to introduce into more general practice the work of Handel, Haydn, and other eminent composers.

HAND SIGNS. The use of specific motions by the dominant hand, with or without the use of **tonic sol-fa**, as an aid to the development of tonal memory in learning to sing from sight. Differing hand signs represent each pitch syllable from do[h] to do[h]. Originally developed by **John Curwen** in England in 1870, these signs were somewhat changed and adapted by **Zoltan Kodály** for use in the Hungarian schools. Combined with sol-fa, this system of hand signs appears to assist in the development of tonal memory for young children.
    Bib.: Apel, Willi, *Harvard Dictionary of Music*, 2nd ed., 1973; Choksy, Lois, *The Kodaly Concept*, 1981; Choksy, Lois, Robert M. Abramson, Avon E. Gillespie, and David Woods, *Teaching Music in the Twentieth Century*, 1986.
    Lit.: Anderson, William, and Joy E. Lawrence, *Integrating Music into the Classroom*, 1985.

HANSON, HOWARD H. (1896–1981). An American composer of large works such as the *Second ("Romantic") Symphony*, the choral cantata *The Lament for Beowulf* (1925), and the opera *Merry Mount* (1933). Hanson was more lastingly remembered as a teacher and as director of the Eastman School of Music, where from 1925 he produced annual festivals of American music. One of his well-known works for high school and college choral groups is *The Song of Democracy*, often used in patriotic concerts or in baccalaureate or commencement services.

HARDING, ALBERT AUSTIN (1880–1958). Founder of the Department of Bands at the University of Illinois (1905) for the purpose of keeping his bands under the Music Department with their budgetary and policy authority. Harding was a key figure in the marching band movement, and the University of Illinois Marching Band was imitated throughout the country. It was the most influential force in the development of high school marching bands.

HARGREAVES, DAVID. (UK.) Hargreaves made a significant contribution to the field of music education through his book *Musical Development and Learning: The International Perspective* (2001), coauthored with A. North.

HARMONICA. *See* DIATONIC HARMONICA.

HARMONIC SOCIETY. (Can.) Among the earliest musical societies of Canada was Quebec's Harmonic Society of 1820. Frédérick Glackemeyer became the first president and director of this society. He was an immigrant from Germany who offered music instruction as a musician and bandmaster. His activities influenced and enriched musical life in Quebec.

HARMONY. The simultaneous sounding of notes, giving what is known as vertical music, as opposed to horizontal music, as found in counterpoint (line against line).

HARP AND EISTEDDFOD. (UK.) A Welsh competitive festival of poetry and singing.

HARTSHORN, WILLIAM C. (1907–1974). A supervisor of music for the Los Angeles, California, schools. He became board chairman of the *Music Educators Journal* (**MENC**) when he succeeded **Wiley Housewright** during his 1968–1970 MENC presidency. During the 1960s MENC published an increasing number of publications, including Hartshorn's *Music for the Academically Talented*, as part of the **NEA** (National Education Association) project on gifted students.

HARVARD GLEE CLUB. In the early part of the 20th century, the a cappella choir came to prominence. The Harvard Glee Club, directed by Archibald Davison, took an all-male *social society* and turned it into a choral ensemble that performed well-prepared selections of art music.

HAWAII MUSIC CURRICULUM PROGRAM. (U.S.) Began in 1968 under the sponsorship of the Hawaii Curriculum Center in Honolulu. It was established to "create a logical, continuous educational program ensuring the competent guidance of the music education of all children in the state's public schools and to test and assemble the materials needed by schools to realize this program." It was designed to implement **comprehensive musicianship** concepts and practices in the public school music program. The book *Comprehensive Musicianship through Classroom Music* (1974) by William Thomson resulted from the Hawaii Music Curriculum Program.

HAYDEN, PHILIP C. (1854–1925). (Can.) Born in Ontario, Canada, he studied at New York University and Oberlin College. He became supervisor of music in Quincy, Illinois, and later in Keokuk, Iowa. His work as a public school music teacher covered a period of 35 years. Some of his major contributions to music education included the founding of the magazine *School Music*, at first called *School Music Monthly*, in 1900. The literature of the school music profession may be said to have begun with Hayden's magazine; Hayden's role in the creation of the **Music Supervisors National Conference** came from his pioneering spirit and his willingness to try things that had never been done. Hayden was the one who issued the call that led to the organization of the future *Music Educators National Conference* in Keokuk, Iowa, in 1907. As an experiment in his teaching he also developed the Hayden Staff Liner, which continues today in a somewhat altered form. Philip Hayden was greatly admired by many professionals throughout the U.S. because of his contribution to the cause of public school music.

HEAD VOICE. The vocal upper register of vocal production, which gives the illusion of being generated from the top of the head. Some singers experience a sensation of vibration toward the front portion of the head.

HEBRIDEAN LABOR SONGS. (From the Hebrides Islands.) (UK.) These songs accompanied milking, churning, moving infants up and down, rowing, and other activities integral to pastoral society. Also, there are songs for *waulking* (shrinking) the tweed (rough woolen fabric). Waulking songs involve a **call-and-response** pattern and draw their themes and melodies from diverse sources.

HELLER, GEORGE NORMAN (1941–2004). Music educator, performing musician, and music historian. Graduated from the University of Michigan in 1963 and served in the army bands at Fort Sheridan, Illinois, and in Heidelberg, Germany, from 1967 to 1969. He was a tuba soloist, assistant conductor, and staff arranger. He returned to Michigan to teach instrumental and general music and in 1973 earned a doctorate in music education, with minors in music history and music theory. Dr. Heller joined the University of Kansas faculty in 1973 as assistant professor in music education. He became a full professor in 1985, and retired from KU in May 2002. Dr. Heller had been a visiting professor at a number of American universities. He published more than 100 articles, book chapters, and books during his career. In 1994 the History Special Research Interest Group of **MENC** awarded him its first Distinguished Service and Scholarship Award. He was also an honorary member of the International Biographical Centre and Biography Council, Cambridge, England. Dr. Heller performed as a pianist, vocalist, and tuba player in schools and churches, as well as in the military. In February 2003, the Kansas Music Educators Association inducted Dr. Heller into its Hall of Fame.

HELLER, JACK J. Professor of music at the University of South Florida and music director of the Tampa Bay Symphony and Spanish Lyric Theater of Tampa. He has held postdoctoral fellowships at Ohio State and Yale Universities. Taught in the public schools of Ohio and Iowa and was concertmaster of the Toledo Orchestra for several years. He has served on the editorial committees of the *Council for Research in Music Education Bulletin*, the *Journal of Research in Music Education*, *Research Perspectives in Music Education*, and *Psychomusicology*.

HELPMANN, SIR ROBERT (1909–1986). (Aus.) Dancer, choreographer, actor, and director; co-artistic director of the Australian Ballet 1965–1974 and sole artistic director 1975–1976.

HEXACHORD. A six-tone scale; a mnemonic device first described by **Guido of Arezzo**. Each chord has six adjacent pitches (named *ut, re, mi, fa, sol*, and *la*) that are a whole tone apart, except for the middle two pitches that are separated by a semitone (mi-fa).

HINDSLEY, MARK (1906–1999). Longtime director of University of Illinois bands and marching band. Hindsley graduated from Indiana University as a member of Phi Beta Kappa and a Rhodes nominee. He had a 45-year career at Illinois as a full-time director of concerts and marching bands. He was known for innovative and intricate formations on the football field. He was inducted into the National Hall of Fame for Distinguished Band Conductors. His awards include being named a fellow in the International Institute of Arts and Letters, the highest award of the American School Band Directors Association and the **NBA**, a Meritorious Service Award from Illinois MEA, a certificate of Merit from the UI Foundation, and the Sudler Medal of the Order of Merit from the **John Philip Sousa** Foundation. He developed new wind instrument intonations that led to changes in the manufacturing of several instruments in the U.S., France, and England.

HITCHCOCK, HUGH WILEY (1923–2007). American musicologist who was a founding director (1971–1993) of the Institute for Studies in American Music at Brooklyn College for the City University of New York. He was the coeditor (with Stanley Sadie) of the four-volume *New Grove Dictionary* of *American Music* (1986), which was considered a premier reference work because of its inclusiveness. Another notable work and vital college text was *Music in the United States: A Historical Introduction* (1969, rev. 2000).

HOFFER, CHARLES R. (1929–). A highly regarded music educator having served in the public schools, Indiana University–Bloomington, and the University of Florida as head of music education from 1984 to the present. His professional activities include: president of Indiana MEA; president of the North Central Division of **MENC,** as well as the national MENC president. He served on the National Standards in Music (MENC) and the Sunshine State Standards for Florida. Dr. Hoffer is author of more than 30 books including *Teaching Music in the Secondary School* (five editions) used by many music-education majors throughout the U.S. He was elected to the **Music Educators Hall of Fame** in 2006.

HOFFMAN, MARY E. (1927–1997). A professor of music education at the University of Illinois, author of numerous music-education publications, and president of **MENC** from 1980 to 1982. Elected to the **Music Educators Hall of Fame** in 1998. Hoffman was well known for her contributions to junior high and middle school general music and, later in her career, for her work with lifelong learning for older adults. She is remembered for her cooperative efforts in joining the Texas Music Educators with MENC in a joint conference in San Antonio (1982) as well as with the new organization, the Texas Music Educators Conference.

HOLISTIC EDUCATION. In education, this is usually associated with the idea that schools should be concerned with the students' behavior, health, emotional development, and social development, as well as their academic performance.

THE HOLLY AND THE IVY. A traditional English carol that reflects great joy rather than a quiet manger carol. The use of holly and ivy is a custom from pre-Christian times. It is sung both at Christmas and Lent. According to legend, the crown of thorns used in the crucifixion was made of holly, and the red berries symbolize the droplets of blood.

HOLT, HOSEA (1836–1898). Developed a new method of teaching music reading through the school music readers. He taught singing schools at night, and during the Civil War he served as a bandsman. He taught music at Wheaton Seminary and the Bridgewater Normal School in Boston. He later became a music supervisor in the Boston Schools from 1869 until 1898. He worked out a new plan of music instruction for all elementary grades, and it became known as the *Holt Method.*

HONK FEST. Protest bands that began as SLSAP (Second Line Social Aid and Pleasure Society Brass Band) formed in 2003 in Boston for an antiwar protest. Band members had so much fun that it continued as a community band after that. The Honk Festival began as a way for SLSAP to reach out and fraternize with similar bands around the country.

HOOD, MARGARET VIVIAN (1903–1992). A valiant leader and teacher for the improvement and recognition of music education; Hood was an impressive and respected voice for all music educators. She was a strong advocate for improved music education in the rural schools. A performing musician as a pianist and conductor of bands, and with an international reputation as a leader in training music teachers, Hood spoke and wrote with authority, and earned respect from colleagues. She was a driving force in uniting **MTNA**, **NASM**, and **MENC** for standard criteria for music accreditation in higher learning. For 30 years Hood was professor of music education and chairman of the Music Education Department at the University of Michigan in Ann Arbor. Her major publications include *Singing Days* (with Gildersleeve), *Learning Music through Rhythm* (with Schultz), *Teaching Rhythm and Using Classroom Instruments in School*, and a *Standard Children's Dictionary*.

HOPE, SAMUEL. Executive director of the **National Association of Schools of Music**; assisted the **Music Teachers National Association** in developing its teacher certification program. He holds degrees in music composition and is well known as a writer on arts and arts education policy.

HORNE, MARILYN (BERNICE) (1934–). Born in Bradford, Pennsylvania, she studied voice with William Vennard at the University of Southern California, attended Lotte Lehman's master classes, and made her opera debut at the Gelsenkirchen Opera in Europe, where she remained on their roster until 1960. She made her U.S. debut with the San Francisco Opera in 1960, London's Covent Garden in 1965, appeared at Milan's La Scala in 1969, and made her debut at the Met in 1970. She subsequently became one of its principal singers. Horne was acclaimed for her brilliant portrayal of roles by Handel, Rossini, and Meyerbeer, including her dazzling vocal ability with runs and arpeggios. She won equal praise as an outstanding concert artist.

HOUSEWRIGHT, WILEY L. (1913–2003). Dr. Housewright was a professor of music at Florida State University beginning in 1947. Among his accomplishments during his tenure were initiating a graduate program, and founding and conducting the University Singers, which he developed into one of the nation's top choral organizations. He was appointed the third dean of the FSU School of Music in 1966 and served until his retirement in 1980. Dr. Housewright was president of **MENC** from 1968 to 1970.

After retirement he focused his research on early Florida music. His Pulitzer Prize–nominated book, *A History of Music and Dance in Florida 1565–1865*, was published by the University of Alabama Press in 1991. His *Anthology of Early Music in Florida* was published in 1999 by the University of Florida Press. During his career, Dr. Housewright traveled for many professional conferences and appointments. The Housewright Archives contain manuscripts and drafts of Dr. Housewright's books about early Florida music and include notes on Native Americans, African Americans, and the Spanish and other settlers of European descent; as well as church music, military music, folk music, and the role music played in early social life.

The collection covers his many professional interests, such as **music education**, and correspondence and speeches written for professional organization meetings such as MENC, the Sonneck Society, and the **International Society for Music Education** (ISME). *See also* HOUSEWRIGHT SYMPOSIUM.

HOUSEWRIGHT SYMPOSIUM: VISION 2020 (2000). Presented at Florida State University, where **Wiley Housewright** had been dean of the School of Music for many years. The *Housewright Declaration* is the statement of belief that summarized the symposium. It was intended to create a vision for music education that would guide the profession for the next 20 years. It was the first such symposium sponsored by **MENC** since the **Tanglewood Symposium** of 1967.

HOWARD, FRANCIS "FRANK" EDWARD (ca. 1857–1945). He is best known for his book *The Child's Voice in Singing* (1858). His methods were in keeping with some of the new psychological ideas being introduced at the close of the century. He taught children to sing new music in a musical manner and exposed them to as much beautiful music as possible.

HULLAH, JOHN (1812–1884). (UK.) Composer and teacher who studied G. L. Wilhelm's method of teaching singing in classes, which he adopted with great success in England. Hullah's system eventually failed because of his attempt to use a pedantic, overly scientific reliance on the **fixed-doh** system for teaching children. Secondly, his songs were created for use in British schools and were designed to illustrate theoretical aspects of music. Head inspector James Keenan reported that these songs "do not pretend to any national character . . . belong to no country," even though Australia, Canada, and Ireland had adopted Hullah's system. His system was considered deeply flawed and was eventually replaced by **John Curwen**'s **tonic sol-fa** approach.

HUMBERT, STEPHEN (1766–1849). (Can., U.S.-born.) A general merchant involved in shipping who owned a book and music shop and operated a singing school. He was a lay reader in the Methodist Church at St. John, publishing a history of Methodism in New Brunswick, and compiled the first English-language collection of tunes published in Canada.

HUMPHREYS, JERE T. (U.S.) Researcher, teacher, and consultant in the field of music education. Professor of music at Arizona State University (ASU), a Fulbright Senior Scholar (2002), and Fulbright Senior Specialist (2010), who has presented 15 keynote and other major speeches worldwide. A prolific scholar, he has produced more than 170 publications with translations into six languages, including the *New Grove Dictionary of American Music* and *Sage Directions in Educational Psychology*. He has had an intensive international career as a lecturer, consultant, and presenter in 30 U.S. states and 30 countries on six continents. Among his many academic awards are the Senior Researcher Award from **MENC** (2006) and the MENC Citation of Excellence in Research (1985). He has been nominated for ASU Professor of the Year, ASU Distinguished Mentor of Women, and ASU College of Fine Arts Distinguished Teacher of the Year.

HWYL NOFIO. From Welsh, meaning "emotional swimmers"; an experimental music group whose only permanent member is Steve Parry, who was born in 1958 in Pontypool, South Wales Valleys, UK. This band was formed in 1997 with an approach that touches on various diverse styles and genres, including industrial music, drone, ambient, and noise. *Hwyl Nofio* is referred to as a marriage of dilemmas being resolved in another space whereby the music explores and exploits an ongoing collision between harmony and disharmony. Influences include **John Cage** and Harry Partch.

I

IDIOPHONE. Older classification of **percussion instruments** whose sound is produced by shaking a metallic, wooden, or other surface directly, thus producing their sound through the substance of the instrument itself. (Concussion sticks are a subcategory as in *claves*, **clapsticks**, and paired **boomerangs**.)

The class contains most of the *pitched* instruments, including instruments made of wood or other organic material, such as **xylophones**. They also include pitched percussion instruments that are struck or plucked and are made of metal or other inorganic material (triangle, glockenspiel, vibraphone, celesta, tubular bell, gong, steel drum, cymbal, **glass harmonica**, etc.).

Idiophones *without pitch* include such instruments as the percussion board, castanets, and rattles, all of which are made of wood or other organic materials and are struck, scraped, rubbed, brushed, or shaken.

IMMERSION METHOD. (Whole song learning.) The teaching of songs to young children through aural memory. Short songs are usually taught in their entirety (e.g., *Hot Cross Buns*, *Mary Had a Little Lamb*).

IMPROVISATION. The art of spontaneous performance without preliminary plan.

INBHEAR. *The Journal of Irish Music and Dance.*

INCLUSIVE CLASSROOM. 1. Fully inclusive schools, which are rare, no longer distinguish between "general education" and "special education" programs; instead, the school is restructured so that all students learn together. **2.** In Ireland, *Travelers* are extremely mobile groups of people—circus workers, gypsies, seasonal workers. Very few children attend school. In 1995, the Department of Education and Science attempted to increase the number of traveler children in their special needs schools. Through initiatives of inclusion and antiracism, Ireland hopes to integrate all primary children enrolled in school.

IN DERRY VALE. (UK.) This song is known as "Londonderry Air" and is one of the loveliest folk melodies in any part of the world. The words by W. G. Rothery are most often sung in the British Isles: "In Derry Vale, beside the singing river . . ."

INDIANA MUSIC TEACHERS ASSOCIATION (IMTA). Formed in 1877, it was one of the first of the state **MENC (NAƒME)** associations.

INDIGENOUS MUSIC. (Aus.) Originating in, and characteristic of Australia, the most important trait is that it is mainly vocal, through songs. Most of these songs are sacred, or at least refer to sacred realms. Uses of these songs include initiation and mortuary ceremonies, ceremonies for managing conflict, religious ceremonies, healing and bewitching, attracting a desired member of the opposite sex, and inducing rain.

INDIGENOUS MUSICAL INSTRUMENTS. (Aus.) Aborigines use instruments of their own making, typically used to accompany songs and often played solo: mostly **idiophones**—paired **boomerang** (rhythm clappers), paired sticks, rasps, seed pods, **membranophones**—and **aerophones**—the **bullroarer** and **didgeridoo**. Relatively few instruments are found in the indigenous music of Australia, and in their traditional use are chiefly confined to specific regions. Most are percussion.

INDIGENOUS PEOPLES. Any ethnic group of peoples who inhabit a geographic region with which they have the earliest known historical connection; aboriginal, native peoples.

INDIVIDUALIZED EDUCATION PROGRAM (IEP). A plan of instruction mandated by the Education for All Handicapped Children Act of 1975, and by the **Individuals with Disabilities Education Act** (IDEA) of 1990, for all children classified in any category of special education.

INDIVIDUALS WITH DISABILITIES EDUCATION ACT (IDEA). Public Law 94-142 in 1990. The name given to the new and expanded version of the Education for All Handicapped Children Act of 1975. The term *handicapped* was replaced with *disability* to more accurately reflect current trends in educational thought.

INDUSTRIAL BANDS. (UK.) Bands that receive financial support from the sponsoring companies whose name they bear. In most cases, the bandsmen are employees of the sponsoring company. These bands tend to be in Great Britain rather than the U.S.

INFANT SCHOOLS. (UK.) Schools or classes attached to a primary school for children from about five to seven years of age; much like **kindergarten** experiences in the U.S.

INNER HEARING. A part of **Kodály** training includes developing the concept of *inner hearing*—the ability to *think* musical sounds without external voicing. Developing this ability is the mark of a literate musician who can look at a musical score and *think* the sounds.

INSTRUMENTAL CLASS INSTRUCTION. *See* MAIDSTONE MOVEMENT.

INSTRUMENTAL MUSIC. Any device or set of devices used to express ideas through organized sounds that create *music*. Australian schools favor concert bands (featuring woodwinds, brasses, and percussion) over symphonic orchestras (featuring strings); and string instruction is less popular because of student preferences, fewer tutors, and budgetary constraints.

INTEGRATED LEARNING. The combining of a variety of subject areas in music through writing, analyzing, listening, composing, reading, and performing in order to reinforce the musical learning process into an interrelated whole.

INTEGRATED SCHOOLS. Schools that include members of different racial, religious, and ethnic groups as equals.

INTEGRATION OF MUSIC. (Can.) The elementary school music teacher supports the general curriculum by providing musical materials and information for the integration of music that reinforces the social studies, math, science, and language arts areas of the curriculum.

INTER-AMERICAN MUSIC COUNCIL (CIDEM). Founded in 1956 by the general secretariat of the Organization of American States, Washington, DC, in compliance with Resolution IX of the First Meeting of the Inter-American Cultural Council, which refers to the "creation of an inter-American musical organization that will function with a permanent character, centralize inter-American musical activities and work closely with the **International Music Council** of **UNESCO**."

INTERDISCIPLINARY STUDIES IN MUSIC. The combining or involving of two or more academic or fields of study (e.g., music theory and music history).

INTERLOCHEN CENTER FOR THE ARTS. (U.S.) Privately owned arts education institution in Interlochen, Michigan. An umbrella organization for *Interlochen Arts Camp* (formerly the *National Music Camp*); a *National High School Orchestra Camp*, founded by **Joseph Maddy** and **T. P. Giddings** in 1928; *Interlochen Arts Academy* boarding high school (founded 1962); *Interlochen Public Radio* (founded 1963); *Interlochen College of Creative Arts* (founded 2004); and the *Interlochen Presents* performing arts series. It has now grown to become one of the premier sites for developing young musicians, dancers, actors, visual artists, and writers. It is a year-round fine arts school in addition to its extensive summer program and annual *Interlochen Arts Festival*. Current director is Jeff Kimpton.

INTERNATIONAL ASSOCIATION OF JAZZ EDUCATORS (IAJE). An organization that promoted jazz curricula in the public schools in America and internationally as a legitimate and serious art form. *Jazz Education Journal* was its official publication. Originally formed in 1968 as **National Association of Jazz Educators** (NAJE) and changed its name in 1989 to reflect global perspective and outreach. The 35th Annual IAJE Conference (its last) was held January 9–12, 2008, in Toronto, Canada. On April 18, 2008, the International Association for Jazz Education (IAJE) ceased daily operations and filed for bankruptcy under Chapter 7 of the United States federal bankruptcy law. All future events were canceled, and it ceased as a corporation 2009. *See also* COUNCIL FOR JAZZ EDUCATION (NAfME).

INTERNATIONAL COUNCIL ON TRADITIONAL MUSIC (ICTM). A UNESCO-recognized academic organization focused on musicology and dance research. Founded in London in 1947, it publishes the *Yearbook for Traditional Music* once a year, and a twice-yearly bulletin. It was previously known as the International Folk Music Council (IFMC). In 1949, it helped found the **UNESCO International Music Council**.

INTERNATIONAL MILITARY MUSIC SOCIETY. Founded in the UK in 1977 from members of the Band Section of the Military Historical Society. The society expanded rapidly with the formation of overseas branches, and in 1998 an international committee was formed to govern the society. The United Kingdom membership was established as a branch of the society rather than as the central nucleus.

INTERNATIONAL MUSIC COUNCIL (IMC). Founded in 1949 at the request of **UNESCO** as a nongovernmental advisory body on musical matters. The IMC *World Forum on Music* is the continuation of IMC's biennial conference, held in conjunction with the General Assembly. Launched in 2005, the IMC World Forum on Music developed into a high-level conference that attracts key people from the international music world and related sectors.

INTERNATIONAL MUSIC EISTEDDFOD. (UK-Wales.) Annual music festival and competition featuring choral singing and dancing, with groups from around the world. This has been an annual event held usually in August at Llangollen since 1947.

INTERNATIONAL SOCIETY FOR MUSIC EDUCATION (ISME). Founded in 1953. An organization that promotes and coordinates international perspectives in music education. It was organized by **UNESCO** and the **IMC**. ISME's mission is to enhance those experiences by building and maintaining a worldwide community of music educators characterized by mutual respect and support; fostering global intercultural understanding and cooperation among the world's music educators; and promoting music education for people of all ages in all relevant situations throughout the world. Based in Australia. ISME publishes the *International Journal of Music Education* (IJME), founded in 1980 to help promote international music education.

INTERNATIONAL SOCIETY FOR THE PHILOSOPHY OF MUSIC EDUCATION (ISPME). (Int.) An international organization that examines such fundamental questions as "why and how should music be taught and learned?" Held its first symposium in 1990. Several prominent music scholars have taken leadership roles over the years, most notably **Estelle Jorgensen** of Indiana University (U.S.). Other well-known participants have included **Bennett Reimer** and **David Elliott**.

INTERPRETATIVE MOVEMENT. This movement focuses on the simple expressiveness of musical elements, text, or programmatic ideas in music. The term describes bodily movement that may be free and creative or carefully planned, either abstract or dramatic. **Dalcroze** was one of the first to consider using the body as interpretive in a system of rhythmic movement known as **eurhythmics**.

INUIT PEOPLES. (Can.) A member of the Eskimo peoples inhabiting northernmost North America from northern Alaska to eastern Canada and Greenland. Moravians in Labrador were first to teach the Inuit on the Labrador coast. They had great capacity to learn music. In 1824 they were able to accompany voices instrumentally. The Inuit were taught not only to sing and play instruments, but also to read music notation. It was observed that by 1899 they were able to sight-sing simple melodies. Since the mid-20th century, the Inuit have sought to discover their own musical heritage.

IPAD. A line of tablet computers designed and marketed by Apple, primarily as a platform for audiovisual media, including books, periodicals, movies, music, games, apps, and Web content. Its size and weight fall between contemporary smartphones and laptop computers. The iPad is controlled by a multitouch display and has a virtual onscreen keyboard in lieu of a physical keyboard. It was launched in 2010 and is currently in its third generation.

IPOD. A line of portable media players created and marketed by Apple, including the hard drive–based iPod classic, Touchstone Touch, compact iPod nano, and ultracompact iPod shuffle. The iPods serve as external data-storage devices primarily for music listening. The iPod line was released in November 2001. The most recent redesign occurred in 2010.

IRISH EDUCATION SYSTEM. Composed of three levels of schooling serving some one million students. First level consists of *junior* and *senior infant* groups, and first through sixth classes, called *primary schools*. Second level consists of three years of instruction leading to the Junior Certificate exam, and the further two or three years culminates in the Leaving Certificate exam. These have various names: *secondary*, *vocational*, *comprehensive*, *community schools*, or *colleges*. Third level consists of universities, technical institutes, and colleges for education of primary teachers.

The primary school curriculum (revised) affirms the centrality of the arts within the schools and includes broad-based offerings in music, dance, drama, visual arts, poetry, and storytelling. Study of the arts is considered to be a key way to assist children in becoming more tolerant, aware, and confident, nurturing creativity and artistic expression.

IRISH FOLK MUSIC STUDIES. The **Folk Music Society** (1971) publishes an occasional journal, *Irish Folk Music Studies*. It has also produced books, pamphlets, and tapes.

IRISH HARPS. From the 1800s Irish harps were made on the old model and strung with gut. Since the 1960s, a few makers have reconstructed the medieval harp so that its tone—much more sonorous than that of modern harps—can be heard again.

IRISH SCHOOL SYSTEM. This system was begun in 1831 by Lord Stanley. By 1920 the system had evolved into three separate parts comparable to the English schools. They operated independently, and the national schools, though funded by the state, were operated by local churches. The schools were either Protestant or Catholic. The third part of the system was composed of technical schools, which were never much of an influence in the nation's early history. For over 400 years, the history of education in Northern Ireland was a history of two separate school systems.

Today's bilateral school system can be traced to the **Lynn Report** of 1922. This report recommended three kinds of schools for primary children: 1) local authority schools (state schools), 2) partially controlled state schools (four local board members, two from churches), and 3) voluntary schools independent of state control. Funding was to be in proportion to the degree of local control. State schools received full funding, and voluntary schools received none.

The Education Act of 1930 was passed to settle the funding issue. The state schools reflected the Protestant and British ethos, and Catholics received half-funding for their voluntary schools. The gap in funding diminished somewhat, but it remained in place as late as the 1990s.

Bib.: Green, James E., *Education in the United Kingdom and Ireland*, 2001.

I STILL CALL AUSTRALIA HOME. A popular song with words and music by Peter Allen and performed in 1980. Allen sings of Australian expatriates longing for home, and the song is filled with nostalgia for the Australian countryside and its customs. Has been used in a number of venues, including advertisements for Qantas airline, and it has been recognized, as has "Waltzing Matilda," as a national Australian song.

ITINERANT SPECIALISTS. (Aus.) Singing masters were chosen from a list of part-time singing teachers, referred to as *itinerant specialists*. After Victoria hired music teacher specialists (1853), they subsequently dismissed the itinerant teachers. Public protests caused them to be reinstated, with payment of extra fees by the parents. This made music an extracurricular subject. Eventually, music was returned to the regular music curriculum.

ITUNES. A media player computer system used for playing, downloading, saving, and organizing digital music and video files on personal computers. It can also manage contents on **iPod**, iPhone, iPod Touch, and **iPad** devices. iTunes was introduced by Apple on January 9, 2001.

IVES, ELAN, JR. (1802–1864). A church choir director and singing-school master. Established the Philadelphia Music Seminary in 1830. Later moved to New York, where he established a new music seminary and where he remained until returning to Connecticut, where he died in 1864. He was the first to apply **Pestalozzian** principles to music teaching in the U.S. He completed the manuscript of his *American Elementary Singing Book*. It was probably the first American book to advocate Pestalozzian principles. His second book was *The Juvenile Lyre*, published in 1831. One of the major principles was "to teach sounds before signs—to make the child sing before he learns written notes or their names." Ives was important in establishing a foothold of music in the public schools in the latter half of the 19th century. He was the one who divided music instruction into three "departments"—rhythm, pitch, and dynamics—which **Lowell Mason** began to use as headings in 1839.

IWAN, DAFYDD (1943–). (UK-Wales.) From the 1960s he was the leader of a movement to save the Welsh language. He sang songs of Bob Dylan and Woody Guthrie to his own guitar accompaniment. Fitting traditional Welsh words to the tunes, or translating American folk songs into Welsh, finally led him to write his own words and music. He is now considered the most prolific song composer in Wales. Iwan is one of the founders of the Sain record company, which produces an immense amount of recorded music.

J

JAMES, WILLIAM (1842–1910). America's first philosopher developed the school of thought eventually known as *pragmatism*. After graduating from Harvard in 1870, he became widely known as a brilliant and original lecturer. His position in American philosophy and psychology was greatly enhanced in 1890 when he wrote his *Principles of Psychology*. Turning to religious and moral problems, and later to metaphysics, he produced a large number of writings that gave ample evidence of his ability to cut through cumbersome terminology. One of his main works is *The Will to Believe and Other Essays in Popular Philosophy.*

THE JAMES REPORT (1972). (UK.) During the 1970s, the professional preparation of teachers received increasing attention. The professional training of teachers was integrated into general higher education. Most of these changes occurred as a result of the James Report, which is credited with providing a framework for teacher education that continues into 1995 and beyond.

JAQUES-DALCROZE, EMILE (1865–1950). (Also referred to as *Dalcroze, Emile.*) A Swiss musician who stressed the importance of training what he described as musical faculties, and not just teaching musical technique. The **Dalcroze method** was derived from his ideas about **eurhythmics**. His method emphasized tone and rhythm, using movement to express musical interpretation; he was one of the first to explore the new science of psychology. Dalcroze studied with Edouard Clarapede, who recognized the potential of the Dalcroze method in teaching children. Dalcroze presented his first training course for teachers in 1906 and repeated it several times until 1909, when the first diploma was awarded.

While the Dalcroze method has not become a specific part of the American music curriculum, many elementary general music teachers have studied it and have incorporated many of its techniques into the American music-education process. A common example of these techniques is the use of the terms *walking* and *running* as designations for quarter and eighth notes. **Mabelle**

Glenn's graded series, *World of Music*, and **Mary Ruth Tolbert**'s *This is Music* (Grade 2) incorporated the use of Dalcroze eurhythmics.

Bib.: Mark, Michael, and Charles L. Gary, *History of American Music Education*, 3rd ed., 2007.

JAPANESE OPERA. Opera known as *Noh* developed in the Japanese musical and theatrical tradition. It features a falsetto singing style; elaborate costumes, masks, and headdresses; and energetic swordplay and acrobatics. It is also a part of the Japanese opera culture known as *Kabuki*.

JAZZ. A term covering several musical styles of African-American origin, including New Orleans/Dixieland, Chicago, big band/swing, bebop, cool/third stream, free jazz, fusion, neo-traditionalism; usually characterized by improvisation and an unlimited variety of dotted or syncopated melodic rhythms against a steady duple or quadruple meter, producing a synthesis known as "swing."

JAZZ BAND. This term actually has two basic definitions. In its early period of the 1920s, the reference was generally the *Dixieland band*. However, small groups of instrumentalists, including the proliferation of high school and college groups in the 1940s and beyond, were generally referred to as *jazz*, *stage*, or *rock bands*, even though they mainly played "swing" tunes for dancing. This ensemble had no fixed instruments. There is generally a large percussion section for a rhythmic background, shared by plucked string instruments (bass) and by the piano, which is used also as a solo instrument. Other solo instruments are clarinet, saxophone, trumpet, and trombone.

JAZZED MAGAZINE (JAZZed). *See* JAZZ EDUCATION NETWORK.

JAZZ EDUCATION. This term came about as a result of instrumental music teachers' desire to promote jazz curricula in the public schools in America and internationally as a legitimate and serious art form. The **International Association of Jazz Educators** (IAJE) was originally formed in 1968 as the **National Association of Jazz Educators** (NAJE) and changed its name in 1989 to IAJE in order to more accurately reflect the organization's global perspective and outreach. It became one of the **MENC (NAfME)** association organizations in 1988. The *Jazz Education Journal*, IAJE's official publication, includes philosophical and practical articles about jazz education.

JAZZ EDUCATION JOURNAL. Official journal of the **International Association for Jazz Education** (IAJE) until 2008 when it ceased to exist. Antonio García served as editor of the *Jazz Education Journal* from July 1993 through June 2003, and he is still the contact for articles from the journal archives.

JAZZ EDUCATION NETWORK (JEN). This organization began in June 2008 when the **International Association for Jazz Education** (IAJE) ceased operation. Cofounders are Mary Jo Papisch, Fine Arts chair at Highland Park High School, Illinois; and Lou Fischer, professor of music at Capital University in Columbus, Ohio. In 2008 at an invitational meeting of jazz educators in Chicago, this volunteer group drafted a name for the organization, a set of bylaws, and a mission statement. The statement reads: "*The Jazz Education Network* is dedicated to building the jazz arts community by advancing education, promoting performances, and developing new audiences." The organization has an elected board that elects its own officers: president, vice president, secretary, and treasurer. JEN currently maintains a partnership with *Symphony Publishing*, which publishes *JAZZed* magazine. It includes six to eight pages of JEN information in every issue.

JAZZ ENSEMBLES. *See* JAZZ BAND.

JAZZ IMPROVISATION. Jazz has raised the art of improvisation to a new height of brilliance, especially in collective improvisation occurring in jam sessions. Depending on the style involved, jazz improvisation is affected by tonality, accompaniment, or length allotted, from a quick "fill" to essentially unlimited time space.

JELLISON, JUDITH. (U.S.) The Mary D. Bold Regents Professor in Music and Human Learning, and a University Distinguished Teaching Professor at the Butler School of Music at the University of Texas at Austin. She has taught in public schools at all levels (general, choral, and instrumental music) and is the founder of the **music therapy** program at the University of Minnesota, where she served as director and taught for more than a decade. Her experiences working with diverse populations as a music teacher and music therapist in schools and hospitals have shaped her philosophy and her research, which focuses on the musical development of children with disabilities, and inclusive educational practices. Dr. Jellison has a sustained record of scholarly publications in premier research journals and books, and she regularly presents her work at national and international clinics and conferences. She has served on the editorial boards of major journals in music education and music therapy and is the recipient of both the prestigious Senior Researcher Award from **NA***f***ME**, and the Publications Award from **AMTA**. She also has been honored with several teaching awards, including being selected as a member of the Academy of Distinguished Teachers and as a recipient of the Regents' Outstanding Teaching Award.

JEPSON, BENJAMIN (1832–1914). Prior to the Civil War and the work of Luther Whiting Mason, Jepson had been very successful training choruses of children. While his work was done out of schoolhouses, he always felt it should have a place in the public schools and that the schools should teach children to read music. After the Civil War (1865), Jepson persuaded the school board to try the experiment of introducing music into the schools of New Haven, Connecticut. During his 50 years of service to these schools, he was prominently successful. For his instruction, he designed a musical chart that eventually was included in his book *The Elementary Music Reader* (1865). The experiences included sight singing by individuals and classes. Eventually, there were six books used in his teaching. The last series, published in 1904, was titled *The New Standard Music Reader*.

JESUIT RELATION OF 1645. (Can.) The earliest written record of a violin in Canada came from the Jesuit Relation of 1645. They additionally had the first documented organ sale, imported for their Quebec City chapel in 1657. The Notre Dame de Quebec Cathedral, built in 1647, is the primate church of Canada. It is the site of the first documented choir in Canada.

JOHNSON, EDWARD (1878–1959). (Can.) World-renowned tenor of the Metropolitan Opera, who showed an interest in providing opportunities for the youth of Guelph, Ontario, his native city. In 1928, he pledged $5,000 annually for five years to establish a Department of Music within the collegiate-vocational institute and public schools.

JOLLIET, LOUIS (1645–1700). (Can.) He is on record as *one of the first classically trained practicing musicians in New France*, although history recognized him more as an explorer, hydrographer, and voyager. Jolliet is said to have played the organ, flute, and trumpet.

JOLTING. (Aus.) A playing technique used with log idiophones, by which the player hits the instrument with the end of a thick stick or a bundle of sticks.

JORGENSON, ESTELLE (1945–). (Aus./U.S.) Currently, since 1987, professor of music education at Indiana University School of Music. Her background includes degrees and studies from Australia, Canada, and the U.S. As a teacher of graduate courses in the foundation of music education, she also serves as editor for *Philosophy of Music Education Review*, and is founding cochair of the **International Society for the Philosophy of Music Education** (ISPME). Among her many books and articles, she is the author of *In Search of Music Education* (University of Illinois Press, 1997), *Transforming Music Education* (Indiana University Press, 2003), and *The Art of Teaching Music* (Indiana University Press, 2008).

JOTHEN, MICHAEL J. (1944–). Music educator. Professor of music emeritus, Towson University, Towson, Maryland. Jothen earned a BA from St. Olaf College, an MA from Case-Western Reserve University, and a PhD from Ohio State University. He is coauthor of three pre-K–8 textbook series published by McGraw-Hill, *Music and You* (1987), *Share the Music* (1995), and *Spotlight On Music* (2005, 2008), and lead author of McGraw-Hill-Glencoe/Hal Leonard Publishing's *Master Strategies for Choir* (2007). His choral compositions have been published by Bechenhorst Press, Broadman Press, Choristers Guild, Coronet Press, Hal Leonard, Laurel Press, Walton Music, and World Library Publications. Jothen has taught in the public schools of Michigan and Ohio, served as a middle school/high school public school music supervisor in Maryland, and was professor at the University of Northern Colorado. He has assisted others as a clinician, consultant, or conductor in more than 40 states, Canada, and Europe. Professional memberships have included **MENC (NA*f*ME)**, where he assisted in the development of national teacher certification and was a member of the music standards writing team, guided by the **NCCAS**. He is also a lifetime member of the **ACDA**, as well as the *Choristers Guild*, of which he served as national president.

***JOURNAL OF MUSIC TEACHER EDUCATION* (JMTE).** A music-education journal founded by Irma H. Collins in 1991, focusing on topics related to music-teacher training and issued twice per year in online format. Previous issues were published in **MENC** booklet form. The JMTE is a refereed journal and publishes articles regarding teacher-education reform, curricular issues, and topics related to teacher education. JMTE is the official journal of the **Society for Music Teacher Education** (SMTE).

***JOURNAL OF RESEARCH IN MUSIC EDUCATION* (JRME).** (U.S.) Official publication for **SRME** since 1963. Considered the premier research journal in music education, with the first issue of volume I appearing in 1953. Marguerite Hood (University of Michigan), Warren Freeman (Boston University), and Allen Britton (University of Michigan) participated in initial discussions regarding the necessity for a scholarly research journal in 1952. Allen Britton served as its first editor, and it became a quarterly journal with volume 12 in 1964. Published by **MENC**, JRME contains information about the latest music-education research and related topics.

JOURNAL OF THE FOLK-SONG SOCIETY. (UK.) The term *folklore* was introduced into scholarship by W. J. Thoms in 1846. The cognate terms *folk song* and *folk music* followed, and growing interest in musical idioms led to the founding of the Folk-Song Society in 1898. As a result of the founding of this society, the first volumes of the *Journal of the Folk-Song Society* (1899) explained how collectors' encounters with traditional music did not follow the conventions of the major-minor systems of Western theory and practice. This difference was explained as "modal survival."

JOURNAL OF THE IRISH FOLKSONG SOCIETY. (UK-Ire.) It began publishing in the early 20th century (1905–1939). Unfortunately, a member of the society, Donal O'Sullivan, was almost the only scholar writing on traditional Irish music at that time. As a result, this journal did not last more than 34 years in this form. In 1971, **Breandán Breathnach**, founder of the journal *Ceol* (1963–1986), was closely involved with Uilleann pipers, and in 1968 was the prime mover of the pipers' society, Na Piobairí Uilleann. It was then that he and others founded the **Folk Music Society of Ireland**.

JUBILEE. A season or occasion of celebration, such as a 50th anniversary. **Patrick Gilmore** organized a **National Peace Jubilee** in 1869 that involved 1,000 army bandsmen, an orchestra of 500, and a chorus of 10,000.

JUILLIARD REPERTORY PROJECT (1967). A tangible result of the **Yale Seminar**; Dean Gideon Waldrop of the Juilliard School applied for and received a grant to enable Juilliard to develop a large body of authentic and meaningful music to augment and enrich the repertory available to music teachers in grades K–6.

JUNG, CARL (1875–1961). An eminent Swiss psychiatrist whose writings influenced many fields, including psychology, education, **music education**, and, to an extent, religion. He founded the field of analytic psychology, and his ideas about introvert and extrovert personalities, archetypes, and the collective unconscious are now classic. Jung believed that an individual's place in the collective unconscious was expressed in dreams and in one's imagination. Carl Jung's book *Psychological Types* influenced Isabel Myers and Kathryn Briggs in their 1950s questionnaire for identifying kinds of personalities. It was called "The Myers-Briggs Type Indicator." A short version of this questionnaire was developed later by David Keirsey in 1978. Some teachers and music educators have used the questionnaire in their classrooms and seminars toward developing instructional strategies for meeting the learning styles of their students.

Lit.: Keirsey, David, *Please Understand Me I* and *II*, 1978 and 1998.

JUNIOR SCHOOLS. (UK.) The name usually given in England to schools for pupils aged 7–11, delivering Key Stage 2 of the national curriculum.

K

KALIMBA. *See* LAMELLAPHONE.

KANGAROO. (Aus.) Any herbivorous marsupial of the family *Macropodidae*, of Australia and adjacent islands, having a small head, short forelimbs, powerful hind legs used for leaping, and a long thick tail.

KANGAROO DANCE. (Aus.) An aboriginal dance in which the movements of the kangaroo are imitated.

KEEP THE BALL A-ROLLING. (Can.) French-Canadian song that Canadian voyageurs sang the rhythm of paddling their canoes. This song was originally a French nursery song.

KEIL, CHARLES (1939–). (U.S.) Ethnomusicologist who spent 30 years as an American studies (AMS) professor at the State University of New York at Buffalo before retiring in 2000. He played an integral role in establishing the PhD program in AMS and helped make this department one of the most prestigious in the country. Though a dedicated performer, his true passion is fostering musical expression in young people. In 1990, Keil founded **Musicians United for Superior Education** (MUSE) because he wanted his two children to attend a school that was committed to creative thinking and expression. *See* BORN TO GROOVE; MUSE; CAMPBELL, PATRICIA SHEHAN.

KEOKUK, IOWA. Sometimes referred to as the "call to Keokuk" because of the work of Phillip C. Haydn, music supervisor in Keokuk, who was the primary force in the founding of the **Music Supervisors National Conference** (later **MENC**) in 1907.
  Bib.: Mark, Michael L., and Charles L. Gary, *A History of Music Education*, 2007; Ponick, Terry L., ed., *MENC: A Century of Service to Music Education: 1907–2007*, 2007.

KEYBOARD. (Piano.) An instrument that is played by depressing keys that cause hammers to strike tuned strings and produce sounds.

KEYBOARDS IN THE CLASSROOM. Set of depressible or struck keys or levers, usually laid out in horizontal manuals, activating sound-inducing mechanisms as in pianos. Classroom keyboards are usually arranged with 12 chromatic notes within an octave, seven white keys on the lower level and five shorter black keys, slightly elevated. White keys are diatonic, and black keys are pentatonic. Small keyboards (referred to as melody bells) in the classroom are generally made of wood with metal keys and extend an octave and one half. Played with wooden mallets. There are also electronic keyboards available. Other instruments of this genre are resonator bells, **xylophones**, and keyboard instruments developed by **Carl Orff**.

KEY STAGES. (UK.) In England and Wales, the curriculum is organized into four key stages that cover the years of compulsory schooling:

- Key Stage 1 corresponds to the first two years, for children ages 5 and 6.
- Key Stage 2 corresponds to the 3rd–6th years, for children ages 7–10.
- Key Stage 3 corresponds to the 7th–9th years, for children ages 11–13.
- Key Stage 4 corresponds to the 10th–11th years, for adolescents ages 14–16.

Each subject in the national curriculum includes *programs of study* and *attainment targets*; these terms are similar to the terms *courses* and *goals* that are in common use in the U.S.

KIDSON, FRANK (1855–1926). English folk song collector and music scholar. One of the founders of the **Folk-Song Society** in 1898.

KINDERGARTEN. ("Children's garden.") Based on the work of **Friedrich Fröebel**, whose goal was that children should be taken care of and nourished in "children's gardens," like plants in a garden. He put forth principles in which games play an important role. In the U.S., a kindergarten class is to prepare children, usually five-year-olds, for school. In Australia, it is usually the first year of *infant school*.

KINDERMUSIK. A music-education program designed to provide musical experiences that are both fun and educational for children from birth through age seven. Integration of music and movement activities into age-appropriate curricula that typically include singing, chanting, listening, and playing instruments.

KINDLE. A portable **e-reader** developed by Amazon.com and introduced November 2007. Its Kindle Fire was introduced in September 2011.

KING'S COLLEGE CHOIR. (UK.) Owes its existence to King Henry VI (1422–1461), who envisaged the daily singing of services in his magnificent chapel. It is an important part of the lives of its 16 choristers, who are educated on generous scholarships at King's College School; and the 14 choral scholars and two organ scholars, who study a variety of subjects in the college.

THE KING'S SINGERS. (UK.) Male ensemble of six singers (two countertenors, one tenor, two baritones, and one bass) formed in 1968 and so called because original members, with one Oxonian exception, were choral scholars at King's College, Cambridge. Specialize in part songs and in arrangements of various genres, including humorous songs. Range from Monteverdi to Noel Coward. Some songs written for them.

KLEZMER. A Jewish folk musician traditionally performing in a small band. (In Yiddish, the word *klezmer* literally means "vessels of the music." Before the 17th century in Central and Eastern Europe, klezmer meant a musical instrument. By the mid-17th century, however, the word had begun to be used to denote the musician.) Sometimes referred to as *Klezmer music*.

KNELLER HALL. (UK.) Former home of painter Sir Godfrey Kneller, it became headquarters of the **Royal Military School of Music** at Whitton, Twickenham, Middlesex. In 1857, a Military Music Class (later the **Royal Military School of Music**) was formed to train Army bandsmen as bandmasters, and by 1872 all bandmasters had to be enlisted men with a certificate from Kneller Hall.

KNIETER, GERARD L. (1931–). Music educator who held a variety of positions in higher education, including Temple University, University of Akron, and University of California–Northridge. Speaker and organizer for interdisciplinary arts programs. Received ARCH Award at NYU (1953). Contributed to *Encyclopedia of Education—Toward an Aesthetic Education*. Research involved applying psychology of creativity to teacher education in the arts. Knieter, with Jane Stallings, edited the Central Midwest Regional Educational Laboratory (CEMREL) conference materials, *The Teaching Process and the Arts and Aesthetics*, 1979.

KODÁLY, ZOLTAN (1883–1967). A composer and teacher from Hungary. The first part of his life was spent as a performing musician, teacher, and composer. He collected folk songs because of his belief that folk music was the basis of national culture. He was closely involved with the Hungarian music curriculum, and with Bartok, formed an organization for the performance of contemporary music. Some of his best-known works are: *Hary Janos*, *Summer Evening*, *Concerto for Orchestra*, and *Psalmus Hungaricus*. In the last 30 years of his life, he created a pedagogical system for Hungarian schools by using nationalistic and folk songs. His pedagogical approach, developed in Hungary, is called the *Kodály method*. This method was not invented by Kodály per se; rather, its practices were developed from the use of **sol-fa** (It.), **tonic sol-fa** (Eng.), rhythm syllables from **Chevé** (Fr.), and **Jaques-Dalcroze** hand singing from **John Curwen**'s approach (Eng.). The teaching process was basically **Pestalozzian**. Kodály combined these approaches into one unified whole now called the *Kodály method. See also* MOTHER TONGUE.

Bib.: Choksy, Lois, *The Kodály Method: Comprehensive Music Education from Infant to Adult*, 1974; Choksy, Lois, et al., *Teaching Music in the Twentieth Century*, 1986.

KODÁLY CENTER OF AMERICA (KCA). Established in 1977 by Denise Bacon, at first in Wellesley, Massachusetts, and later in Newton, Massachusetts, and Providence, Rhode Island. Its purposes were essentially the same as those of the KMTI.

KODÁLY METHOD. *See* KODÁLY, ZOLTAN.

KODÁLY MUSIC EDUCATION INSTITUTE OF AUSTRALIA (KMEIA) (1973). (Aus.) A professional association dedicated to supporting Australian music teachers and providing Kodály information to them. A result of the 1971 **Kodály Pilot Project**.

KODÁLY PILOT PROJECT (1971). (Aus.) Deanna Hoermann established this project under the auspices of the NSW Department of Education in the West Metropolitan Region of Sydney. The success of this program led to the wide promotion of Kodály teaching in NSW and other states. It has become well established in Australia as the *Developmental Music Program*. The **Kodály Music Education Institute of Australia** was established in 1973.

KOHLBERG, LAWRENCE (1927–1987). A Jewish-American psychologist who served as a professor at the University of Chicago and Harvard University. He specialized in research on moral education and reasoning. He is best known for his theory of stages of moral development. These stages are planes of moral adequacy conceived to explain the development of moral reasoning. He was inspired by Jean Piaget's theory of cognitive development and by a fascination with children's reactions to moral dilemmas. He proposed a form of "Socratic" moral education and reaffirmed Dewey's idea that development should be the aim of education. Kohlberg was found to be the 30th most eminent psychologist of the 20th century.

KONOWITZ, BERT. (Can.) A retired professor of music at Teachers College, Columbia University, he is known for his work in jazz improvisation. He is the founder, conductor, and pianist of *Spirit*, the Columbia University improvisational arts ensemble. His pioneering work in improvisation is reflected in his many publications that are used around the world, including texts, compositions, and teaching guides for piano/keyboard, chorus, orchestra, and classroom activity. He has taught at every level of the public school system. He was commissioned to write a new curriculum, *Music in American Society*, and has contributed jazz/rock sections to the New York State Department of Education middle school curriculum.

KOTO. (Japan.) Japanese zither, having 13 silk strings set on movable bridges and played with ivory picks.

KOUKIAS, CONSTANTINE (1965–). (Aus.) Composer and flautist. One of Australia's most prolific composers in opera and musical theater. His works range from large-scale, site-specific works to gallery pieces. His compositions are remarkable for their peculiar, mesmerizing atmosphere, created by temporal, spatial, and sound effects. His work *Prayer Bells—Pentekostarion*, which draws on traditions of religious chant, was commissioned for the Melbourne Federation Festival in 2001. He has created and presented laboratory works for his Young Singer Laboratory Program.

KRONE, MAX THOMAS (1901–1970). Founder and president (1946–1962) of the Idyllwild School of Music and the Arts, he was interested in what the arts, in a beautiful and inspiring outdoor setting, in a creative approach to teaching and learning, would do in the lives of people. He was also director of choral activities at Northeastern University and dean of the Institute of the Arts at the University of Southern California. He possessed vision and imagination in his teaching, conducting, arranging, and administrative leadership. His publications raised the standards of choral music and the elementary school music program. He supported **MENC** at local, state, regional conferences, and at the national office.

KWALWASSER, JACOB (1894–1977). A pioneer in research in the field of music testing and member of the **Music Educators Hall of Fame**. Helped to develop the **Kwalwasser-Dykema Music Test** and the Kwalwasser-Ruch Music Achievement Test.

KWALWASSER-DYKEMA MUSIC TEST (1930). Developed by Jacob Kwalwasser and Peter Dykema to measure auditory perception. Test given to groups or individually for the purpose of individual diagnosis and prognosis. Phonograph records were used to measure tonal memory, quality discrimination, intensity discrimination, feeling for tonal movement, time discrimination, melodic tastes, and rhythm imagery.

L

LABAN, RUDOLPH VON (1879–1958). Developed an approach to music education labeled *Laban movement education* in the early 20th century that centered on movement activities. This movement emphasized developing awareness of the body and its movement in space.

LAMELLAPHONE. Class of handheld musical instruments indigenous to sub-Saharan Africa; the sound is produced by thin tongues of metal or wood vibrating when plucked by the thumbs. The tongues are attached to a rectangular wooden or metal resonator. *See also* KALIMBA; MBIRA; THUMB PIANO.

LANGER, SUSANNE K. (NÉE KNAUTH) (1895–1985). An American philosopher of mind and art who was influenced by Ernst Cassirer and Alfred North Whitehead; one of the first women to achieve an academic career in philosophy and the first to be popularly and professionally recognized as an American philosopher. As a girl, Langer learned to play both the cello and piano; for her early education she attended Veltin private school, and she studied at Radcliffe College, receiving her bachelor's degree in 1920 and her doctorate in 1926.

Langer's first major work, *Philosophy in a New Key* (1942), was one of the most influential books on the field of music (education) and art, and it put forth an idea that has become commonplace today: that there is a basic and pervasive human need to symbolize, to invent meanings, and to invest meanings in one's world. Her impact on the thinking of **Charles Leonhard** and **Bennett Reimer** has been immeasurable. Langer's statement, "music is the tonal analogy of emotive life," continues to be discussed and debated among music educators who are familiar with her work. Langer's final work, *Mind: An Essay on Human Feeling*, a three-volume work, represents the culmination of her attempt to establish a philosophical and scientific underpinning of aesthetic experience.

LAVALLÉE, CALIXA (1842–1891). A French Canadian–American musician and Union officer during the American Civil War who composed the music for "O Canada," which officially became the national anthem of Canada in 1980.

Born in Quebec, Calixa began his musical education with his father and studied in Montréal with Charles Wugk Sabatier. In 1857, he moved to the U.S. and lived in Rhode Island, where he enlisted in the 4th Rhode Island Volunteers of the Union army during the American Civil War, attaining the rank of lieutenant. During and after the war, he traveled between Canada and the United States building his career in music. Lavallée resided in Louisiana, California, and in the French Canadian community of Lowell, Massachusetts, where he married an American woman, Josephine Gentilly (or "Gently"), in 1867.

To celebrate St. Jean-Baptiste Day in 1880, the lieutenant governor of Québec, Théodore Robitaille, commissioned Lavallée to compose "O Canada" to a patriotic poem by Adolphe-Basile Routhier.

LAWLER, VANETTE (1904–1972). Lawler's professional leadership of **MENC** promoted an ever-increasing involvement on the part of the individual music educators in an organized effort to improve music education. She was executive secretary to MENC for 38 years. Her accomplishments included the doubling of MENC membership, meaning that it had more members than any other subject matter department of the **NEA** (National Education Association). Lawler played a vital role in the establishment of the **International Society for Music Education** (ISME).

LEARNING. The act or process of acquiring knowledge or skill. For music learning, *see* GORDON, EDWIN ELIAS; SKILL LEARNING SEQUENCE.

LEARNING THEORIES. In general, any theory that attempts to explain how learning occurs. Four of the most notable theories are:

1. Behavioral psychology: Learning theories based on the idea that most behavior is learned from environmental experiences (nature) as opposed to inborn capacity (nurture). All are based on a form of reinforcement within their environment.
2. Cognitive psychology: Learning theories based on the idea that learning results from thinking processes within the brain.
3. Humanistic psychology: Learning theories based on the idea that every human being possesses a natural goodness that helps promote or enhance individual development according to personal needs and desires.

4. **Edwin Gordon**'s music learning theory focuses on **audiation**, the ability to hear music that is no longer or may never have been physically present. *See also* INNER HEARING; KODÁLY, ZOLTAN.

LEARNING TO LIVE, LIVING TO LEARN: **PERSPECTIVES ON ARTS EDUCATION IN CANADA.** *See* CANADIAN COMMISSION FOR UNESCO.

LEE, ANN (1736–1784). She was the founder of a celibate religious sect that originated in England as an offshoot of the Quakers known as the "Shaking Quakers." She was illiterate, had worked in a cotton factory in Lancashire, and had suffered from an unhappy marriage followed by the death of her four children. Lee was known as "Mother Ann" and had the power of being spiritually possessed and seeing visions. She had a "vision of America in which she believed that God had a chosen people in America." In 1774, she and eight of her followers arrived in Albany and then New Lebanon, New York, where they built their first meetinghouse. The Shaker movement grew to include communities in Connecticut, Massachusetts, New Hampshire, Maine, and in 1805, Kentucky and Ohio. Music was important in their culture as a means of expressing their faith. From Mother Ann they received a number of songs that had been revealed to her in visions. She also received through visions her own system of musical notation used by the Shakers. Singing, dancing, shaking, running, leaping—all these were means by which the Shakers expressed the joy of their religious faith. A famous Shaker song is "The Gift To Be Simple."

LEHMAN, J. F. (1840–). (Can.) Important for his earliest publication of a song in sheet music format with piano accompaniment—"The Merry Bells of England."

LEHMAN, PAUL R. (1931–). Served as president of the **Music Educators National Conference** (MENC), 1984–1986. Chair of MENC's National Commission on Instruction, which produced *The School Music Program: Description and Standards*. Commission formed to implement the recommendation of the **Tanglewood Symposium (GO Project)**. Lehman also served as chair of the **Ann Arbor Symposium** on Research in the Psychology of Music Learning (1978–1982), which provided the opportunity for music educators to meet with leading psychologists and learning theorists. The first two meetings focused on the applications of psychology to music teaching and learning, and the third meeting concentrated on motivation and creativity. Two of Lehman's influential books are *Tests and Measurement in Music* (1968) and *The Sesquicentennial Music in Our Schools: The First 150 Years* (MCJ, Feb. 1981). Lehman was recognized as a Lowell Mason Fellow in 2002 and inducted into the **Music Educators Hall of Fame** in 2000.

LEONHARD, CHARLES (1915–2002). An American music educator and academic; first to argue for a focus on **aesthetic education** within **music education**. Most of his career was spent as a professor at the University of Illinois at Urbana-Champaign. He was the primary adviser on nearly 100 doctoral dissertations, including those of **Eunice Boardman**, **Wayne Bowman**, and **Bennett Reimer**.

As a doctoral student at Teachers College of Columbia University, many of his teachers were former students of **John Dewey**, whose ideas influenced him throughout his career. Leonhard studied aesthetics with **Susanne Langer**.

In 1953, as the music-education profession was beginning to rethink its philosophy, Leonhard published his article "Music Education—Aesthetic Education." He urged music educators to avoid the use of the "instrumental values" of music education and to stress the aesthetic value of music. Along with his student Robert House, Leonhard published *Foundations and Principles of Music Education* in 1959, with a second edition in 1972. It was this book that promoted emphasis on the "unique role of music education as a part of aesthetic education. . . . The music education program should be primarily aesthetic education" (Leonhard and House, p. 116).

In the 1970s, Leonhard edited a series of books called *Contemporary Perspectives on Music Education*. The series aimed to establish "a pattern for music teacher education based on the areas of knowledge and processes involved in music education rather than on the levels and specializations in music education." Six titles were published in this series of books. One of these, *A Philosophy of Music Education*, by his student Bennett Reimer, "succeeded in articulating what were then the emerging philosophical premises of modern music education" (C. Leonhard).

Many important philosophers of music education can trace their lineage back to Charles Leonhard. For example, Bennett Reimer, his student at the University of Illinois, who worked with Leonhard and **Harry Broudy**. In 1986 Leonhard retired from his position at the University of Illinois. In 1988 he was appointed the director of research at the National Arts Education Research Center.

In 1994, the **Music Educators National Conference** (MENC) placed Leonhard's name alongside those of William Billings, **Lowell Mason**, **Frances Elliott Clark**, **Karl Gehrkens**, **Mabelle Glenn**, **James Mursell**, **Lila Belle Pitts**, and **Allen Britton** in the **Music Educators Hall of Fame**. George N.

Heller wrote Leonhard's biography, *Charles Leonhard: American Music Educator*, published in 1995 by the Scarecrow Press.

Lit.: Heller, G. N., *Charles Leonhard: American Music Educator*, 1995.

LESCARBOT, MARC (1570–1641). A French author, poet, and lawyer, best known for his *Histoire de la Nouvelle-France* (1609), based on his expedition to Acadia (former French colony in southeastern Canada) (1606–1607) and research into French exploration. It is considered to be one of the first great books in the history of Canada, printed in three editions, translated into German and twice into English.

LETTERS TO PAT **(1953).** A professional book for midlevel school music teachers who teach boys' changing voices in their classrooms. This small, paperback book was written by **Irvin Cooper**; its design is similar to the format of *Gradus ad Parnassum*, in which Cooper exchanges letters with his music teacher's nephew on how to discern and work with the boy's changing voice, including the kinds of literature appropriate for the early adolescent voice.

LIFE GUARDS. (UK.) A cavalry regiment of the British Household Brigade, distinguished by their scarlet uniform, jackets, and white helmet plumes.

LINDEMAN, CAROLYNN A. (1940–). A past president of **MENC** (NA*f*ME), 1996–1998, she has been actively involved in the promotion of music education throughout the United States, Canada, Europe, Southeast Asia, Mexico, South Africa, and Israel. She serves on the board of directors for the International Society for Music Education and on the National Committee of Examiners in Music for the Educational Testing Service. Lindeman is a widely published author of more than 50 articles on music education and several books—including, with Patricia Hackett, *The Musical Classroom: Backgrounds, Models, and Skills for Elementary Teaching*, and *PianoLab: An Introduction to Class Piano.* She has also been a series editor for 23 publications related to MENC (1995–2002). Lindeman was a member of the Music Writing Committee that produced the 14-volume *Strategies for Teaching* series, (MENC, 1995–2002). She was also appointed by President Clinton to the President's Advisory Committee on the Arts. Lindeman is a graduate of Oberlin, the Mozarteum Academy, San Francisco State University, and Stanford University, from which she earned a DMA. Until her retirement, she was a professor of music at San Francisco State University. She has recently been appointed to the next generation of music standards committee for MENC—the Music Writing Team, **National Coalition for Core Arts Standards**.

LINING OUT. The practice of singing psalm tunes in which a line of psalm was read by deacon or precentor, who provided the pitch for its tune, and the congregation repeated the line to a prescribed tune that was a part of their memorized repertoire. "Lining out" was a tradition in England and in the New World for those who could not read music.

LISTENING. There are basically two ways of listening to music, sonorously and perceptively. Sonorous listening tends to be purely emotive. Perceptive listening involves focusing on specific musical events in melody, rhythm, harmony, and form.

LISTENING GUIDES. In order for students to listen to music perceptively, teachers develop guidelines for listening experiences. These guidelines may include mapping (linear icons), written listening guides that ask students to answer questions regarding the elements of music in specific compositions, and the use of chart information to follow while listening to a musical composition.

LITTLE, WILLIAM. *See* SHAPE-NOTE.

LLATAI. (UK-Wales.) A less-common trait of love songs in Welsh folk song is the device of sending a bird as a messenger of love. This is called *llatai* in classical Welsh poetry, but it is also popular among folk poets. The chosen messenger is usually a blackbird—but some have sent a nightingale, a lark, or some little mountain birds.

LOCAL EDUCATION AUTHORITIES (LEA). (UK.) The basic political entity for operating schools in England and Wales. England's LEAs correspond to other political subdivisions—counties, metropolitan districts, and London boroughs. Currently, LEAs must be responsive, rather than resistant, to the demands for change in education.

LOMAX, ALAN (1915–2002). (U.S.) Folklorist and musicologist, who as a writer and producer spent his life capturing in sound, photograph, video, and research what today is termed our "intangible heritage." The central value of his career was the promotion of cultural equity as the right of every culture to express and develop its distinctive heritage, believing it should be recognized as a fundamental human right. Lomax's search to find and record songs and singers took him on lengthy journeys through the rural southern U.S. to farms, churches, small nightclubs, and prison farms. Lomax found and documented an American folk heritage with the blues steeped in African roots, and a Western heritage flavored with cowboy lore. He was the son of John Lomax.

LOOMIS, GEORGE BRACE (1833–1887). An American music teacher who began teaching in Indianapolis, Indiana; he was recommended for the position by **Lowell Mason**, a well-known American music educator, and worked for several years without instructional materials. In response to this void, he created *Loomis' Progressive Music Lessons*, a series of texts widely used in Indiana and surrounding states during the late 19th century. He later became the first superintendent of music in the Indianapolis system. Loomis was also one of the charter members of the Indiana Music Teachers Association, founded in 1877, one of the first such organizations in the country.

LUNDQUIST, BARBARA REEDER. (U.S.) Author of numerous articles on music education and systematic musicology, Lundquist is an internationally known author and clinician in multiethnic/multicultural music education. She has been president of the **College Music Society**, and has served on the CMS board and committees in various capacities. She has been a member of the executive boards of the **MENC Council for General Music** and the **Society for Music Teacher Education**, of the Standing Committee for Music Education of the **Society for Ethnomusicology**, and of the editorial board of Design for Arts in Education. She has served as curriculum consultant for music education in Malawi and Mozambique–Central Africa for the U.S. Information Service. Her research and curricular philosophy are featured in several articles within music-education publications.

LUTKIN, PETER CHRISTIAN (1858–1931). American music educator, organist, conductor, and composer. Main achievement was the founding and development of the Northwestern School of Music, of which he was the first dean. Founder of the American Guild of Organists (AGO) in 1896. Lutkin's compositions were mainly church music compositions, which were often sung by college/university choral groups.

LYNN REPORT (1922). (NIre.) Northern Ireland's first official report on education; considered the foundation of today's bilateral school system. Its central purpose was to recommend the structure for a national school system of the "new" nation. Recommended three kinds of schools for primary children: local authority (state schools); partially controlled state schools; voluntary schools, independent of state control. Funding was available for all but the voluntary schools. These eventually became Catholic schools.

   Bib.: Green, James E., *Education in the United Kingdom and Ireland*, 2001.

MACMILLAN PUBLISHING CO. There are two companies by this name:

1. MacMillan Publishers, LTD, owned by Georg von Holtzbrinck Publishing Group, founded in 1843 in the UK. From the beginning, they published major writers such as Yeats, Walpole, and C. P. Snow. Also published the *Grove Dictionary of Music and Musicians* (1877). In 1954, it became known in the U.S. as St. Martin's Press. Eventually sold to Holtsbrinck, which then ended the MacMillan family ownership.
2. MacMillan Publishing became an American company in 1896 and was renamed the MacMillan Company. This company split from its parent company in Britain, and George Brett Jr. then served as publisher of works by Winston Churchill, Margaret Mitchell, and Jack London. After mergers and acquisitions, *MacMillan Publishers USA* became the name of Simon & Schuster's reference division. Pearson then acquired the MacMillan name in 1998. It was sold to Thomas Gale in 1999. McGraw-Hill continues to market its prekindergarten through elementary school titles under its MacMillan/McGraw-Hill brand. MacMillan Publishing USA is now mostly defunct.

MACRONIC VERSE. (UK.) Incorporates words of the writer's native tongue into a work in another language and subjects them to its grammatical laws, thus achieving a comic effect. Loosely speaking, the term has also been applied to any verse mingling two or more languages together.
   Lit.: Preminger, Alex, ed., *Princeton Handbook of Poetic Terms*, 1986.

MADDY, JOSEPH EDGAR (1891–1966). The 25th president of **MENC**, whose philosophy, "mutual understanding through music is the first step in promoting mutual understanding of all peoples," permeated his life and work as a teacher, performer, and administrator. Most remember him as the cofounder, president, and director of the Interlochen Arts Academy. He was primarily involved in orchestral teaching, as well as several publications: *Willis Graded School Orchestra, Graded Orchestra Series No. 4, Standard*

Orchestra Folio, and *Symphonic String Course*. He was also a professor of public school music at the University of Michigan, 1930–1938.

MADELINE COLLEGE. (UK.) Music school at Oxford, which has awarded degrees in music since 1499.

MADRIGAL. Vocal composition of Italian origin for several voices, usually unaccompanied, but sometimes with instrumental accompaniment. Texts usually secular, but there are also *madrigali spirituali*. Madrigals first sung in Italy toward the end of the 13th century. Early Italian composers: Jacopo da Bologna, Lassus, Palestrina, Monteverdi. English composers in late 1500s and 1600s: Byrd, Morley, Weelkes, and Wilbye.

MADRIGAL SOCIETY (1741). Founded in London by the elder John Immyns, this association has met regularly for the performance of English and foreign madrigals by its members for their own enjoyment. Briefly interrupted during the WWII aerial bombing of London. Originally known as the *Monday Night Club*, for the night on which it first met.

MADSEN, CLIFFORD. Distinguished professor of music, coordinator of music education/music therapy/contemporary media at Florida State University, Tallahassee. Teaches music education, music therapy, research, and psychology of music. He serves on various international and national editorial and research boards, and he is widely published throughout scholarly journals in music education and therapy. He has authored and coauthored many books, and is best known for his prolific research publications on music education and music therapy. He has been a member of the FSU faculty since 1961.

THE MAGNA CARTA OF MUSIC EDUCATION (1838). A vote passed by the Boston School Board that permitted the committee on music to contract with a vocal music teacher to teach in several Boston public schools. **Lowell Mason** (1792–1872) was hired to fill this position. It is considered by many to be *the beginning of public school music education in America*. Its real significance was the fact that music was included in the curriculum by a public authority.

MAIDSTONE MOVEMENT (1897–1939). (UK.) A movement toward instrumental class instruction as a result of the formation of the first violin class in Maidstone, England, ca. 1897. The G. J. Murdock Company, a publisher and instrument manufacturer, supported the movement by supplying instruments, music, and other equipment. Students were charged a small amount to participate. Many children, including poor children, participated in the program. The Murdock Company formed the Maidstone School Orchestra Association (MSOA) to promote this method of teaching. This movement is considered to be an influential British precursor of American public school instrumental classes, after **Albert G. Mitchell** visited England in 1910. In 1911 he formed the first public school violin class in the United States. Although the movement does not appear to have had a significant *methodological* impact on American instrumental classes in general, widely circulated reports of the Maidstone movement motivated school music educators throughout the U.S. to develop their own group instrumental programs. *See also* CLASS METHOD FOR VIOLIN.

MAINSTREAMING. As a result of Public Law 94-142, the **Education for All Handicapped Children Act of 1975**, students who might be classified as handicapped or disabled, or learning disabled, were placed in regular classrooms for all or part of the school day. Music classes were subject to this law as well.

THE MANHATTANVILLE MUSIC CURRICULUM PROJECT (MMCP). A program whose purpose was to develop a sequential music-learning program for primary and secondary school students. It was funded by the U.S. Department of Education in 1965–1970 and was named for Manhattanville College, where it originated. The MMCP was influential in developing comprehensive musicianship in school music programs. Its premise, developed by **Ronald Thomas**, was that learning is based on a spiral curriculum, as described in **Jerome Bruner**'s theory of learning. A book by Ronald B. Thomas, *MMCP Synthesis*, describes this spiral approach in the teaching and learning of music. MMCP was not widely used in its original form, but the concepts and strategies have often been adapted for use in traditional school music programs.

THE MAPLE LEAF FOREVER. (Can.) One of Canada's two national anthems, written by **Alexander Muir**. The song speaks of the origins of Canadians: the thistle of Scotland, the shamrock of Ireland, and the red rose of England. Canada's coat of arms uses the coats of arms of England, Scotland, Ireland, and France on its shield. Three maple leaves represent Canada. The other national anthem, "O Canada," is used by French Canadians.

MARCHING BAND. (U.S.) A group of instrumentalists, usually brass, woodwinds, and percussion, that plays for marching or open-air performances. Originating in the military, it began to appear in schools around the turn of the 20th century. The key figure in this movement was **Albert Austin Harding**, who became director of the University of Illinois band in 1905 as head of the Department of Bands. At Illinois, Harding developed creative field maneuvers, including the forming of words while marching and playing. According to **Richard Colwell**, the marching band has been the vehicle through which instrumental programs (including the orchestra) have flourished, obtaining equipment, music, building space, professionally trained teachers, and public attention. The marching band, though not strictly a playing organization, plays enough so that there are opportunities to teach some music, technique, range, breathing, endurance, and understanding. School marching bands are found from late elementary to high school, colleges, and universities.

MARIACHI OR CONJUNTO. (Known as *mariachi* in California and the Southwest, and as *conjunto* in Texas.) A form of traditional Mexican-American dance music, as played by a group of strolling players dressed in native costumes. Consists of violins, guitarrón (large guitar), a short five-string rhythmic guitar called a *vihuela*, and a six-string guitar, trumpets, and Mexican percussion instruments, particularly marimba.

MARIE DE CHAUVIGNY DE LA PELTRIE. *See* MARIE DE L'INCARNATION.

MARIE DE L'INCARNATION (1599–1672); MARIE DE CHAUVIGNY DE LA PELTRIE (1603–1671). (Can.) Two nuns who founded the **Ecole des Ursulines** and the Ursuline Convent. These were North America's oldest schools and the first institutions of learning for women in North America in 1639. They were the first Canadian institutions to have music as part of the curriculum.

MARI LWYD (GRAY MARE). (UK-Wales.) Some of the oldest songs in Welsh tradition are probably those associated with calendric customs. Around the winter solstice, farm work was suspended so people could indulge in seasonal festivities, including a horse ceremony (*Mari Lwyd*, or "Gray Mare") in which a party outside sang to gain admittance, and defenders inside answered in song.

MARIMBA. A musical instrument in the percussion family. It consists of a set of wooden bars with resonators. The bars are struck with mallets to produce musical tones. The bars are arranged as those of a piano, with the accidentals raised vertically and overlapping the natural bars to aid the performer both visually and physically. This instrument is a type of xylophone, but with broader and lower tonal range and resonators. A classroom instrument designed by **Carl Orff**, but referred to as bass **xylophones** (wood) and **metallophone** (metal).

MARITIME PROVINCES. (Can.) Also called the *Maritimes* or the *Canadian Maritimes*, this is a region of eastern Canada consisting of three provinces: New Brunswick, Nova Scotia, and Prince Edward Island.

MARK, MICHAEL. A graduate of the Catholic University of America (CUA), Mark taught music in Maryland public schools and was supervisor of music in two New York school districts before earning his DMA from CUA as the first music-education student to graduate with this degree. He received his master's degree in 1962 at the University of Michigan. He continued in higher education as a music professor, and as dean of Towson University's graduate school. In his retirement, he has written numerous articles and 13 books on music, including the popular *A History of American Music Education* with Charles L. Gary, now in its third edition. In 2004, Mark was inducted into the **Music Educators Hall of Fame** for his distinguished teaching career and for his prolific publications on music education.

MASLOW, ABRAHAM (1908–1970). Credited with the initial development of third-force psychology, which is sometimes referred to as *humanistic psychology*. This view was in opposition to associationist psychology with its broader view of the study of man, which includes motivation, affect, creativity, and general fulfillment of human potential. Maslow's primary contribution is in his theory of motivation, found in his two books: *Motivation and Personality* (1970) and *Toward a Psychology of Being* (1968). He does not provide a theory of learning, but does provide general information as to the desired characteristics of the learning situation. Emphases include encouraging the desire to learn, learning how to learn, adaptability to changing situations, and self-evaluation. The role of the arts and music is most important, and it is this rationale that prompted Maslow to regard music education as intrinsic, basic, and as belonging at the core of educational experience.

MASON, LOWELL (1792–1872). A gifted composer, conductor, and teacher who traveled widely and applied himself to the training of teachers. Mason believed that the music teacher must be a master of his subject matter—a person cannot teach what he does not know. A comprehensive musical approach should be used, including composition, history of music, theory, and an adequate philosophy of music education. To illustrate this philosophy, he organized the New York Normal Institute for professional development of teachers of music.

Mason is often referred to as the *Father of Music Education* in the U.S., because of his early work as a teacher of music for a year without pay in the Boston schools to convince the Boston School Board that children could learn to sing and enjoy it. As a result of his efforts, music was officially added to the Boston schools curriculum. He incorporated the **Pestalozzian** principles of teaching singing using his book *Manual of Instruction*. This was the beginning of modern principles of teaching music to the youth of the U.S. public schools. Mason also supervised music in all Boston grammar schools, and became the first supervisor of public school music in the history of the world.

Not only was Mason involved in public schools, but also his composing and conducting of church music for choirs, choral societies, and congregational singing made him one of the foremost church musicians in America. Lowell Mason's influence on American musical life was profound and long lasting.

MASON, LUTHER WHITING (1818–1896). Often confused with Lowell Mason, Luther may have been a distant relative. He studied with Lowell Mason at the Boston Academy of Music, and then became a music teacher in Louisville schools in 1853. In 1856, he moved to Cincinnati, where he invented the National System of music charts and books, which had instant success and made him famous. He settled in Boston in 1864, and reformed instruction in the primary schools. In 1880, he was invited by the Japanese government to supervise music in the schools of Japan, where he taught for three years with notable results. (School music in Japan was termed *Mason-song*.) He spent some time in Germany perfecting his principal work, *The National Music Course*. His fundamental purpose was to demonstrate that every child can sing. Mason surrounded children with beautiful song literature, as well as a musical background, in order to develop in them a sense of taste and appreciation.

MASSACHUSETTS BAND. Formed in Boston in 1783, it was known from about 1812 as the **Green Dragon Band**, changing its name again in about 1820 to the **Boston Brigade Band**. It was this band that in 1859 became **Gilmore's Band**, the first great American band and undoubtedly one of the finest that has ever played.

MASTER CLASS. A lesson, usually in music, given by a virtuoso to a small group of gifted students and taking the form of performances by the students while the **master teacher** comments.

MASTER TEACHER. Formally, a title used to label a music educator who, through academic completion, educational achievement, political appointment, or peer election, has been identified as being qualified to assist others inside or out of the discipline. Informally, used to refer to a music educator who consistently exhibits and demonstrates certain qualities and characteristics when engaged in the music teaching-learning process—these qualities and characteristics include knowing who master teachers are as a person as differentiated from who they are as a teacher; knowing the qualities, needs, dynamics, and characteristics of varied individuals and groups; knowing the discipline of music and appropriate content and pedagogy for a specific age or level of individual or group; and knowing the sociocultural characteristics within which they provide instructional leadership. Such *knowing* is evident in a master teacher through his high level of proficiency in adjusting and modifying instruction throughout the music teaching-learning process, thus enabling a high level of musical development individually and/or collectively; apart from formal considerations, a master music teacher is recognized by peers as being without equal.

(Entry by **Michael Jothen**, Nov. 2012.)

MAYDAY GROUP. (Can.) An international community of scholars and practitioners with a twofold purpose: (1) to apply critical theory and critical thinking to the purposes and practices of music education, and (2) to affirm the central importance of musical participation in human life and, thus, the value of music in the general education of all people. *ACT* (**A**ction, **C**riticism, **T**heory for Music Education) is the MayDay Group's scholarly, refereed e-journal. It invites critical, analytical, theoretical, and policy-development articles of international interest that illuminate, extend, or challenge the action ideals of the MayDay Group.

MBIRA. Sometimes called a *thumb piano*. *See also* LAMELLAPHONE.

MCALLISTER, A. R. (ARCHIE RAYMOND) (1883–1944). Music educator and band director. Around 1912, McAllister instituted in Joliet, Illinois, a band program whose reputation for excellence continued for half a century. In 1926, the first national band contest sponsored by the **Music Supervisors National Conference**, held in Fostoria, Ohio, was won by McAllister's band from Joliet (Illinois) Township High School.

MCBETH, W. FRANCIS (1933–2012). A prolific American composer whose wind band works are highly respected. His primary musical influences included Clifton Williams, Bernard Rogers, and Howard Hanson. The popularity of his works in the U.S. during the last half of the 20th century led to many invitations and appearances as a guest conductor, where he often conducted the premier performances of some of his compositions, the majority of which were commissioned. His conducting activities took him to 48 states, three Canadian provinces, Japan, and Australia. At one time, his "double pyramid balance system" was a widely used pedagogical tool in the concert band world.

McBeth spent most of his career (1957–1996) at Ouachita Baptist University, Arkansas, until his retirement in 1996. Major awards include: ASCAP Special Award annually for more than 30 consecutive years; the Howard Hanson Prize of the Eastman School of Music for his *Third Symphony*; and the John Philip Sousa Foundation's Sudler Medal of Honor in 2000.

Bib.: Colwell, Richard J., *Basic Concepts in Music Education II*, 1991, pp. 104–6.

MCBURNEY, SAMUEL (1847–1909). Born in Scotland, died in Melbourne, music educator, **tonic sol-fa** advocate. Early training in tonic sol-fa, with degrees from Trinity College in Dublin. Immigrated to Victoria in 1870, and after public school teaching became principal of Geelong Ladies College. He published numerous school textbooks, songbooks, choral works, and articles. After touring eastern Australia, the U.S., and the UK promoting tonic sol-fa, he gained approval for this approach in state schools and was appointed as inspector of music, Victorian Department of Education. He later taught at the University of Melbourne Conservatorium of Music.

MCCARTHY, MARIE. (Ire.) A general music specialist who has taught at all levels, from elementary and secondary classes to the University of Maryland and the University of Michigan. Her teaching has included elementary and secondary music methods, research methods in music education, and music-teacher education. Her research studies have focused on the sociocultural and sociohistorical foundations of music education. Her current research interests include the application of sociological perspectives to music-transmission contexts, and exploration of the spiritual dimensions of arts education.

Dr. McCarthy received undergraduate preparation in Limerick, Ireland, and the University College of Dublin. Graduate degrees are from the University of Michigan. She has written numerous articles for major music-education journals, including the *Journal of Research in Music Education*. Two of her major book publications are *Passing It On* and *Toward a Global Community: The International Society for Music Education*, *1953–2003*.

A former public school teacher in Ireland, she has received numerous awards. She has also served as chair of the Music Education Department at the University of Michigan, and is currently serving as chair of the International Society for Music Education.

MCCARTHY, MARY. (Can.) In the fall of 1904, McCarthy, a local music teacher, asked permission to address the school board in Moncton, New Brunswick, Canada, "in respect to the introduction of the systematic instruction in music into the schools of the city." The board received her suggestion favorably, and she began work on a six-month trial basis in January 1905. She requested no materials other than a staff-lined blackboard for each school building. The experiment proved so successful that she continued in the position until 1915, when she retired and was replaced first by Blanche O'Brien and later by Bertha Flanagan. McCarthy was praised by the school board for her outstanding work. She placed emphasis on singing as an enjoyable experience, but also included drills in **tonic sol-fa** and gave theory tests. The chief superintendent noted the work of Mary McCarthy and stated that Moncton had the distinction of being the first place in the province "to provide regular instruction in vocal music to all the pupils of the schools, by employing permanently a professional teacher for that subject."

MCCONATHY, OSBORNE (1875–1947). A gifted music educator, author, and conductor, he became the 12th president of **MENC**. He was also president of **MTNA** (1922), **NEA** (National Education Association), and chair of the **Music Education Research Council**. He was an early advocate of allowing high school credit for private study of music. McConathy believed that "every child should be educated in music according to his natural capacities, at public expense, and his studies should function in the musical life of the community." He also thought that every child has the capacity to enjoy and participate in music. McConathy was author and coauthor of several books on the teaching of music, including the popular *The Music Hour*, published by **Silver Burdett**. He studied school music with **Luther Whiting Mason**.

MCKENZIE (MCKENSIE), DUNCAN. (Scot.-Can.) Born in Scotland and moved to Canada as a young man. A public school teacher in Montreal and on the staff of McGill Conservatory. Later he became the director of public schools in Toronto. McKenzie was best known for his pioneering work with the boy's changing voice. His book, *Training the Boy's Changing Voice* (1956), introduced the controversial alto-tenor concept in allowing boys to sing through puberty. Following this writing were two other pioneers in the training of mutational voices: **Frederick Swanson** and **Irvin Cooper**. McKenzie's description of the alto-tenor is as follows: "The term was applied not only to the voice but also to the part. The voice is still alto, but it has lowered to the extent that the boy can sing in the tenor range; the quality, however, has not yet become masculine, that is, either tenor or bass." *See also* ALTO-TENOR PLAN.

MCPHERSON, GARY. (Aus.) Professor and chair of music, and also head of the School of Music at the University of Melbourne. A multifaceted music professional whose career includes performances as a trumpeter and conductor throughout Australia. As a researcher and writer, his work involves studies in motivation for music among young people, and several longitudinal studies of music learning in Australia and the U.S. His academic teaching areas include music education, research techniques, music psychology, performance science, and musicianship. Former president of both the **Australian** and the **International Society for Music Education**. His current project includes the coediting of the *Oxford Handbook of Music Education*, which includes over 90 chapters and a website that updates and redefines music-education practice internationally. As of this writing, it is in process.

MELBA, DAME NELLIE (1861–1931). (Aus.) Born *Helen "Nellie" Porter Mitchell*, in 1887 she adopted her stage name, *Melba*, in tribute to her native city, Melbourne. One of the most outstanding singers of opera's "Golden Age," and one of the two most famous musicians produced by Australia, she appears on the Australian $100 banknote. Melba studied with Picho Ceechi and Mathilda Marchosi, whose vocal method is still used today with young singers. Her artistic "home" was Covent Garden, where between 1888 and 1923, *The Times* advertised on 355 occasions her appearance that day in a complete opera. Of her 25 operatic roles, the most important, except Lucia, were studied with their composer: Marguerite, Juliette, Ophelia, Mimi, and Gilda. She also studied Manon with Massenet and Lakmé with Delibes. Of her voice there was near-unanimous praise; as the great critic W. J. Henderson wrote, "It had splendour. The tones glowed with a star-like brilliance. The scale was beautifully equalized throughout and there was not the slightest change in the quality from bottom to top. All the tones were forward; there was never even a suspicion of throatiness."

From 1904, when she was 42 and vocally past her prime, she made numerous commercial recordings, although the primitive technology was incapable of preserving adequately the quality of her voice. Among her writings, she published *The Melba Method* in 1926, and was created DBE in 1918 and GBE in 1927.

MELE. (Aus., U.S.) A Hawaiian poetic text and its vocalization: *mele hula*, singing with dancing; *mele oli*, singing without dancing.

MELODEON. (UK.) Friction-bar keyboard instrument; steel bars are pressed against a revolving cylinder in place of strings; invented by J. C. Dietz in the early 19th century; also a small reed organ (1840–1850 U.S.).

MELODY BELLS. A series of chromatically tuned metal bars mounted horizontally on a frame in the form of a piano keyboard. Smaller sets contain pitches ranging from C to G. Uses wooden or metal mallets.

MEMBRANOPHONE. The oldest of all instruments that produce sound by a vibrating membrane. The group consists most notably of the timpani or kettledrums, which can be tuned by increasing or decreasing the tension of the membranes that form the heads of the enclosed cavities. Other membranophones consist of drums *without* fixed pitch, such as side drums, bongos, and various non-Western types with indefinite pitch. Tone quality and character are the result of the player's skill in controlling intensity and overtone character of the sound. Even though original instruments have a playing area made of stretched animal skin (membrane), today many of these instruments use plastic instead of skin. *See also* PERCUSSION INSTRUMENTS.

MEMPHIS SOUND. This Memphis style (1960) originated at Stax Records, where multiracial studio bands and songwriting teams joined forces. These artists mixed a Memphis "stew" of rhythm and blues (R&B), country, rock and roll (R&R), and the raw emotion of gospel that resulted in the "Memphis soul sound." Memphis soul is known as *Memphis sound*. It is stylish, funky, uptown soul music; a shimmering, sultry style produced in the 1960s and 1970s and featuring melodic unison horn lines, organ bass, and a driving beat on the drums. After the rise of disco in the late 1970s, Memphis soul declined somewhat in popularity.

MENC. *See* MUSIC EDUCATORS NATIONAL CONFERENCE.

MENC EDUCATIONAL COUNCIL (1918–1923). Responsible for publishing materials related to music education. *See also* MUSIC EDUCATION RESEARCH COUNCIL (MERC).

MENC: NATIONAL ASSOCIATION FOR MUSIC EDUCATION (1998–2011). *See* NATIONAL ASSOCIATION FOR MUSIC EDUCATION (NA*f*ME).

MENDELSSOHN SOCIETY (1858). (UK.) The untimely death of Mendelssohn shocked the world, and as a result Mendelssohn societies were formed all over the world; in the U.S., the Mendelssohn Quartet Club was formed (1849); a Mendelssohn Scholarship was established in England (1856), and its first recipient was Arthur Sullivan, of Gilbert and Sullivan fame.

THE MERRY BELLS OF ENGLAND. (Can.) One of the earliest surviving publications in Canada of a song for the piano in sheet music format, published by **J. F. Lehman** in 1840.

METALLOPHONE. A percussion instrument consisting of a graduated series of metal bars struck with either handheld or keyboard-controlled hammers.

MIDDLE SCHOOLS. (UK.) Nearly all middle schools in the United Kingdom are found in England. Wales has only one local education authority that offers a middle school, and Scotland has none. Though the age range of children in middle schools varies widely, a middle school enrolling children 8–12 years is classified as a primary school, whereas children 10–14 is considered a secondary school. Some middle schools enroll children 9–13, and they might be classified as either primary or secondary, depending on the local authority's preference.

MID-WEST CLINIC. 1946: *Band Clinic*—Approximately 120 directors from the Chicago area met for a six-hour clinic and reading session for new music. As a result of this event, the clinic expanded each year by adding more days, and a variety of clinics and performances. It has been renamed several times to reflect the expanded nature of its conferences. 1947: *Mid-West Band Clinic*. 1951: *Mid-West National Band Clinic*. 1968: *Mid-West National Band and Orchestra Clinic*. 1986: *Mid-West International Band and Orchestra Clinic*. 1996: *Mid-West Clinic: An International Band and Orchestra Conference*.

It is now attended by some 17,000 people from 36 countries. The focus of the Mid-West Clinic has continued to be on bringing music directors into contact with the best published music, teaching new techniques, and offering the latest in products and services for the music educator.

MILITARY BAND. (UK.) In 1663, the fifes and trumpets of the French army were replaced by *hautbois* (oboes), and shortly after, they were fixed as four for each company. This practice was copied by the British Army, and the year 1678 is considered the year of the institution of the military band in England by the first official recognition in the army of instruments other than fifes, trumpets, and drums.

MILITARY BAND "JOURNALS." (UK.) In the middle of the 19th century, military band "journals" offered regular publication of music arranged and edited by notable bandmasters, the result being that a standard system of instrumentation was adopted. Along with this important occurrence was the formation of a Military Music Class at **Kneller Hall** in 1857.

THE MILLER AND HIS LASS. (UK.) One of many English songs that can be traced back to the later Middle Ages and that survive into the present.

MINIMALISM. 1. A school of composition, influenced by **John Cage** and contemporaneous painting of the 1950s, in which a pointillistic musical texture prevails. **2.** From the 1960s, a term denoting work based on repetition and gradual alteration of short rhythmic and/or melodic figures; also referred to as *process music*. Two American pioneers of this school were Steve Reich and Philip Glass.

MINISTERIAL COUNCIL FOR EDUCATION, EARLY CHILDHOOD DEVELOPMENT AND YOUTH AFFAIRS (MCEECDYA). (Aus.) *See* STANDING COUNCIL ON SCHOOL EDUCATION AND EARLY CHILDHOOD (SCSEEC).

MINISTERIAL COUNCIL FOR VOCATION AND TECHNICAL EDUCATION (MCVTE). (Aus.) *See* STANDING COUNCIL ON SCHOOL EDUCATION AND EARLY CHILDHOOD (SCSEEC).

MINISTERIAL COUNCIL ON EDUCATION, EMPLOYMENT, TRAINING AND YOUTH AFFAIRS (MCEETYA). (Aus.) *See* STANDING COUNCIL ON SCHOOL EDUCATION AND EARLY CHILDHOOD (SCSEEC).

MITCHELL, ALBERT G. (1833–1916). Leader of the class violin movement in America. In 1910, he left his supervisory post in Boston for England, where he studied class violin instruction. Upon his return to Boston, he introduced the *Mitchell Class Method*, published by Oliver Ditson. Classes were held after school, and no fees were charged. Students provided their own violins. Later, Mitchell revised his book as a *Class Method for the Violin*. Dr. Mitchell adopted several mechanical aids to assist in instruction: nonslip pegs, metal first strings, paper fingerboard charts, and chin and shoulder rests.

MIXED A CAPPELLA. In the early part of the 20th century, the **a cappella** choir came into vogue. The mixed group at Northwestern University was the first to use the term *a cappella*. **Peter Christian Lutkin** developed this approach to be able to demonstrate how music of the Renaissance composers should be performed.

MONSOUR, SALLY (1931– 2013). (U.S.) Nationally known music consultant, lecturer, and clinician. Dr. Monsour served at Georgia State University in Atlanta from 1970 until her retirement in 1995 as professor emerita. A graduate of Manhattanville College (NY), Teachers College of Columbia University (NY), and the University of Michigan in Ann Arbor, her teaching experience included public schools in Winter Park, Florida, and Ann Arbor, Michigan. In higher education she concentrated on college methods courses at Rollins College (FL), the University of Michigan, and the University of Colorado at Boulder. In 1970 she began her 25-year tenure at Georgia State, where she initiated the music-education degree program.

Dr. Monsour traveled extensively throughout the U.S. and taught in Australia at the Conservatorium of Music in Sydney. She visited over 85 colleges, and 65 state, regional, and national music-educators meetings as guest lecturer or clinician. Monsour authored or coauthored several books and computer software programs, including: *Handbook for Teaching Junior High Music*, *Music in Recreation and Leisure*, and *Movement Experiences in the Primary Curriculum*. She was the editor of nine *Classroom Enrichment* books for the primary grades, as well as teaching strategies for the recordings on *Music of the Middle East*, published by **MENC**.

Her contributions to the field of music education have been notable. She was a consultant for the **Juilliard Repertory Project**; member of the resource team for Curriculum Development in Higher Education (NASM); member of the **Go Project** team for the National Assessment of Educational Progress; and vice president of the **College Music Society**. Dr. Monsour also served as the U.S. representative on the Commission on Music in the Schools and Teacher Education of the **International Society for Music Education**.

MONTESSORI, MARIA (1870–1952). First woman in Italy to receive a medical degree (MD). She worked in the fields of psychiatry, education, and anthropology. She believed that each child is born with a unique potential to be revealed, rather than as a "blank slate" waiting to be written upon. Her message to those who emulated her was always to turn one's attention to the child, to "follow the child." One of her main contributions to educating children was "the continual adapting of the environment in order that the child may fulfill his or her greatest potential physically, mentally, emotionally, and spiritually." This premise is also followed by music educators.

MOORE, THOMAS (1779–1852). (UK-Ire.) During a visit to Canada in 1894, Moore composed the poem used in the song "Canadian Boat Song." It became so popular that it was published several times over the next 20 years in Boston, New York, and Philadelphia.

MORAVIAN TEACHERS CHORAL MOVEMENT. The 19th century was a great age for amateur part-singing groups. In Czechoslovakia, the Moravian Teachers Choral Movement was recognized with high distinction for its involvement in choral music.

MORAVIUM COLLEGIUM MUSICUM. A society of Moravian citizens meeting to play and sing for their own pleasure. This term was in use in Germany in the 17th and 18th centuries. The primary purpose of a collegium musicum is to study music (particularly old music) by playing it, rather than to give public performances. Haydn's *Creation* was premiered by the Moravium Collegium Musicum in 1811, two years after his death.

MORGAN, HAZEL NOHAVEC. A distinguished editor, author, and teacher, and a recognized authority on graduate music education. She edited two major sourcebooks for **MENC** (1955) and served as MENC North Central Division president. Morgan was a member of the research council, executive committee, and editorial board of the *Music Educators Journal*.

MORGAN, RUSSELL VAN DYKE (1893–1952). A major contributor to **MENC**, he was national MENC president (1930–1932), a member of the editorial board of the *Music Educators Journal*, chairman of the **Music Education Research Council**, and a main force behind the first MENC Source Book. He also served communities involved in the arts, such as the Cleveland Orchestra and Cleveland Music School Settlement, and was a member of the Advisory Council on Music in the State Department. Morgan was supervisor of music in the Cleveland Public Schools, and was a longtime organist for the Old Stone Church (First Presbyterian) in Cleveland.

MORLAN, GENE (1917–2010). Supervisor of music in Shenandoah County, Virginia; was appointed assistant secretary to **Vanette Lawler** and was charged with moving material and equipment from Chicago to Washington when **MENC** was offered free space by the **National Education Association**. In the 1960s, Morlan, who for 30 years was director of professional programs for MENC, arranged to have many of the biannual and division meeting sessions available on cassette tapes. He was the founder, and director for 20 years, of the Mormon Choir of Washington, DC.

MORLY COLLEGE. (UK.) London College of Adult Education. Founded in the 1880s, it offers courses in a wide variety of fields, including drama, dance, and music. Located in the Waterloo district of London, on the South Bank, close to the city's arts center.

MORRIS DANCE. (UK.) A vigorous central and southern English dance, performed by costumed men wearing bells.

MORROBALAMA. (Aus.) An Australian Aboriginal language from the Princess Charlotte Bay area of the eastern coast of Cape York Peninsula; an endangered aboriginal language. Also *Umbuygamu.*

MOTET. Any of several distinct types of polyphonic composition in European art music; a variety of sacred or secular medieval works in which multiple voices simultaneously sing different verbal texts; a sacred work of the Renaissance and later, employing several voices that sing a single text not drawn from the Ordinary of the Mass.

MOTHER TONGUE. An important philosophy of both **Kodály** and **Suzuki** approaches is their concept of the "mother tongue."

1. Kodály: The "musical mother tongue" is found in the folk songs of a child's own linguistic heritage and should be a vehicle for all early instruction in learning music. The use of natural patterns of rhythm and melody are found in folk music of all cultures. Children, through folk music, can gain a sense of identity in the present and continuity with the past. Some adaptations and changes in syllables have been, and should be, made to compensate for the languages found in other countries, as well as in different localities in the United States.
2. Suzuki: The "mother tongue method" is based on the premise that all children learn to speak their own language with relative ease, and if the same natural learning process is applied in teaching other skills, these can be acquired as successfully. Suzuki referred to the process as the *mother tongue method* and to the whole system of pedagogy as ***talent education***.

See also SUZUKI TEACHING METHOD.

MOTIVATION. The will or incentive to learn. There are two sources considered: **1.** *Intrinsic motivation*, which comes from within the learner and typically offers the satisfaction gained by doing something for its own sake, as in discovering the pleasure of gaining and understanding or skill. **2.** *Extrinsic motivation* is motivation for learning that comes from the outside. This involves the use of rewards or sanctions by the teacher, such as praise, disapproval, or withholding of enjoyable learning activities.

MOTOR LEARNING. A process of learning through movement activities. Young children are usually involved in clapping, marching, running, jumping, and swaying from side to side. As they mature, activities include more thoughtful consideration of movement useful to developing skills in the playing of various instruments.

THE MOUNTAIN LAKE COLLOQUIUM FOR TEACHERS OF GENERAL MUSIC METHODS. (U.S.) Biennial gathering in Mountain Lake, Virginia, founded by Nancy Boone Allsbrook and **Mary Goetze** and sponsored by Middle Tennessee State University, the **Society for Music Teacher Education**, and **NAⳚME**: The National Association for Music Education.

MOUTH ORGAN. Colloquialism for **harmonica**.

MOUTHPIECE. A piece or part of an instrument to which the mouth is applied, or which is placed upon the lips (for brass instruments) or between the lips (for reed instruments), such as a trumpet.

MOUTHPIECE "PULLER." An indispensable aid to those who teach wind instruments requiring a brass mouthpiece, such as a trumpet. From beginners to professionals, a mouthpiece puller is a mechanical device similar in appearance to a workman's vise that attaches to a lead pipe to remove stuck mouthpieces. The "Bobcat" Mouthpiece Puller is often recommended. Fits most brass instruments.

MOVABLE DO[H]. A **solfège** method used to teach **sight singing**, in which the major diatonic scale is sung to the original syllables of **Guido of Arezzo**, with the leading tone designated by the syllable *ti*. With *movable doh*, the tonic note is also called *doh*, whatever the key.

MOVEMENT. 1. Tempo. **2.** Principal division or section of a musical composition.

MOZART EFFECT. 1. First described by French researcher Dr. Alfred A. Tomatis in his 1991 book *Porquoi Mozart?* (Why Mozart?). He used the music of Mozart in his efforts to "retrain" the ear, and believed that listening to the music presented at differing frequencies helped the ear; and promoted healing and the development of the brain. This research is ongoing. **2.** A set of research results that indicate that listening to Mozart's music may induce a short-term improvement on the performance of certain kinds of mental tasks, known as "spatial-temporal reasoning."

MP3. (MPEG-1, MPEG-2, Audio Layer III.) A patented encoding format for digital audio that uses a form of *lossy* data compression. It is a common audio format for consumer audio storage, as well as a de facto standard of digital audio compression for the transfer and playback of music on digital audio players.

MUIR, ALEXANDER (1830–1906). A Canadian songwriter, poet, soldier, and school headmaster. He was the composer of "The Maple Leaf Forever," which he wrote in October 1867 to celebrate the confederation of Canada. He was born in Lesmahagow, Scotland, but immigrated to Toronto (Can.), where he grew up and was educated by his father. A formal garden and park in Toronto, the Alexander Muir Memorial Gardens, are named in his honor.

MULTICULTURALISM. Of, relating to, reflecting, or adapted to diverse culture.

MULTICULTURAL PERSPECTIVES IN MUSIC EDUCATION. A book published by **MENC** in 1989, with an expanded second edition in 1996, edited by William M. Anderson and Patricia Campbell. A description of the world's culture and a collection of lessons for upper-elementary and secondary general music classes.

MULTIPLE INTELLIGENCES. A theory associated with **Howard Gardner**, who described seven intelligences in his book *Frames of Mind* (1983). An important part of the seven intelligences is his theory of musical intelligence.
    Lit.: Guilford, J. P., "The Structure of Intellect," *Psychological Bulletin* 53, no. 4 (July 1956).

MURSELL, JAMES LOCKHART (1893–1963). (Aus., UK, U.S.) An internationally famous author, music psychologist, philosopher, and distinguished teacher who has had a profound influence on music teaching and curriculum throughout the world. Mursell thought that all music-education experience should be conceived and taught in a process of musical growth. Of his 23 major publications from 1927 to 1956, one of the most important for music education is *Education of Musical Growth* (1948). His most fruitful years were spent at Columbia University Teachers College (1935–1958).

He wrote extensively about music education and the use of music in a classroom setting. He emphasized the student's role in learning and believed that unless students are intrinsically motivated to learn, their musical growth will be minimal at best. In Mursell's view, the best motivator is the active, participatory musical experience—singing, playing, listening, and being actively involved with good music. This is the all-important starting point for motivation, and it is from these experiences that musical growth can occur. He applies his "synthesis-analysis-synthesis" (or whole-part-whole) pattern of learning to music education, and speaks of musical understanding as "unfolding or evolving, rather than adding or accumulating." Instead of teaching the rudiments of music in isolation from the context that gives them meaning, Mursell *suggests that factual knowledge about music will gradually be gleaned from songs that students have learned and enjoy singing.* Each time they sing a particular song, they do something different with it and learn a little more about it. In this way their understanding of melody, rhythm, and dynamics deepens gradually as an outgrowth of meaningful music making, rather than drill and practice. At the end of each such activity, when students sing the song through once more, it means more to them that it did prior to their "analysis" of it.

MUSIC. The art of sound in time that expresses ideas and emotions in significant forms (as in organization) through the elements of rhythm, melody, harmony, and counterpoint.

MUSICAL. A term describing the desired outcome for each participant, or learner, as the result of music-education experiences; exhibiting sensitivity to and with the nuances of sound as presented in music; the condition which enables the shaping, refining, and presentation of sound for expressive purposes.

(Entry by **Michael Jothen**, Nov. 2012.)

MUSICAL ACHIEVEMENT TEST. Musical achievement is concerned with measuring what has been learned to date; its value is diagnostic. **Richard Colwell**'s book *The Evaluation of Music Teaching and Learning* (1970) emphasizes the importance of overlapping of cognitive and affective domains to help simplify the problems of measuring affective responses.

MUSICAL APTITUDE PROFILE (MAP). Considered to be the most widely used aptitude test in music education. Devised by **Edwin E. Gordon** in 1965, this test is to be used in grades four through 12 to measure musical aptitudes. It consists of three main sections: 1) tonal imagery, which includes melody and harmony; 2) rhythm imagery, which involves tempo and meter; and 3) musical sensitivity, which includes phrasing, balance, and style.

MUSICAL BOX. (Aus.) A box or case containing an apparatus for producing music mechanically, as by means of a comb-like steel plate with tuned teeth sounded by small pegs or pins in the surface of a revolving cylinder or disc. Also called a *music box.*

MUSICAL CHAIRS. (Aus.) A children's game in which the players walk to music around a number of chairs (one less than the number of players), with the object of finding a seat when the music stops. The player failing to find a seat is eliminated, and one chair is removed before the next round. A musical game found universally.

MUSICAL FOUNDATIONS OF MUSIC THERAPY. Music therapists use music's expressive, dynamic, evocative, stimulating, relaxing, and nonverbal qualities to achieve therapeutic goals. Music therapists must be qualified musicians and therapists.

MUSICAL FUTURES. (UK.) An initiative funded by the Paul Hamlyn Foundation that aimed to devise new and imaginative ways of engaging young people in music activities as an entitlement for 11- to 19-year-olds. It attempts to bring together formal education and informal learning. The work of Musical Futures in Britain is a sign of the renewal of general music, with its emphasis on informal learning and greater connection with popular music in the classroom.

MUSICAL GLASSES. *See* GLASS HARMONICA.

MUSICALLY EDUCATED PERSON. An individual possessing knowledge, understanding, skills, and attitudes encouraging interaction with music beyond the superficial; having the ability and desire to apply multiple musical intelligences, including performing, creating, evaluating, analyzing, listening, and relating music to other disciplines and historical and cultural contexts when encountering and/or engaging in musical experiences.
(Entry by **Michael Jothen**, Nov. 2012.)

MUSICAL SOCIETY OF LONDON (1858–1867). The society's purpose was to promote social interaction among its members and with other musicians nationally and internationally; to form a musical library for the use of members; to hold meetings in which papers on musical subjects could be read; and, among other activities, to give orchestral, choral, and chamber concerts. This was a splinter group of the New Philharmonic Society.

MUSIC AND MOVEMENT. (Aus.) Part of the Australian Research Council's national educational programs.

MUSIC APPRECIATION. A type of musical training designed to develop the ability to listen intelligently to music. This subject matter is usually found in high school and college general studies electives. Basically, this course is concerned with the study of music literature and its many types through guided listening and musical experiences. Guided listening may be through written graphs or maps that students can follow as they listen. It may include performances by students or by professionals. Music-appreciation classes may involve visual arts, literature, and a global-cultural history of man and his music. The focus, however, should always be on the music and not on the composer without the music. Students should be introduced to a wide repertoire of listening events with attention to the aesthetic and feelingful aspects of the music itself. Today's students have available a wide variety of electronic means of exploring music. Learning about music through the leadership of a sensitive and competent music teacher, students should develop a greater understanding of and sensitivity to expressiveness in music.

MUSIC AT LEEDS. (UK.) A music festival, principally choral, held in Yorkshire City of Leeds since 1858, when it marked the opening of town hall. Second festival held in 1874, third in 1880, after which it was held triennially until 1970. Some important works *first* performed were: Elgan's *Caractus* (1898) and *Falstaff* (1913), Vaughn Williams's *A Sea Symphony* (1910), Holst's *Choral Symphony* (1925), Walton's *Belshazzar's Feast* (1931), Britten's *Nocturne* (1958), and Blake's *Lumina* (1970).

MUSICA VIVA AUSTRALIA. A private Australian organization founded in 1945; primarily an entrepreneurial body promoting chamber music; considered the largest entrepreneurial organization in the world. Formerly *the Musica Viva Society*.

MUSICA VIVA IN SCHOOLS. (Aus.) **Musica Viva Australia** manages a touring program in 25 regional centers around Australia, at which the best Australian ensembles are featured, and presents an extensive schools-visit program featuring more than 25 ensembles annually.

MUSIC BATH. As Oliver Wendell Holmes (1809–1894) once said, "Take a music bath once or twice a week for a few seasons, and you will find that it is to the soul what the water bath is to the body."

MUSIC BOARD. (Aus.) A board of the Australian Council established in 1975.

MUSIC BOX. *See* MUSICAL BOX.

MUSIC EDUCATION. The acquisition and dissemination of knowledge about music through a variety of means in study, schooling, and experiential involvement. It is systematic and intentional toward synthesizing knowledge and understanding from music history, music theory, performance, and other disciplines such as learning theory, assessment, philosophy, psychology, sociology, and ethnomusicology for the purpose of assisting others in developing their musical potential.

    Bib.: Apel, Willi, *Harvard Dictionary of Music*, 2nd ed., 1973; Mark, Michael L., and Charles L. Gary, *A History of American Music Education*, 3rd ed., 2007; Reimer, Bennett, *A Philosophy of Music Education*, 2nd ed., 1989.

    Lit.: Leonhard, Charles, and Robert W. House, *Foundations and Principles of Music Education*, 2nd ed., 1972.

MUSIC EDUCATION COUNCIL (MEC). (UK.) The umbrella body for all organizations connected with music education in the United Kingdom. It exists to bring together and provide a forum for those organizations to debate issues affecting music education and to make representation and promote appropriate action at local, national, and international levels.

MUSIC EDUCATION JOURNALS. See separate listing in appendix B.

MUSIC EDUCATION RESEARCH COLLABORATIVE. (Can.) Focuses on regenerating music education in Canada through research and action in areas such as networking, leadership, new technologies, advocacy, inclusivity, and accessibility, and by seeking funding. It seeks to examine and promote music and arts education in Canada. Canadians are seen as the leaders in this initiative.

MUSIC EDUCATION RESEARCH COUNCIL (MERC). The governing body of the **Society for Research in Music Education**. MERC began as the **MENC Educational Council** in 1918, responsible for publishing materials related to music education. In 1923 the name was changed to the *National*

Research Council and eventually to the *Music Education Research Council* (MERC) in 1932.

MUSIC EDUCATION SOURCE BOOKS I (1947), II (1955), III (1966). Materials developed by **MENC** commissions after 1942. **Hazel Morgan** edited Book I, which contained ideas from some 2,000 members who had been involved in the project for five years. Eight years later (1955), another Source Book appeared, Book II: *Music in American Education*, also edited by Hazel Morgan. **Vanette Lawler** initiated the idea of a Book III, titled *Perspectives in Music Education*, published by MENC in 1966. This third Source Book includes theoretical and philosophical aspects of music education.

MUSIC EDUCATOR. One who intentionally organizes, implements, assesses, and refines instructional experiences in music for the purpose of assisting others in developing their musical understanding.
   (Entry by **Michael Jothen**, Nov. 2012.)

MUSIC EDUCATORS HALL OF FAME. Established by **MENC** in 1984 to honor those individuals who are considered the most highly regarded professional leaders in American music education. It is a means of preserving the most notable aspects of the heritage of music education in the United States. Any music educator may submit a nomination for the Hall of Fame. A letter of nomination should be no more than a page in length. It should summarize the most important contributions of the nominee to music education and explain why he or she deserves induction into the Hall of Fame. A letter of nomination for a living nominee may, but need not, be accompanied by a curriculum vitae. If it is submitted, the nominee will be given an opportunity to revise and update it. If none is submitted, the nominee will be invited by **NAfME** to submit one. A letter of nomination for a deceased nominee, however, must be accompanied by a curriculum vitae. No nomination will be considered until a curriculum vitae has been received.

MUSIC EDUCATORS JOURNAL **(MEJ).** Est. 1914. Now published by SAGE Publications on behalf of **NAfME**. Offers peer-reviewed scholarly and practical articles on music-teaching approaches and philosophies, instructional techniques, current trends, and issues in music education in schools and communities.

MUSIC EDUCATORS NATIONAL CONFERENCE (MENC) (1934–1998). *See* NATIONAL ASSOCIATION FOR MUSIC EDUCATION (NAfME).

MUSICIANS UNITED FOR SUPERIOR EDUCATION (MUSE). (U.S.) Founded in 1990 in Buffalo, New York, by **Charles Keil**. Interested in sociomusicology, he brought together artists, teachers, and parents committed to encouraging schoolchildren to participate actively in music. MUSE brings professional artists together with Buffalo-area children to get kids moving, drumming, and dancing. Physical activities strengthen their bodies, and as part of the process, they learn about diverse cultures, thus fostering cultural vitality in the community. The primary objective is to help children develop fundamental personal, social, leadership, academic, and artistic skills. MUSE teaching artists are among the region's top performers. The program surpasses the New York State Standards for music and dance education. Teaching artists share their professional experience and belief in the power of music and movement with the children.

MUSIC IN OUR SCHOOLS MONTH (MIOSM). This public outreach program designed to support school music programs and to highlight the importance of music education has been in effect since 1985, when it became a part of *Music in Our Schools* outreach initiatives. One of the highlights of the MIOSM program has been the performance of a selected choral piece by public school students throughout the U.S. at the same time and broadcast by cooperating radio stations.

MUSIC IN THE IRISH CURRICULUM. The arts, particularly music, are given a place of prominence in the national curriculum and are viewed as a way to help students to become more human. The arts are an integral part of the Irish curriculum.

MUSICKING. Christopher Small, a cultural musicologist, brought attention to this term through his book *Musicking*, published in 1998. He argued that music is an action, not an object—a verb, not a noun. All aspects affecting the concertgoer—the experience of the building, ticket taking, the seating arrangement of players, excellence in individual performance, and the discussion following a concert—are what Small describes as "musicking." He writes of the rise of Western music as a mercantile, nonparticipating art. He also spoke of written music as being a matter of "black dots."

MUSIC LEARNING THEORY. A comprehensive theory of the music-learning process, developed by **Edwin E. Gordon** (1927–), that attempts to explain how individuals learn music skills and music content. Gordon borrowed from the work of **Robert Gagné** (1916–2002) and **Jean Piaget**

(1896–1980). His learning theory is a theory explaining how individuals learn music and a skill-learning hierarchy of musical development.

MUSICOLOGY. A study of the science of music; the concept includes all branches of music, including theory, history, aesthetics, lexicography, and bibliography. The term originated in France early in the 19th century, and was later adopted by German, English, and American music theorists.

MUSIC PLAY. A resource for early childhood music based on the book *A Music Learning Theory for Newborn and Young Children* by **Edwin E. Gordon**. *Music Play* is designed to assist teachers, parents, and caregivers of newborn and young children in the development of basic music skills, such as singing, rhythm chanting, and moving.

MUSIC ROLL. A roll of perforated paper for use in a player piano (pianola, self-playing piano, auto-piano).

MUSIC SUPERVISORS JOURNAL **(1914).** The official publication of the **Music Supervisors National Conference** (MSNC). It was issued quarterly under the title *Music Supervisors Bulletin*, with its name changed to *Music Supervisors Journal* in 1916. The journal kept the plans and problems of the conference constantly before all the supervisors of the country. When MSNC changed its name to **Music Educators National Conference** in 1934, the periodical became the *Music Educators Journal* (MEJ), available to all members.

MUSIC SUPERVISORS NATIONAL CONFERENCE (MSNC). In early April of 1907 in Keokuk, Iowa, 69 supervisors out of 104 attendees attended an important first national conference; it would ultimately be named the Music Supervisors National Conference at the Cincinnati meeting in 1910. At the 1934 Chicago conference, the executive committee voted to change the MSNC name to the *Music Educators National Conference* (MENC) in order to clarify the notion that a music supervisor was indeed a music educator. Discussion topics from this new organization ranged from how to deal with monotones to making music a required subject in state schools. Music educators continue to be involved in addressing the topic of music as a required subject. *See also* NATIONAL ASSOCIATION FOR MUSIC EDUCATION (NA*f*ME).

MUSIC TEACHER. *See* GENERAL MUSIC TEACHER.

MUSIC TEACHERS ASSOCIATION (MTA). (UK.) Founded in London in 1908 by Stewart MacPherson to be the rallying ground of the teaching profession. It is associated with the educational, professional, social, or benevolent activities of musicians in the capital and beyond.

MUSIC TEACHERS MANUAL. *See* JULIA ETTA CRANE.

MUSIC TEACHERS NATIONAL ASSOCIATION (MTNA). (U.S.) An organization founded in 1876 to promote the welfare of music education, music study, and music making in American society. Theodore Presser, with his colleagues from Delaware and Ohio, founded MTNA, which is the oldest nonprofit music teachers' association in the U.S.

MUSIC TECHNOLOGY. The music technology of the 21st century involves musical sounds that are generated, modified, and controlled by electronic means. Its roots can be found in Edison's phonograph. Thaddeus Cahill in 1900 invented the *telharmonium* (Dynamophone), a machine that used electrical current to produce sound. Leon Theremin introduced the Theremin in 1923 (aetherophone). It generated only a single pitch of an eerie and haunting sound that composers often used in their music for special effects. Eventually, the Hammond organ (1934) became the most sophisticated of electronic instruments. *See* COMPUTER MUSIC; SYNTHESIZER; TAPE RECORDER MUSIC.

MUSIC THEATER. Combines the art of drama with music (and dance) in order to tell a story with greater emotion. Forms of musical theater include the Broadway musical and opera.

MUSIC THEORY. The study of how music works through fundamentals, music writing, **solfège**, and advanced studies in harmony, as well as counterpoint, form, and orchestration.
  Bib.: Apel, Willi, *Harvard Dictionary of Music*, 2nd ed., 1973.

MUSIC THERAPY. The use of music as a therapeutic tool for the restoration, maintenance, and improvement of psychological, mental, physical, and social skills—all within the context of a client-therapist relationship. A nonverbal treatment modality that is applicable to both the verbal and nonverbal person, it serves a wide age range with a wide diversity of disorders. It can be a diagnostic aid and can reinforce other treatment modalities.

Lit: Boxill, Edith Hillman, *Music Therapy for Developmental Disabilities*, 2nd ed., 2007.

MUSIC THERAPY IN SPECIAL EDUCATION. (U.S.) Promotes development of skills, knowledge, and understanding through the use of therapeutic musical approaches in the classroom.

MUSIC THROUGH MOVEMENT. 1. In Australia: The concept of music through movement came from the work of **Emile Jaques-Dalcroze**, "**Dalcroze eurhythmics**" (1865–1950). **Heather Gell** was the first Australian to obtain a diploma at the Institut Jaques-Dalcroze and subsequently broadcast the national program, *Music and Movement*, in 1940 through the Australian Broadcasting Company (ABC). **2.** In the U.S.: Phyllis Weikart of the University of Michigan developed a similar program, which was published in her book *Teaching Movement in Dance* in 1982.

MUSIQUE CONCRETE. *See* TAPE RECORDER MUSIC.

MUSO. (Aus.) A colloquial term for a musician in Australia.

MYERS, DAVID. Professor and director of the University of Minnesota School of Music since 2008; was for 21 years professor, associate director of the School of Music, and founding director of the Center for Educational Partnerships in Music (CEPM) at Georgia State University (GSU). He founded the PhD in music education at GSU and served as visiting lecturer at the University of Sydney (Aus., 1993). CEPM was cited in Harvard's *Qualities of Quality* report for its *Sound Learning* program, which united community musicians, Atlanta-area schools, and preservice music-education students in sustained collaborations. Myers is the U.S. consultant for the joint *European Master's Degree for New Audiences and Innovative Practice* and has served on and chaired panels for the **National Endowment for the Arts** (NEA). His seminal research on adult music learning led to numerous publications and presentations on life-span music learning, and he has published, presented, and consulted widely on music and the public good. He serves on editorial committees of a number of important journals in music education. He cofounded MENC's Special Research Interest Group on Adult and Community Music Education. His 1996 research for the National Endowment for the Arts, *Beyond Tradition: Partnerships Among Orchestras, Schools, and Communities*, remains a leading publication in the field of orchestra education and community engagement. He edited a section and authored a chapter on engagement and partnerships in the *Second Handbook of Research on Music Teaching and Learning* and coedited a section on life-span learning for the *Oxford Handbook of Music Education* (2012). He is a former curriculum consultant for *Live from Lincoln Center*, and from 1998 through 2008 served as principal investigator for evaluation research with the League of American Orchestras. In addition to NEA, his work has been funded by the Texaco Foundation, the Fund for Improvement of Post-Secondary Education, and the Cousins Foundation.

N

NATIONAL ABORIGINAL ISLANDER SKILLS DEVELOPMENT ASSOCIATION (NAISDA). (Aus.) Organization that evolved from the *Aboriginal Islander Skills Development Scheme*, established in early 1975, when the **Arts Council of Australia** and the **Aboriginal Arts Board** wished to stimulate and initiate Aboriginal and Torres Strait Islanders' artistic activities. NAISDA involves the study of dance, theater, and songs from indigenous Australian cultures as well as contemporary arts.

NATIONAL AFFILIATION OF ARTS EDUCATORS (NAAE). (Aus.) In 1991 this group, representing the nation's arts associations, officially recognized fine arts—music, dance, drama, media, and visual arts—as a key learning area (KLA). Development of the **National Arts Statement and Profile** followed. NAAE is concerned with ensuring that the arts maintain and improve their position in the school education systems, and with related curriculum and professional issues.

NATIONAL ANTHEM PROJECT. A project launched in 2005 by **MENC** as a public awareness campaign "to restore America's voice through music education."

NATIONAL ARTS CURRICULUM. (Aus.) A curriculum published in 1994 by the **Australian Education Council** as a national curriculum for Australian schools; it included music as one of six subject strands. The significance of this national curriculum is that it places music as an integral element in the general education of young people in Australia.

NATIONAL ARTS STATEMENT AND PROFILES. (Aus.) In 1991, the Australian federal government recognized fine arts—music, dance, drama, media, and visual arts—as a key learning area. The National Arts Statement and Profiles followed as suggested outcomes for each of eight bands (levels of learning), ranging from kindergarten to tenth grade. Each band has five strands: creating, making, presenting; exploring and developing ideas; using skills, techniques, and processes; presenting criticism and aesthetics; and understanding past and present artistic contexts.

NATIONAL ASSESSMENT OF EDUCATIONAL PROGRESS (NAEP). (U.S.) A battery of achievement tests mandated by Congress to assess the effects of schooling across the U.S. **Educational Testing Service** (ETS) was responsible for their development.

NATIONAL ASSOCIATION FOR MUSIC EDUCATION (NA*f***ME).** The history is as follows:

> 1907: Meeting in Keokuk, Iowa, considered to be the founding date of the music-education organization known as the **Music Supervisors National Conference**.
> 1910: The organization approved a constitution and adopted the name *Music Supervisors National Conference* (MSNC).
> 1934: **Music Educators National Conference** (MENC)
> 1998: MENC: National Association for Music Education
> 2011: National Association for Music Education (NA***f***ME)

The organization began in 1907 when **Philip Hayden** and 30 music supervisors came together in Keokuk, Iowa, to observe Hayden's new method, "Ear Training in Rhythm Forms." In 1909, a committee was appointed from the 1907 meeting to consider an organizational structure for music supervisors. In 1910, about 150 music educators from 23 of the 46 states registered. They approved a constitution, adopted the name *Music Supervisors National Conference* (MSNC), and thought of themselves as representing the entire country. MSNC actually was an outgrowth of the Department of Music Education that was then under the **National Education Association**, and the school-music section of **Music Teachers National Association**. At the 1922 conference in Nashville, newly elected president **Karl W. Gehrkens** put forth the motto (*originally* conceived by **Osborne McConathy**) "Music for Every Child, Every Child for Music," and the organization has kept this theme in many ways since 1923.

In 1926 to 1931, the various divisions known today were developed and had their separate conferences throughout the years apart from the national conference. In 1934, the Music Supervisors National Conference changed its name to *Music Educators National Conference* (MENC). A new constitution in 1940 officially recognized the arrangement of six regional divisions with a central headquarters under the jurisdiction of the national board of directors. The new constitution made clear that the affiliated state units were an important part of the design. The concept of a totally unified organization working at national, divisional, and state levels was the critical element of the new document.

In 1998 the name changed to *MENC: National Association for Music Education*. On September 1, 2011, the name change of *National Association for Music Education* officially went into effect, and the new logo, NA*f*ME, incorporates the "f" as a forte music symbol.

NATIONAL ASSOCIATION FOR MUSIC THERAPY (NAMT) (1950–1997). An organization devoted to the scientific application of the art of music to accomplish therapeutic aims. It is the use of music and the therapist's self to influence changes in behavior. In 1998 NAMT joined with AAMT to become **AMTA**. *See also* MUSIC THERAPY.

NATIONAL ASSOCIATION OF JAZZ EDUCATORS (NAJE). Became **International Association of Jazz Educators** (INAJE) in 1989, an organization that ceased to exist in 2009. *See also* COUNCIL FOR JAZZ EDUCATION (CJE).

NATIONAL ASSOCIATION OF MUSIC EDUCATORS (NAME). (UK.) A professional network with key links to government and educational bodies. It advocates on behalf of all music educationalists, similar to **NA*f*ME** in the U.S. The history is as follows:

1942: Dr. Charles Hooper of Bradford, both inspector of schools and music adviser, arranged for the first annual conference of MANA (Music Advisers National Assoc.) to take place in London.
1954: MANA represented at the UNESCO conference on music education in Brussels.
1993: A *Common Purpose Group*, comprising MANA and other music organizations, produced a joint statement about the current state of music education. The association seeks closer collaborative partnerships with other associations and organizations concerned with music education.
1996: **NAME** was founded when AATEM (Assoc. for the Advancement of Teacher Education in Music) joined forces with MANA.
2011: The *National Plan for Music Education* was unveiled.

NATIONAL ASSOCIATION OF SCHOOLS OF MUSIC (NASM). Accrediting agency for music and music-education programs at the university/college level. It was created in 1924 at the suggestion of Burnett Tuthill of the Cincinnati Conservatory of Music.

NATIONAL BAND ASSOCIATION (NBA). (U.S.) Founded in 1960 by **Traugott Rohner**, who founded and published *The Instrumentalist* magazine in 1946. This association is dedicated to the promotion of excellence in all aspects of wind bands, including performance, education, and literature.

NATIONAL BAND CONTEST. The first of these contests was held in Chicago in 1923, when the instrument manufacturers sponsored a national band contest as a promotional device. It is interesting to note that the history of the band contest became the history of school bands. Many of these contests flourished until the end of WWII. Today, band contests are usually held only at state and local levels.

NATIONAL COALITION FOR CORE ARTS STANDARDS (NCCAS). (U.S.) A partnership of organizations and states formed in February 2011 and committed to developing the next generation of voluntary national arts education standards; partnering organizations include the **National Association for Music Education**, American Alliance for Theatre and Education, **Arts Education Partnership**, the College Board, Educational Theatre Association, National Art Education Association, National Dance Education Organization, and the State Education Agency Directors of Arts Education; the partnership seeks to build on the foundation created by the voluntary 1994 national standards documents, support the 21st-century needs of students and teachers, help ensure that all students are college and career ready, and affirm the place of arts education in a balanced core curriculum. The standards are being designed to provide common understandings for arts education in American schools and to describe what students should know, understand, and be able to do as a result of engaging a quality curricular arts education program in each of the disciplines; drafts for review were released in the spring of 2013.
(Entry by **Michael Jothen**, Nov. 2012.)

NATIONAL COMPETITION FOR YOUNG PERFORMERS. (Can.) *See* CBC NATIONAL COMPETITION FOR YOUNG PERFORMERS.

NATIONAL COUNCIL FOR THE ACCREDITATION OF TEACHER EDUCATION (NCATE). (U.S.) From 1927 to 1970, several organizations came together to form NCATE. In 1970, it was named the "solo agency for the accreditation of teacher, educational administrators and school personnel" by the National Commission on Accrediting. In 1988, NCATE and **NASM** ratified a policy that made it possible for an institution to avoid duplication of requirements of both organizations.

NATIONAL CURRICULUM FOR AUSTRALIAN SCHOOLS. This curriculum, published in 1994, included music as one of the six subjects within the National Arts Curriculum. The significance of the National Curriculum is that it reaffirms the place of music as an integral element of the general education of Australian young people. The development of a new Australian (National School) Curriculum was in process from 2009 to 2012, and music will still be represented.

NATIONAL CURRICULUM FOR SCHOOLS. (UK.) The Education Reform Act of 1988 instituted the national curriculum for both England and Wales. Eventually, it included Northern Ireland. Both England and Wales have English, mathematics, and science as core subjects. Welsh is also a core subject for those schools that use Welsh as the primary medium of instruction. England and Wales include the same set of *foundation* subjects: art, history, geography, *music*, physical education, and technology. Each subject includes *programs of study* and *attainment targets*, which are similar to *courses* and *goals* in the U.S. Revisions occurred in 2000, 2002, and 2007.

NATIONAL EDUCATION ASSOCIATION (NEA). (U.S.) In 1857, the National Teachers Association (NTA) was founded, and as a result, in 1866, it was responsible for the creation of the U.S. Department of Education. Horace Mann, president of the American Association for the Advancement of Education (1848), attended the NTA meeting in Cincinnati, where he agreed to a merger between his group and the NTA to form the NEA in 1879. Two other teachers' associations also merged with NTA to become the NEA.

NATIONAL EISTEDDFOD. (UK-Wales.) *See* EISTEDDFOD.

NATIONAL ENDOWMENT FOR THE ARTS (NEA). Created by the U.S. Congress in 1965. An independent agency of the U.S. government that offers support and funding for projects exhibiting artistic excellence.

NATIONAL FOUNDATION ON THE ARTS AND HUMANITIES (NFAH). A foundation created in 1965 by Congress (Public Law 89-209) as an independent federal agency to support the practice of the arts and the study of the humanities.

NATIONAL HIGH SCHOOL ORCHESTRA AND BAND CAMP (NHSO). (U.S.) The first NHSO was assembled for the 1926 meeting of the **Music Supervisors National Conference** in Detroit, Michigan. A National

High School Band was included as part of the camp program. *See also* IN-TERLOCHEN CENTER FOR THE ARTS.

NATIONAL MOD. (UK.) **1.** A British teenager of the 1960s who affected a very neat, sophisticated appearance and wore fancy clothing inspired by Edwardian dress and also affected by the modernist movement in design and music. **2.** In education, a self-contained subdivision of a program of study that is taught and assessed as a discrete "unit."

NATIONAL MUSIC CAMP (NMC). (Can.) Camping and music organization that has been in existence for more than 50 years, and in 1980s it became the NMC. Serves children 9–10 years old through high school.

NATIONAL MUSIC CAMP. (U.S.) *See* INTERLOCHEN CENTER FOR THE ARTS.

NATIONAL NURSERY EXAMINATION BOARD (NNEB). (UK.) The examining body for nursery teachers. A nursery nurse is qualified to work with children aged birth to seven years in a variety of settings with the title of *teaching assistant* and qualifications gained through the National Nursery Examination Board. They are responsible for all aspects of physical care and safety, and for social and educational development.

NATIONAL PEACE JUBILEE (1869). (U.S.) A celebration organized by **Patrick Gilmore** to recognize the end of the Civil War. Held in Boston; an orchestra of 1,000 and a chorus of 10,000 performed. In the production, the concertmaster was the famous Norwegian violinist and composer, *Ole Bull*. Canons were fired by electricity, with a simultaneous ringing of every church bell in Boston.

NATIONAL RESEARCH COUNCIL (1923–1932). *See* MUSIC EDUCATION RESEARCH COUNCIL (MERC).

NATIONAL REVIEW OF SCHOOL MUSIC EDUCATION (2005). (Aus.) Following an earlier report by Robin Stevens, Professor Margaret Scares, chair of the Steering Committee of this review, stated that music education in Australian schools is at a critical point where immediate action is needed to right the inequalities in school music. As a result of this review, *Guidelines for Effective Music Education* were developed to provide tools for individual schools to revise the health of their own programs.

NATIONAL ROCK BANDS. (Aus.) The government has encouraged the popular music industry by establishing and funding **Ausmusic**, a training and promotion organization encouraging popular musical training in secondary schools and technical colleges. Since the 1980s, Aboriginal bands have had success in rock, which is the urban equivalent of country music. The most widely known Aboriginal band nationally and internationally is the *Yothu Yindi*, from northeastern Arnham Land. It performs indigenous songs and rock.

NATIONAL SCHOOL BAND AND ORCHESTRA ASSOCIATION (NSBOA). Originally called the *National School Band Association*, it expanded in 1929 to become the National School Band and Orchestra Association. By 1932, three organizations were formed: band, orchestra, and vocal. They each became auxiliary organizations under **MENC**. Because of the emphasis on state and district competition, this eventually led to the establishment of state music associations.

NATIONAL SCHOOL ORCHESTRA ASSOCIATION (NSOA). Merged with **American String Teachers Association** (ASTA) in the 1990s.

NATIONAL STANDARDS FOR MUSIC EDUCATION. (U.S.) These standards, developed through **NAfME**, are arranged according to three grade levels: K–4, 5–8, and 9–12. They describe the skills and knowledge students are to have learned by the end of grades four, eight, and 12. The movement toward developing national standards began in 1992. While they are voluntary, many states have adopted them, and others have used the national standards for developing their own standards according to their needs.

NATIONAL SURVEY OF SCHOOLS. (Aus.) In 2004, at the request of the minister of education, a National Review of School Music Education was initiated. In order to obtain needed information from the schools, a National Survey of Schools was performed. It had two components: a stratified sample of 525 schools ("sample schools"), and an additional sample of 147 schools nominated through the submission process as "effective music" schools ("music schools") to enable comparison. Due to a response rate of only 47.6 percent, the findings are to be considered with caution. One form of data collection was *site visits*, in order to report on effectiveness and exemplary practice in music education. Evidence gathered from the surveys indicates that both parents and teachers shared perception and understanding of the importance of music and how it is to be taught in the school curriculum. They also believed that music should be taught as a separate subject rather than integrated with other subjects.

NATIONAL YOUTH BAND OF CANADA (NYB). The **Canadian Band Association**'s flagship project. Since 1994, the National Youth Band of Canada has offered an unparalleled musical opportunity for outstanding Canadian woodwind, brass, and percussion instrumentalists between the ages of 16 and 21.

A NATION AT RISK. A 1983 report from the National Commission on Excellence in Education; the full title is *A Nation at Risk: The Imperative for Education Reform*. The report indicated that American students were academically behind other industrialized nations in certain areas. Criticisms included that of teaching and learning in America. Controversy ensued throughout the country regarding this report. Music and arts were left out of the report. Only the "new" basics were included: English, math, science, social studies, and computer science. This report helped change American education, and brought about changes in curriculum design and content, and school schedules. The development of alternative school schedules such as **block scheduling** is one of the outcomes. The chair of this report was David Pierpont Gardner.

NATIVE AMERICAN MUSIC. (U.S.) Prior to European and African settlements, their music education was entirely oral.

NETTL, BRUNO (1930–). (U.S.) Although a native of Czechoslovakia, Nettl was educated in the U.S. and has spent his entire career at the University of Illinois School of Music. He is professor emeritus of music and anthropology, with his main interest being **ethnomusicological** theory and method, music of Native American culture, and music of the Middle East, especially Iran. In recent years, he has focused on the study of improvisatory music, the understanding of musical change throughout the world, and the intellectual history of ethnomusicology. Currently, he is chair of a committee to organize an international and intercultural conference on the study of improvisation.

His teaching philosophy includes his concern for students who should be encouraged to develop a curiosity about fundamental questions and issues in music and culture. He believes that ethnomusicology has a significant role in music education, in order to expose students to many intellectual and artistic options and to a large variety of approaches and teaching philosophies.

Among his many publications is his professional memoir, *Encounters in Ethnomusicology* (2002). He continues teaching part-time in the University of Illinois School of Music.

NEW AGE. In music, of or pertaining to a nonintrusive style of music using both acoustical and electronic instruments, and drawing on classical music, jazz, and rock. The New Age movement occurred basically from 1970 to 1975.

NEW ENGLAND PUBLIC SCHOOL MUSIC TEACHERS ASSOCIATION. (U.S.) Toward the end of the 19th century, state and district associations of school music teachers began to be formed. The movement to form independent bodies of school music teachers began as early as 1885 at a meeting of music teachers at Pilgrim Hall, Boston, with the title New England Public School Music Teachers Association.

NEW HANDBOOK I AND II. *See* COLWELL, RICHARD.

NEW UNION SINGING SOCIETY (1809). (Can.) One of the earliest musical societies in Canada, located in Halifax; it eventually became the Halifax Choral Society.

N'KET. A large, closed drum with a carved-out base on which it stands; from the music of Cameroon. Used in music-education classes in multicultural instruction.

THE NOBLE DUKE OF YORK. (UK.) An English children's nursery rhyme often performed as an action song; and sometimes referred to as the "Grand Old Duke of York." Origins of the song are much debated and remain unclear. The Duke has often been identified with Prince Frederick, Duke of York and Albany (1763–1827). The oldest version of the song that survives is from 1642 ("Old Tarlton's Song"), attributed to the stage clown Richard Tarlton (1530–1588). This song is also sung to the tune of "A-Hunting We Will Go," and is often used as an action song within many Scouting organizations.
  Lit.: Opie, I., and P. Opie, *The Oxford Dictionary of Nursery Rhymes*, 1997.

NOBLEMAN'S CATCH CLUB. (UK.) It should be mentioned that **glee clubs** had a highly beneficial effect upon the vocal art, and as a result, several societies were founded for the cultivation of this and kindred forms of vocal music. *The Nobleman's Catch Club*, which still exists, was founded by a number of amateurs in November 1761. King George III was a member.

NO CHILD LEFT BEHIND (NCLB). (U.S.) Legislation of 2001 that reauthorized the **Elementary and Secondary Education Act of 1965** (ESEA). Four main strategies were enacted: 1) increased accountability for states, school districts, and schools, which caused increasing friction among administrators and teachers; 2) increased opportunity for school choice; 3) increased flexibility in the use of federal education funds; 4) increased emphasis on reading in the younger grades. As a result of dissatisfaction with NCLB, on June 30, 2012, some 24 states have been granted waivers (or freedom) from NCLB rules. The waivers allow states to develop their own measuring sticks to reduce the failure rate in math and reading by 50 percent. This means that "waiver" schools will no longer receive the annual accountability grades, or *Adequate Yearly Progress* ratings, which have been tied to school funding.

NOISE POLLUTION. An excessive, displeasing human, animal, or machine-created environmental noise. In music performances such as rock bands with electronically produced sound, the noise level can be so high as to cause noise-induced hearing loss. Musicians now use musicians' earplugs to protect their hearing during concerts. These plugs allow clear and natural sound while reducing exposure to extreme noise.

NO-NO LANGUAGE. (Aus.) Any of several Australian aboriginal languages, the names of which consist of the local words for *no* and *with*.

NOOK. A portable **e-reader** developed by Barnes & Noble Booksellers and introduced in October 2009.

NORMAL INSTITUTES. A type of convention that offered pedagogy for teachers, developed by Lowell Mason and George Root. These institutes consisted of courses in methods, theory, voice and piano, and they were usually held during the summer. *See* CRANE, JULIA ETTA; CRANE NORMAL INSTITUTE OF MUSIC.

NORMAL SCHOOL. A school offering a two-year course and certification to high school graduates preparing to be teachers, especially elementary school teachers. Most of them are now called *Teachers Colleges* and are four-year programs.

NORTHERN IRELAND. (UK.) Six counties that are a part of Great Britain as a result of the Irish War of Independence in 1916. Their schools have continued to be segregated—Protestants attend state schools and Catholics attend parochial schools. Currently, the two systems are close to being evenly divided in terms of enrollment, and integration may soon become a reality.

The War of Independence was an Irish rising against the British government, resulting in the political organization of Ireland. In 1921 the lower 26 counties of Ireland became an independent country known as the Republic of Ireland, while the northern six counties are called Northern Ireland and remain part of Great Britain.

Bib.: Green, James E., *Education in the United Kingdom and Ireland*, 2001.

NORTHUMBRIAN PIPERS SOCIETY. (UK.) Encourages practice of the **Northumbrian small pipes**; highly skilled players live in many parts of England. Hornpipes, jigs, polkas, and reels form the mainstay of the repertory. Some triple-time hornpipes survive in Northumbria. There is a strong Scottish influence on the repertory.

NORTHUMBRIAN SMALL PIPES. (UK.) Bellows-blown bagpipes from northeastern England. A bag of the small pipes is supplied with air from a bellows held under the arm. The bagpipe survives in England only as Northumbrian small pipes.

NORWICH SOL-FA METHOD. A system developed by **Sarah Anne Glover** (1785–1867) of Norwich, England. Europeans at that time favored numbers to represent degrees of the scale or based on the **fixed-doh** sol-fa. In England an old gamut (scale)-derived sol-fa, far removed from **Guido of Arezzo**'s original concept, was still in use. Glover rejected traditional methods, and devised her own adaptation of Guido's sol-fa system, extending it to a full *relative* (**movable-doh**) sol-fa system.

NO-SING THEORY. The influence of vocal training in boy choirs led to the theory that when a young male entered puberty and the voice "broke" or "cracked," he should stop singing until the voice stopped changing. Unfortunately, this approach caused young men to stop singing, and choirmasters lost many future male singers for their choirs. *See also* CAMBIATA.

NOTATION SYSTEMS. A system of symbols designed to represent the elements of time and sound (tones). It took a millennium to develop a musical-notation system capable of even an approximate rendition of the pitch and duration of each individual note.

NOTE TO ROTE OR ROTE TO NOTE. Early in American music-education history were two conflicting approaches to the teaching of singing:

- "Note to rote" was the learning to sing by "reading" the symbols *mi-fa-sol-la*. This was eventually displaced by the seven-scale *ut-doh-re-mi-fa-so-la*. This approach was called singing by "rule and art."
- The "rote to note" approach was essentially learning "by ear." The singing teacher sings a short melody, and the students imitate the teacher.

Both of these approaches were used in the early singing schools, and were referred to as singing from "lining out the tune" (rote to note), to singing by the "recall of notes" (note to rote), which led to the formation of singing societies. In public schools today, both approaches are still used, and the debate continues. With the advent of the **Kodály** and **Orff** approaches, "note to rote" has been successful in schools where these are a part of instruction in singing. Some teachers continue to use the "rote to note" approach because it is a quicker way to teach many songs in the early grades.

N'TO. A medium-sized tubular drum that is open on one end. Useful for music-education classes of multicultural instruction.

OATES, DR. J. P. (UK.) Acoustician. From the ancients until the 19th century, researchers have worked to improve a valve system for brass instruments. While Gottfried Weber invented the valve system, others worked to overcome the prevailing defects. It was in 1851 and 1852 that Dr. J. P. Oates made his equilateral valves, adopted by Antoine Courtois for his cornets; the same clever acoustician invented a piston with four straight windways, afterward patented by A. Sax of Paris.

OBERLIN CONSERVATORY OF MUSIC (1865). Oldest continuously operating conservatory in the U.S. The Oberlin College Conservatory of Music in 1921 established America's first four-year college degree program in **music education**.

OCARINA. A simple musical wind instrument shaped somewhat like an elongated egg, with finger holes.

OCEANIA. (Aus.) The islands of the central and southern Pacific, including Micronesia, Melanesia, and Polynesia; sometimes also called *Australia and the Malay Archipelago*.

O'CONOR, JOHN (1947–). An Irish pianist known for his formidable technique and unique sound. Has been called a true "poet of the piano." Born in Dublin, he has performed throughout the world with many of the leading orchestras, including the London, Vienna, Cleveland, Dallas, and Montreal symphonies. After winning first prize at the Beethoven International Piano Competition in Vienna, Austria, in 1973, he continues to be regarded as a Beethoven specialist.

In August 2010, O'Conor retired as director of the Royal Irish Academy of Music, having served some 16 years in this position. He is considered one of the most important piano teachers in the world. In an interview with O'Conor at Shenandoah University in Winchester, Virginia, he revealed his great love for teaching through one-on-one piano instruction, as well as through group interaction in seminars and master classes. He expressed the importance of "passing on" musical information to young musicians through his work as a performer.

John O'Conor has been awarded honorary doctorates by the National University of Ireland, Trinity College in Dublin, and Shenandoah University in Virginia; and honored with the title "Officier de L'ordre des Arts et des Lettres" by the French government and the "Ehrenkreuz für Wissenschaft und Kunst" by the Austrian government. He is currently the Distinguished Artist-in-Residence and professor of piano at Shenandoah Conservatory of Shenandoah University. He also continues as professor of piano at the Royal Irish Academy of Music in Dublin.

OFFICE FOR STANDARDS IN EDUCATION (OFSTED). (UK.) An independent agency apart from the Department of Education that is responsible for the inspection of schools. It is similar to state accreditation. "Inspectors must report on the quality of education; educational standards achieved, efficiency of financial management, and the 'spiritual, moral, social, and cultural development' of pupils."

OLD HALL MANUSCRIPT. (UK.) The most important manuscript of English sacred music of the late 14th and early 15th centuries, found in the Library College of St. Edmund's College Old Hall, near Ware, Hertfordshire, first described in 1903 and published 1933–1938. Sold to a British Library, 1973, it comprises 140 folios of church music by composers of the Chapel Royal.

OLD STYLE SINGING OR OLD WAY. This approach originated in England for the benefit of illiterate parishioners, when few people could read music. A psalm was read (or sung) by a deacon or pre-cantor, and the congregation then repeated the line to the prescribed tune. This was known as *lining out*. This continued in the New World until approximately 1721–1723, when **John Tufts**'s innovation in musical notation simplified music reading. Singing schools began to appear in 1723 for the purpose of learning to read music notation and to improve singing in the churches.

OMNICHORD. An electronic instrument similar to an **autoharp**, in that one can push down marked buttons and play chords, and play rhythms, too. It is self-contained, executed like the autoharp, with a built-in amplifier, and is completely portable. It has a variety of tone colors and rhythmic features not available on the autoharp. The omnichord does not need tuning.

ONE SWEETLY SOLEMN THOUGHT. (Can.) Song written by Robert S. Ambrose in 1876. It became one of the most popular songs ever to be published in the 19th century. It was an appropriate song to sing in the parlors of homes that would not permit any nonsacred music to be performed on Sundays. It could be sung in dance halls or on the stage in operas and operettas.

O, NO JOHN! An English folksong collected by **Cecil J. Sharp**. A song to be dramatized by boys and girls, regarding a courtship between the two.

OPERA. Opera is a drama set to music, to be sung, with instrumental accompaniment, by singers, who are usually in costume. Recitation (*recitative*) or spoken dialogue may separate the numbers, but the essence of opera is that the music is integral, rather than incidental as in a musical or play with music. Opera is generally said to have originated in Florence toward the close of the 16th century.

OPERETTA. Little opera. Strictly, a play with overture, songs, entr'actes, and dances. It has become synonymous with *light opera*.

OPHICLEIDES. (UK.) Obsolete keyed brass instrument of conical bore and played with a cup mouthpiece. Was used in military bands and also included in early scores of Mendelssohn, Berlioz, Verdi, and Wagner. Superseded by the bass tuba.

ORCHESTRA. (Gen.) A *large ensemble* of instruments (as distinct from small ensembles—one player to a part), divided into four main sections: **strings**, **woodwinds**, **brass**, and **percussion**.

ORFF, CARL (1895–1982). (Ger.) As a composer, his most famous score is the scenic oratorio *Carmina Burana* (1937), with the text in Latin and Middle German. His fame rests in his highly influential approach to music education, adopted not only in Germany, but also in the U.S., England, Australia, Canada, and other countries involved in music education for children. His approach stemmed from the Günther School for gymnastics, dance, and music, which he cofounded with Dorothee Günther in Munich (1924), in the promotion of instrumental playing and understanding of rhythm among children. He commissioned K. Maendler to construct special percussion instruments that were easy to play, the *Orff instruments*.

ORFF INSTRUMENTS. These instruments were designed by **Carl Orff** to provide children with simple instruments especially suited to them; they play a vital part in every aspect of the Orff approach. Orff instruments are used almost entirely as an accompaniment to singing, and occasionally for instrumental compositions. A basic purchase plan for Orff instruments is as follows: alto **xylophone**, 16- and 20-inch timpani, soprano xylophone, alto **metallophone**, alto glockenspiel, and brass metallophone. This set of instruments is known as the *Instrumentarium*, and includes recorders, metals, and some strings.

ORFF-SCHULWERK. In 1924, Dorothy Günther used **Carl Orff**'s works in the training of dancers and gymnasts. They were the forerunners of the Orff-Schulwerk, or *Orff approach*. Orff and Günther's philosophy was based on students physically experiencing beat, meter, tempo, and rhythm through *doing* rather than *learning about*. Gunild Keetman became a student at the Günther School in 1926. As a result, Orff asked her to become his helper and colleague. She translated Orff's ideas into techniques for playing his newly developed instruments, especially the xylophones. Keetman composed the first piece for these instruments, which became central to the Orff style. The actual development of Orff instruments was a direct result of Orff's exposure to the African xylophone and Indonesian instruments. After many years of Orff's performing and teaching, the Orff Institute was established in Salzburg in 1961, and in 1963 this became the music-education division of the Mozarteum. It is now known and referred to as the *Orff-Schulwerk Music for Children*. Orff and Keetman detailed Günther's method in the book *Music for Children*.

ORGAN HISTORICAL TRUST OF AUSTRALIA. (Aus.) Formed at a public meeting held in St. Paul's Cathedral Chapter House, Melbourne, on May 13, 1977. It extends the work of the National Trust of Australia in order to: 1) preserve historic pipe organs and organ building records; 2) stimulate public interest in pipe organs that are of national or local importance; and 3) encourage scholarly research into the history of the organ, its musical use, and organ music.

ORGANIZATION OF AMERICAN KODÁLY EDUCATORS (OAKE). An organization founded in 1974 to support Kodály education in the U.S., and to act as a catalyst to help it grow and develop. Its official journal is the *Kodály Envoy*.

ORGANUM. A plainchant melody developed in the Middle Ages, with at least one added voice to enhance the harmony.

OSCILLOSCOPE. Device that makes the shape of a voltage wave visible on the screen of a cathode-ray tube or other device to depict changes in an electric quantity, voltage, or current, as in sound waves. Used in early (1965–1969) **synthesizers**.

OSSIAN. (UK.) A legendary hero, poet, and son of Finn; supposed to have lived during the 3rd century AD; represented in Gaelic poems and in imitations of them written by James MacPherson in 1760.

OUTCOMES-BASED EDUCATION (OBE). An educational approach that emphasizes what students are to learn or to be able to do as a result of their instructional activities.

OXFORD UNIVERSITY. (UK.) English university, which has awarded degrees in music since 1499.

P

PACIFIC FESTIVAL OF THE ARTS. (Aus.) A quadrennial international festival featuring cultural displays from the nations of **Oceania**; first held in 1972.

PANPIPE. (Aus.) A set of differently pitched tubular flutes, usually bound in a bundle or row, sometimes made of cane (reed).

PARENTS COALITION FOR MUSIC EDUCATION (PCME). (Can.) A music-education organization that helped fund the participation of various scholars in the initial meeting of the **Canadian Music Education Research Collaborative**, whose purpose is to examine and promote music and arts education in Canada.

PARIS, AIMÉ (1798–1866). *See* GALIN-PARIS-CHEVÉ METHOD.

PARTNERSHIP AND PROCESS. A shortened title for the MENC publication *Music Teacher Education: Partnership and Process* (2007). *See also* TASK FORCE ON MUSIC TEACHER EDUCATION.

PARTNER SONGS. Songs that have identical harmonization and can be combined and sung together; for example, "Row Your Boat" and "The Farmer in the Dell." This approach has been used to assist in learning to sing in parts. Frederick Beckman developed this idea into his two collections, *Partner Songs* and *More Partner Songs*, published by Ginn and Company.

PAYNTER, JOHN (1931–2010). (UK.) British composer and music educator. Known for his advocacy of music making and his emphasis on the importance of music as a subject in the general education of all children. Emeritus professor of the University of York from 1982 to 1994. Taught in primary, secondary modern, and grammar schools, which helped shape his view that music should be at the heart of the curriculum. He is considered by many as the most influential figure in music education. Paynter placed creativity at the core of his teaching. He wrote the book *Sound and Silence* (1970) with Peter

Aston. It was a triumph and has remained a touchstone for music education. Between 1973 and 1982, he directed the Schools Council Project, *Music in the Secondary School Curriculum*. This culminated in a book with the same title (1982) that influenced the National Curriculum in music (England and Wales). Paynter was general editor of the *Resources of Music* series for Cambridge University Press, 1969 and 1993. He was joint editor of the *British Journal of Music Education* from 1984 to 1997.

PEARSE, PATRICK (1849–1916). (UK-Ire.) A teacher, poet, writer, and political activist who led the Irish "Easter Rising" in 1916. As a cultural nationalist, Pearse believed that language was intrinsic to the identity of a nation. He believed that the Irish school system taught Ireland's youth to be good Englishmen, and he felt that an alternative was needed. Saving the Irish language from extinction was of utmost importance. As a result, he started his own bilingual school, *St. Enda's School* in Dublin, in 1908. Students were taught both Irish and English languages.

Unfortunately, Pearse became involved with the Irish Republican Brotherhood (IRB), which was dedicated to the overthrow of British rule in Ireland and its replacement with a republic. His reputation and writings were vigorously criticized by historians, who saw him as a dangerous and fanatical influence. Following the Good Friday Agreement in 1998, his complex personality remains a subject of controversy for those who wished to debate the evolving meaning of Irish nationalism. It was, however, Pearse who proclaimed a republic during the Easter Rising of April 24, 1916, and after several days of fighting, Pearse, his brother, and 14 others were court-martialed and executed by firing squad. He was one of the first to be shot on May 3, 1916. His former school, St. Enda's, is now the Pearse Museum, dedicated to his memory.

Lit. *Encyclopedia Britannica*; Wikipedia.

PEG DOPE. (Peg paste; peg stick; peg compound.) A substance used to coat the bearing surface of the tuning peg of string instruments, mainly violins, cellos, and violas. Commercial varieties include a small stick (resembling lipstick), a block, or a liquid in a bottle. Home treatments include soap and chalk, depending on whether the peg sticks or slips.

PENNYWHISTLE. (UK-Ire.) A small, simple, and cheap wind instrument, usually consisting of a tin or plastic pipe with finger holes. *See also* TIN WHISTLE.

PEP BANDS. Usually a small group (no more than 20 performers) of brass and percussion performers who play for athletic events to increase the student support for events such as basketball games.

PERCUSSION INSTRUMENTS. Generic name for instruments that are sounded by shaking, or by striking one object with another. In general classification of instruments, they are divided into two categories—**membranophones** and **idiophones**.

PERFECT PITCH. *See* ABSOLUTE PITCH.

PERFORMANCE-BASED TEACHER EDUCATION (PBTE). Also known as competency-based teacher education (CBTE). Since about 1970, prospective teachers are required to demonstrate predetermined competencies as part of teacher-training programs. These competencies include knowledge of subject matter, teaching methods (or approaches), professional attributes, personal characteristics, and teaching style.

PESTALOZZI, JOHANN HEINRICH (1746–1827). Swiss educator and founder of a method for the education of young children. He believed that children should learn through activity and through the handling and use of material objects rather than simply through words; they should be given a balanced, whole-child approach to learning through psychomotor, affective, and cognitive development: as suggested by Pestalozzi, learning by "hand, heart, and head." In 1801, he published *How Gertrude Teaches Her Children*, which encapsulated much of the Pestalozzian method, and is a major source of his influence on pedagogical theory and philosophy of education. *See also* MASON, LOWELL.

PHILOSOPHY OF MUSIC EDUCATION. A search for the meanings found in fundamental questions about the nature and value of music through the acquisition of knowledge contained in the discipline of music education in learning, teaching, and experiential involvement in music.
  Bib.: Reimer, Bennett, *A Philosophy of Music Education.*
  Lit.: Elliott, David, *Music Matters: A New Philosophy of Music Education.*

PHI MU ALPHA SINFONIA. An American collegiate social fraternity for men with a special interest in music (also known as Phi Mu Alpha, or simply *Sinfonia*); founded as the *Sinfonia Club* at the New England Conservatory of Music in Boston, Massachusetts, in 1898.

PIAGET, JEAN (1896–1980). A Swiss biologist who worked as a professor of psychology at the University of Geneva from 1929 to 1975. He produced over 60 books on children and learning. Piaget was interested in the nature of thought and the development of thinking in young children. He developed, through observations of his own children, four descriptive schemas: 1) sensorimotor (0–2); 2) preoperational-symbolic (2–7); concrete-logical operations (7–11), and formal-abstract operation (12+). In music education, **Marilyn Zimmerman** provided extensive research into the musical characteristics of children, based on the work of Piaget. While there has been much criticism of Piaget's work because he studied his own children, nonetheless, Piaget's theories about the stages of development have provided a broad overview of how children think in their early years. His thought on education, developmental psychology, and the evolution of human intelligence is still highly regarded by many educationalists.

PIANO. English term for keyboard instrument whose full name is *pianoforte* (Italian), "soft-loud." A descendant of the dulcimer (string and hammers), and through its keyboard, a descendant of the harpsichord and clavichord. The modern piano has an iron frame and is either *grand* (strung horizontally) or *upright* (vertical strings). It normally has 88 keys, with a standard compass of 7 1/3 octaves, but some models by Bösendorfer have a compass of eight octaves. It is generally accepted that the earliest of its type was made in Florence ca. 1698–1700 by Bartolomeo Cristofori, who produced a *granicombalo col piano e forte*, a harpsichord with loudness and softness.

Bib.: Kennedy, Michael, *Oxford Concise Dictionary of Music*, 2004.

PIANO PEDAGOGY. The field of piano pedagogy is generally studied through academic programs in colleges and conservatories. A study of materials, methods, and repertoire for the teaching of piano includes how to teach beginning through intermediate piano students.

Piano pedagogy may be an undergraduate or graduate course as part of a music performance or music-education degree requirement. Schools require prior piano studies or previous teaching experience.

PIANO PROFICIENCY. This term is used in a variety of collegiate institutions to ensure that music-education students meet the demands for piano skills (such as accompanying) necessary for teaching general music programs in the classroom. Each school has its own set of requirements, which may be listed as keyboard skills for different levels.

PIPERS. (UK.) Those who play bagpipes in Great Britain and many European cultures. The basic instrument consists of an air-holding bag and pipes. Pipers were part of the clan retinue, and whole families evolved traditions of teaching and compositions (e.g., by the use of mnemonic syllables) that influence pipers today. Realizing the powerful effect of massed bagpipers, the British government enlisted pipers as part of its army, and still does. Bagpipe music includes song, march, and dance tunes.

PITCH. In music, the position of a tone in the musical scale, which is today designated by a letter name, and which is determined by the frequency of vibration of the source of the tone. Pitch is an attribute of every musical tone; the fundamental, or first harmonic, of any tone is perceived as its pitch. The earliest successful attempt to standardize pitch was made in 1858, when a commission of musicians and scientists appointed by the French government settled upon an "A" of 435 cycles per second; this standard was adopted by an international conference at Vienna, Austria, in 1889. In the U.S., however, the prevailing standard is an "A" of 440 cycles per second. Before the middle of the 19th century, pitch varied according to time, place, and medium of musical performance; since the classical period the trend has been gradually upward. The *relative pitch* of a tone, in contrast to *absolute pitch*, is an expression of its pitch in relation to the pitch of some other tone taken as a standard.

Bib.: Kennedy, Michael, *Oxford Concise Dictionary of Music*, 2004.

PITCH MATCHING OR PITCH ACCURACY. According to a number of research studies with young children, these two terms are related. Pitch matching must occur by at least ages four or five through kindergarten experiences. In vocal and/or pitch accuracy, musical experiences and maturation are important factors in the development of vocal accuracy. Individual differences can and do occur in the process of pitch matching and pitch accuracy.

Bib.: Zimmerman, Marilyn, *Musical Characteristics of Children*, 1971.

Lit.: Boardman, Eunice, *An Investigation of the Effect of Pre-School Training on the Development of Vocal Accuracy on Young Children*, 1964; Swears, Linda, *Teaching the Elementary School Chorus*, 1984; Goetze, Mary, *Factors Affecting Accuracy in Children's Singing*, 1985.

PITCHPIPE. Small wooden (17th–18th century) or metal reed pipe that sounds one or more tones of fixed pitch, to give the tone for tuning an instrument, or for a choral group. Often found as a small round disc marked with notes C to C, with chromatic notes on the opposite side.

PITTS, LILLA BELLE (1884–1970). An authority on junior high school music, Pitts was the originator of the general music concept. To her, general music was a part of the general education of the child. She believed that the arts "is to make people more acutely aware of life—to hear more, feel more, see more, and be more." Pitts also believed that singing activity was the basic activity in music education. All children are involved in singing, and it involves the most basic instrument—the voice. She thought that the active precedes the perceptive understanding and that "sensing meaning comes before attempting to translate symbols back into meanings for which they stand merely as reminders" (from a class presentation at Teachers College, NY).

Pitts was very active in **MENC**, serving as president (1942–1944), a member of the Research Council (1950–1954), and on the editorial board of the *Journal of Research in Music Education*. A southerner in schooling, she eventually found her way to Teachers College, Columbia University, as a graduate and eventual lecturer and professor.

Bib.: Blanchard, Gerald L., *Lilla Belle Pitts: Her Life and Contributions to Music Education*, 1966.

A PLACE CALLED SCHOOL (1984). *See* GOODLAD, JOHN.

PLAYER PIANO. A self-playing piano containing a pneumatic or electro-mechanical mechanism that operates the piano action via preprogrammed music, using perforated paper or metallic rolls. The rise of the player piano grew with the rise of the mass-produced piano for the home in the late 19th and early 20th centuries. Sales peaked in 1924, then declined as the improvement in phonograph recordings due to electrical recording methods developed in the mid-1920s. *See also* MUSIC ROLL.

THE PLOWDEN REPORT. (UK.) This 1967 report raised the level of public awareness about primary education in England and Wales. While many of its practical recommendations did not receive decisive action by Parliament, it did create an agenda for improvement that would surface in various acts of Parliament 10 years later.

PLYGAIN CAROLS (1600s and 1700s). (UK-Wales.) Associated with the winter solstice in the Christian tradition, they were sung to complex, extended tunes, including non-Welsh melodies, with words in *cynghanedd*, a verbal embroidery including alliteration and interval rhyme. In the 19th century under the influence of hymns, carols became simpler in text and tune.

PORTFOLIO ASSESSMENT. A collection of a student's works over a specified period of time for the purpose of assessment. Often contains samples of the student's coursework with a variety of critiques, both student self-assessment and teacher assessments.

PRAIRIE PROVINCES. (Can.) The Canadian Prairies is a region of Canada, specifically in western Canada, which may correspond to several different definitions, natural or political. Generally, the Prairie Provinces, or simply the Prairies, comprise the provinces of Alberta, Saskatchewan, and Manitoba, as they are largely covered by prairie. In a more restricted sense, the term may also refer only to the areas of those provinces covered by prairie. Prairie also covers portions of northeastern British Columbia, though that province is typically not included in the region in a political sense.

THE PRAXIS SERIES. Devised by educators for the **Educational Testing Service** (ETS), it replaced the National Teacher Exam (NTE). Used to measure teacher candidates' knowledge and skills for licensing and certification processes.

PRAXIS I measures basic skills in reading, writing, and mathematics. In addition to licensure, these tests are often used to qualify candidates for entry into a teacher-education program.

PRAXIS II measures subject-specific content knowledge, as well as general and subject-specific teaching skills that are needed for beginning teaching.

PRAXIS II. One of the first in a series of tests devised by a committee of music educators for the **Educational Testing Service** (ETS) to assess the skills and knowledge of beginning music teachers. This series of tests were designed to replace the National Teacher Exam (NTE), used by many states in the late 1980s. It was an attempt to measure students' musical abilities by testing both written and aural skills as well as teaching behaviors in the classroom and ensembles.

PRIMARY EDUCATION. (UK.) In England and Wales, this refers to provision for the education of children age 5–11. It is usually divided into two phases: the infant school for children age 5–7, which delivers key stage 1 of the **national curriculum**, and the junior school for children age 7–11, which delivers key stage 2. It has been in effect since the **Butler Act** (1944).

PRIMARY MEASURES OF MUSICAL AUDIATION (PMMA). A music aptitude test developed by **Edwin Gordon** in 1979 for students from kindergarten through third grade. The test has two sections: tonal stimuli (40 sets) and rhythm stimuli (40 pairs). The test has an interval consistency reliability of .90 and a test-retest reliability of .75. This is one of the first developmental aptitude tests.

PRIMARY SCHOOLS.
(UK.) A maintainer school for pupils in the age range from 5 to 11-plus.
(Aus.) Primary schools may be from 5 to 12 or 13 years of age.

(U.S.) It loosely applies to *elementary school* or *grade school* for teaching in grades 1, 2, 3, 4. Referred to as *primary grades*.

PROFESSIONAL TOURING BANDS. These bands had their beginnings in the post–Civil War era under the direction of **Patrick Gilmore** and **John Philip Sousa**. They each brought polished musical performances to more Americans than any other ensemble. In 1892 Sousa formed the band that set the standard from that time forward. Professional groups included circus bands and even family bands (complete with wives and daughters) that toured on entertainment circuits in amateur ranks; lodge bands, industrial bands, ethnic bands, children's bands, and institutional bands (including prison groups) also flourished. It was Sousa's tours, plus the growth of phonograph recordings, that brought the sound of published playing to more and more American communities and listeners. His band spent half the year or more touring North America by rail. European tours were organized in the early 1900s and a world tour in 1910–1911. By 1931 the professional band was a thing of the past, with the advent of the school band, which had begun to flourish.

PROGRESSIVE EDUCATION. This term became synonymous with the entire movement to change the practices of the traditional school, although no official organization formed until 1919. By that time, **John Dewey** had developed a philosophy and theory of education that came to represent "progressivism." School bands and orchestras found meaningful support in this new philosophy. **Lawrence Cremin** described progressive education as the broadening of the program and function of the school to include direct concern for health, vocation, and the quality of family and community life. It is considered student centered rather than teacher centered. Critics felt that progressive education lacked structure and placed too little emphasis on academic rigor.

PROGRESSIVE MUSIC SERIES. First published in 1914; three leading editors of MSNC—**Osborne McConathy**, Edward Bailey Birge, and W. Otto Miessner—contributed to the series. No exercises or scales for drill; "observation songs" to observe notation for tonal and rhythmic elements; songs and singing games with large bodily motions were students' music education for three years. Themes from Mozart, Beethoven, Dvorak, and others were in student texts and related to musical elements experienced in the singing.

PROJECT ZERO. An educational research group at the Harvard University Graduate School of Education. Its mission is to understand and enhance learning, thinking, and creativity in the arts, as well as humanities and scientific disciplines, at the individual and institutional levels. *See also* ARTS PROPEL.

PROMISE RESEARCH (2001). (UK-Wales.) A nationwide research investigation into the special education needs of children in England. This became known as the PROMISE (**Pr**ovision **O**f **M**usic **I**n **S**pecial **E**ducation) project. It was found that "there is considerable variation in the quantity and quality of music education and music therapy available to pupils." This research occurred in 2001, with Welch et al. as researchers. Within the special school populations in England, it was found that more than 30,000 children have complex needs. The age range was from early years to 16+.
  Lit.: *British Journal of Special Education* 29, no. 4 (Dec. 2002).

PROTEST SONGS. Songs reflecting social change through individuals and groups have been a part of human music history for hundreds of years. These songs range from folk material to composed songs reflecting the consensus of musicians who became involved in movements of social reform. "We Shall Overcome" is a familiar folk song made famous during the American civil rights movement of 1964–1965.

PSALTER. A collection of psalms for liturgical or devotional use. The Puritans brought this with them from England. Considered a manual of psalmody, it was used as a basis for teaching music to members of the choir and congregation. *See AINSWORTH PSALTER*; *BAY PSALM BOOK*.

PUBLIC LAW 94-103, 1975. A law requiring due process and a "free appropriate public education" (FAPE) for all disabled children. The act went into effect in 1977.

PYTHAGORAS (6TH CENTURY BCE). An Ionian Greek philosopher and mathematician. "There is geometry in the humming of the strings. . . . There is music in the spacing of the spheres. . . . Everything is created out of whole numbers. From their ratios, differences and sums everything is made. The spheres are arranged by their immutable laws, rotating in eternal **harmony**. In the same way we can attain perfect harmony with the cosmos by opening our minds to the truth of numbers."
  Bib.: Apel, Willi, *Harvard Dictionary of Music*, 2nd ed., 1973.

Q

QCHORD. This instrument is a digital version of the **Omnichord** and is used with **autoharp** in the elementary classroom. Because of its unique features, the QChord can be strummed like a guitar, can play melodies like a keyboard, can play chords like a piano, and contains over 100 MIDI voices and rhythms that can be used throughout the music-education spectrum and beyond. It is a Suzuki product.

QIN (CH'IN). Early Chinese zither, most honored of Chinese instruments, associated with the Confucian ruling class, who played meditatively upon it while pondering life.

QUADRILLE. A type of square dance in five sections popular at the court of Napoleon I in the early 19th century. Music selected from popular tunes, operatic arias, and sometimes sacred works.

QUADRIVIUM. From medieval Latin, "the four mathematical studies." The division of mathematics into four groups—geometry, astronomy, arithmetic, and **music**. The higher division of the seven liberal arts needed for a bachelor's degree in the Middle Ages (the lower division of the liberal arts comprised the *trivium*—grammar, logic, and rhetoric).

QUÉBEC. A province in eastern Canada. A seaport in and the capital of New France from 1663 to 1759, when it was taken by the English. Formal education came to New France in the 17th century, and like the first settlers in Jamestown, Virginia, in the 1600s, missionaries attempted to instruct the Indians in their faith. Most of the priests who arrived in Québec had undergone musical training in the monastic colleges of France. Upon the arrival of the Ursulines in 1639, education for young women included instruction in music. Following the conflict of 1759, Québec became a British colony. The educational system established in Québec remained in effect almost unchanged until educational reform occurred in the 1960s with the implementation of the Parent Commission Report.

QUEEN'S QUARTERLY. (Can.) A multidisciplinary journal aimed at the generally educated reader. Prints articles, essays, reviews, short stories, and poetry.

QUERFLOTE. Name for the transverse flute in German (Querflöte).

QUESENEL, JOSEPH (1746–1809). (Can.) New France composer, poet, and playwright who published sheet music from two operas written in the late 18th century.

QUODLIBET. (Latin for "what pleases.") Lighthearted compositions comprising several popular tunes or fragments of tunes ingeniously put together, such as the finale of Bach's *Goldberg Variations*, where two popular melodies of the day are combined within the harmonic outline of the theme. *See also* PARTNER SONGS.

R

RAMEAU, JEAN PHILLIPE (1683–1764). Composer and theorist who wrote *Traité de L'Harmonie reduite à ses Principes naturels* (1722), in which he laid the foundation of the modern theory of harmony by setting forth the principles of key-center, fundamental bass, and the roots and inversions of chords.

RAP. A style of urban black popular music that emerged in the mid-1970s, characterized by (often) improvised rhymes, performed to a rhythmic accompaniment, frequently performed **a cappella**, with sexual, socially relevant, or political lyrics. The music itself became known as *hip-hop*.

RECORDER. An end-blown vertical flute ca. 1800 with a whistle mouthpiece popular during the Baroque period; later superseded by the transverse flute. In the 20th century there was a revival of interest in the recorder, which is now used not only in professional groups but also in public school music classes. These recorders are generally inexpensive and made of wood, plastic, or other synthetic materials.

REED. A flexible thin strip of cane, wood, plastic, or metal (e.g., organ, harmonica) attaches to the open end of a woodwind instrument so that the opening is almost completely closed. With oboes and bassoons, they have two reeds that vibrate against each other, hence the name *double-reed instruments*.

REEL. A line dance of Britain and Ireland, usually in 4/4 time, with little or no syncopation and reprises of eight-measure sections; a dance in a four-couple set.

REES, STEPHEN. (UK-Wales.) One of the prominent members of the Society for the Traditional Instruments of Wales (1996), an organization that wished to preserve the instrumental tradition in Wales. Rees, a former fiddler with the folk song group *Ar Log*, lectures in music at the University of Wales at Bangor.

REGIMENTAL BANDS. (Can.) The arrival of British regimental bands, as well as immigrants from Great Britain, Germany, and the U.S., stimulated the growth of secular music during the second half of the 18th century. Because of this influx of regimental band members, instrumental music instruction began to spread throughout the Canadian provinces, especially in Newfoundland. The rise of instrumental instruction in Canadian schools has been due to the influence of two or three outstanding teachers who set high standards for others to emulate.

REGISTER OF CULTURAL ORGANIZATIONS (RCO). (Aus.) Est. 1991. Assists qualifying cultural bodies to attract support by enabling them to offer donors the incentive of a tax deduction; aims to strengthen private-sector support for the arts and encourages Australians to contribute to the nation's vibrant cultural life.

REGULAR SINGING. One of the methods used in singing psalm tunes imported from the Old World was the *regular way*, which consisted of singing by note, or reading music. The *old way*, inherited from England, was the practice of "**lining out**."

REIMER, BENNETT (1932–). A prolific author of some two dozen books and over 145 articles and chapters on a variety of topics in music and arts education. Reimer is best known for his landmark book, *A Philosophy of Music Education*, first published in 1970, which had a significant impact on students, scholars, and university teachers because of its emphasis on aesthetic education, or that branch of philosophy concerned with the "essential nature and value of music education, which are determined by the nature and value of the art of music." As a student, Reimer was influenced by **Charles Leonhard** and **Harry Broudy**, both of whom were his teachers at the University of Illinois. He began his career in music as a clarinetist, oboist, and public school music teacher. Later he became a specialist in the philosophy of music education; curriculum development, with emphasis on the "special curriculum"; theory of research; and comprehensive arts education programs. Always interested in teaching and the education process, Reimer's textbooks on music for grades one through eight, *Silver Burdett Music*, were the most widely used throughout the U.S. and the world for two decades.

From 1978 until his retirement in 1997, Reimer held the John W. Beattie Endowed Chair in Music at Northwestern University, where he was chair of the Music Education Department, director of doctoral programs in music education, and founder and director of the Center for the Study of Education and Music Experience. He also taught at Case Western Reserve University from 1965 to 1978, where he held the Kulas Endowed Chair in Music, and was chair of the Music Education Department.

RELIABILITY. A statistical term that in lay terms means the extent to which a test is dependable, stable, and consistent, when given to different people and/or administered on different occasions. Together with *validity*, reliability is a fundamental property that test constructors hope to achieve.

RELIEF TEACHER. (Aus.) A substitute teacher or supply teacher.

RELIGIOUS STUDIES IN THE UK. The national schools continue to have the right to provide religious education according to the ethos of the school and community. Parents may withdraw their children from religious education, but schools continue to provide religious instruction.

REPORT OF THE CANADIAN CONFERENCE FOR THE ARTS. A project of the Canada Council and UNESCO, *Learning to Live; Living to Learn*, that outlines 50 values that the arts bring to Canadian society. Arts education allows one to learn in, about, and through the arts in formal and informal ways, in schools and communities both *intrinsically* and *extrinsically* (or, instrumental value).

REPUBLIC OF IRELAND. *See* NORTHERN IRELAND.

RESONATOR BELLS. Tuned metal (or plastic) bars mounted individually on a block of wood or plastic that serves as its own resonator. Individual bells can be removed; two or more bells can be used to play harmony as well as melodies.

REVELLI, WILLIAM (1902–1994). (U.S.) Director of bands, including the Michigan Marching Band, at the University of Michigan for 36 years from 1935 to 1971. He won international acclaim for the musical precision of the marching band. The band also was known for intricate formations and high-stepping style. Among his other innovations for marching bands, Revelli was the first to score original music for band shows, to synchronize music and movement, to use an announcer for marching band events, to do a postgame show, and to host a high school band day. He was dedicated to furthering musical education in high schools, as witnessed by his work with the Hobart (Indiana) High School Band from 1925 to 1935. Revelli influenced band directors throughout the country when he founded the **College Band Directors National Association** in 1942. He had a roster of over 300 active members in 1959, and it continued to grow among college band directors as well as those with the most highly developed band programs. Revelli had a fierce dedication to excellence and was known as a tough taskmaster. At Michigan, he was known as *The Chief.*

RHYTHM ENSEMBLE. This refers to an ensemble in grades K–3. A classroom percussion ensemble made up of musical characteristics such as high/low, strong beat/weak beat, dynamics, and accents. Instruments are divided into woods, metals, and skins. Children are matched to instruments according to their developmental ability from sticks and claves, finger cymbals and triangles, to bongo drums and conga drums, as well as **Orff instruments** when available.

RHYTHM SECTION. Percussion section in a jazz band consisting of piano, bass, and drums, supplying the main beat; if a guitar is used, it will function within this section at times.

RHYTHM SYLLABLES. Systems of notation used by elementary teachers to teach note values. **Kodály** used a system based on *ta* and *ti*. These, with additions and variations, are still used in French conservatories. **Edwin Gordon** used a system of *du-de* and *du-di*.

RICHARDS, MARY HELEN (1921–1998). A pioneer adapter of Kodály concepts who organized the Richards Institute of Music Education and Research, which concentrated on how children learn. Her *Threshold to Music* is based on the work of **Zoltan Kodály**. Kodaly advised Richards personally to use the language and songs native to the people in the U.S. American folk songs and games were selected that reflect the rhythm, accents, and inflections of American English. Kinesthetic experience is stressed in the many singing games or games with songs, and through body motions that the child is led to discover through repeated words, rhythm patterns, phrases, and tonal patterns. Important rhythmic and vocal patterns are learned in notation to encourage sight singing. Curwen hand signs and corresponding syllables are employed. In Richards's *Experience Charts* (1–3), from her *Threshold to Music*, there are pictorial ways of teaching rhythmic notation (e.g., animals for quarter notes, replaced by stick notation as the children move through each section). She also uses the "empty dog house" to teach rests. She created a program called **Education through Music** (ETM) as a result of the Richards Institute of Music Education and Research, of which she was the founding director.

RICHARDS INSTITUTE OF MUSIC EDUCATION AND RESEARCH.
See MARY HELEN RICHARDS.

RICHARDSON, MARILYN ANN (1936–). (Aus.) Opera singer. Born in Sydney and studied singing and piano at the Conservatorium of Music. In 1971 she was awarded a Churchill Fellowship to study in Europe, where she made her international debut in Theater Basel in the title roles of *Lulu* and *Salome*, 1972–1975. She returned to Australia to perform the title role in *Aida* in 1975 for the Australian Opera. She has performed with all of the Australian state operas and has given numerous concerts and recitals specializing in 20th-century music. Since 1958 she has given the first Australian performance of over 300 songs and vocal works by Messiaen, Dallapiccola, Berio, and **Cage**. She is coordinator and voice teacher for the Australian National Academy in Melbourne, and coaches Opera Queensland's Young Artists.

RING UP. (Aus.) To telephone.

RITCHIE, JEAN (1922–2012). An American folk music singer, songwriter, and Appalachian dulcimer player. Ritchie attended Cumberland College (University of the Cumberlands) and later the University of Kentucky in Lexington. In 1946, she graduated with a BA in social work. She taught elementary school, and in the summer of 1946 worked at the Henry Street Settlement in New York. There she met Oscar Brand, Leadbelly, and Pete Seeger. They began to sing family songs again. Ritchie sang unaccompanied folk songs, but occasionally accompanied herself on guitar or lap dulcimer. She was awarded a Fulbright to trace the links between American ballads and the songs of the British Isles. In 1955, Ritchie wrote a book about her family, who lived in Viper, Kentucky, of the Cumberland Mountains; this was *Singing Family of the Cumberlands* (1955). She became known as "the Mother of Folk," as well as for work songs and ballads.

Ritchie performed at Carnegie Hall and at the Royal Albert Hall in London. She received a National Endowment for the Arts National Heritage Fellowship, the nation's highest honor in the folk and traditional arts.

RITCHIE, JOHN (1921–). (Aus.-NZ.) A composer, teacher, and administrator, Ritchie is known for choral music, music for brass, concerto-type works, and church music. He has served as a professor of music, head of music, and deputy vice chancellor. Ritchie has conducted many choirs and formed the John Ritchie String Orchestra and the Christ Church Civic Orchestra. He guest-conducted the New Zealand Symphony Orchestra and Ballet. His roles as secretary general of the **International Society for Music**

Education from 1976 to 1984 and president from 1990 to 1992 have been important to music educators. He was elected an individual member of the **International Music Council** in 1979. Ritchie is currently professor emeritus at Canterbury University.

RIVETT FAMILY. (Aus.) An Australian family noted for their contribution to the fields of welfare, science, and education. A daughter of the family, Elsie, founded the Children's Library and Crafts Movement.

ROBERTS, ELEAZAR (1825–1912). (UK-Wales.) Welsh musician and writer who wrote for several Welsh journals and traveled Wales setting up music classes. Most notable for pioneering the **tonic sol-fa** method of **sight singing** in Wales, having adapted and translated the works of **John Curwen** into Welsh. His most important publication on the topic was *Llawlyfr y Tonic Solfa*, a handbook that was designed to help in the teaching of the tonic sol-fa method. His work also led to the strengthening of the practice of congregational singing.

ROBIN HOOD AND THE TANNER. (Traditional English ballad.) This is a ballad, or storytelling song, that lends itself to choral speaking and dramatization. The singing is interrupted by dialogue. The May Day celebrations in early England were called *Robin Hood's Festivals*. Robin Hood was king of May, and Maid Marian was his queen. **Morris dances**, archery contests, and bonfires were features of the celebrations.

THE ROCKEFELLER REPORT. *See COMING TO OUR SENSES*—THE ROCKEFELLER REPORT.

ROCK MUSIC. A popular music style begun in the 1950s with a blending of gospel, rhythm and blues, and country music. It originated as a rebellion against the social mores and rigidity of the 1950s. Many individual groups and styles emerged from rock, with Elvis Presley (1935–1977) being one of the first to bring rock and roll to the public.

ROCK OPERA. A work of rock music that presents a story line told over multiple parts or sections, similar to a traditional opera. It tells a story that may involve songs performed as if sung by separate characters in a drama, as in classical opera. One of the earliest attempts at rock opera appeared in the 1960s in Canada; later, informally, Peter Townsend and The Who released their first attempt at rock opera. Two of the more familiar works are *Tommy*, the first of The Who's two full-scale rock operas; and *Jesus Christ Superstar*, composed in the 1970s by Andrew Lloyd Webber and Tim Rice. Even though billed as a *rock opera*, the latter became more famous as a Broadway musical.

The rock opera concept has continued developing, as in the nonprofit Boston Rock Opera (1993), and the Baltimore Rock Opera Society, formed out of Baltimore, Maryland (2009). They both have featured original scores.

ROGERS, CARL (1902–1987). One of the most influential American psychologists, and among the founders of the humanistic approach to psychology, Rogers is considered to be one of the founding fathers of psychotherapy research. His contributions to music education and the arts field in general come from his person-centered approach, his own unique approach to understanding personality and human relationships. These approaches found wide application to client-centered therapy, education through student-centered learning, organizations, and other group settings. Two of his most important books are *On Becoming a Person* (1961) and *Freedom to Learn for the 80s* (1983). Rogers's therapeutic approach is based on the belief that the individual has the ability to work out his own problems, and that it is preferable that he do so. The role of the therapist is one of a facilitator who assists the individual in clarifying, understanding, and working out his own problems as indicated above. His concepts of learning and teaching are primarily a matter of facilitation. As a believer in third-force or humanistic psychology, Rogers shared Abraham Maslow's approach to learning, in that it is learning geared to the "whole" person—both intellect and feelings—that results in learning that is most lasting and pervasive.

Rogers won many awards within his profession for his work in psychotherapy research, and as a result of his involvement with the national intergroup conflict in South Africa and Northern Ireland, he was nominated for the Nobel Peace Prize. Unfortunately, the nomination arrived just days after his death in February 1987.

ROHNER, TRAUGOTT (1906–1987). (U.S.) In 1946, while he was directing a junior high and high school orchestra every day, and teaching instrumental music at three grade schools and several classes at Northwestern University for future band and orchestra directors, Rohner decided that he could produce a better publication for school band and orchestra directors. He proceeded to found and publish *The Instrumentalist* magazine. In 1960 he founded the **National Band Association**, dedicated to the promotion of excellence in all aspects of wind bands, including performance, education, and literature.

ROHRBACHER, MICHAEL. Professor and certified music therapist who teaches courses in music therapy at Shenandoah University (VA). He began undergraduate studies as a piano performance major at the Peabody Conservatory and later completed the bachelor of music degree with a concentration in music therapy from East Carolina University. He holds a master's of science in education with a concentration in communicative disorders from Johns Hopkins University, and a PhD in ethnomusicology from the University of Maryland, Baltimore County. Prior service includes six years as a music therapist with the Baltimore City Public Schools, former board director with the Certification Board for Music Therapists, and former president of the Mid-Atlantic Region of the American Music Therapy Association, Inc. Training Program. He currently is a visiting professor at Tokushima Bunri University, Japan. Awards include an honorary doctorate from Tokushima Bunri University (2003), and Shenandoah's 2002–2003 Exemplary Teacher Award, presented by the General Board of Higher Education and Ministry of the United Methodist Church. His fieldwork and research interests include health-care arts in Bali, Indonesia, and medical ethnomusicology. Dr. Rohrbacher's students have field experience in hospitals, schools, and a variety of assisted living facilities throughout the city and county each semester. His students are also involved in learning how to play Indonesian musical instruments, which they perform each spring for the general university population.

ROLLAND, PAUL (1911–1978). A violinist born in Budapest and an influential American violin teacher who concentrated on the pedagogy of teaching fundamentals to beginning string students. He emphasized that the physical demands of most violin techniques can be taught in the first two years of violin education.

Rolland earned a BM from Simpson College (Iowa), and an MM from the Franz Liszt Academy of Music in Budapest. He was first violinist with the Budapest Symphony, but when asked to choose between performing and teaching, he chose teaching.

He published a book and a set of videos titled *The Teaching of Action in String Playing.* His ideas and methods were also documented in the University of Illinois String Research Project films. He helped found the **American String Teachers Association** (ASTA), and in 1950 became the first editor of its journal, *American String Teacher*. Rolland was chairman of the String Department at the University of Illinois, and he also founded the International String Workshop.

Before his death, he collaborated with his son Peter and Norman Burgess to develop a pedagogical method using folk fiddle tunes to develop playing skills in a logical sequence. He also believed in the pedagogical value of *fiddling* as a means of developing good motion patterns for young violinists.

ROM. 1. (*read-only memory*) A computer storage device that holds data that can be read, but not altered, by program instructions. **2.** (*rom*) (Aus.) A ceremony performed by the Aboriginal Australians of Arnhem Land as a mark of friendship, with singing and dancing.

ROOT, F. GEORGE (1820–1895). His autobiography offers a detailed look at Lowell Mason's influence on Root's musical life. He grew up on a farm wanting to be a musician but never played organ or piano until at 18 he went to Boston. He eventually won national fame as a teacher of vocal music. He taught as one of Mason's assistants in the Boston Public Schools. After teaching in New York, he went to Paris for further musical study. As a result of further positive performance activities in New York, he was urged to complete instructional tune books by Bradbury and Woodbury. These tune books failed in the elementary music series because of their "lofty" approach. Root then chose to adapt his work to the practical needs of the people. His approach was to move from simple music to more complex compositions. In the 1850s, he began to write popular songs, which moved his career beyond the realm in which Mason worked.

Root wrote "The Battle Cry of Freedom," which became a recruiting song for the Union army. It became one of the Union's most popular martial songs. It was also taken over and adapted by the Confederates for their use. The "Vacant Chair" was also a very popular Civil War song. Later, it was discovered that Root had written "Tramp, Tramp, Tramp, the Boys are Marching," another memorable song of this period.

George Root made a significant contribution to the National Music Convention (1840), where he and others taught music pedagogy, harmony, conducting, and voice culture. This convention eventually led to **normal institutes** that became purely pedagogical enterprises. For Root's continued efforts in many areas of music teaching, he was considered one of the leaders in public school music.

ROOT MUSIC. The fundamental of a chord or a series of harmonics.

ROTE. 1. Learning facts mechanically by repetition. **2.** Learning to sing songs by repetition.

ROTE TO NOTE. *See* NOTE TO ROTE.

ROWLEY, ALEC (1892–1959). (UK.) Composer, pianist, and organist. Teacher and examiner, Trinity College of Music, 1920. Received Carnegie Award for his ballet, 1927.

ROYAL ACADEMY OF MUSIC (1822). (UK.) College of music in London supported by government grant, subscription, donations, and fees. Moved to Marylebone Road in 1912. Has a wide range of facilities, including concert hall (Duke's Hall), lecture hall, opera theater (opened 1977), and library.

ROYAL ARTILLERY. (UK.) The British Royal Artillery has had an organized band since 1762, which accompanied the regiment on active duty. On the battlefield, the band played lovely airs and patriotic music to inspire the soldiers. They were not armed for battle. Drummers and fifers were not officially part of the band, but fought in the ranks with the other men.

The regiment band's patron, the Duchess of Kent, died in 1861. She, it is claimed, wrote the Royal Artillery Slow March for the Regiment.

THE ROYAL COLLEGE OF MUSIC. (UK.) London music college, successor to National Training School of Music (NTSM). Founded by Prince of Wales in 1882 and opened in 1883, and received Royal Charter. Originally housed in the NTSM building, but in 1894 a new building was opened. Large concert hall opened in 1901 and later an opera theater, later replaced by Britten Theater in 1986. Has superb music library and valuable collection of historical instruments.

ROYAL MANCHESTER COLLEGE OF MUSIC. (UK.) Founded in Manchester, 1893, with title *Royal* from inception. Royal Charter, 1923. In 1972, merged with Northern School of Music to become Royal Northern College of Music, Manchester.

ROYAL MILITARY SCHOOL OF MUSIC (RMSM). (UK.) Formed in 1857 at **Kneller Hall** near Twickenham, a Military Music Class was created for the purpose of training army bandsmen as bandmasters. In 1875 the class was recognized to train bandmasters, and in 1887 it became known as the Royal Military School of Music.

ROYAL NATIONAL EISTEDDFOD. (UK-Wales.) This is the most important gathering of the competition festival in Wales. In early times, it was a gathering of Welsh bards, usually confined to music and a celebration of Welsh language and culture. It now includes nearly all forms of the arts, with international competition. It takes place annually in towns in northern and southern Wales. An International Eisteddfod has had choirs and dancers from all over the world compete in Llangollen since 1947. It aims to include all aspects of culture in Wales, classical and traditional. It attracts thousands each day to the arts and crafts exhibition, the literary pavilion for the poetry competitions, the music studio for the competitions and instrumental performances, and the main pavilion for competition in the traditional arts of dancing, folk singing, *cerdd dant* recitation, and classical singing and playing.

ROYAL NAVAL SCHOOL OF MUSIC (1903). (UK.) The primary function of this school is to train and supply bands for service in royal ships and naval establishments. Instruction is given in orchestral and military band playing. All are eligible for advancement to higher ranks, and those selected are given extensive training at the school to qualify for bandmaster.

ROYAL NORTHERN COLLEGE OF MUSIC, MANCHESTER. Opened in 1972 by amalgamation of the Royal Manchester College of Music and the Northern School of Music. Housed in a new building on Oxford Road containing a concert hall, opera theater, recital room, tutorial room, etc.

ROYAL SCOTTISH ACADEMY OF MUSIC (1929). (UK-Scot.) Music college in Glasgow. In 1929, a Scottish National Academy of Music was formed to combine with university faculty of music. The *Royal* prefix added in 1944. In 1968 there was a name change to the **Royal Scottish Academy of Music and Drama**, in order to reflect the broadened scope of teaching in the academy.

ROYAL SCOTTISH ACADEMY OF MUSIC AND DRAMA (1968). Formerly the **Royal Scottish Academy of Music** (1944–1968), which was formerly the Scottish National Academy of Music (1929–1944), formerly Glasgow Athenaeum (Limited) School of Music (1890–1929). The name change in 1968 was made due to the widening teaching activities of the institution.

RUBANK ETUDES. An etude series for all instruments was a mainstay for many years among instrumental teachers. It was a three-way partnership of George A. Finder (1894–1962), Joseph J. Urbanek (1894–1953), and Harry Ruppel Sr. (1888–1957) under the name Finder & Urbanek, in Chicago. In 1927, Finder sold his interest to the other partners—Ruppel and Urbanek—who changed the name of the company to just Rubank. Rubank eventually moved to Miami, and in 1988 the company was dissolved. There were a number of composers for the Rubank series. Some of these were:

H. Lawrence Walters (1918–1984), chief composer until his death; Himie Vexman (1912–2011); Hale Ascher Vandercook (1864–1949); and Clifton Williams (1923–1976).

RUTKOWSKI, JOANNE. Music educator. Professor of music education at Pennsylvania State University, serving as graduate program chair and area coordinator for music education. She has been a faculty member since 1984, teaching undergraduate and graduate music-education courses, with emphases on music learning and development, research design, curriculum development, assessment, and music for children from birth through age 12. Rutkowski has written a number of articles for major music-education publications, including the *Handbook of Research on Music Teaching and Learning* (ed. Colwell). She currently serves on the editorial committee for several journals and is a member of the **ISME** Early Childhood Commission.

RYERSON, EGERTON (1803–1882). (Can.) The first superintendent of education in western Canada in 1844 was a follower of **Pestalozzi** and Rousseau. He thought of vocal music as a vehicle for promoting middle-class values, and he recognized the potential of music to foster loyalty and patriotism in Canadian life. Ryerson supported teachers in the **Hullah** system of singing. Since he prescribed vocal music as a subject in the Common School Act of 1846, Ryerson has been regarded as the champion of music education in the schools of Ontario. Ryerson was a Methodist minister, educator, and politician, as well as a public education advocate in early Ontario. His study of educational systems led to four school acts that revolutionized education in Canada. Major innovations included: 1) libraries in every school; 2) professional development conventions for teachers; 3) a central textbook press using Canadian authors; and 4) securing land grants for universities. Ryerson University (Toronto) and the Township of Ryerson, Ontario, were named after him.

S

SACKBUT. Early form of trombone, dating from about 1000 AD.

SACRED HARP. A well-known **shape-note** hymnal.

SACRED HARP SINGING. Predominantly religious, but not denominationally specific. It comes from the **fa-so-la** tradition in England, but uses the American system of **shape-note** notation. Singing style includes a full-throated sound from each singer. The tenor line is the melody. All parts have an octave range with some parts of the melody included. Harmonies are formed in parallel fifths and octaves, as well as a few thirds and an occasional fourth. It is always sung **a cappella**, and singers arrange themselves in a hollow square with chairs or pews arranged as tenors, trebles, altos, and basses. Treble and tenor sections are usually mixed, with men and women singing an octave apart. The relative pitch is given by a leader, who chooses the song. He or she intones the pitch, and the singers respond with their own parts, at which time the singing begins.

SAKURA. One of the most popular folk songs in Japan. It celebrates the national flower, cherry blossoms, which in springtime provide a profusion of pink and white blossoms through the countryside, much like the cherry blossoms in Washington, DC. Stylized movements are often added to express ideas in the song.
   Lit.: Wolfe et al., *Voices of the World*, "Movement," 1963.

SALSA. A raucous Latin American dance originating in the Caribbean islands, notably Cuba, with African roots. The name may have come from its peppery, pervasive rhythm over a hypnotically repetitive melodic line.

SAMBA DRUMMING. A characteristic accompaniment to the Brazilian dance, marked by a fast rolling rhythm in 2/4 time and vigorous syncopation.

SAMISEN. Japanese three-string guitar or lute, without frets, with string of waxed silk played by a plectrum called *batsi*. Often used in *Kabuki*, the popular musical drama of Japan.

SAND BLOCKS. Small blocks of wood covered with varying grades of sandpaper. Handles for each are attached. Percussion instrument for children to provide accompaniment to songs or ensembles.

SAX, ADOLPHE (1814–1894). Inventor of the saxophone (1842), an instrument that is made of metal with a single-reed clarinet-type mouthpiece and conical bore. Sax went to Paris in 1842, where he exhibited brass and woodwind instruments at the Paris Exposition of 1884, winning a silver medal. He taught the saxophone at the Paris Conservatory (1858–1871) and published a method for it. It was adopted by jazz musicians ca. 1918. He received the Grand Prix in Paris (1867).

SCAT SINGING. A style of jazz performance in which a singer improvises nonsense syllables, usually quickly with a rhythmic impulse. Sometimes singers imitate sections of instrumental sounds or short melodic phrases. Ella Fitzgerald made this technique her trademark. Louis Armstrong was its major proponent in the 1920s.

SCHAEFFER, PIERRE (1910–1995). *See* TAPE RECORDER MUSIC.

SCHAFER, RAYMOND MURRAY (1933–). Canadian-born composer, writer, music educator, and environmentalist, perhaps best known for his *World Soundscape Project*, an important project relating to acoustic ecology.

SCHOOL BANDS. (U.S.) Instrumental music in public schools began slowly, with school orchestras preceding bands. Instrument manufacturers led to much of the school band and orchestra development, and the 1920s proved to be a time of healthy growth and development for bands. As a result of the **progressive education** movement, bands and orchestras caught the attention of the **MSNC** in 1922. Research indicates that a number of school bands were formed across the country around 1910, but they were not endorsed by any national organization at the time. After WWI, school bands began to proliferate, and **William D. Revelli**, who was later an important figure in collegiate bands, began an instrumental music program at Hobart, Indiana. The high school band program at Hobart was so successful that the band movement was solidified during these years, and as a result, bands have become an integral part of school and community life throughout the U.S.

Band programs often begin as early as the third grade, creating opportunities for students to be band members from elementary through high school.

SCHOOL CURRICULUM AND ASSESSMENT AUTHORITY (SCAA). (UK.) Formed in 1997 as a result of the Education Act of 1993 to take over the responsibilities of both the National Curriculum Council (NCC) and the School Examinations and Assessment Council (SEAC). It subsumed the curriculum and assessment functions in one body.

SCHOOL MUSIC PROGRAM: DESCRIPTION AND STANDARDS (1986). (U.S.) A list of goals for school music programs established by **MENC**, which was a revision of the goals established in 1974. These standards and descriptions served as the basis for the National Standards in Music developed in the early 1990s.

THE SCHOOL OF SCOTTISH STUDIES (1951). Located at Edinburgh University and founded in 1951, created by an archive that houses an extensive collection of Gaelic and Lowland music.

SCHOOL ORCHESTRAS. School orchestras preceded school bands. As early as 1896, Connecticut had a number of grammar school orchestras. In 1912, **MSNC** advocated high school orchestra ensembles. Jesse Clark formed an orchestra in Wichita, Kansas, in 1896. W. Earhart created a high school orchestra with full instrumentation in Richmond, Indiana. **Joseph Maddy** became the first supervisor of instrumental music in America in 1918. In 1926, he formed the first National High School Orchestra to perform for the MSNC. Maddy organized two other events, including the Chicago MSNC meeting. This third meeting inspired Maddy and **Thaddeus P. Giddings** to found the National High School Orchestra and Band Camp at Interlochen, Michigan. It is now a prestigious year-round arts academy.

SCHWADRON, ABRAHAM (1925–1987). Musician, composer-arranger, scholar, and educator. His doctorate is from Boston University. His music publishing included nearly 40 original works, both chamber instrumental and choral, and numerous transcriptions for woodwind and brass ensembles. He probed all aspects of music education, especially his support of music specialists over the classroom teachers. His strong philosophical position on aesthetics was established with the publication of *Aesthetics: Dimensions for Music Education*, by MENC in 1967. He wrote over 40 articles and numerous reviews of books and dissertations. His contributions on philosophy of music education guided many toward deeper levels of understanding and higher levels of achievement. He was a professor at UCLA from 1969 to 1987. While he was there, his interest in world music led to the development of the graduate program in ethnomusicology and music education, the first joint graduate program of its kind in the U.S.

SCOTS GUARDS. Formed in 1642 by order of Charles I to raise a regiment of personal guards in Scotland. Although annihilated during the Civil War (1646–1647), it was reformed as part of Scotland's army in the reign of Charles II, following the restoration of the monarchy in 1660. Interestingly, the drummers and drum majors do not swing their sticks as in other Scottish regimental bands. The practice is considered undignified and is prohibited in the bands of the Scots Guards.

SCOTTISH CURRICULUM. Scottish language and literature, in combination with Scottish history, define the basic curriculum in Scotland. Students learn Gaelic through courses in Scottish culture. They are also introduced to *Scots*, a dialect of English, when studying their literature. English is introduced gradually in primary schools. Learning is focused on a core academic curriculum that includes the three Rs plus religion. Additionally, national guidelines include social studies, environmental studies, the arts, and physical education.

SCOTTISH GENERAL TEACHING COUNCIL. This council is the national policy and regulatory body for preparing and licensing teachers for nursery, primary, and secondary schools. It represents all the public interests in education, not just those of teachers. The council is responsible for maintaining a list, or registry, of teachers eligible to teach in Scotland's public schools. They are responsible for ensuring high quality in the Scottish education system.

SCULTHORPE, PETER (1929–). (Aus.) Composer known for his orchestral and chamber music. His work is known for its distinctive use of percussion. He was born in Tasmania, and indigenous music became very important to him because of the stories told by his father about past wrongs in Tasmania. His *Requiem* is possibly his most serious and substantial work at this time. Sculthorpe became a lecturer at the University of Sydney in 1963 and remained there until his retirement. He also served as a composer-in-residence at Yale University. His *Sun Music I* was the result of an interesting commission by Sir Bernard Henize, who asked Sculthorpe to write "something without rhythm, harmony, or melody."

SEASHORE, CARL EMIL (1866–1949). Born in Sweden and immigrated with his family to the U.S. in 1870. A leader of the psychology of hearing, he is best known for his battery of tests for aptitude in music, showing the relationship between physical phenomena of sounds and our perception of them. He devised the *Seashore Tests of Musical Ability*, a version of which is still used in the U.S.

SEASHORE MEASURES OF MUSICAL TALENT (1919). (U.S.) An aptitude test consisting of six measures of musical talent: 1) the sense of pitch, 2) the sense of intensity, 3) the sense of time, 4) the sense of consonance and dissonance, 5) tonal memory, and 6) auditory imagery. The basic and fundamental factors measured represent an undercurrent of musicianship from which all musical expression and interest originate. Even with minor revisions, it remains basically the same as the 1939 text version.

SECONDARY COLLEGE. (Aus.) A school providing years 11 and 12 of education.

SECONDARY EDUCATION. That which follows primary education. In most countries, it begins at approximately 11 years of age.

SECONDARY MODERN SCHOOLS. (UK.) A nonselective school introduced in England and Wales by the Education Act of 1944, selective schools being either grammar schools or technical high schools. *See also* TRIPARTITE SYSTEM.

SECONDARY SCHOOL MUSIC. (U.S. and Can.) Music courses at this level are usually classified as either *performing groups* (band, orchestra, chorus) or specific *classes*, such as general music, theory, and music appreciation. Performance groups perform, and the other type of class uses books, tests, and discussions.

SECOND FIDDLE. 1. A part to be written and played by the second violin. **2.** One who takes a minor or secondary role.

THE SEEKERS. (Aus.) Folk-influenced music group—Athol Guy, Bruce Woodley, and Keith Potger—that achieved major international success in 1962 and was joined soon afterward by lead singer Judith Durham. After a debut album in Australia, The Seekers traveled to the UK in 1964 and performed alongside Dusty Springfield, whose brother, Tom, subsequently wrote several of their hit singles. "I'll Never Find Another You" topped the

UK charts in 1964, while their 1966 hit "Georgy Girl" went to Number 1 in the U.S. and was nominated for an Academy Award. They returned to Australia in 1967 and are the only group ever to have been named joint Australians of the Year.

SEE SAW MARJORY DAW. (UK.) A popular nursery rhyme, folk song, and playground singing game published in London in about 1765. It was first recorded by the composer and nursery rhyme collector James W. Elliott in his *National Nursery Rhymes and Nursery Songs* (1870). May have originated as a work song for sawyers to keep rhythm in sawing. This game first appeared in print in about 1700.

Lit.: Opie, I., and P. Opie, *The Oxford Dictionary of Nursery Rhymes*, 1997.

SEGMENTED METHOD. Early American approach to the teaching of hymns, through a practice also known as ***lining out***. A leader sings a phrase, and the congregation repeats the phrase throughout the tune.

SEMINAR ON COMPREHENSIVE MUSICIANSHIP. In 1965, the Contemporary Music Project (CMP) sponsored a four-day seminar titled *Seminar on Comprehensive Musicianship—The Foundation for College Education in Music*. After years of use and differing terminology, ***comprehensive musicianship*** has come to mean the teaching of music from a holistic, comprehensive perspective.

SEQUENCE INSTRUCTION. Arrangement of instruction in a planned and logical sequence.

SEQUENCING. A sequence is an electronic system that stores data about music. A sequence simplifies the process of constructing a musical score with many parts that are synchronized. It can become a whole band or orchestra; hence the word *sequencing*.

SERPENTS. (UK.) **1.** A bass cornet invented by C. E. Guillaume in 1590; constructed of several pieces of wood bound together by a leather covering in the shape of a snake. By the 18th century, the serpent was providing the deep bass in military bands, supporting the bassoons; it was also known as the *Russian bassoon* because of its use in Russian military bands. Berlioz decided it was a laughable monstrosity in the early 19th century. It was rarely in use by the 20th century. **2.** A reed stop in the organ.

SHADOW MARCH. (UK.) Comes from *A Child's Garden of Verses* by Robert Louis Stevenson, and also a short cantata, *The Garden of Childhood*, which is a setting of Stevenson's poems by the late-20th-century English composer **Alec Rowley**.

SHAKUHACHI. Japanese end-blown notched flute that came from China at the end of the first millennium AD. Made of lacquered bamboo, it is used in musical pieces that are typically programmatic and contemplative in character. Its sounds are low and deep throated, as in a bass recorder.

SHAPE-NOTE SINGING. *See* SACRED HARP SINGING.

SHAPE-NOTE. A music notation system begun in the late 1770s. Designed to facilitate congregational and community singing and to be used as a teaching device in **singing schools** in the northeastern U.S. Introduced in 1801 in the publication *The Easy Instructor* by William Little and William Smith for use in singing schools, mostly in the southern states. They used the traditional **fa sol la** teaching method used in England (fa-sol-la-fa-sol-la-mi-fa) for the major scale, so only four shapes were needed (placing note heads on the staff), but instead of oval note heads, they added shapes to the note heads, allowing the shapes—a *triangle* (fa), a *circle* (sol), a *rectangle* (la), and a *diamond* (mi)—to be the means of expressing pitch. The American notation was *fa*, for the tonic *doh*. Shape-note singing continues today among groups who enjoy this approach to reading and singing from the ***Sacred Harp***, a well-known shape-note hymnal.

    Lit.: Hinton, M., and E. Hinton, *Awake My Soul: The Story of the Sacred Harp*, 2006.

SHARP, CECIL J. (1859–1924). (UK.) English folk song and folk dance collector and editor, organist, and writer. Trained as a lawyer and practiced in Australia. Began systematic collection of English folk dances in 1899, and folk songs in 1903. In 1916–1918, with M. Karpeles, collected folk songs in Appalachian Mountains of North America. Published many collections of folk songs and dances. Wrote *English Folk Song* and other books. After his death, Cecil Sharp House in London was built as headquarters of amalgamated **English Folk Dance and Song Society**.

SHENG. Chinese free-reed mouth organ; the earliest known example of this instrument family (ca. 1100 BCE). Involves a mouthpiece, wind chest, and bamboo pipes. Each pipe has a small finger hole, which must be closed in order to sound. Much like the harmonica, pitches are created by inhaling and exhaling.

SHIGIN. (Aus.) Japanese chanted poetry, usually composed of four or more lines. Can be chanted individually or within a group.

SHOFAR. Ancient Jewish ritual trumpet made from a ram's horn, usually blown at the beginning of the Jewish New Year.

SHOW CHOIR. (Swing choir, jazz ensembles.) These three vocal groups all have similar types of structures. They tend to be smaller in size and are usually drawn from the larger choral organization. The differences among them are based on repertoire and approach to movement within each group. The show choir and swing choir usually have colorful attire to match their performance. Jazz ensembles generally tend to be smaller, and less attention is given to specific flashy attire.

SHROVE TUESDAY. (UK.) The last day of Shrovetide (before Ash Wednesday—a time of confession and absolution), long observed as a season of merrymaking before Lent; Pancake Day.

SIGHT-READING or SIGHT SINGING. To read or sing unfamiliar music at first sight. Most English-speaking countries use a system based on **movable doh** or **fixed doh**. Sight-reading differs among the various areas of musical activity.
   Bib.: Apel, Willi, *Harvard Dictionary of Music*, 2nd ed., 1973.

SIGN LANGUAGE. Also known as *dactylology*, a method of visual communication in which the fingers are used to form an alphabet (finger spelling) and to construct words. Used by the deaf and the partially hearing.

SILBERMAN, CHARLES E. *See* CRISIS IN THE CLASSROOM.

SILENT MOVIES. Motion pictures not having spoken dialogue or a soundtrack. Pianists or organists played background music to accompany the action on screen; such music was often used to drown out the noise of the projector. Ca. 1915–1920. In about 1929, with the invention of the soundtrack, silent movies no longer existed, and musicians were no longer employed in movie houses.
   Bib.: Apel, Willi, *Harvard Dictionary of Music*, 2nd ed., 1973.

SILVER BURDETT SERIES. One of the earliest textbook companies (1888) to publish graded or basic series texts for elementary music classes in the public schools. It is now owned by Pearson Education.

SINFONIA. *See* PHI MU ALPHA SINFONIA.

SINGING SCHOOLS. The first American school created solely to teach singing was created at Brattle Street Church in Boston, Massachusetts, in 1717. Its aim was singing in religious celebrations. During the following years, similar schools were opened in other colonies.

SINGING SOCIETIES. An outgrowth of **singing schools**, these societies became permanent organizations. Stoughton, Massachusetts, is the home of the oldest singing society in existence (1786), and William Billings conducted singing schools there. By 1812, they outnumbered those in Germany. The *Handel Society* at Dartmouth College dates from 1807, and its name indicates interest in European music rather than the music of the singing school. The most famous singing society was the Boston *Handel and Haydn Society*, organized in 1815. There was also the *Saint Cecilia Society* of Charleston, South Carolina, probably dating from 1762. The *Ukrainian Academy Chorus* of Philadelphia began after the Revolutionary War, and both the *New York Choral Society* and the *New York Sacred Music Society* were founded in 1823.

SINOR, JEAN (1946–1999). A master's and doctoral graduate of the Indiana University School of Music, Bloomington, Sinor chaired the Music Education Department and, for a number of years, was director of undergraduate studies. She was cofounder of the IU Children's Choir and was dedicated to the teaching principles of **Zoltan Kodály**. Her work as a clinician and author of teaching materials became internationally known. Professor Sinor was known by colleagues and students as a versatile and gifted teacher. She served as a visiting lecturer at 20 institutions and taught over 70 workshops, nationally and internationally. She served two terms as the president of the International Kodály Society.

SITE-BASED MANAGEMENT. (U.S.) Also called *school-based management*, this approach became popular in the 1980s and 1990s. It is based on the principle of shared decision making. People affected by educational decisions should be involved in the decision-making process. Unfortunately, a lack of clear vision or mission in articulating specific goals has limited the success of this approach.

SIXTH FORM. (UK.) The most senior class in a secondary school, to which pupils, usually above the legal leaving age, may proceed to take "A" (Advanced) levels or retake **GCSE** (General Certificate of Secondary Education) courses. Appropriately equivalent to the 11th and 12th grades in U.S. schools, it is the over-16 form in UK secondary schools, many of the students having passed **GCE** (General Certificate of Education) "O" (Ordinary) levels, or GCSE subjects, "A" (Advanced) levels.

SIXTH-FORM COLLEGE. (UK.) Educational institution where students aged 16 to 19 typically study for advanced school-level qualifications. Similar to a junior or community college in the U.S.

SKIFFLE BANDS. (UK.) British popular music style of the 1950s, in which percussion included washboard, and harmonica and kazoo were often part of the ensemble; the goal was a more acoustic, less electrified sound. Many performers were jazz musicians and future rock and rollers; others became leaders of the 1960s British Invasion, such as the Beatles.

SKILL LEARNING SEQUENCE. A learning process developed by **Edwin Gordon** in his book *Learning Sequences in Music*, suggesting that there are two types of music learning where learning occurs sequentially, and each level combines and interacts with previous levels. These two types of music learning are as follows: 1. Discrimination learning, including aural/oral, verbal association, partial synthesis, and symbolic association. 2. Inference learning, which includes generalization, creativity/improvisation, and theoretical understanding.

    Lit.: Gordon, E., *Learning Sequences in Music: Skill, Content, and Patterns*, 1984.

SKINNER, BURRHUS FREDERIC (B. F.) (1904–1990). An important psychologist in the development of learning theory, it was Skinner who, in the 1950s, was the major proponent of behavior modification. His approach was based on animal research that resulted in the refinement and extension of **E. L. Thorndike**'s law of effect. The behavior modification area includes operant learning research, programmed instruction, teaching machines, and many others that have been applied extensively to music education and therapy. Skinner developed the idea of operant conditioning, which is based on the premise that, if behavior is reinforced, the probability of recurrence of that behavior is increased. He recognized two types of behavior: respondent and operant. Respondent behavior comes from reflexive behaviors, whereas operant behavior is emitted by the organism. He emphasized reinforcement of the operant response, and learning occurs because of the consequences that follow the response. Skinner wrote about positive and negative reinforcement, either of which can strengthen the probability of repetition. Music scholars and researchers have applied Skinner's views extensively. It is recommended that readers read further in the work of Skinner to understand his concept that learning is controlled primarily by its consequences, and not merely as a result of association.

Lit.: Hodges, Don, *Handbook of Music Psychology*, 2nd ed., 1999.

SKOOG. A new type of switch technology that allows the user to program any pentatonic scale pattern in almost any range. Instrument sounds can easily be changed to include any MIDI instrument option. The five "buttons" can sound independently or in pairs (monophonic or polyphonic) and can be programmed to suit any sensitivity level needed (to meet fine motor needs and challenges). Students can "read music" using color-coded scores. Some teachers use Skoog for students who are unable to play traditional band, orchestra, or classroom instruments, to increase the level of participation in inclusive music settings.

SKYE BOAT SONG. An old Highland rowing song, with words by Harold Boulton. The song tells of the escape of Bonnie Prince Charlie to the Isle of Skye off the northwest coast of Scotland. Flora Macdonald, referred to in the second stanza, was a loyal supporter who helped Prince Charlie to escape. *Claymore* refers to a large two-edged sword used by the Scottish Highlanders.

SMALL, CHRISTOPHER (1927–2011). (NZ.) Writer and musicologist whose three books, published in Britain, influenced American academic and music critics from the 1970s to the 1990s. He used jargon-free prose to make broad comparisons among musical traditions in Africa, Asia, Europe, and America. Small wrote about ritual, cultural identity, and the rise of Western music as a mercantile, nonparticipatory art form. He also wrote about the classical tradition as well as popular music using the term *vernacular*, in order to understand Western music as a phenomenon of capitalist societies. In *Musicking* (1998), he argued that music is an action, not an object—a verb, not a noun, as the title implies. The philosopher Nicholas Wolterstorff writes that ***musicking***, to him, is used interchangeably with *performing*. Unfortunately for those who believe in the power of music education when appropriately promoted, Small has left no doubt in his writings that music education should be removed from the classroom to a network of music centers, where people could engage in "musicking."

Lit.: Small, Christopher, *Music, Society, Education*, 1977.

SMART BOARD. (Can.) An interactive whiteboard produced by the Calgary, Alberta–based company Smart Technologies. It uses touch detection for user input, as in scrolling, right mouse-click, etc. A projector is used to display a computer's video output on the interactive whiteboard, which then acts as a large touchscreen. It comes with four pens, which use digital ink and replace traditional whiteboard markers. Since December 2010, the Smart Board technology has grown to include many companies that have developed products that either support Smart Boards or compete with Smart Boards using similar technologies.

SMITH, ELEANOR (1858–1942). An important contributor to the graded music book series, Smith studied voice in Berlin with Julius Hey and composition with Moritz Moszkowski. She arrived in Chicago in 1890 and taught music to adults and children at Hull House. There, she taught singing, **ear training**, and reading and writing of music. Smith's pedagogical methods were consistent with those of **John Dewey** and Francis W. Parker. She became a leader in introducing music to the Chicago Public Schools in 1898 through the publication of her textbook series *Modern Music Series*. Smith also taught at the Chicago Kindergarten College, where she authored a number of books of vocal music for children, including the multivolume *Eleanor Smith Music Course* (1908–1911). The American Book Company publishes this series.

SMITH, WILLIAM. *See* SHAPE-NOTE.

SNAP. (UK.) The most characteristic element in Welsh song is the *snap*. Snapping feminine endings vocally gives syncopation; if the cadence is snapped at a slow tempo, it has the effect of an appoggiatura. Used vocally to break suddenly with a sharp sound, or sharp cracking noise.

SNYDER KNUTH ACHIEVEMENT TEST. A test designed to assess the musical achievement levels of college/university students majoring in elementary education who are required to take music courses as part of their curricula. Can also be used to establish a basis for remedial work at the high school level, or to assess basic achievement at any level. Music written by Alice Snyder Knuth.

SOCIALIZATION. *See* ACCULTURATION; ENCULTURATION.

SOCIETY FOR ETHNOMUSICOLOGY (SEM) (1953, officially 1955). By the second half of the 20th century, musicologists became interested in

African and Asian music, and their new interest influenced music educators. In 1953, the Society for Ethnomusicology and the **International Society for Music Education** were founded. Several events promoted interest in this new discipline of ethnomusicology: the desegregation of America's schools; the **Tanglewood Symposium**; the **GO Project** of 1968–1969; the **MENC** National Black Caucus, 1972; a special-interest edition of *Music Education Journal* that featured music of world cultures; the **Wesleyan Symposium** (CT); and the 1989 publication of *Multicultural Perspective in Music Education*, edited by William M. Anderson and Patricia Campbell. The *Music Educators Journal* continued its support of multicultural music education in 1995–1996 through a series of interviews with ethnomusicologists.

SOCIETY FOR GENERAL MUSIC. (U.S.) Formed in 1981 and immediately recognized by **MENC**. This society was brought about through the efforts of **Charles Leonhard** and a number of general music teachers. It is currently known as the **Council for General Music**.

SOCIETY FOR MUSIC TEACHER EDUCATION (SMTE). An NA*f*ME society, founded in 1982 by Dr. **Charles Leonhard**, University of Illinois.

SOCIETY FOR RESEARCH IN MUSIC EDUCATION (SRME). Founded in 1960 by Clifford V. Buttleman, executive secretary of **MENC**. Its purpose is "the encouragement and advancement of research in those areas pertinent to music education." Official publication is the *Journal of Research in Music Education* (JRME).

SOCIETY FOR THE PRESERVATION AND ENCOURAGEMENT OF BARBERSHOP QUARTET SINGING IN AMERICA. *See* BARBERSHOP HARMONY ASSOCIATION.

SOCIETY FOR THE TRADITIONAL INSTRUMENTS OF WALES (1996). This society was founded to "safeguard the instrumental tradition in Wales and to reinstate it to its rightful place in Welsh life" (*Society Newsletter*). The society hopes to awaken interest in *cruit* (lyre), *pigborn*, harp, and fiddle by organizing workshops for traditional music making and teaching and performing sessions at various locations throughout Wales.

SOL-FA METHOD. (Also called *solfège, solfeggio,* or *solfa.*) A pedagogical **solmization** technique for teaching of sight singing, in which each note of the score is sung to a special syllable, called a *solfège syllable* (or *sol-fa* *syllable*). The seven syllables commonly used for this practice in English-speaking countries are: *do* (or *doh* in **tonic sol-fa**), *re*, *mi*, *fa*, *sol* (*so* in tonic sol-fa), *la*, and *ti/si* (*si* is used for the seventh scale tone in the diatonic scale). Some of the *history* of the sol-fa method includes:

- The use of syllables in the 11th century by the monk **Guido of Arezzo** (ca. 991–1050).
- The cipher notation proposed by Jean-Jacques Rousseau in 1746.
- Its further development by **Pierre Galin** (1786–1821) and popularization by Aimé Paris (1798–1866).
- **Emile Chevé** (1804–1864), French theorist and music teacher.
- The **Norwich sol-fa method** of **Sarah Anne Glover** (1785–1867) of England.
- Reverend **John Curwen** (1816–1880) was instrumental in the development of tonic sol-fa in England ca. 1865, and was chiefly responsible for its popularity.
- **Zoltán Kodály** (1882–1967) of Hungary championed the system in more modern times, building on Curwen's work. He introduced a set of hand signals that correspond to each solfège syllable.

SOLFÈGE. (Fr.) A term used in the **Dalcroze** method of music instruction, in which **sight readings** or vocal exercises include the names of notes used in the **fixed-doh** system (e.g., *doh* for C, etc.). This term is also used to cover all rudimentary music instruction throughout North America and around the world. *See also* SOL-FA METHOD.

SOLMIZATION. A method of teaching the scales and intervals by syllables; its invention is ascribed to **Guido of Arezzo**, based on the **hexachord**.

SOMATRON. (U.S.) Widely used and recommended music-vibration equipment used in hospitals, universities, private, and government facilities. Invented by Byron Eakin in 1985, this *vibroacoustic therapy* involves the conversion of music to tactile sensations that permeate the whole body with stimulating and soothing sound vibrations. Useful for autistic children, age-related dementia, pain management, and post-traumatic stress victims.

SONGLINE. (Aus.) Term popularized by Bruce Chatwin to denote the geographical path evoked or taken by a series of related Aboriginal Australian ceremonial songs. *Songline* might seem to be an Aboriginal term for the Western term *melodic line*, but their similarities are nonexistent.

SOUND POST. In the violin and other stringed instruments, a small cylindrical wooden prop set inside the body, between belly and back, just behind and beneath the treble foot of the bridge.

SOUNDS AUSTRALIAN. Quarterly journal of the Australian Music Centre (AMC), originally *AMC News*, appearing under its present title from no. 15 (Oct. 1987), to discuss issues pertaining to the practice of musical composition in Australia.

SOUSA, JOHN PHILIP (1854–1932). Born in Washington, DC, Sousa studied violin, orchestration, and harmony, and acquired considerable efficiency on wind instruments. After playing with the Marine Band, he was active in theater orchestras and as a violinist with the Philadelphia Orchestra. He then was appointed director of the Marine Band (1880–1892). Sousa composed and played his famous marches around the world. He was influential in American instrumental music education when public schools began to establish bands. As a close friend of **Albert Austin Harding**, founder of the University of Illinois Department of Bands, Sousa gave his extensive library of printed and manuscript band music to the University of Illinois, where it remains today.

SPECIAL EDUCATION. (UK-Scot.) For a number of years, Scotland has provided a free public education to all children regardless of their special needs. Some 3 to 5 percent of these students receive some kind of instruction in connection with special needs. About half of special-education teachers have special credentials, but they all must have regular primary or secondary teaching credentials as well. Children with social or emotional disabilities are not integrated into the same assessment and identification system as are children with cognitive or physical disabilities.

SPECIAL LEARNERS IN MUSIC. (U.S.) Although special learners may be in separate classes or "mainstreamed," they are generally very responsive to music and the arts. The same teaching materials or basic techniques can be used as with typically developing students. Hands-on experiences with music are encouraged for all students at any level of development. Through an IEP (individualized education program) designed by an instructional team including parents, music teachers may need to modify expectations regarding the ability of each special learner to participate in all or specific musical experiences. Special learners are of two general types: 1) normal intelligence but physically disabled, visually impaired, or hearing impaired; 2) mentally challenged.

SPECIAL POPULATION. (Can.) The Canadian elementary music program for special populations has not realized its full potential. Who should do the teaching and implementation of training programs remains a problem for the country because of the differences in the provinces. The Atlantic region uses music specialists, whereas other regions tend to use classroom teachers. **Orff** and **Kodály** programs have been and continue to be used for gifted children as well as for mentally and physically challenged students. The need for adequate teacher training remains a major concern for those providing leadership in elementary music.

SPECIAL RESEARCH INTEREST GROUPS (SRIG). Formed at the 1978 **MENC** Convention, the SRIGS, under the guidance of the **Music Education Research Council** (MERC), have been vehicles to serve music educators with similar research interests. There are currently 13 SRIGS that publish their own newsletters and sponsor sessions at state and national conferences.

SPEECH CANONS. A repeating form in which the same thing is spoken at a precise interval of time. Speech canons are spoken in rhythm, with separate groups beginning one or two measures apart, as in singing.

SPIRAL CURRICULUM. Based on **Jerome Bruner**'s idea that any subject can be taught to a student at any age in an intellectually honest form as long as the concepts and materials are presented in an age-appropriate manner. *See also* MANHATTANVILLE MUSIC CURRICULUM PROJECT.

SPIRITUALS. Term derived from the European spiritual song. It was shortened later by white abolitionists to religious songs cultivated by African-American slaves in the antebellum South. It is a form of the American gospel hymn, a term usually applied to white church music. *See also* GOSPEL MUSIC.

SPUTNIK. In October 1957, the Soviet Union launched Sputnik I, the first artificial orbiting satellite, and established itself as the leader in space technology. As result of this event, school improvement became a national priority, and leaders such as Admiral Hyman Rickover recommended stronger academic programs in mathematics, science, foreign language, and reading. Unfortunately, many people thought that other subjects, including music, were frills. Music educators went on the defensive to justify the place of quality music in the curriculum.

STAGE BANDS. Selected high school bands form the best players into a small ensemble to expand students' musical experiences by involving them with the jazz and rock idioms.

Students are able to devote attention to proper technique, good tone quality, and other attributes of artistic performance. These groups also engage in improvisation. The earliest stage bands of the 1950s and 1960s were usually all male, and were the precursors of the jazz and rock bands of the late 20th century to the 21st century. By 1980, 70 percent of America's 30,000 junior and senior high schools had at least one stage band or jazz ensemble. The Canadian Stage Band Festival increased from 18 groups in 1975 to 1,500 groups in 1983.

Lit.: Murphy, Daniel, "Jazz Studies in American Schools and Colleges: A Brief History," *Jazz Educators Journal* 26 (1994).

STANDIFER, JAMES. Professor emeritus at the University of Michigan and director of the oral history archive of the African American music collection. He was a fellow for the Ford Foundation, the National Endowment for the Humanities, and the U.S. Information Agency. He has coauthored several books and has served as an adviser to educational television. He was producer and director of a PBS documentary on the history of *Porgy and Bess*.

STANDING COUNCIL ON SCHOOL EDUCATION AND EARLY CHILDHOOD (SCSEEC) (2012). (Aus.) Formerly the Ministerial Council for Education, Early Childhood Development and Youth Affairs (MCE-ECDYA), which was formed in 2009 to realign the roles and responsibilities of two previous councils: the Ministerial Council on Education, Employment, Training and Youth Affairs (MCEETYA) and the Ministerial Council for Vocation and Technical Education (MCVTE).

ST. ANDREWS MUSIC BOOK. (UK-Scot.) A medieval link to Europe is the famous mid-13th-century *St. Andrews Music Book*, compiled at St. Andrews (a town in eastern Scotland) and removed to Wolfenbüttel, Germany, in 1553. It contains music of the French school of Leonin and Perotin and important native pieces (conductus, tropes, motets) written for the Cathedral of St. Andrews in the late Middle Ages.

Lit.: Hiley, David, *The New Grove Dictionary of Music and Musicians, Organum and Discant*, 1980.

ST. ENDA'S. (UK-Ire.) A school founded by **Patrick Pearse** that began to change the intellectual landscape of Ireland in the early 20th century from the devastating effects of the Irish famine from 1845 to 1849. At St. Enda's, bilingualism was advocated, and nearly all instruction returned from the requirement of the English language to Irish language. Music and drama were again made important parts of the curriculum, along with the heroic literature of Ireland and the classical literature of Europe.

ST. OLAF LUTHERAN CHOIR (1912). F. Melius Christiansen, a Norwegian immigrant, became the conductor of this choir after he combined the male and female segments of the Choral Union into one choir, known as the *St. John's Church Choir*. The choir's name was changed to the *St. Olaf Lutheran Choir*. By 1920, the choir had developed a national reputation, and as a result the St. Olaf Choir set the standard that became the performance practice of the **a cappella tradition** in high schools and colleges throughout the country. Their vocal trademark was the straightness of tone achieved throughout the vocal range.

STEEL GUITAR. An acoustic, handheld guitar having a metal resonator and producing a *wailing*, variable sound. Can be a pedal steel guitar or a Hawaiian guitar. All strings used are metal.

STEEN, ARVIDA (1937–). A renowned American **Orff** specialist from the University of St. Thomas (UST), St. Paul, Minnesota. She taught in the UST **Orff-Schulwerk** Certificate Program from 1972 to 2003 and served as the director for four years. Steen received the Distinguished Service Award from the **American Orff-Schulwerk Association** (AOSA) in 1997 and was vice president and president of AOSA between 1978 and 1981. She is the author of *Exploring Orff*, an important resource for Orff practitioners. The *Arvida Steen Orff Schulwerk Studies Scholarship* was established in 2004 to recognize her extensive and generous support of music education.

STEM NOTATION. (Also known as *stick notation*). Found in *Threshold to Music* books by **Mary Helen Richards** and based on **Kodály** principles, this notation begins with stems to quarter notes (no note heads), with eight notes using two stems connected by a bar across the top of the stems. Children learn by looking at large charts that have this notation to simple chants.

STEPBELLS. A smaller set of **melody bells** constructed vertically as "steps"; encompasses only one octave without sharps or flats. The pitches go higher as the bells go up the ladder. Bells are played with a short stick with a mallet head made of wood or hard rubber.

THE STOUGHTON SINGING SOCIETY (1786). Stoughton, Massachusetts, is the home of the oldest singing society still in existence. William Billings conducted **singing schools** there. It antedates the Berlin *Singakademie* by five years.

STRINGS. (Gen.) Colloquial abbr. for the stringed instruments of the **orchestra** (string section), or the string quartet, quintet, etc.

STROLLING STRINGS. High school orchestra string groups. Stan Nosal, a Wisconsin high school orchestra teacher, is credited with the beginning of groups of high school string players who strolled at local social, non-school-related activities. He had observed the *Flame Room Golden Strings* from Minneapolis, who were well-known strolling string players in that area, performing frequently in restaurants. Nosal was inspired to begin a similar group with his high school orchestra students. Word of the group's success began to spread, and by the 1970s other strolling groups began to appear in school string programs throughout the country.
   (Entry by **Robert Gillespie**, Nov. 2012.)

STUBER, B. F. (1878–). Member of the **MSNC** (1922) Committee on Instrumental Affairs and the author of *Instrumental Class Course*, published by Root and Sons, 1923.

STUDENT MUSIC EDUCATION NATIONAL CONFERENCE (SMENC). A **MENC**-sponsored organization for college/university music-education students, found in most participating states.

SULLIVAN, JOHN DWIGHT (1813–1893). He was Harvard educated and was considered the first influential American music critic and arbiter of taste. His journal, ***Dwight's Journal of Music***, included critical reviews, analyses, reports on concert life, and many other aspects of the field of music in both Europe and the U.S. Sullivan believed in music—fine art music—as the language of feeling and of "natural religion" (from a lecture in 1941 to the Harvard Musical Association).

SUMMERHILL. (UK.) Experimental coeducational boarding school founded in 1921 at Leiston, Suffolk, by A. S. Neill. Students have complete freedom, except in matters of health, safety, and interference with rights of others. Class attendance is optional.

SUTHERLAND, DAME JOAN (1926–2010). (Aus.) Opera singer. She won the Sydney Sun Aria Competition in 1949 and the Mobil Quest in 1950.

She traveled to the UK and studied at the Royal College of Music Opera School. She joined the Royal Opera House Covent Garden in 1952, where she made her debut as the First Lady in *Die Zauberflöte*. Her husband, Richard Bonynge, recognized her potential to sing the great *bel canto* roles, and he coached and encouraged her in this repertoire. A major international career followed in the leading opera houses of the world. In 1959 she was given the title of *La Stupenda*, which remained with her throughout her career. She returned to Australia in 1965 to head the Sutherland-Williamson International Grand Opera Co. From 1976 until her retirement from the stage in 1990, she returned regularly to the Australian opera in many of her greatest roles. Her unique vocal quality, seamless legato, secure coloratura, great dynamic range, and a career that lasted more than 40 years have ensured that she is regarded as one of the greatest singers since Melba and Tetrazzini, and one of the greatest singers of all time. She continued to work as a master teacher in Australia's National Vocal Symposium. She was awarded the CBE (1961), the AC (1975), and the OM (1991).

SUZUKI, SHINICHI (1898–1998). (Japan.) Violinist and founder of a method devoted first to the teaching of violin to children. He maintained that any child, given the right stimuli under proper conditions in a group environment, could achieve a high level of competency as a performer. The **Suzuki teaching method** is defined as the process of musical education based on the repetition of (and adaptation to) external stimuli. His program appears to be most successful with very young children—ages four through eight—who are taught to play by imitating the physical movements and the visual placement of the fingers on the strings.

SUZUKI TEACHING METHOD. A method of teaching music conceived and executed by Japanese violinist **Shinichi Suzuki** in the mid-20th century. The central belief of Suzuki, based on his language-acquisition theories, is that all people are capable of learning from their environment. The essential components of his method spring from the desire to create the "right environment" for learning music. He also believed that this positive environment would help to foster character in students. The important elements of the Suzuki approach to *instrumental teaching* include:

- An early start (age three to four is normal in most countries)
- The importance of listening to music
- Learning to play before learning to read
- The involvement of the parent
- A nurturing and positive learning environment

- A high standard of teaching by trained teachers
- Core repertoire, used by Suzuki students across the world
- Social interaction with other children: Suzuki students from all over the world communicate through the language of music

See MOTHER TONGUE; TALENT EDUCATION.

SWANSON, BESSIE (1921–). Music educator. A graduate of the University of the Pacific (CA), where she obtained her BA, BM, and MM degrees. She was a vocal music teacher, as well as an accomplished cellist who toured with an all-female USO ensemble during WWII. After completing her doctorate in music education at Stanford University (CA), she taught at the University of Washington and the University of Michigan, and in San Luis Obispo, California, where she served as head of the Music Department for 13 years. Swanson is known primarily for her music-education textbook, *Music in the Education of Children*, first published by Wadsworth Publishing in 1969. This popular college text had its fourth and final printing in 1981.

SWANSON, FREDERICK (1910–1990). Pioneer in the male "changing-voice" theory. Founder of the Moline Boys Choir. *See also* ADOLESCENT BASS THEORY.
   Bib.: Collins, Don L., *Teaching Choral Music*, 2nd ed., 1999.

SWANWICK, KEITH (1936–). (UK.) Professor emeritus, University of London, Institute of Education. Graduated with distinction from the **Royal Academy of Music**. Taught in schools and has been a choral and orchestral conductor, orchestral musician, and a church organist. His doctoral dissertation was a study of *Music and the Education of the Emotions*. A past editor, with **John Paynter**, of the ***British Journal of Music Education***, he has had a number of important leadership positions as chair, advisory professorships, and international invitations, including New Zealand, Australia, Finland, Sweden, Italy, Greece, Canada, and the U.S. He is the editor of *Music Education*, a major four-volume reference work published by Routledge in 2012.

SWEET ADELINES INTERNATIONAL. A worldwide organization of women singers committed to the advancement, through education and performance, of this musical art form of barbershop harmony. The original *Sweet Adelines* was established in 1945 by Edna Mae Anderson of Tulsa, Oklahoma, and became international in 1953, when the first chapter of *Sweet Adelines* was chartered in Bradon, Manitoba, Canada. The name did not officially change until May 1991, when other international chapters were added.

SWING CHOIR. *See* SHOW CHOIR.

SWING-STYLE BANDS. A smooth, sophisticated style of jazz playing, popular in the 1930s and early 1940s. An important characteristic of this time was the movement away from small jazz groups toward a well-organized larger ensemble of professional instrumentalists. As a result, the larger band became the band of the "swing era," which became synonymous with the "big band" era. Duke Ellington wrote a song, "It Don't Mean a Thing If It Ain't Got that Swing." And Benny Goodman, the jazz clarinet player, became known as the *King of Swing*. Even Stravinsky endorsed the big band and swing sounds when he wrote his *Ebony Concerto* for "ebony stick" (a swing term for the clarinet) and band.

SWUNG SLATS. (Aus.) A pseudomusical instrument or device that produces a howling or whirring sound when whirled through the air. A flat piece of wood measuring from 4 to 14 inches in length is classified as a free **aerophone**, and its pitch is determined by the speed with which it is whirled. *See also* BULLROARER.

SYMPHONIC CHOIR. Label describing an accompanied vocal ensemble consisting of a large number of mixed voices; may or may not be auditioned; repertoire emphasizes performing extended choral works with varying accompaniments; contrasts with **chamber choir**.
    (Entry by **Michael Jothen**, Nov. 2012.)

SYMPOSIUM ON MULTICULTURAL APPROACHES TO MUSIC EDUCATION. (U.S.) This event occurred in 1990 at the **Music Educators National Conference** in Washington, DC. The symposium was planned to promote a great national discussion among music teachers on the importance of a broad, multicultural curriculum in music at all educational levels. William Anderson, symposium director, compiled the contents of the symposium in the MENC publication *Teaching Music with a Multicultural Approach* in 1991.

SYNTHESIZER. A class of electronic devices that make possible the creation of any sound via electronic synthesis. While a synthesizer is now a self-contained unit, the first synthesizers were composed of several modules, as in *Turner boxes*, each of which represented a specific waveform. These early synthesizers were driven by the use of dials, unlike those of the 21st century, which use computers, with an increasingly large number of software programs available. Currently, synthesizers are able to create any desired instrumental timbre.

SYSTEMATIC AURAL TRANSMISSION. The audiation-based approach to music instruction developed by **Edwin Gordon**.

TAIKO. (Aus.) A Japanese large barrel-shaped two-headed drum.

TAKE THE "A" TRAIN. A jazz standard written in 1939 by Billy Strahorn (1915–1967), who was a member of Duke Ellington's band as a lyricist and arranger.

TALENT EDUCATION. A method of teaching music developed by the Japanese violinist **Shinichi Suzuki** (1898–1998), based on his language-acquisition theories that all people are capable of learning from their environment. The center of his movement was established as the Talent Education Research Institute in Matsumoto, Japan. Suzuki traveled to the U.S. in 1964, where his 10 students performed at the 1964 **MENC** convention. John Kendall, of Southern Illinois University at Edwardsville, traveled to Japan to study the **Suzuki method**, and with others, adapted the method for American string educators as *talent education* in public and private schools.

TALKIES. During the first decades of motion picture production, there was no sound, only motion, with words added as in the closed-captioning used in TV today. When sound was added in the form of synchronized dialogue and music, people referred to the motion pictures as "talkies," or "talking pictures."

TANGLEWOOD SYMPOSIUM (1967). A music-education symposium that was held in Tanglewood, Massachusetts, from July 23 to August 2, 1967. It was a gathering designed to discuss and define the place of music education in the public school curriculum at a time when many changes were occurring throughout society. One of the most important documents resulting from the symposium was the *Tanglewood Declaration*, which provided a philosophical basis for the future of music education.

TANGLEWOOD II: CHARTING THE FUTURE. A Symposium on Music Learning for the 21st Century held in 2007 at Williams College, 40 years after the 1967 **Tanglewood Symposium**. Specific goals were the cultivation of a new understanding of music learning; to examine values of music in culture and its effect on transmission processes; and to explore how schools at all levels, public and private, can meet the challenges of the decades ahead with a deeper understanding of the role they can play in supporting a musical future.

TAPE RECORDER MUSIC. Recorded sound that is manipulated with editing, speed and direction alteration, loops, mixing, or processing. Composition on tape using recorded natural sounds, as well as editing and processing, to produce a piece. This is referred to as *Musique Concrete*, which was discovered and named in 1948 by **Pierre Schaeffer** (1910–1995), a French radio engineer.

TAPPER, THOMAS (1864–1958). American music educator and writer. One of his early works, *The Natural Music Course*, written with Frederick Ripley (American Book Company, 1895), was the outstanding series of the last decades of the 19th century. Tapper was an authority on music teaching, and this book contained some new and innovative approaches to simplifying music instruction. He also edited *The Musician*, taught at New York University (1908–1912), at the Institute of Musical Art in New York (1905–1924), and, among many other publications, he produced 19 volumes of *The Modern Graded Piano Course*.

TASK FORCE ON MUSIC TEACHER EDUCATION (1984). MENC appointed a 10-member task force for the nineties to gather information from music educators and other interested persons throughout the country to make recommendations for change. The task force made several recommendations, which were implemented in collegiate teacher-preparation programs. In 1987 MENC published the report *Music Teacher Education: Partnership and Process*.

TEACHER-CENTERED INSTRUCTION. An approach to teaching in which the lecture method is used with little student input, involvement, or discussion. Lectures, drills, and recitation are often used as modes of delivery.

TEACH FOR TRANSFER. *Transfer* in teaching refers to the process that occurs when one uses previously learned knowledge and skills toward the learning of something new. For example, it is recommended that teachers plan their teaching approach to include ways for students to apply knowledge and skills gained in a general music class to an instrumental class.

TEACHING MUSIC. An official publication for members of **MENC** (**NAfME**), which contains a variety of practical ideas for teaching at all levels. Issued five times yearly, it began publishing in 1993.

TEAM TEACHING. This occurs when two or more teachers work closely together in planning, producing, and evaluating learning experiences for a group of students.

TELHARMONIUM. A musical keyboard instrument operating by alternating currents of electricity that, on impulse from the keyboard, produce music at a distant point via telephone lines.

TELYN. (UK-Wales.) Symbolically the most important Welsh musical instrument, the harp is somewhat obscure. There are medieval references to it, but no native instrument survives from before about 1700. Literary references suggest that the early harp was small, with about 30 strings. Later Welsh harps became increasingly large.

TEX-MEX MUSIC. A derivative of Texan Mexican-American cultural mix. Also known as *conjunto*, a dance music created by Texan Mexican-Americans, especially the polka and waltz, which were brought to Mexico from European countries in the 19th century. They also brought the button **accordion** with them and incorporated the polka rhythm into their songs and dances.

THEATER ORCHESTRA. A small, flexible ensemble for which arrangements were made with separate instrumental parts cued into other parts when a particular instrument was not available. Instrumentation included first and second violins, an occasional bass and cello, cornets, trombones, clarinets, flutes, drums, and piano. In large cities, theater orchestras played for silent films.

THEMATIC APPROACH. Teaching approach that organizes subject matter around broad themes, topics, or units.

THIRD-HAND CAPO. A device that can clamp any combination of strings at any fret on any guitar. This device is similar to the earlier single-purpose **capo**.

THOMAS, THEODORE (1835–1905). Although born in Germany, he is considered the first renowned American orchestral conductor. Prior to its name change in 1913, the Chicago Symphony Orchestra was known as the Theodore Thomas Orchestra. He also worked hard to promote the standard of singing in schools, churches, and choral societies. Throughout his life as a teacher of violin, he advised violinists to study singing, and singers to study violin. He was greatly influenced by two women singers in New York in 1851: Jenny Lind and Henrietta Sontag.

THORNDIKE, E. L. (1874–1949). A renowned educational psychologist, he studied with **William James** (1842–1910) at Harvard, and later taught at Columbia Teachers College. As a result of his early animal lab experiments, he constructed the first internally consistent learning theory. He developed three major laws of learning: law of readiness, law of exercise, and law of effect. Learning by trial and error was an important part of his theories about learning, and he thought of learning as the result of connections between stimuli and response, a view often referred to as *connectionism*. He was one of the first to promote the use of scientific method in psychology. Thorndike also wrote the *Thorndike-Century Junior Dictionary*, published by Scott Foresman & Company in 1935, which was used by many elementary students throughout the U.S.

THOUSAND VOICE CHOIR. (Aus.) Formed in 1891 by **Alexander Clark**, the choir is part of the Festival of Music and an important state icon of South Australian life. It reaches over 23,000 primary children, with choral music as its core. The festival assists schools in achieving excellence. **Francis Lymer Gratton**, an important music educator of the **tonic sol-fa** system of **sight singing**, was the acclaimed conductor of the Thousand Voice Choir for many years. This choir is still a prominent part of South Australian life, and continues to this day.

THE THREE RAVENS. (UK.) One of three songs that were important to the repertoire of English songs current in the Tudor period (1485–1603) and that survive into the present.

THRESHOLD TO MUSIC. An elementary music method by **Mary Helen Richards** that represented her own music-education program based on the work of **Zoltan Kodály**.

THUMB PIANO. *See* LAMELLAPHONE.

THUNDERSTICK. *See* BULLROARER.

THYROARYTENOIDS. A set of complex muscular fibers that, when used, become shorter and thicker than when they are not active. When singing in the chest voice, phonation occurs throughout most of the length of the folds, the thyroarytenoids.

TIN WHISTLE. (UK-Ire.) A six-holed whistle flute that has a long, millennial history. Its use is almost entirely recreational and it has no ritual significance.

TIOMPDN. (UK-Ire.) An old Irish *timpan* was not a drum, but a plucked or bowed **chordophone**. It is often mentioned in literature but fell from use before the harp. The *tiompdn* instrument in medieval texts has not been discovered in physical form.

TIPTON, GLADYS (1905–1996). A supervisor of music and a state music consultant, Tipton was a longtime professor of music education in four different universities, with Teachers College, Columbia University, being the last. Tipton endeavored throughout her teaching career to enrich both the content and process of listening to music. Through workshops, classroom demonstrations, teacher guides, and her *Music for Living Series* (Silver Burdett, 1956), she helped teachers to become actively engaged with the children in exploring music "by ear." Her major national contributions to music education were through **MENC**, **MTNA**, the Association for Childhood Education and Development, and the Association for Supervision and Curriculum Development.

'TIS IRISH I AM. (UK-Ire.) A frolicking type tune known originally as "Top O' Cork Road," the movement and patter are characteristic of many Irish folk songs. The tune is from an old Irish **reel** (dance). It probably was played on the piano and at a faster tempo than can be sung.

TITLE IX. From the Education Amendments of 1972, it states that "no person in the United States shall, on the basis of sex, be excluded from participation in, be denied the benefits of, or be subjected to discrimination under any education program or activity receiving Federal financial assistance."

T.MUS.A. (Teacher of Music Australia). A diploma awarded by the Australian Music Examinations Board (AMEB) based on written and practical examinations in studio teaching methods. Taken after the completion of prerequisites in AMEB's advanced practical and theoretical examinations. This award does not certify completion of a course and has no formal status with Australian education authorities, but it tests knowledge relevant to studio music teaching. It takes more than a year to complete, and has served as the primary qualification of many Australian private music teachers.

TOLBERT, MARY RUTH (1915–2012). Professor emeritus in music education at the Ohio State University (OSU). She was a graduate of OSU, the Juilliard School, and international studies in Europe, Russia, China, Africa, and Mediterranean countries. She taught at OSU School of Music for over 40 years. Tolbert authored many music publications, including coauthoring *This is Music*, which is still used in many elementary schools. She spearheaded

MENC's Early Childhood **Special Research Interest Group**, of which she became the first chairperson. Mary Tolbert was an outspoken advocate for arts, music, and history throughout her career and in her retirement.

TOLMIE, FRANCES (1840–1926). By the 1900s, research into Scotland's songs became increasingly important. Tolmie's collection of songs from Skye (1911) is accurate and important, notably for the study of women's songs. *See also* SKYE BOAT SONG.

TONIC SOL-FA. A system of "**movable doh**"; a system of syllables, as in *doh, re, mi, fa, so, la, ti, doh*, in which *doh* is considered to be the keynote, or tonal center, in all *major* keys. *La* is considered to be the keynote, or tonal center, in all *minor* keys. This is considered to be the "movable-doh" approach. It was developed by **Sarah A. Glover** (ca. 1840) and perfected by **John Curwen** (ca. 1865). Curwen chose the term *tonic sol-fa method* to distinguish his use of relative sol-fa from the prevailing **fixed-doh** method. He used the first letter (lower case) of each of the solmization tones (*doh, re, me, fa, sol, la, ti*), and a rhythmic system that used bar lines (prefixing strong beats), half-bar lines (prefixing medium beats), and semicolons (prefixing weak beats) in each measure. In his system, the seven letters refer to key relationship (relative pitch), and not to absolute pitch.

    Bib.: Apel, Willi, *Harvard Dictionary of Music*, 2nd ed., 1973; Choksy, Lois, et al., *Teaching Music in the Twentieth Century*, 1986.

    Lit.: Anderson, William, and Joy E. Lawrence, *Integrating Music Into the Classroom*, 1985.

TONIC SOL-FA ASSOCIATION (1853). *See* JOHN CURWEN.

TONIC SOL-FA COLLEGE OF MUSIC. (Aus.) Opened in 1863. The college later became the Curwen Memorial College. In 1944, the college moved to Queensborough Terrace and took the name *Curwen Memorial College*. The Curwen Institute was formed in 1973 by members of the college under the auspices of the **John Curwen** Society. The institute concentrates on the applicability of the Curwen method of **tonic sol-fa** to primary education. It formerly offered a diploma in tonic sol-fa.

TORRANCE TEST OF CREATIVE THINKING. Test designed by P. E. Torrance (1966, 1988, 1990) to measure the creative abilities of students, K–12. Two tests are available—a verbal content test and a figural content test. Written responses are scored and identified according to the theoretical constructs of J. P. Guilford (1897–1988), which include fluency, originality, flexibility, and elaboration.

TOVEY, DONALD FRANCIS (1875–1940). (UK.) English pianist, composer, conductor, teacher, and writer. Professor of music at Edinburgh University from 1914. He wrote celebrated program notes for the Reid Orchestra, and published them in six volumes as *Essays in Musical Analysis*, 1935–1938. Used by music students over the years. He was knighted in 1935.

TOWN BANDS. Bands that consisted of members of the community and that served civic functions. Individuals established bands in the 1900s throughout the U.S. They sometimes owned as many as 28 bands in one state. Family members made simple uniforms for the bandsmen. Town bands eventually became a part of school districts, and their directors were paid teacher salaries. In most cases the band director's salary continued to come from state fees.
   Bib.: Dissertation by Samuel Meredith.

TRADITIONAL MUSIC AND SONG ASSOCIATION OF SCOTLAND. In 1965, the founding of this association paved the way for folk festivals in Scotland that continue to flourish. *See also* GLASGOW SCHOOL TEACHERS.

TRADITIONAL TUNES OF THE CHILD BALLAD (1959–1972). (UK.) The American scholar Bertrand Bronson (1902–1986) sought to understand melodic variation through points of difference between one mode and another, and the points that are nonexistent in the pentatonic system. In the *Traditional Tunes*, Bronson demonstrates that it is possible to find the same essential tune cast in different modes.

TRAINING SCHOOL. (UK.) A secondary school that, in partnership with a local university or other higher education institution involved in teacher training, develops strategies for initial teacher training. Introduced in 2000.

TRAINING THE BOY'S CHANGING VOICE. (Can.) In 1956 **Duncan McKenzie** presented the **alto-tenor plan** for keeping adolescent boys singing in church and school choirs throughout the period when their voices are changing. McKenzie believed that the alto-tenor idea was first found in a music text, *The Third Reader for Mixed Voices*, from a series, *The Normal Course*, edited by John W. Tufts.
   Bib.: Collins, Don, *Teaching Choral Music*, 2nd ed., 1999.

TRAVELER CHILDREN. The children of Gypsies.

TRAVELERS OR TRAVELLERS. (Gypsies.) (UK.) Chiefly British; a member of a number of traditionally itinerant peoples of the British Isles and other English-speaking areas, including those of Gypsy origin who use *Shelta*, a private language based in part on the Irish language and used among Travelers in the British Isles. Additionally, see Glinka's (1804–1857) "Life of the Czar," *The Traveller's Song* (literally, *Passing Song*), a choral text by the poet Zhukovsky.

TRINIDADIAN STEEL DRUMS. Percussion ensemble developed in Trinidad using steel oil bands discarded by local oil companies. Players, called *panmen*, select drum tops with dents, each producing a different pitch; by further manipulation, a whole diatonic scale and chromatic notes can be produced.

TRINKA, JILL. Director of graduate and undergraduate programs in music education at the University of St. Thomas in St. Paul, Minnesota, where she teaches methods, musicianship, and American folk music. She holds Kodály Certification and a Ford Foundation Ringer Fellowship from the Liszt Academy of Music in Budapest. She has served as director of the Kodály Institute of Texas and Kodály Certificate Program at Portland State, Oregon. A past president of the **Organization of American Kodály Educators**, she received its Outstanding Educator Award in 2003. She recorded and has written four volumes of folk songs for children of all ages, and is a frequent lecturer and clinician. She presents workshops on topics ranging from music literacy pedagogy to folk music performance practice.

TRIPARTITE SYSTEM. (UK.) The division of the secondary sector into three types of schools: grammar schools, technical schools, and modern schools, as suggested in the Spens Report (1938). Following the 1944 Educational Act (**Butler Act**), local authorities could choose between the tripartite system and others, including the dual system of grammar and secondary modern schools. Both involved the selection of pupils by ability at age 11. Both systems were replaced by the Education Act of 1976. *See also* EDUCATION ACT OF 1980.

TROWSDALE, G. CAMPBELL (1938–). (Can.) An educator and violinist appointed in 1961 to the faculty of education at the University of British Columbia and retired as professor emeritus in 1988. A performer and chamber orchestra musician, he had been active as a teacher of **Orff**, **Kodály**, and **R. Murray Schafer** methods at the elementary level. He believed in a fully integrated musical curriculum, and that music education should produce listeners as well as performers. After retirement from the university, he continued to be active as a performer and as a consultant for a number of organizations, including the Banff Music and Sound Program, **Canada Council**, Ontario Arts Council, and a variety of institutional program assessments.

TUCKWELL, BARRY EMMANUEL (1931–). (Aus.) French-horn player and conductor. Had perfect pitch and studied at the NSW State Conservatorium. Played French horn with the Sydney Symphony (1947–1950) before going to Britain and playing with the Hallé Orchestra, among others. He became principal hornist with the London Symphony for 13 years, and was a horn soloist on many recordings. Professor of horn at the **Royal Academy of Music**, London (1963–1974). Has written several books on horn playing, and has been called both "the leading horn player of his generation" and, in Italy, *Il Corno d'oro* (The Golden Horn). Conductor of the Tasmanian Symphony (Aus., 1980–1983) and the Maryland Orchestra (U.S., from 1982). After retirement, he and his wife live in Maryland (U.S.). Honored with the OBE (1963), AC (1992), and an honorary DMUS from the University of Sydney.

TUFTS, JOHN (1689–1750). (U.S.) Considered the "grandfather" of American music education, he is credited with writing the first music instruction books in the early 18th century. His book, *Introduction to the Singing of Psalm-Tunes*, was first published ca. 1714 and was the first music "textbook" published in the colonies. His goal, shared with other singing masters of the time, was to improve church singing by teaching congregations to read by note rather than through the **lining-out** method. His system of notation was based on tetrachords (E-F-G-A and B-C-D-E), an approach that was later adapted to the **shape-note** system (four separate note-head shapes used to indicate **solfège** syllables.)

TUNING FORK (1711). Two-pronged metal object invented by the trumpeter John Shore (ca. 1662–1752). When the object is set in vibration, it produces a sound to check the pitch of instruments, and to give the pitch to singers. Gives a "pure" tone, without upper harmonics. Generally, the tuning fork produces A above middle C, most commonly 440 cps.

TURKISH MUSIC. Also called *Janizary* or *Janissary music*. Military music of the Janizary guards of Turkish sultans. A raucous, loud, and rhythmically vibrant music made up of Turkish drums, (large) cymbals, and the Turkish crescent, overhung with bells and jingles. These instruments provide exotic color for Gluck and Mozart operas, Haydn's *Military Symphony No. 100*, and the Mozart Piano Sonata No. 11 in A, marked as *Rondo alla turca*, a good example of rondo form.

TWENTY-FIRST CENTURY SKILLS. Led by the University of Melbourne (Aus.), ATCS (Assessment and Teaching of 21st Century Skills), and a variety of other educational, business, and governmental organizations, 21st-century learning skills have been divided into four broad categories. These are: ways of thinking, ways of working, tools for working, and skills for living in the world. Other teams identified cognitive skills, interpersonal skills, and intrapersonal skills. An outgrowth of these broader terms is the focus on critical and analytical thinking, the ability to transfer knowledge along with "deeper learning," or the process through which a person becomes capable of taking what was learned in one situation and applying it to new situations. *See also* SPIRAL CURRICULUM.

UKULELE. Popular smaller guitar-like instrument with four strings. Originally imported by Portuguese sailors into Hawaii in the 1870s; came to the U.S. in the early 20th century. Both treble and baritone instruments are useful in the classroom for teaching a variety of musical skills.

UKULELE METHOD FOR CLASSROOM TEACHING. See DOANE UKULELE SYSTEM.

UNDERSTANDING BY DESIGN (UbD). A framework for improving student achievement by emphasizing the teacher's critical role as a designer of student learning. Developed by nationally recognized educators Grant Wiggins and Jay McTighe, and published in 1998 by the Association for Supervision and Curriculum Development (ASCD). UbD works within the standards-driven curriculum to help teachers clarify learning goals, devise revealing assessments of student understanding, and craft effective and engaging learning activities.

UNITED NATIONS EDUCATIONAL, SCIENTIFIC AND CULTURAL ORGANIZATION (UNESCO). An international nongovernmental organization that encourages international peace and universal respect by promoting collaboration among nations. At its request, the **International Music Council** (IMC) was founded in 1949 as the world's largest network of organizations, institutions, and individuals working in the field of music.

UNITED STATES MARINE BAND. Formed in 1775 when the Continental Congress passed a bill for the raising of two battalions of marines. It provided for a Marine Band of "one drum-major, one fife major, and 32 drums and fifes." The new band, *The Musics*, was stationed in Philadelphia. After moving to the new capital of Washington, its debut occurred at a reception given by President John Adams on New Year's Day in 1801.

UNIVERSITY OF TORONTO. (Can.) Events of paramount importance for music in postsecondary education took place in 1946 at the Toronto Conservatory of Music. In order to keep Canadians from going to the U.S. for advanced degrees, Toronto's Faculty of Music initiated a three-year BMUS degree in "school music." A name change took place to *the Royal Conservatory of Music*, which allowed for the expansion of degree programs in the 1950s to include musicology, composition, and music education. Eventually, enrollment in music education increased by more than 200 percent between 1960 and 1967. However, even in the late 20th century, graduate study in music education has been mainly at the master's level. Apart from a few who obtained EdD degrees, Canadians have had little opportunity to do doctoral work in music education at Toronto or elsewhere in Canada.

Bib.: Peters, Diane E., *Canadian Music and Music Education: An Annotated Bibliography of Theses and Dissertations*, 1997.

Lit.: Green, J. Paul, and Nancy F. Vogan, *Music Education in Canada*, 1991.

UPDATE: APPLICATIONS OF RESEARCH IN MUSIC EDUCATION. Established in 1982 by Charles Elliott at the University of South Carolina, this journal focuses on practical applications of research in general, choral, and instrumental music. It also contains information on special topics in music education. Published by **NA***f***ME**, it is offered twice a year.

URSULINE CONVENT. *See* ECOLE DES URSULINES.

URTEXT. Ideally, a score presenting the most "authentic" version of a musical work. An *urtext* attempts to present the original manuscript as set down on paper by the composer.

VALIDITY. Content validity is the extent to which test instruments measure what they are supposed to measure. There are seven other types of validity used in assessment.

VALVE OIL. A special type of oil used in lubricating valves or slides for musical instruments such as trumpet and trombone.

VIBRATO. A pulsating of the tone by slight variations in pitch, intensity, or both. It is generally used in lyrical passages, providing a warm quality to the tone. There are a variety of ways to produce vibrato on instruments and the voice.
    Bib.: For wind instruments, see Colwell, Richard J., and Thomas Goolsby, *The Teaching of Instrumental Music*, 1992. For voice, see Collins, Don, *Teaching Choral Music*, 2nd ed., 1999. For strings, see Green, Elizabeth A. H., *Teaching Stringed Instruments in Classes*, 1996.

VICTROLA. *See* CLARK, FRANCES ELLIOTT.

VIRGINIA REEL. An American country dance in which the partners start by facing each other in two lines.

VOCAL CONCERTO. An all-encompassing term that means about the same as *motet*; however, it is mostly understood as a solo concerto for one voice with orchestra, and dates from the early 18th century.

VOCAL JAZZ. Jazz singers from Louis Armstrong to Ella Fitzgerald developed the jazz style of singing from many of the techniques of the jazz instrumentalists—a natural brassy tone, a rhythmic delivery, and the ability to improvise. Fitzgerald is known for her **scat singing**, the vocal approach to instrumental improvisation.

VOCAL JAZZ ENSEMBLE. Generally, this group is made up of at least two singers to a part. Literature is usually drawn from arrangers such as Kirby

Shaw. They may perform **a cappella** or with any instrumental combination. These ensembles are usually found in high school or college settings.

VOLUNTARY GRAMMAR SCHOOLS. (UK.) These are highly selective secondary schools in Northern Ireland. Only about 40 percent of students eligible by age are accepted. Usually churches or other religious organizations sponsor and manage these schools through a board of governors.

VOLUNTARY MAINTAINED SCHOOLS. (UK-Ire.) Schools that are independent of the control of the education and library boards. These schools may be either primary or secondary. They do not charge tuition or fees for attendance, and are usually sponsored by the Catholic Church.

VYGOTSKY, LEV SEMYONOVICH (1896–1934). A Russian psychologist and founder of an original, holistic theory of human cultural and historical development, referred to as *cultural-historical psychology*. Influenced by **Jean Piaget** and **Gestalt psychologists**, he was very interested in the arts as well as developmental psychology, in which he focused on how children acquire the higher cognitive functions during development. Some consider his most important contribution to be his work with the interrelationship of language development and thought. This was explored in his book *Thought and Language*.

W

WALSH, BRENDAN. *See* BREATHNACH, BREANDÁN.

WALTZING MATILDA. (Aus.) Best known of all Australian songs. There have been several unsuccessful attempts to have it declared the national anthem. Words by A. B. "Banjo" Paterson (ca. 1895) and music coming from an old Scottish ballad. It was first sung in public in Winton, Queensland, in 1895. Colloquially known as *Wander as a tramp with a swag*. The most widely known version was arranged by Marie Cowan (1900), but the authorship has long been disputed.

WANGGA. (Aus.) Public singing and dancing in northwestern Northern Territory (NT). An Australian Aboriginal dance with music, generally one that is performed publicly. Aboriginal songs, usually received from spirits in dreams. Aboriginal words for public singing and dancing vary among different language groups in other parts of Australia.

WARNOCK REPORT (1978). (UK.) This report in the UK recommended important changes in education policy for students with special needs. It was the impetus for the Education Act of 1981 with regard to special education. The Warnock Report, along with Swan in 1985, was instrumental in continuing the plan for social reform through education.

WAR OF INDEPENDENCE. *See* NORTHERN IRELAND.

WASHINGTON SYMPOSIUM (1990). MENC, the Smithsonian Institution, and the **Society for Ethnomusicology** cosponsored a symposium in Washington, DC, on the Multicultural Approach to Music Education, which was directed by William M. Anderson. Music educators, ethnomusicologists, and culture bearers came together to teach and learn about the music of African Americans, Chinese, Cuban/Caribbean, Mexican, and Native American cultures.

WATKINS-FARNUM PERFORMANCE SCALE. Written by John Watkins and Stephen Farnum in 1954, this test is most often used to assess **sight-reading** skills at the secondary school level. This may be used as a standard achievement test for all band instruments, with its purpose being the measurement of performance and progress on a musical instrument. The authors believe it to be useful in a variety of applications, not only for testing sight-reading ability, but also for band tryouts, seating placement, and annual or semiannual testing to measure individual improvement.

WEBSTER, PETER. Professor emeritus from Northwestern University, he has served as chair of the Department of Music Studies, which includes the programs of music education, musicology/ethnomusicology, music theory/cognition, technology, and composition. His publications include over 75 articles and book chapters on technology, music-education practice, and creative thinking in music. He is coauthor of *Experiencing Music Technology*, 3rd ed., which is considered the standard textbook used in introductory college courses in music technology. He is well known for his work in creative thinking and is the author of *Measures of Creative Thinking in Music*, an exploratory tool for assessing music thinking using quasi-improvisational tasks. His doctoral dissertation from Eastman, *A Factor of Intellect Approach to Creative Thinking in Music*, served as a foundation for much of his later research in *Creative Thinking in Music*.

WEIKART, PHYLLIS. A longtime member of the kinesiology faculty of the University of Michigan, Weikart is principally known for her work in rhythmic movement and folk dance, which has won her international recognition. She has published five books and produced or directed 14 albums, audiotapes, and videotapes. Her program, "Education through Movement: Building the Foundation," has certified teachers from across the country. She is also the creator of "Fitness Over Fifty," an exercise program for older people. She continues to be in demand as a keynote speaker and workshop presenter at conferences throughout the U.S. The Regents of the University of Michigan have named Weikart associate professor emeritus of kinesiology.

WELCH, GRAHAM. (UK.) Chair of Music Education, University of London, and president of the **International Society of Music Education** (ISME). He is in demand as a visiting professor and a specialist consultant for government departments and agencies in the UK, Italy, Sweden, the U.S., Ukraine, United Arab Emirates, South Africa, and Argentina on aspects of music, education, and teacher education. His publications include some 300 articles on musical development and music education, teacher education, the psychology of music, singing and voice science, as well as music in special education and disability. He is also a member of the editorial board of many of the world's leading journals in music education.

WELSH FOLK-SONG SOCIETY. From the standpoint of traditional music, the most important development in Wales was the founding of the Welsh Folk-Song Society in 1906 to collect, preserve, interpret, and make known the folk songs of Wales and to foster interest in folk song and folk literature in general. Aside from a number of amateur collectors, the most important collector was the botanist **John Lloyd Williams** (1854–1945), who established sound analytical principles for Welsh songs. *Canu Gwerin*, the society's journal, appears every August, and there is an annual meeting for lectures, discussion, and song as well as a lecture at the National Eisteddfod.

WELSH HARP SOCIETY. Formed in 1961, traveling harp teachers popularized the instrument in schools. Eventually, young people even in mountainous rural districts have been able to rent or buy harps, leading to a great number of performers, among whom women predominate.

WELSH OFFICE EDUCATION DEPARTMENT. Composed of four divisions: curriculum, administration, further and higher education, and culture and recreation. It is Wales's own central education agency.

WELSH WORK SONGS. The oldest known category of these songs is oxen songs, mentioned in the 1100s and still used in plowing until about 1900. The singer was the plowboy (**geilwad**), whose job it was to walk backward facing the oxen and sing to keep the oxen calm. Twenty-one of these songs survive, including several tunes. Other examples include one sung by the blacksmith while striking the anvil. The only known Welsh language sea shanty was used as a capstan or rope shanty, sung while sailors pulled together on a rope to help to secure rhythmic unanimity. Similar to *What Shall We Do With the Drunken Sailor?*

WESLEYAN SYMPOSIUM (1984). The Symposium on the Application of Social Anthropology to the Teaching and Learning of Music, sponsored by **MENC**, Wesleyan University (CT), and the Theodore Presser Foundation, was held in 1984 to examine the relationship between social anthropology and music education.

WEST AFRICAN PERCUSSION. Features the use of a *time line*, or basic rhythmic pattern that provides the foundation of the complex rhythm played by multiple drums. Often the pattern is played on an iron bell and struck wooden sticks, as in claves.

WESTMINSTER CHOIR COLLEGE. Founded in 1925 by John Finlay Williamson from the Westminster Presbyterian Choir of Dayton, Ohio. In the early 1930s, the college and choir moved to Princeton, New Jersey. The Westminster Choir maintained the **a cappella tradition** throughout Williamson's tenure. His vocal approach included a very dark, full-throated sound with a full vibrato. Some describe this as *a tremolo*.

WHISTLE REGISTER. An extremely high area of the child and female voice. Sometimes referred to as the *squeak register*. This register is not considered useful for true and enjoyable singing.

WHITE, PORTIA (1911–1968). First a mezzo-soprano, and then a contralto, who made her formal debut in Toronto at age 30. She became the first black Canadian concert singer to win approval across North America. After a successful Town Hall recital in New York in 1944, she continued on a highly successful tour of Canada and the northern U.S. She attracted comparison to the African-American contralto Marian Anderson. Her early work includes teacher training, and she became a schoolteacher in Nova Scotian black communities. White has been called "the singer who broke the colour barrier in Canadian classical music."
   Lit.: Editorial, *Halifax Chronicle-Herald*, April 27, 1996.

WHITE PAPER. (UK.) A government discussion document that sets out government policy on a specific issue. It usually precedes legislation and gives opportunity for discussion before it is presented to Parliament as a bill.

WHITE PAPER ON EDUCATION. (RIre.) A policy formed through the Ireland Department of Education and Science (IDES) on the education of **traveler children** in the **Republic of Ireland**. Its goal is to increase the number of traveler children in the successful education community. Therefore, all schools in Ireland must include provisions for travelers in their school plans. A visiting-teacher service is funded by the department to act as a liaison between the settled and traveler communities.

WHITTLE AND DUB. A related instrument to the **fipple flute** is the three-holed pipe that is played with one hand only, leaving the other free to beat a small drum, called a *tabor*; the combination was called *whittle and dub* (whistle and drum). This primitive one-man band, used since the Middle Ages, was a common accompaniment for **Morris dancing**.

WHOLE-PART-WHOLE. An education term referring to an instructional approach using a holistic method, or a series of separate steps or parts, as in the movement from general to specific or from specific to general. This has been debated for centuries among educators, but studies indicate that a combination of both approaches is used.

WIEPRECHT, WILHELM FRIEDRICH (1802–1872). German musical conductor, composer, and inventor. While credited with Stolzel and Moritz as the inventors of the bass tuba, the date for its invention is often given as 1935; however, it was first used *before* 1835 by Wieprecht in the Trompeteer Corps of the Prussian Dragon Guards in Berlin. He studied acoustics in order to improve the valves of brass instruments to increase their volume and purity of tune. In 1835 he was honored by the Royal Academy of Berlin.

WILLIAMS, DR. J. LLOYD (1854–1945). (UK.) Considered the most important figure in the history of the **Welsh Folk-Song Society**. He contributed more than all others in collecting and publishing Welsh folk songs in the *Journal of the Welsh Folk-Song Society*. He lectured and promoted the use of folk songs in schools and in the **eisteddfod**, and established sound analytical principles for Welsh songs.

WILLIAMS, JOHN CHRISTOPHER (1941–). (Aus.) Classical guitarist and long-term resident of the UK, after having moved there in 1952. He created a Guitar Department at the Royal College of Music in London; he has maintained links with this school and with the Royal Northern College in Manchester. He has recorded almost the entire repertoire for the guitar. Williams believes that student education should include ensemble playing, sight-reading, and a focus on phrasing and tone production/variation, rather than focusing only on solo playing. Williams received the BRIT Award for Best Classical Recording (1983). He is visiting professor and honorary member of the **Royal Academy of Music** in London.

WIND BAND. *See* BRASS BAND; WIND ENSEMBLE.

WIND ENSEMBLE. (Also symphonic wind ensemble, wind band). In 1952, as an adjunct to the symphony band, the **Eastman Wind Ensemble** was organized by Frederick Fennell with a minimum rather than a maximum number of players. The instrumentation of this first group consisted of 52 players: three flutes (piccolo), three oboes (English horn), one E-flat clarinet, eight B-flat clarinets, one bass clarinet, one contrabass clarinet, two bassoons, one contrabassoon, two alto saxophones, one tenor saxophone, one baritone saxophone, five French horns, six trumpets, four trombones, two euphoniums, two tubas, six percussion players, one contrabass (string), and one harp. Fennell was looking for a different sound from that of a large band. He chose to find contemporary composers of that era to write for the specific wind band instrumentation. Fennell used the term *ensemble* rather than *band* because of its suitability as a chamber ensemble. According to David Whitwell, Fennell's intention was not "to replace the traditional band and its literature with that of the wind ensemble, but to expand the performance repertoire possibilities for all wind groups."

Lit.: Battisti, Frank L., *The Twentieth Century American Wind Band/ Ensemble: History, Development and Literature*, 1995; Goldman, Edwin Franko, *The Wind Band: Its Literature and Technique*, 1974; Whitwell, David, *A Concise History of the Wind Band*, 1985.

WIND INSTRUMENTS. Musical instruments that contain some type of resonator in which a column of air is set into vibration by the player blowing into (or over) a mouthpiece set at the end of the resonator. The main wind instruments are the **brass instruments**, with sound produced by lip vibration, which causes the air within the instrument to vibrate (e.g., trumpets, horns, trombones, tubas), and **woodwinds**, with sound produced by blowing through one or two reeds to create vibration (e.g., flutes, clarinets, oboes). *See also* AEROPHONE.

WING MUSIC APTITUDE TEST. (UK- Eng., Wales.) Also referred to as the *Wing Standardized Tests of Musical Intelligence*. It is a battery of seven tests designed to measure music aptitude and preference. The tests were designed to identify children who were musically talented and who would be good candidates for instrumental instruction and performance at the secondary level. Initially published in 1939, with revisions in 1957, 1960, and 1961.

WOLFE, IRVING W. (1903–1977). A consummate musician and music educator, Wolfe worked tirelessly throughout his career to uphold the highest standards in music and education. Known particularly at Peabody College, Nashville, Tennessee, as a teacher and administrator, he served as head of the Music Department and brought about its inclusion as a full member of **NASM** in 1950. He also established the doctor of philosophy degree with a major in music, which was granted in 1942. It was one of the first such programs in the South. Wolfe was active in a variety of choral experiences at Peabody, including the founding and directing of the *Madrigalians*, who were well known throughout the South. He compiled the first State Certification of Music Teachers for **MENC** in 1972; developed the elementary music series *Together We Sing* with Margaret Fullerton in 1950, and later edition for upper grades; and was one of the first to introduce recordings to accompany his song series (1950, 1952). He was also known for his interest in folk songs from around the world, and for his promotion of **singing schools** and the **shape-note** tradition during his tenure at Peabody in Nashville.

WOODBLOCKS. *See* CHINESE WOOD BLOCK.

WOODBRIDGE, WILLIAM CHANNING (1794–1845). (U.S.) Woodbridge championed the cause of music as a branch of common education. He also promoted the idea that all children could be taught to sing through public performance by children's choirs. As a follower of **Pestolozzian** principles, he wrote out Pestolozzian lesson plans for **Lowell Mason** to use in teaching children to sing. Because of his observance of Nägeli using Pestolozzian principles of instruction, Woodbridge thought this approach was superior to that of American **singing schools**. These principles were the first formulation of modern principles of teaching music in the U.S.

WOODS HOLE CONFERENCE. Held at Woods Hole on Cape Cod in 1959, its primary purpose was to identify the problems with science education in the primary and secondary schools and to recommend solutions. During this conference there was recognition of the need for balanced curriculum, and this included music and the other arts. Music was recognized by this distinguished group of nonmusic educators as being an important part of curriculum at one of the most influential conferences in history. *See also* JEROME BRUNER.

WOODWINDS. A family of musical instruments within the more general category of wind instruments. There are two main types of woodwind instruments: flutes and reed instruments (reed pipes). What differentiates these instruments is the way in which they produce their sound. As a general description, *flutes* produce sound by directing a focused stream of air across the edge of a hole in a cylindrical tube; *reed instruments* produce sound by focusing air into a mouthpiece that then causes a reed (or reeds) to vibrate. Woodwinds can be soprano, alto, tenor, or bass.

WOODWINDS, GUIDE TO TEACHING. A highly recommended method book for the teaching of beginning woodwinds in the public school, written by Frederick Westphal, 4th ed., W. C. Brown, 1985.

WORLD FEDERATION OF MUSIC THERAPISTS (WFMT). An international nonprofit organization bringing together music therapy associations and individuals interested in developing and promoting music therapy globally through exchange of information, collaboration among professionals, and actions. Founded in 1985 in Genoa, Italy, it is the only worldwide professional organization representing music therapy in many areas of the world. As of January 1, 2013, Dr. Annie Heiderscheit of the U.S. is the new interim president.

WORLD MUSIC PEDAGOGY. This term was coined by **Patricia Shehan Campbell** to describe world music content and practice in elementary and secondary school music programs. Pioneers of the movement are **Barbara Lundquist**, **William Anderson**, Bryan Burton, **Mary Goetze**, Ellen McCullough-Babson, and Mary Shamrock, who designed and delivered curricular models to teachers of music of various levels and specializations.

WORLD MUSICS. A term credited to ethnomusicologist Robert E. Brown, who in the early 1960s at Wesleyan University in Connecticut developed undergraduate through doctoral programs in the discipline. The term became current in the 1980s as a marketing/classificatory device in the media and the music industry. It is often used to classify any kind of non-Western music. This is only one of several conflicting definitions for world music; however, it appears to be the most useful at this particular time.

WORLD PEACE JUBILEE AND INTERNATIONAL MUSIC FESTIVAL (1872). (U.S.) After the Franco-Prussian War, **Patrick Gilmore**, who believed that music had the power to change the world, created this jubilee to express a profound relief that there was peace in the world. He visited Europe's capital cities and royal courts, imploring presidents and kings to send their finest musicians to Boston to help celebrate this peace. He staged the event in Boston's new Coliseum, holding an audience of 50,000, containing 20,000 choristers and almost 2,000 instrumentalists. Johann Strauss attended the jubilee and composed a *Jubilee Waltz* for the occasion.

XENAKIS, IANNIS (1922–2001). Greek composer, music theorist, and architect-engineer. Born in Brăila, Romania. Educated in Greece, where he studied engineering. In 1945, having been involved with the Greek resistance against the Nazi occupation forces, he was captured, but escaped to the U.S. In 1947 he went to Paris, became a naturalized citizen, studied architecture with Le Corbusier, and then studied with Honegger, Milhaud, and Messiaen.

With his background of engineering and architecture, Xenakis worked to connect mathematical concepts with the organization of a musical composition. He founded the Center for Mathematical and Automated Music at Indiana University (U.S.), where he served on the faculty from 1967 to 1972. His influence on the development of advanced composition in Europe and America was considerable. One of his more important works is *Metastasis for 61 Instruments*, which influenced Penderecki's cluster pieces.

XENOPHOBIA. Hatred existing between the races of mankind.

XYLOPHONE. Keyboard percussion instrument with hardwood keys arranged and tuned like a piano. Each key has a resonator tuned to it. It is played with two or more sticks. The early xylophone reached its height in Southeast Asia in the 14th century; spread into Africa, then to the Americas; it arrived in Europe by the 16th century. Saint-Saëns used it his *Danse Macabre*, and Khachaturian included it in his "Sabre Dance" from the *Gayane Suite*.

XYLORIMBA. A hybrid keyboard instrument developed in the early 20th century with a five-octave range as found in the xylophone and marimba. Used in popular music as the *marimba-xylophone*. Used also by Berg, Stravinsky, and others of the early 20th century.

X-Y-Z GROUPING. Grouping students according to ability into three sections for separate teaching.

Y

YALE SEMINAR ON MUSIC EDUCATION (1963). A federally funded arts education seminar held in New Haven, Connecticut, to discuss developments in the arts, including music education. Unfortunately, out of the 31 participants, only a few music educators were included. The seminar focused on major criticisms of the teaching of science in the public schools. The conference participants believed that music teachers spent too much time on performance-related activities. The major publication from this seminar is the *Juilliard Repertory Project*.

YOUNG, PHYLLIS. Professor emerita of violincello and string pedagogy, and professor emerita of music from the Butler School of Music, the University of Texas. Internationally acclaimed as a string teacher, she has presented workshops/master classes in 32 countries on six continents and in 41 American states. Author of two widely distributed books, *Playing the String Game: Strategies for Teaching Cello and Strings* (8th printing), and *The String Play: The Drama of Playing and Teaching Strings*, she has served as national president of the **American String Teachers Association** (ASTA) and was the recipient of its 1984 Distinguished Service Award. ASTA and the **National School Orchestra Association** (NSOA) honored her again with the 2002 Paul Rolland Lifetime Achievement Award for "Grande Dame du Violoncello."

In addition to teaching cello performance majors, for 35 years she directed the University of Texas String Project, a large teacher-training program that has been a model for numerous string programs throughout the U.S. and abroad. She is an honorary member of the European String Teachers Association and is listed in *Who's Who in America*.

YOUNG COMPOSERS PROJECT. Founded in 1959, this was a union between composers and public school music programs. Norman Dello Joio proposed this project, which placed young composers, under age 35, in public school systems to serve as composers-in-residence. These composers wrote music for a school's performing ensembles in order to expose students and teachers to new music, and to increase repertoire. As a result of this project, the Ford Foundation awarded **MENC** a $1.38 million grant, through which it initiated the *Contemporary Music Project for Creativity in Music Education* (CMP).

THE YOUNG PERSON'S GUIDE TO THE ORCHESTRA. Orchestral work for speaker and orchestra by Benjamin Britten. The narration (written by Eric Crozier) describes the uses and characteristics of various sections of the orchestra. The orchestral theme is from Purcell's incidental music to the play *Abdelazer* (1695). One of the first recordings used to introduce children to the sounds and organization of the orchestra.

YOUPE! YOUPE! SUR LA RIVIÈRE. A Canadian lumberjack song found in the **Silver Burdett** series.

Y-TEENS. (U.S.) Organization for high school girls aged 12–18 and designed to promote world understanding between races and religions.

Z

ZAUBEROPER. "Magic opera" or "fairy-tale opera," in which supernatural forces intervene in human affairs; examples include Weber's *Der Freischütz* and Mozart's *Die Zauberflöte* (The Magic Flute).

ZIGEUNERMUSIK. Gypsy music. A good example is the music of Fritz Kreisler (1875–1962), brilliant violinist and composer.

ZIMMERMAN, MARILYN PHLEDERER (1929–1995). Music educator and researcher, she is known for her work in early childhood education and the study of cognitive influences on the musical learning of children. In 1968 she conducted with Lee Sechrest a Health, Education, and Welfare research project titled "How Children Conceptually Organize Musical Sounds." As a result of this and her study of **Piaget**'s research, she wrote a monograph for the MENC series, From Research to the Music Classroom, no. 1: *Musical Characteristics of Children*, which became a major contribution to the college music educator's library for early childhood. During her research career, she published more than 50 articles in various journals in her field. She also participated regularly in the **International Society for Music Education**. Her writings are available in the book *On Musicality and Milestones: Selected Writings of Marilyn Pflederer Zimmerman: With Contributions from the Profession*, edited by Mark Robin Campbell. In 1991 she and her husband, Vernon Zimmerman, established the Vernon and Marilyn Pflederer Zimmerman Foundation.

ZITHER. A folk instrument consisting of a flat wooden soundbox, over which are stretched four or five melody strings and up to 37 accompaniment strings. Melody strings nearest the player are stopped on a fretted keyboard with the fingers of the left hand and plucked by a plectrum on the right thumb. Accompaniment strings are plucked by fingers of either hand. The zither is similar to the Appalachian **autoharp**.

ZUMPE, JOHANNES (1726–1790). Born in Germany, buried in London, UK. A leading maker of early English square pianos—a form of rectangular piano with a compass of about five octaves. The piano sounded like a mellow harpsichord.

List of Organizations

Aboriginal Education Council (AEC)
P.O. Box 3120
Redfern, NSW 2016
Tel (toll-free): 1800 989 185 / (02) 9699 2299
Fax: (02) 9699 2399
E-mail: admin@aec.org.au
Website: http://www.aec.org.au

Australian and New Zealand Association for Research in Music Education
(ANZARME)
Website: http://www.anzarme.org/

Australian Band and Orchestra Directors Association (ABODA)
Contact: Cathy Chan
ABOD National
P.O. Box 132
Surrey Hills, Victoria 3127
E-mail: secretary@aboda.org.au
Website: http://www.aboda.org.au

Australian Music Association (AMA)
Website: http://www.australianmusic.asn.au/

Australian Music Therapy Association (AMTA)
MBE 148/45 Glenferrie Road
Malvern, Victoria 3144
Tel: 03 9525 9625
Fax: 03 9507 2316
E-mail: info@austmta.org.au
Website: http://www.austmta.org.au

Australian National Association of Teachers of Singing (ANATS)
ANATS Secretariat
P.O. Box 576
Crows Nest, NSW 20265
Tel: 02 9431 8640
Fax: 02 9431 8677
Website: http://www.anats.org.au

Australian National Council of Orff-Schulwerk (ANCOS)
President: Kerry Raynor
P.O. Box 707
Brighton, South Australia 5048
E-mail: info@ancos.org.au
Website: http://www.ancos.org.au/

Australian Society for Music Education (ASME)
President: Dr. Kay Hartwig
Griffith University
Queensland
E-mail: K.Hartwig@griffith.edu.au
Website: http://www.asme.edu.au

Australian Strings Association (ASA)
President: John Quaine
P.O. Box 187
East Brunswick, Victoria 3057
Tel/Fax: +61 3 9443 0234
E-mail: admin@austa.asn.au
Website: http://austa.asn.au

The Kodály Music Education Institute of Australia (KMEIA)
P.O. Box 8299
TooWoomba Mail Centre, Queensland 4352
E-mail: info@kodaly.org.au
Website: http://www.kodaly.org.au

Music Council of Australia
Administrator: Sara Hood
MBE 148/45 Glenferrie Road
Malvern, Victoria 3144
Tel: +61 (0)3 9507 2315

Fax: +61 (0)3 9507 2316
E-mail: admin@mca.org.au
Website: www.mca.org.au/

Music Education New Zealand Aotearoa (MENZA)
Website: http://www.menza.org.nz

Suzuki Talent Education Association of Australia
Contact: Natalie Alexander
P.O. Box 18
Nedlands, Western Australia 6909
Tel: (08) 9386 3882
Fax: (08) 9389 1240
E-mail: info@suzukimusicwa.com.au
Website: http://suzukimusicwa.com.au

West Australia Music Teachers Association
P.O. Box 4385
Victoria Part, Western Australia 6979
Tel: (08) 9470 5595
Fax: (08) 9470 2193
E-mail: info@musicteacherswa.org.au
Website: http://www.musicteacherswa.org.ua

CANADA

British Columbia Music Educators' Association (BCMEA)
Contact: Jeff Weaver
Tel: 250-386-3591
Fax: 250-361-7191
E-mail: bcmusiced@gmail.com
Website: http://bctf.ca/BCMEA/Welcome.html

Canada Council for the Arts (CCA)
350 Albert Street
P.O. Box 1047
Ottawa, Ontario K1P 5V8
Tel: 1-800-263-5588
Fax: 1-613-566-4390
Website: www.canadacouncil.ca

Canadian Association for Music Therapy (CAMT)
110 Cumberland Street, Suite #320
Toronto, ON M5R 3V5
Tel: 1 800 996-2268
Website: http://www.musictherapy.ca

Canadian Band Association (CBA)
President: Wendy McCallum (Manitoba)
5 Pincrest Bay
Winnipeg, MB R2G 1W2
Tel: 204-727-7368
Fax: 204-663-1226
E-mail: mccallumw@brandonu.ca
Website: http://www.canadianband.ca/

Canadian Folk Music
Contact: Gillian Turnbull
Ryerson University
350 Victoria Street
Toronto, ON M5B 2K3

Canadian Music Educator's Association (CMEA)
Contact: Theodora Stathopoulos, President
E-mail: theodoraks@gmail.com
Website: http://www.cmea.ca/

Canadian Society for Traditional Music (CSTM)
E-mail: cstmsctm@ualberta.ca

Canadian University Music Society (CUMS)
Formerly *Canadian Association of University Schools of Music* (CAUSM)
Website: http://www.cums-smuc.ca/

Federation of Canadian Music Festivals (FCMF)
Exec. Director: Heather Bedford Clooney
14004 75th Avenue
Edmonton, AB T5R 2Y6
Tel (toll-free): 1-877-323-3263
Fax: 1-780-758-1227
E-mail: info@fcmf.org
Website: http://www.fcmf.org/

Kodály Society of Canada (KSC)
Website: http://www.kodalysocietyofcanada.ca

Manitoba Music Educators' Association (MMEA)
President: Eric Marshall
E-mail: emarshall@sjsd.net
Website: http://www.mymmea.ca/

National Youth Band of Canada
NYB Coordinator/Manager: Barbara Stetter
67 Catherine Street
Glace Bay, Nova Scotia B1A 2K1
Tel: (902) 849-5846
E-mail: nybmanager@hotmail.com
Website: http://www.canadianband.ca/nyb2013/nyb2013.html#

Nova Scotia Music Educators' Association (NSMEA)
President: Donalda Westcott
E-mail: djwestcott@nstu.ca
Website: http://nsmea.nstu.ca/

Ontario Music Educators' Association (OMEA)
Website: http://www.omea.on.ca/

Quebec Music Educators' Association
Contact: Therese Marcy
1034, Fort St-Louis, Apt. 3
Boucherville, QC J4B 0G5
Website: http://www.apmqmta.org/

Saskatchewan Music Educators' Association (SMEA)
Exec. Director: Val Kuemper
Box 632
Cudworth, SK SOK IBO
Tel: 1-306-256-7187
Fax: 1-306-256-3489
E-mail: smea@sasktel.net
Website: http://elecqlx.sasktelwebhosting.com/smea/smea.html

INTERNATIONAL

European Society for the Cognitive Sciences of Music (ESCOM)
Contact: Prof. Jukka Louhivuori
University of Jyväskylä
Department of Music
P.O. Box 35 (M)
40014 University of Jyväskylä
Finland
Tel: +358 40 8054310
Fax: +358 14 617 420
E-mail: escom@escom.org

International Council for Traditional Music (ICTM)
Contact: Dr. Svanibor Pettan
Department of Musicology
Faculty of Arts
University of Ljubljana
Aškerčeva 2
1000 Ljubljana
Slovenia
Tel: +1 410 501 5559
E-mail: secretariat@ictmusic.org
Website: http://www.ictmusic.org/

International Federation for Choral Music (IFCM)
E-mail: office@ifcm.net
Website: http://www.ifcm.net/

International Kodály Society (IKS)
P.O. Box 67
1364 Budapest
Hungary
Tel: (+36-1) 3434503
Fax: (+36-1) 4130138
Website: http://www.iks.hu

International Montessori Council (IMC)
Contact: Margot Garfield-Anderson
1001 Bern Creek Loop
Sarasota, FL 34240

United States
Tel: 800-632-4121
Fax: 941-359-8166
E-mail: Margot@montessori.org
Website: http://www.montessori.org/imc/

International Music Council (IMC)
1 Rue Miollis
75732 Paris
Cedex 15
France
Tel: +33 1 45 68 48 50
Fax: +33 1 45 68 48 66
Website: http://www.imc-cim.org/

International Music Education Research Centre (IMERC)
Contact: G. Welch
Tel: +44(0)20 76126503
Fax: +44(0)2076126741
E-mail: g.welch@ioe.ac.uk
Website: http://www.imerc.org

International Society for Music Education (ISME)
ISME International Office
P.O. Box 909
Nedlands, West Australia
Australia
Tel: +61-8-9386-2654
E-mail: isme@isme.org
Website: http://www.isme.org

International Society for Philosophy of Music Education (ISPME)
Website: http://www.ispme.net/

International Suzuki Association (ISA)
Contact: Gilda Barston, CEO
Music Institute of Chicago
300 Green Bay Road
Winnetka, IL 60093
United States
Tel: 214-783-3671

Fax: 847-446-3876
E-mail: info@internationalsuzuki.org
Website: http://www.internationalsuzuki.org/

MayDay Group
(International Music Education think-tank connected through E-mail, Internet, and Mail)
Contact: David Elliott
E-mail: mdgacted@gmail.com
Website: http://www.maydaygroup.org/

Music Education Research International (MERI)
Center for Music Education Research
School of Music, MUS 101
College of the Arts
University of South Florida
4202 East Fowler Avenue
Tampa, FL 33620-7350
United States
Fax: 1-813-974-8721
E-mail: fung@usf.edu
Website: http://www.cmer.arts.usf.edu

Women Band Directors International
President: Linda Thompson
E-mail: lkaythomp@gmail.com
Website: http://www.womenbanddirectors.org/
Journal: *BandWorld*

UNITED KINGDOM AND REPUBLIC OF IRELAND

Arts Council of Northern Ireland
MacNeice House/77
Malone Road
Belfast BT9 6AQ
United Kingdom
Tel: +44 28 9038 5200
Website: http://www.artscouncil-ni.org/

British Association for Music Therapy (BAMT)
24-27 White Lion Street
London N1 9PD
Tel: +44 (0)20 7837 6100
E-mail: info@bamt.org
Website: http://www.bamt.org

British Forum for Ethnomusicology (BFE)
Dr. Carolyn Landau, chair
Tel: +44 (0)20 7848 2384,
E-mail: carolyn.landau@kcl.ac.uk
Website: http://www.bfe.org.uk/

British Journal of Music Education (BJME)
Editor: Martin Fautley
Cambridge Journals On-Line
Website: http://journals.cambridge.org/action/displayJournal?jid=BME

British Suzuki Institute (BSI)
Administrator: Minette Joyce
Unit 1.01
The Lightbox
111 Power Road
Chiswick
London W4 5PY
Tel: 020 3176 4170
E-mail: info@britishsuzuki.com
Website: http://www.britishsuzuki.org.uk/

English Folk Dance and Song Society (EFDSS)
Cecil Sharp House
2 Regent's Park Road
London NW1 7AY UK
Tel: (+44) (0)20 7485 2206
Fax: (+44) (0)20 7284 0534
E-mail: info@efdss.org
Website: http://www.efdss.org

National Association of Music Educators (NAME)
Gordon Lodge
Snitterton Road
Matlock
Derbyshire DE4 2JG
Tel: 01629 76091
E-mail: musiceducation@name.org.uk
Website: http://www.name.org.uk

Orff Society UK
Website: http://www.orff.org.uk

Post Primary Music Teachers Association (PPMTA) (Ireland)
Website: http://www.ppmta.ie/

Royal Musical Association
Tel: +44 (0) 207 017 7720
E-mail: agents@tandf.co.uk

Scottish Arts Council
12 Manor Place
Edinburgh EH3 7DD
Tel: +44 (0) 131 240 2444 or 2443
Fax: +44 (0) 131 225 9833
Website: http://www.scottisharts.org.uk

Scottish Association for Music Education (SAME)
Graeme Wilson, secretary
P.O. BOX 26858
Kirkcaldy
Fife KY2 9BP
Tel: 05601921483
Website: http://www.same.org.uk/

Scottish Orff Schulwerk Association (SOSA)
E-mail: enquiries@orffscotland.org
Website: http://www.orffscotland.org/

Society for Music Education in Ireland (SMEI)
Website: http://www.smei.ie

Society for Musicology in Ireland (SMI)
Contact: Dr. Kerry Houston, president
KIT Conservatory of Music and Drama
Rathmines Road
Dublin 6
Ireland
E-mail: Kerry.Houston@dit.ie
Website: http://www.musicologyireland.com

Traditional Music & Song Association of Scotland (TMSA)
c/o The Drill Hall
30-38 Dalmeny Street
Edinburgh EH6 8RG
Scotland
Tel: +44 (0)7922 533 915
E-mail: office@tmsa.org.uk
Website: http://www.tmsa.org.uk/

Welsh Folk-Song Society
Dr. Rhiannon Ifans (honorary secretary)
Rhandir
Penrhyn-coch
Aberystwyth
Ceredigion, SY23 3EQ
Tel: (01970) 828719
E-mail: ymholiadau@canugwerin.com
Website: http://www.canugwerin.com

UNITED STATES

American Bandmasters Association (ABA)
President-Elect: David Waybright
1521 Pickard
Norman, OK 73072-6316
Tel: 1-450-321-3373
Website: http://www.americanbandmasters.org

American Choral Directors Association (ACDA)
545 Couch Drive
Oklahoma City, OK 73102-2207
Tel: 1-405-232-8161
Fax: 1-405-232-8162
Website: http://www.acda.org

American Musicological Society (AMS)
6010 College Station
Brunswick, ME 04011-8451
Tel: 1-877-679-7648
Fax: 1-207-798-4254
Website: http://www.ams-net.org

American Music Therapy Association
8455 Colesville Road, Suite 1000
Silver Spring, MD 20910
Tel: 1-301-589-3300
Fax: 1-301-589-5175
Website: http://www.musictherapy.org

American Orff-Schulwerk Association (AOSA)
Director: Carrie Barnette
P.O. Box 391089
Cleveland, OH 44139-8089
Tel: 1-440-543-5366
E-mail: execdir@aosa.org
Website: http://www.aosa.org

American School Band Directors Association
President: Kevin Beaber
227 N. 1st Street
P.O. Box 696
Guttenberg, IA 52052
Tel: 1-563-252-2500
E-mail: asbda@alpinecom.net
Website: http://www.asbda.com

American String Teacher Association (ASTA)
4153 Chain Bridge Road
Fairfax VA 22030

Tel: 1-703-279-2113
Fax 1-703-279-2114
Website: asta@astaweb.com

Association for Supervision and Curriculum Development (ASCDA)
1703 N. Beauregard Street
Alexandria, VA 22311-1714
Tel: 1-800-933-2723 (press "1")
Fax: 1-703-575-5400
Website: http://www.ascd.org

Association of Waldorf Schools of North America (ASWNA)
Contact: Frances Kane
2344 Nicollet Avenue S.
Minneapolis, MN 55404
Tel: 1-612-870-8310
Fax: 1-612-870-8316
E-mail: awsna@awsna.org
Website: http://www.awsna.org

College Band Directors National Association (CBDNA)
Contact: Thomas Verrier
Blair School of Music
Vanderbilt University
2400 Blakemore Avenue
Nashville, TN 37212
Tel: 1-615-322-7651
Fax: 1-615-343-032
Website: http://www.cbdna.org

College Music Society (CMS)
Contact: Julie L. Johnson
312 East Pine Street
Missoula, MT 59802
Tel: 1-406-721-9616
Fax: 1-406-721-9419
E-mail: cms@music.org
Website: http://www.collegemusicsociety.org

Council for Research in Music Education (CRME)
School of Music, University of Illinois
1205 W. California
Urbana, IL 61801
Tel: 217-333-1027
Website: http://www.crme.uiuc.edu

Dalcroze Society of America (DSA)
Contact: Jessica Schaeffer
310 N. State Street
Ukiah, CA 95482
Tel: 707-489-3006
E-mail: admin@dalcrozeusa.org
Website: http://www.dalcrozeusa.org

Early Childhood Music and Movement Association (ECMMA)
805 Mill Avenue
Snohomish, WA 98290
Tel: 1-360-568-5635
Website: www.ecmma.org/

Early Music America (EMA)
801 Vinial Street, Suite 300
Pittsburgh, PA 15212
Tel: 412-642-2778
Fax: 412-642-2779
E-mail: info@earlymusic.org
Website: http://www.earlymusic.org

Education through Music (ETM)
Richards Institute
Tel: 1-805-701-8140
E-mail: info@richardsinstitute.org
Website: www.educationthroughmusic.com/

Getty Center for Education in the Arts
1200 Getty Center Drive
Los Angeles, CA 90049-1679
Tel: (310) 440-7300
Website: http://www.getty.edu

Gordon Institute for Music Learning (GMIL)
Contact: Jennifer McDonel
P.O. Box 126
Buffalo, NY 14231-0126
E-mail: execdir@giml.org
Website: http://www.giml.org

Interlochen Center for the Arts
4000 Highway M-137
P.O. Box 199
Interlochen, MI 49643-0199
Tel: 1-231-276-7200
Website: http://www.interlochen.org

Jazz Education Network (JEN)
Contact: Larry Green
Tel: 1-573-692-0012
E-mail: JazzerLG@aol.com
Website: http://www.jazzednet.org/

Kodály Center of America (KCA)
10951 Pico Boulevard, Suite 405
Los Angeles, CA 90064
Tel: 1-310-441-3555
Fax: 1-310-441-3577
E-mail: info@oake.org
Website: http://www.kodaly-center-of-america.org/

Montessori Foundation
Exec. Director: Joyce St. Giermaine
1001 Bern Creek Loop
Sarasota, FL 34240
Tel: 1-800-655-5843
Fax: 1-941-745-3111
Website: http://www.montessori.org

Musicians United for Superior Education (MUSE)
475 Beard Avenue
Buffalo, NY 14214
Tel: 1-716-834-6873
Fax: 1-716-834-5666
E-mail: muse475@aol.com
Website: www.musekids.org/

Music Teachers National Association (MTNA)
441 Vine Street, Suite 3100
Cincinnati, OH 45202-3004
Tel: 1-888-512-5278
Fax: 1-513-421-2503
Website: http://www.mtna.org

National Association for Music Education (NA*f*ME)
1806 Robert Fulton Drive
Reston, VA 20191
Tel: 1-800-336-3768
Fax: 1-703-860-1531
Website: http://www.nafme.org

National Association of College Wind and Percussion Instructors (NACWPI)
President-Elect: Patrick Smith
Dept. of Music, Virginia Commonwealth University
922 Park Avenue
P.O. Box 842004
Richmond, VA 23284-2004
E-mail: psmith7@vcu.edu
Website: http://www.nacwpi.org
Journal: *NACWPI Journal*

National Association of Teachers of Singing (NATS)
9957 Moorings Drive, Suite 401
Jacksonville, FL 32224
Tel: 1-904-992-9101
Fax: 1-904-262-2587
E-mail: info@nats.org
Website: http://www.nats.org

National Band Association (NBA)
Box #102
745 Chastain Road, Suite 1140
Kennesaw, GA 30144
Tel: 1-601-297-8168
E-mail: info@nationalbandassociation.org
Website: http://www.nationalbandassociation.org

National Education Association (NEA)
1201 16th Street, NW
Washington, DC 20036-3290
Tel: 1-202-833-4000
Fax: 1-202-822-7974
Website: http://www.nea.org

National Endowment for the Arts (NEA)
1100 Pennsylvania Avenue, NW
Washington, DC 20506
Tel: 1-202-682-5400
Website: http://www.nea.gov

National School Orchestra Association (NSOA)
Orginally a separate organization, now part of ASTA. *See* American String
Teacher Association.

Organization of American Kodály Educators (OAKE)
10951 Pico Boulevard, Suite 405
Los Angeles, CA 90064
Tel: 1-310-441-3555
Fax: 1-310-441-3577
E-mail: info@aoke.org
Website: http://www.oake.org
Journal: *Kodály Envoy*

Society for Research in Music Education (SRME)
National Association for Music Education
1806 Robert Fulton Drive
Reston, VA 20191
Tel: 1-800-336-3768
Fax: 1-703-860-1531
Website: http://www.nafme.org

Suzuki Association of America (SAA)
Chair: Mark George
P.O. Box 17310
Boulder, CO 80308
Tel: 1-888-378-9854
Fax: 1-303-444-0984
Website: http://www.suzukiassociation.org

List of Publications

aMUSE
Association of Music Educators
150 Palmerston Street
Carlton, Victoria 3053
Tel: (03) 9349 1048
Fax: (03) 9349 1052
E-mail: info@amuse.vic.edu.au
Website: http://www.amuse.vic.edu.au/

Australian Journal of Music Education (IJME)
Editor: David Forrest
P.O. Box 5
Parkville, Victoria 3052
Tel: +61 3 9925 7807
E-mail: publications@asme.edu.au
Website: http://www.asme.edu.au/publications.htm

Australian Journal of Music Therapy (AJMT)
MBE 148/45 Glenferrie Road
Malvern, Victoria 3144
Tel: 03 9525 9625
Fax: 03 9507 2316
Website: http://www.austmta.org.au

Australian Online Journal of Arts Education
Website: http://www.deakin.edu.au/arts-ed/education/teach-research/arts-ed/journal.php

Australian Voice
Australian National Association for Teachers of Singing (ANATS)
P.O. Box 576
Crows Nest, New South Wales 2065

Tel: 02 9431 8640
Fax: 02 9431 8677
Website: http://www.anats.org.au

E-Journal of Studies in Music Education
Contact: Susan Gilmour
School of Music
University of Canterbury
Private Bag 4800
Christchurch, New Zealand
Tel: +64 3 364 2183
E-mail: susan.gilmour@canterbury.ac.nz

Interlude
Australian Band and Orchestra Directors Association (ABODA)
Contact: Cathy Chan
ABODA National
P.O. BOX 132
Surrey Hills, Victoria 3127
E-mail: secretary@aboda.org.au
Website: http://www.aboda.org.au

Journal of the Australian National Council of Orff Schulwerk
P.O. Box 707
Brighton, South Australia 5048
E-mail: info@ancos.org.au
Website: http://www.ancos.org.au

Kodaly Music Institute of Australia Journal
Kodaly Music Education Institute of Australia
P.O. Box 8299
Toowoomba Mail Centre, Queensland 4352
E-mail: info@kodaly.org.au
Website: http://www.kodaly.org.au/index.php/journal

Music Education in the Wider Community (e-Journal)
Australian and New Zealand Association for Research in Music Education
(ANZARME)
Contact: Susan Gilmour
Tel: +64 3 364 2183
E-mail: susan.gilmour@canterbury.ac.nz
Website: http://www.merc.canterbury.ac.nz/e_journal.shtml

Music Forum
Music Council of Australia
Editor: Dr. Richard Letts
MBE 148/45 Glenferrie Road
Malvern, Victoria 3144
Tel: +61 (0)2 9251 3816
Fax: +61 (0)2 9251 3817
E-mail: mca@mca.org.au
Website: http://musicforum.org.au/index.shtml

National Review of School Music Education in Australia
National Affiliation of Arts Educators (NAAE)
Education Services Australia
P.O. Box 177
Carlton South, Victoria 3053
Tel: +61 3 9207 9600
Fax: +61 3 9639 1616
E-mail: cl@esa.edu.au
Website: http://www.curriculum.edu.au/leader/school_music_review_report,12505.html

Sound Ideas (e-Journal)
Australian and New Zealand Association for Research in Music Education (ANZARME)
Contact: Susan Gilmour
Tel: +64 3 364 2183
E-mail: susan.gilmour@canterbury.ac.nz
Website: http://www.merc.canterbury.ac.nz/e_journal.shtml

CANADA

Canadian Folk Music Journal
4907 54th Street
Athabasca, Alberta T9S 1L2

Canadian Journal of Music Therapy (CJMT)
Journal of the Canadian Association for Music Therapy
Editor: Jennifer James Nicol
110 Cumberland Street, Suite #320
Toronto, Ontario M5R 3V5
E-mail: journal@musictherapy.ca

Canadian Music Educators' e-Newsletter
Contact: David Gueulette
E-mail: dgueulette@ashbury.ca
Website: http://www.cmea.ca/journal/

Canadian Music Educators' Journal (CMEJ)
Journal for the Canadian Music Educators' Association (CMEA)
Contact: Dr. Ben Bolden
E-mail: benbolden@gmail.com
Website: http://www.cmea.ca/journal/

Canadian University Music Review
Journal for the Canadian University Music Society
Website: http://www.cums-smuc.ca/

Encyclopedia of Music in Canada
http://www.thecanadianencyclopedia.com/index.cfm?PgNm=EMCSubjects

E-NOTZ
Journal for the Saskatchewan Music Educators' Association (SMEA)
Editor: Lauren Campell
E-mail: l.campbell.smea@sasktel.net
Website: http://www.musiceducationonline.org/smea/enotz.html

Ensemble Magazine
Journal for the Canadian Association of Music Therapy
110 Cumberland Street, Suite #320
Toronto, Ontario M5R 3V5
Tel: 1-800 996-2268
E-mail: ensemble@musictherapy.ca
Website: http://www.musictherapy.ca

Intersections: Canadian Journal of Music
(formerly *Canadian University Music Review*)
Journal for the Canadian University Music Society
10 Morrow Avenue, Suite 202
Toronto, Ontario M6R 2J1
Tel: 416-538-1650

Queen's Quarterly
144 Barrie Street
Queen's University
Kingston, Ontario K7L 3N6
613 533-2667

INTERNATIONAL

ACT (Action, Criticism, and Theory)
MayDay Group
Contact: David Elliott
E-mail: mdgacted@gmail.com
Website: www.act.maydaygroup.org/

Bulletin of the International Council for Traditional Music
(Electronic-only publication)
Editor: Carlos Yoder
E-mail: bulletin-editor@ictmusic.org
Website: http://www.ictmusic.org/publications/bulletin-ictm

Bulletin of the International Kodály Society
Website: http://trove.nla.gov.au/version/44973018

International Choral Bulletin
Editor: Andrea Angelini
Viale Pascoli 23-g
47900 Rimini
Italy
Tel.: +39 347 2573878
Fax: +39 02 700425984
E-mail: aangelini@ifcm.net
Website: http://www.ifcm.net

International Journal of Community Music
(North America)
Turpin Distribution
The Bleachery
143 West Street
New Milford, CT 06776
United States
Tel: 1-860-350-0041
Website: http://www.intellectbooks.co.uk/journals/view-journal,id=149/

International Journal of Community Music
(United Kingdom and Europe)
Turpin Distribution
Pegasus Drive
Stratton Business Park
Biggleswade, Bedfordshire, SG18 8TQ
United Kingdom
Tel: +44 (0) 1767 604951
Website: http://www.intellectbooks.co.uk/journals/view-journal,id=149/

International Journal of Music Education (IJME)
Editor: Scott Harrison
ISME International Office
P.O. Box 909
Nedlands 6909, West Australia
Australia
Tel: ++61-(0)8-9386-2654
Website: http://ijm.sagepub.com

International Journal of Musicology (United Kingdom)
Peter Lang Ltd.
International Academic Publishers
52 St Giles
Oxford, OX1 3LU
United Kingdom
Tel: +44 (0)1865 514160
Fax: +44 (0) 1865 604028
E-mail: oxford@peterlang.com
Website: http://www.peterlang.com

International Journal of Musicology (United States)
Peter Lang International Academic Publishers
29 Broadway
New York, NY 10006
Tel: 212-647-7706
Fax: 212-647-7707
E-mail: CustomerService@plang.com
Website: http://www.peterlang.com

International Journal of Research in Choral Singing (IJRCS)
Editor: James F. Daugherty
University of Kansas School of Music
Murphy Hall
1530 Naismith Drive, Suite 448
Lawrence, KS 66045-3013
United States
E-mail: jdaugher@ku.edu

International Review of the Aesthetics and Sociology of Music
Published by JSTOR
Website: http://www.jstor.org

International Suzuki Journal
(Online journal)
Website: http://www.internationalsuzuki.org/docs/ISA_Journal

MERI Journal Archives
Music Education Research International (MERI)
Center for Music Education Research
School of Music, MUS 101
College of the Arts
University of South Florida
4202 East Fowler Avenue
Tampa, FL 33620-7350
United States
Fax: 1-813-974-8721
E-mail: fung@usf.edu
Website: http://www.cmer.arts.usf.edu

Music Education International
ISME International Office
P.O. Box 909
Nedlands 6909, West Australia
Australia

Musicæ Scientiæ
Journal for the European Society for the Cognitive Sciences of Music (ES-COM)
Contact: Reinhard Kopiez
Hochschule für Musik und Theater
Emmichplatz 1

30175 Hannover
Germany
Tel: +49 511 3100 7608
Fax: +49 511 3100 7600
E-mail: reinhard.kopiez@hmtm-hannover.de
Website: http://www.escom.org/

UNITED KINGDOM AND REPUBLIC OF IRELAND

British Journal of Ethnomusicology
British Forum for Ethnomusicology (BFE)
Walton Hall, Open University, Faculty of Arts
Milton Keynes MK7 6AA
United Kingdom
Tel: +44 1908 655798
Website: http://www.bfe.org.uk/Journal.html

British Journal of Music Education (BJME)
Cambridge University Press
100 Brook Hill Drive
West Nyack, NY 10994-2133
United States
Tel: 845-353-7500

British Postgraduate Musicology
E-mail: editor@bpmonline.org.uk
Website: http://www.bpmonline.org.uk/

Canu Gwerin
Journal of the Welsh Folk-Song Society
Dr. Rhiannon Ifans (honorary secretary)
Rhandir
Penrhyn-coch
Aberystwyth
Ceredigion, SY23 3EQ
United Kingdom
Tel: (01970) 828719
Website: http://www.canugwerin.com

EDS Magazine
English Folk Dance and Song Society
Cecil Sharp House
2 Regent's Park Road
London NW1 7AY
United Kingdom
Tel: (+44) (0)20 7485 2206
Fax: (+44) (0)20 7284 0534
E-mail: info@efdss.org
Website: http://www.efdss.org

Folk Music Journal
English Folk Dance and Song Society
Cecil Sharp House
2 Regent's Park Road
London NW1 7AY
United Kingdom
Tel: (+44) (0)20 7485 2206
Fax: (+44) (0)20 7284 0534
E-mail: info@efdss.org
Website: http://www.efdss.org

Inbhear: Journal of Irish Music and Dance
Inbhear General Editor
Irish World Academy of Music and Dance
University of Limerick
Limerick
Ireland
Website: http://www.inbhear.ie/aims.html

Journal of Music (formerly *Journal of Music in Ireland*—JMI)
Editor: Benedict Schlepper-Connolly
An Spidéal, Connemara
County Galway
Ireland
Tel: + 353-86-8241309
E-mail: benedict@journalofmusic.com
Website: http://journalofmusic.com/

Journal of Music, Technology and Education
Contact for the United Kingdom and Europe
Turpin Distribution
Pegasus Drive
Stratton Business Park
Biggleswade, Bedfordshire, SG18 8TQ
United Kingdom
Tel: +44 (0) 1767 60951
Website: http://www.intellectbooks.co.uk/

Journal of Musicological Research (United Kingdom)
Taylor and Francis Group
Tel: +44 (0)207 017 7720
E-mail: subscriptions@tandf.co.uk
Website: www.tandf.co.uk/journals/publish.asp

Journal of the Irish Folk Song Society (JIFSS)
Na Píobairí Uilleann Teoranta
15 Henrietta Street
Dublin 1
Ireland
Tel: +353-1-8730093
Fax: +353-1-8730537
E-mail: info@pipers.ie
Website: http://www.pipers.ie

Journal of the Royal Musical Association
Published by Taylor & Francis Group
Tel: +44 (0)207 017 7720
Website: http://www.tandfonline.com

Journal of the Society for Musicology in Ireland (JSMI)
Executive Editor
Department of Music
Mary Immaculate College South
Circular Road
Limerick
Ireland
Tel: +353 61 204396
E-mail: Gareth.Cox@mic.ul.ie
Website: http://www.music.ucc.ie/jsmi

Music Quarterly
United Kingdom
Oxford University Press
Great Clarendon Street
Oxford OX2 6DP
United Kingdom Tel: + 44 (0)1865 353907
Fax: + 44 (0)1865 353485
Website: http://www.oxfordjournals.org

Teaching Music
National Association of Music Educators
E-mail: info@teachingmusic.org.uk
Website: http://www.teachingmusic.org.uk/

UNITED STATES

American Choral Review (ACR)
Editor: James A. John
P.O. Box 2646
Arlington, VA 22202-0646
Tel: 1-202-331-7577
Fax: 1-202-331-7599
Website: www.chorusamerica.org

American Music
University of Illinois Press
1325 South Oak Street MC-566
Champaign, IL 61820-6903
Tel: 1-217-333-0950
Fax: 1-217-244-8082
E-mail: uipress@uillinois.ed
Website: http://www.press.uillinois.edu

American Music Teacher (AMT)
Music Teachers National Association (MTNA)
The Carew Tower
441 Vine Street, Suite 505
Cincinnati, OH 45202-2814
Website: http://www.mtna.org/publications/

American String Teacher (AST)
American String Teachers Association
57 Antioch Pike
Nashville, TN 37211
Website: http://www.astaweb.com/

American Suzuki Journal
P.O. Box 17310
Boulder, CO 80308-7310
Tel: 1-888-378-9854
E-mail: info@suzukiassociation.org
Website: suzukiassociation.org/news/journal

Arts Education Policy Review
Heldref Publications
1319 18th Street, NW
Washington, DC 20036-1802
Tel: 1-800-354-1420
Website: http://www.tandfonline.com

Bandworld
Managing Director: Scott McKee
407 Terrace Street
Ashland, OR 97520
Tel: 1-541-778-4880
E-mail: scottmckee@bandworld.org
Website: http://www.bandworld.or

Bulletin of Historical Research in Music Education (HRME Bulletin)
311 Bailey Hall
University of Kansas
Lawrence, KS 66045-2344
Website: http://www.jstor.org/stable/40214998

Bulletin of the American Musicological Society
American Musicological Society
Published by University of California Press
2000 Center Street, Suite 303
Berkeley, CA 94704-1223
Tel: 1-510-643-7154
Fax: 1-510-642-9917
Website: http://www.ams-net.org

Bulletin of the Council for Research in Music Education
University of Illinois Press
Interim Editor: Dr. Eve Harwood
1325 South Oak Street
Champaign, IL 61820
Tel: 1-866-244-0626
Fax: 1-217-422-9910
E-mail: journals@uillinois.edu
Website: http://www.bcrme.press.illinois.edu

Choral Journal
American Choral Directors Association (ACDA)
545 Couch Drive
Oklahoma City, OK 73102-2207
Tel: 1-405-232-8161
Fax: (405) 232-8162
Website: http://www.acda.org/cj.asp

Contributions to Music Education
Department of Music
Case Western Reserve University
306 Haydn Hall
Cleveland, OH 44106-7105

Current Musicology
Department of Music
Columbia University
614 Dodge Hall, MC 1812
New York, NY 10027
Tel: 1-212-854-1632
Fax: 1-212-854-8191
E-mail: current-musicology@columbia.edu

Early Music America Magazine
Editor: Benjamin Dunham
801 Vinial Street, Suite 300
Pittsburgh, PA 15212
Tel: 1- 412-642-2778
Fax: 1-412-642-2779
E-mail: info@earlymusic.org
Website: http://www.earlymusic.org/ema-magazine

Educational Leadership
Association for Supervision and Curriculum Development (ASCD)
1703 N. Beauregard Street
Alexandria, VA 22311
Tel: 1-800-933-2723
Fax: 1-703-575-5400
Website: www.ascd.org/publications/educational-leadership.aspx

General Music Today (GMT)
NA*f*ME
1806 Robert Fulton Drive
Reston, VA 20191
Tel: 1-800-336-3768
Website: http://www.gmt.sagepub.com

International Journal of Research in Choral Singing (IJRCS)
American Choral Directors Association
545 Couch Drive
Oklahoma City, OK 73102-2207
Website: http://www.choralresearch.org

JAZZed Magazine
Jazz Education Network
Contact: Sidney L. Davis
21 Highland Circle, Suite One
Needham, MA 02494
Tel: 1-800-964-5150
Fax: 1-781.453.9389
Website: http://www.jazzedmagazine.com/

Jazz Educator's Journal (JEJ)
International Association for Jazz Education (no longer active)
For *archived articles*, contact: ajgarcia@garciamusic.com

Journal for String Research
Institute for Innovation in String Music Teaching
School of Music at the University of Arizona
P.O. Box 210004
Tucson, AZ 85721-0004

Journal of Aesthetic Education
College of Education
University of Illinois at Urbana-Champaign
1310 South Sixth Street
Champaign, IL 61820
Tel: 217-333-0950
Website: www.press.uillinois.edu/journals/jae.html

Journal of Band Research
American Bandmasters Association (ABA)
Editor: Dr. John R. Locke
UNCG School of Music
P.O. Box 26170
Greensboro, NC 27402-6170
Tel: 1-336-334-5299
E-mail: lockej@uncg.edu
Website: http://www.journalofbandresearch.org/

Journal of Conductors Guild
Exec. Director: Amanda Burton Winger
5300 Glenside Drive, Suite 2207
Richmond, VA 23228-3983
Tel: 1-804-553-1378
Fax: 1-804-553-1876
E-mail: guild@conductorsguild.org
Website: http://www.conductorsguild.org/

Journal of Historical Research in Music Education (JHRME)
Editor: Mark Fonder
Ithaca College
School of Music
953 Danby Road
Ithaca, NY 14850-7000
Tel: 1-607-274-1563
Fax: 1-607-274-1727
E-mail: jhrme@ithaca.edu
Website: http://www.ithaca.edu/music/education/jhrme/

Journal of Music, Technology and Education
Contact for North America
Turpin Distribution
The Bleachery
143 West Street
New Milford, CT 06776
Tel: 1-860-350-0041
Website: http://www.intellectbooks.co.uk/

Journal of Musicological Research (United States)
Taylor and Francis Group
Tel: 1-800-354-1420
Website: http://www.tandfonline.com

Journal of Musicology
University of California Press Journals
2000 Center Street, Suite 303
Berkeley, CA 94704-1223
Tel: 1-510-643-7154
Fax: 1-510-642-9917
Website: http://www.ucpressjournals.com/journal.php?j=jm

Journal of Music Teacher Education (JMTE)
National Association for Music Education (NA*f*ME)
1806 Robert Fulton Drive
Reston, VA 20191
Tel: 1-800-336-3768
Fax: 1-703-860-1531
Website: http://musiced.nafme.org/

Journal of Music Theory
Executive Editor: Daniel Harrison
P.O. Box 208310
New Haven, CT 06520-8310
Tel: 1-203-432-2985
Fax: 1-203-432-2983
E-mail: jmt.editor@yale.edu
Website: http://www.dukeupress.edu

Journal of Music Theory
Duke University Press
905 West Main Street, Suite 18B
Durham, NC 27701
Tel: 1-888-651-0122
Website: http://www.jmt.dukejournals.org

Journal of Music Theory Pedagogy (JMTP)
Editor: Alice Lanning
213 Mimosa Drive
Norman, OK 73069
Tel: 1-405-364-7328
E-mail: aLanning@ou.edu
Website: http://www.jmtp.ou.edu

Journal of Music Therapy
American Music Therapy Association
8455 Colesville Road, Suite 1000
Silver Spring, MD 20910
Tel: 1-301-589-3300
E-mail: info@musictherapy.org

Journal of Research in Music Education (JRME)
Society for Research in Music Education (SRME)
National Association for Music Education
1806 Robert Fulton Drive
Reston, VA 20191
Tel: 1-800-336-3768
Fax: 1-703-860-1531
Website: http://musiced.nafme.org/

Journal of Research in Singing
International Association for Experimental Research in Singing
Texas Christian University
Fort Worth, TX 76129
Website: www.choralresearch.org/

Journal of Singing
National Association of Teachers of Singing (NATS)
Moorings Drive, Suite 401
Jacksonville, FL 32257
Tel: 1-904-992-9101
Fax: 1-904-262-2587
E-mail: info@nats.org

Music Educators Journal (MEJ)
NAfME
1806 Robert Fulton Drive
Reston, VA 20191
Tel: 1- 800-336-3768
Website: http://musiced.nafme.org/

Music Quarterly
United States and Canada
Oxford University Press
2001 Evans Road
Cary, NC 27513
Tel: 1-800-852-7323
Fax: 1-919-677-1714

Music Therapy E-News
American Music Therapy Association
8455 Colesville Road, Suite 1000
Silver Spring, MD 20910
Tel: 1-301-589-3300
E-mail: ENews@musictherapy.org
Website: http://www.musictherapy.org

Music Therapy Perspectives
American Music Therapy Association (AMTA)
8455 Colesville Road, Suite 1000
Silver Spring, MD 20910
Tel: 1-301-589-3300
E-mail: info@musictherapy.org
Website: http://www.musictherapy.org

National Band Association Journal
The National Band Association
Box #102
745 Chastain Road, Suite 1140
Kennesaw, GA 30144

Orff Echo
American Orff-Schulwerk Association—Music and Movement Education
P.O. Box 391089
Cleveland, OH 44139-8089
Tel: 1-440-543-536
Website: www.aosa.org/echo.html

Perspectives: Journal of the Early Childhood Music & Movement Association
805 Mill Avenue
Snohomish, WA 98290
Tel: 360-568-5635
E-mail: adminoffice@ecmma.org
Website: http://www.ecmma.org/perspectives

Philosophy of Music Education Review
Indiana University School of Music
12-1 East 3rd Street
Bloomington, IN 47405-7006
Tel: 1-812-855-2051

Psychology of Music
SAGE Publications
2455 Teller Road
Thousand Oaks, CA 91320
Tel: 1-800-818-7243

Research Studies in Music Education (RSME)
SAGE Publications
2455 Teller Road
Thousand Oaks, CA 91320
Tel: 1-800-818-7243

School Band and Orchestra Magazine (SBO)
21 Highland Circle, Suite One
Needham, MA 02494
Tel: 800-964-5150
Fax: 781-453-9389
Website: http://www.sbomagazine.com

Teaching Music Magazine
NA*f*ME
1806 Robert Fulton Drive
Reston, VA 20191
Tel: 1-800-336-3768
Website: http://musiced.nafme.org/

Examining Institutions for Music

AUSTRALIA

Associated Board of the Royal School of Music (ABRSM)
(Examination Board)
Website: http://www.abrsm.org

Australian Music Examinations Board (AMEB)
Rosslyn Feast, state manager
AMEB (Western Australia)
M421
35 Stirling Highway
Crawley, Western Australia 6009
Tel: (08) 6488 3059
Fax: (08) 6488 8666
E-mail: amebwa@usa.edu.au
Website: http://www.ameb.uwa.edu.au

Trinity College London
Examination Board for Music and Drama (first in Australia)
Barry Walmsley, national manager
P.O. Box 1
Parramatta, NSW 2124
Tel: +612 9630 1289
E-mail: barry.walmsley@trinitycollege.co.uk
Website: http://trinitycollege.co.uk

UNITED KINGDOM

Bandsman's College of Music
Founded: 1931
The national college of the brass band movement offers diplomas in brass
band performance and conducting.

British College of Accordionists
Founded: 1936
Rayomond Bodell, exec. director
112, Countesthorpe Rd
South Wigston, Leicester LE18 4PG
Website: http://www.accordions.com/articles/bca.aspx
The British College of Accordionists offers diplomas in accordion performance and teaching, as well as graded examinations in the instrument.

Central Academy of Music
Founded: 1984
Dr. Donald Heath, principal and director of examinations
Empire House
175 Piccadilly
London W1J 9TB
Website: http://www.centralacademy.org.uk
The Central Academy of Music is an active examining body that offers graded examinations in piano and electronic keyboard and diplomas in these and other disciplines via examination centers throughout Britain and the Republic of Ireland.

Council for the Curriculum, Examinations and Assessment (CCEA)
29 Clarendon Road
Clarendon Dock
Belfast BT1 3BG
Tel: +44 (0)2890 261200
Fax: +44 (0)2890 261234
Textphone: (0)2890 242063
E-mail: info@ccea.org.uk
Website: http://www.rewardinglearning.org.uk/about/

Curwen College of Music
Founded: 1863 as the *Tonic Sol-Fa College of Music* (Curwen Memorial College)
Reconstituted under present name in 1972.
Dr. Terry Worroll, warden
259 Monega Rd.
Manor Park, London E12 6YU
The Curwen College of Music offers diploma examinations in most practical disciplines, theory, and composition.

Curwen Institute
Founded: 1863 as the *Tonic Sol-Fa College of Music* (Curwen Memorial College)
The institute was formed by members of the college in 1973.
17 Primrose Avenue
Chadwell Heath
Romford, Essex RM6 4QB
The Curwen Institute concentrates on the applicability of the Curwen method of tonic sol-fa to primary education. Formerly offered a diploma in tonic sol-fa.

Faculty of Church Music (part of the Central School of Religion—CSR)
Founded: 1956. Incorporated into the CSR ca. 1968.
Rev. Geoffrey Gleed, registrar
27 Sutton Park
Blunsdon, Swindon
Wiltshire SN2 4BB
The Faculty of Church Music offers experience-based diplomas in church music.

Guild of Church Musicians
Founded: 1888 as the *Church Choir Guild*; renamed the *Incorporated Guild of Church Musicians* in 1905.
John Ewington, OBE
St. Katharine Cree
86 Leadenhall Street
London EC3A 3DH
Tel: 01883 743 168
Website: www.churchmusicians.org
The Guild of Church Musicians offers several external diplomas in church music.

ICMA (Independent Contemporary Music Awards)
Founded: 1984
P.O. Box 335
Oxon OX18 1 WX
Tel: 0800 089 1219
E-mail: admin@icma-exams.co.uk (preferred contact)
Website: www.icma-exams.co.uk
One of the first to offer examinations in popular music, ICMA offers a wide range of graded exams and external diplomas in both theory and practical studies.

Leicester School of Music
Founded: 1964 by Francis Wright
This school offers its own graded examinations in many musical disciplines, in cooperation with the British College of Accordionists.

Metropolitan College of Music
Founded: 1996; reconstituted 2002
Dr. Michael Walsh, registrar
Website: www.mcom.org.uk
The Metropolitan College of Music elects musicians to fellowship on the basis of distinguished career achievements.

National College of Brass
Founded: 1988
Lana Clough, general secretary
15 Brushes Road
Stalybridge, Cheshire SK15 3EF
Tel: 0161 338 3768
The National College of Brass offers primary grades, theory and practical grades (I–VIII), and diplomas in conducting and performing for brass instruments.

National College of Music
Founded: 1894
Eric Hayward, general secretary
4 Duffield Road
Chelmsford, Essex CM2 9RY
Tel: 01245 354596
Website: www.nat-col-music.org.uk
The *National College of Music* offers graded examinations and external diplomas in all major areas through a number of local examination centers.

North and Midlands School of Music (NMSM)
Founded: 1994. Predecessor: Lancashire School of Music (1986–1993). Incorporates the London Academy of Music since 1999 and the Association of Church Musicians (1984–1999).
Prof. Colin H. Parsons MBE and Bill Thomas, senior executive officers
Website: www.nmsm.musicnw.co.uk
NMSM has an active examining board that offers great flexibility and a wide range of diploma awards. Membership is available without assessment.

Norwich School of Church Music
Founded: 1981
Now part of the Curwen College of Music.
The Norwich School of Church Music offers diplomas in church music by essay scheme or composition.

Bibliography

DICTIONARIES AND ENCYCLOPEDIAS

Apel, Willi. *Harvard Dictionary of Music*, 2nd ed. Cambridge, MA: The Belknap Press of Harvard University Press, 1973 [orig. pub. 1944].

Bebbington, Warren, ed. *The Oxford Companion to Australian Music*. Oxford: Oxford University Press, 1997.

Chaplin, J. P. *Dictionary of Psychology*. New York: Dell, 1968.

Delbridge, A., J. R. L. Bernard, D. Blair, D. Butler, P. Peters, and C. Yallop, eds. *Macquarie: Australia's National Dictionary*, 3rd ed. Sydney: Macquarie Library, 2001.

Ely, Mark, and Amy Rashkin. *Dictionary of Music Education: A Handbook of Terminology*. Chicago: GIA, 2005.

Kaeppler, Adrienne L., and J. W. Love, eds. *The Garland Encyclopedia of World Music*. Vol. 9, *Australia and the Pacific Islands*. New York and London: Garland, 1998.

Kennedy, Michael. *Oxford Concise Dictionary of Music*. Oxford: Oxford University Press, 2004.

Koskoff, Ellen, ed. *The Garland Encyclopedia of World Music Series*. Vol. 3, *United States and Canada*. New York and London: Garland, 2001.

Lee, William F., ed. *Encyclopedia of Music Knowledge*. Danvers, MA: Santorella, 2001 [orig. pub. 2000].

Merriam-Webster's Collegiate Dictionary, 10th ed. Springfield, MA: Merriam-Webster, 1993.

Page, G. Terry, J. B. Thomas, and A. R. Marshall. *International Dictionary of Education*. Cambridge, MA: The MIT Press, 1980 [orig. pub. 1977 in Great Britain by Kogan Page].

Reber, Arthur S., ed. *Dictionary of Psychology*, 2nd ed. London: Penguin Books, 1995 [orig. pub. 1985].

Rice, Timothy, James Porter, and Chris Goertzen, eds. *The Garland Encyclopedia of World Music*. Vol. 8., *Europe*. New York: Garland, 2000.

Runes, Dagobert, ed. *Dictionary of Philosophy*. Totowa, NJ: Littlefield, Adams, 1971 [orig. pub. 1956].

Sadie, Stanley, ed. *The New Grove Dictionary of Music and Musicians*, 2nd ed. Vol. 29. London: MacMillan, 2001 [orig. pub. 1980].

Slonimsky, Nicolas, and Richard Kassel. *Webster's New World Dictionary of Music*. Hoboken, NJ: Wiley, 1998.

Stone, Ruth M., ed. *The Garland Encyclopedia of World Music*. Vol. 10, *The World's Music*. New York: Routledge, 2002.

Unger, Melvin P. *Historical Dictionary of Choral Music*. Historical Dictionaries of Literature and the Arts, 40. Lanham, MD: Scarecrow Press, 2010.

Vergason, Glenn A. *Dictionary of Special Education and Rehabilitation*, 3rd ed. Denver: Love, 1990.

Wallace, Susan, ed. *A Dictionary of Education*. New York: Oxford University Press, 2009 [orig. pub. 2008].

Westrup, J. A., and F. L. Harrison. *The New College Encyclopedia of Music*. New York: W. W. Norton and Co., 1960 [orig. pub. 1959 as *Collins Encyclopedia of Music*, William Collins Sons and Co. Ltd.].

BOOKS AND JOURNAL ARTICLES

Abeles, Harold F., Charles R. Hoffer, and Robert H. Klotman. *Foundations of Music Education*. New York: Schirmer Books, 1984.

Anderson, William M., and Patricia Shehan Campbell. *Multicultural Perspectives in Music Education*, 2nd ed. Reston, VA: Music Educators National Conference, 1996.

Bartle, Graham. *Music in Australian Schools*. Australian Council for Educational Research. Melbourne: Wilke & Company, 1968.

Birge, Edward Bailey. *History of Public School Music in the United States*. Reston, VA: Music Educators National Conference, 1966 [orig. pub. 1928].

Bloom, Benjamin S. *Taxonomy of Educational Objectives*. Handbook 1, *Cognitive Domain*. New York: David McKay, 1956.

Broudy, Harry. *Enlightened Cherishing: An Essay on Aesthetic Education*. Urbana: University of Illinois Press, 1974.

Bruscia, Kenneth E. *Defining Music Therapy*, 2nd ed. Gilsum, NH: Barcelona, 1998.

Campbell, P., and C. Scott-Kassner. *Music in Childhood*. New York: Simon & Schuster Macmillan, 1995.

Choksy, Lois. *The Kodaly Method*. Englewood Cliffs, NJ: Prentice-Hall, 1974.

Choksy, Lois, Robert M. Abramson, Avon E. Gillespie, and David Woods. *Teaching Music in the Twentieth Century*. Englewood Cliffs, NJ: Prentice-Hall, 1986.

Claudson, William D. "The Philosophy of Julia E. Crane and the Origin of Music Teacher Training." *Journal of Research in Music Education* 17, no. 4 (Winter 1969): 399–404.

Collins, Don L. *Teaching Choral Music*, 2nd ed. Upper Saddle River, NJ: Prentice-Hall, 1999.

Colwell, Richard J. *Basic Concepts in Music Education II*. Niwot: University Press of Colorado, 1991.

Colwell, Richard J., and Thomas Goolsby. *The Teaching of Instrumental Music*, 2nd ed. Englewood Cliffs, NJ: Prentice-Hall, 1992.

Daugherty, James F. "Why Music Matters: The Cognitive Personalism of Reimer and Elliott." *Australian Journal of Music Education* 1 (1996): 29–37.

Davey, Henry. *History of English Music*. London: J. Curwen and Sons, 1895.

Dewey, John. *Art as Experience*. New York: G. P. Putnam's Sons, 1979 [orig. pub. 1934].

Dicky, George. *Aesthetics: An Introduction*. Traditions in Philosophy. New York: Pegasus, 1971.

Fowler, Charles, ed. *The Crane Symposium: Toward an Understanding of the Teaching and Learning of Music Performance*. Potsdam, NY: Potsdam College of the State University of New York, 1988.

Gardner, Howard. *Multiple Intelligences*. New York: Basic Books, 1983.

Goodman, A. Harold. *Music Education: Perspectives and Perceptions*. Dubuque, IA: Kendall/Hunt, 1982.

Green, A. H. *Teaching Stringed Instruments in Classes*. Englewood Cliffs, NJ: Prentice-Hall, 1996.

Green, James E. *Education in the United Kingdom and Ireland*. Bloomington, IN: Phi Delta Kappa Educational Foundation, 2001.

Henry, Nelson B. *Basic Concepts in Music Education*. The Fifty-Seventh Yearbook of the Society for the Study of Education. Chicago: University of Chicago Press, 1957.

Jorgensen, E. R. *In Search of Music Education*. Urbana: University of Illinois Press, 1997.

Krathwohl, D. R., G. S. Bloom, and B. B. Masia. *Taxonomy of Educational Objectives*. Handbook 2, *Affective Domain*. New York: David McKay, 1964.

Langer, Susanne. *Philosophy in a New Key*. Cambridge, MA: Harvard University Press, 1942.

Mark, Michael. *Contemporary Music Education*. New York: Schirmer, 1986.

——. *Source Readings in Music Education History*. New York: Schirmer, 1982.

Mark, Michael L., and Charles L. Gary. *A History of American Music Education*, 3rd ed. New York: Rowman & Littlefield, 2007.

Mills, Janet. *Music in the Primary School*, 3rd ed. Oxford: Oxford University Press, 2009.

Mills, Janet, and John Paynter, eds. *Thinking and Making: Selections from the Writings of John Paynter on Music Education*. Oxford: Oxford University Press, 2008.

Ockelford, Adam. *Music for Children and Young People with Complex Needs*. Oxford Music Education. Oxford: Oxford University Press, 2008.

Olson, Gerald B., et al. *Music Teacher Education: Partnership and Process*. Reston, VA: Music Educators National Conference, 1987.

Peters, Diane E. *Canadian Music and Music Education: An Annotated Bibliography of Theses and Dissertations*. Lanham, MD: Scarecrow Press, 1997.

Ponick, Terry L., ed. *MENC: A Century of Service to Music Education: 1907–2007*. Evansville, IN: M. T. Publishing, 2007.

Reimer, Bennett. *A Philosophy of Music Education*, 2nd ed. Englewood Cliffs, NJ: Prentice-Hall, 1970.

Shetler, Donald J., ed. *The Future of Musical Education in America. Proceedings of the July 1983 Conference*. Rochester, NY: Eastman School of Music Press, 1984.

Swanson, Bessie. Interview by author, Winchester, VA, December 4, 2012.

Swanwick, Keith. *Music, Mind and Education*. London: Routledge, 1988.

Zimmerman, Marilyn P. *Musical Characteristics of Children*. From Research to the Music Classroom 1. Washington, DC: Music Educators National Conference, 1971.

About the Author

Irma H. Collins has had an active and diverse teaching career that spans more than 50 years at both the public school and university levels. She received a DMA in music education from Temple University, an MM in voice at Peabody College in Nashville, Tennessee, and a BA in voilin from Ouachita Baptist University in Arkadelphia, Arkansas. She is professor emeritus of music education at Murray State University, Kentucky, and continued teaching as an adjunct professor of music education at Shenandoah Conservatory, Shenandoah University, Virginia, where she also created lifelong learning programs in music. Dr. Collins has taught violin, voice, and music education and has directed choral groups for higher-education institutions. She taught instrumental music for the Pittsburgh Board of Education and directed the Vocal Unit of the Centers for the Creatively Talented. She also served as MENC (NA*f*ME) chairperson for the Society for Music Teacher Education, where she founded the *Journal of Music Teacher Education*.